RANDOM HOUSE

NEW YORK

VANESSA REDGRAVE

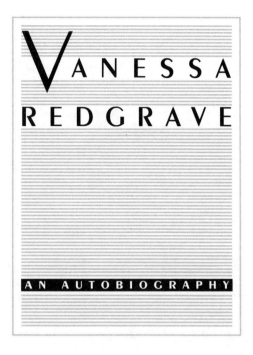

VANESSA REDGRAVE

AN AUTOBIOGRAPHY

This work was originally published in different form as
Vanessa Redgrave: An Autobiography by Hutchinson, a
division of Random House UK, in 1991.

Grateful acknowledgment is made to the following for
permission to reprint previously published material:
Casarotto Ramsay Limited: Excerpt from *The Tiger and the
Horse* by Robert Bolt, published by Faber and Faber
Limited. All rights whatsoever in this play are strictly
reserved, and application for performance, etc., must be
made before rehearsal to Casarotto Ramsay Ltd., National
House, 60-66 Wardour Street, London, W1V 4ND. No
performance may be given unless a license has been
obtained. Reprinted by permission.
CPP/BELWIN, Inc.: Excerpt from "The Trolley Song" by
Ralph Blane and Hugh Martin. Copyright © 1943, 1944
(renewed) c/o EMI Feist Catalog, Inc. International
copyright secured. Made in USA. All rights reserved.
Reprinted by permission of CPP/BELWIN, Inc., Miami,
Florida, 33014.
*Hal Leonard Corporation, Walter Kent Music Co., and Shapiro
Bernstein & Co., Inc.:* Excerpt from "(There'll Be Bluebirds
Over) The White Cliffs of Dover" by Nat Burton and
Walter Kent. Copyright © 1941 by Shapiro Bernstein &
Co., Inc., New York, and Walter Kent Music Co., Los
Angeles. Copyright renewed. All rights reserved.
International copyright secured. Reprinted by permission
of Hal Leonard Corporation, Walter Kent Music Co., and
Shapiro Bernstein & Co., Inc.
Ludlow Music, Inc.: Excerpt from "If I Had a Hammer (The
Hammer Song)," words and music by Lee Hays and Pete
Seeger. Copyright © 1958 (renewed) and 1962 (renewed)
by Ludlow Music, Inc., New York, New York. Reprinted
by permission.

Library of Congress Cataloging-in-Publication Data
Redgrave, Vanessa.
Vanessa Redgrave: an autobiography / Vanessa Redgrave.
p.   cm.
Includes index.
ISBN 0-679-40216-0
1. Redgrave, Vanessa.   2. Actors—Great Britain—
Biography.   I. Title.
PN2598.R422A3   1994   792'.028'092—dc20   94-14307

Manufactured in the United States of America on
acid-free paper
Book design by J. K. Lambert
9 8 7 6 5 4 3 2
First U.S. Edition

FOR RACHEL, MY MOTHER

FOR TASHA, JOELY, AND CARLO

FOR MY GRANDCHILD AND ALL THE OTHERS TO COME

"[I believe] that the universe is governed by an order that we can perceive partially now and that we may understand fully in the not-too-distant future. It may be that this hope is just a mirage; there may be no ultimate theory, and even if there is, we may not find it. But it is surely better to strive for a complete understanding than to despair of the human mind."

Stephen Hawking
Black Holes and Baby Universes

VANESSA REDGRAVE

I was born in the middle of a snowstorm on Saturday, January 30, 1937. My mother was in a maternity clinic in Blackheath, London, at the time, about six o'clock in the evening, and my father was fighting a duel with Laurence Olivier at the Old Vic. Laertes versus Hamlet. Someone signaled to my father from the wings, "It's a girl," and at the curtain call Olivier stepped forward and announced to the audience that Laertes had a daughter. My father was rather proud of this story. He told it to my mother, and, according to her, Olivier said, "Ladies and gentlemen, tonight a great actress has been born."

The earliest memory I can recall in sharp focus, with sound and smells, is of an August morning in 1940 when I was three years old. I am alone in a garden, eating a bowl of milk and Kellogg's Rice Krispies. The sun shines, the air is cool and sweet and damp with the moisture from the grass and the leaves of a large chestnut tree. A few midges and flies hover; their buzzing and the popping noise from the Rice Krispies are the only sounds breaking the silence. Suddenly a vast wailing fills the whole sky. A wooden window sash on the top floor bangs up. Dulcie Shave, my baby brother's nurse, thrusts her

head out and shouts, "Vanessa! Come indoors. Come indoors AT
ONCE!"

The wailing came from a siren sounding the first air-raid warning
I ever heard. My mother remembers us spending that afternoon, and
every night for a week, in the basement of our rented house in St.
John's Wood in North London, while the bombs fell on the City and
the densely populated East End. She laid out mattresses on the floor,
told stories by candlelight, and sang baby Corin and me to sleep:

> Golden slumbers kiss your eyes,
> Smiles awake you when you rise.
> Sleep, pretty darlings, do not cry,
> And I will sing a lull-a-by.

Soon after the bombing, we left St. John's Wood and Daddy to go to
Bromyard in Herefordshire. My father was performing every night
in *Thunder Rock* by Robert Ardrey, waiting to be called up to serve
in the navy.

In 1938 Prime Minister Neville Chamberlain had returned from a
summit meeting in Munich with Hitler. He waved a piece of paper
and said he had brought "peace in our time." Some years ago, I asked
my mother, "What did you think when you heard that?" "We didn't
know what we know now," she said. "I was just so relieved that there
wouldn't be a war for a little while longer. We knew there *would* be
a war, but I was so thankful that we would all have a little more time
together before it started."

My mother, Rachel, and my father, Michael—whom Rachel,
when she was very happy, used to call "Mikey," or "Misha"—fell in
love in 1935 while they were performing in a season of repertory plays
in Liverpool. Rachel was twenty-four and had been a wage-earning
actress for two years. She had played Juliet with great success in her
very first engagement at Stratford-upon-Avon. Her father, Eric
Kempson, was a schoolmaster who taught science at Rugby and later
became headmaster at the Royal Naval College at Dartmouth. Her
mother was Beatrice Ashwell, the youngest of a homeopathic pharmacist's three daughters. Beatrice was a very beautiful woman in her
youth, but rather melancholy and disappointed when we knew her.
Married life, my mother told us, had not come up to Beatrice's

expectations. My mother adored her father, and found her mother rather a trial, especially after Eric's death in 1948. "If ever *I* become like her," she used to say, "please warn me." "You *couldn't* become like her," we reassured her. Mother's family was beset with strange, inexplicable feuds, fierce likes and dislikes, and arguments that simmered on for thirty or forty years, long after some unforgivable, absolutely unspeakable thing had been said or done. We thought it very funny and never asked the reason why.

Michael and Rachel were married a year after they met. Lilian Baylis then asked them both to join her Old Vic Theatre Company in London. The leading actors, Laurence Olivier and Edith Evans, were already great names. Others, like Alec Guinness, were playing their first small parts that season. Michael had only two years' experience in repertory behind him, but he was given some of the best roles. By the end of 1936 he was playing Orlando in *As You Like It*, with Edith Evans as Rosalind, and Mr. Horner in Wycherley's *The Country Wife*, with Ruth Gordon.

By August 1940, when my first memory begins, my father had become the most popular film star in Britain. Alfred Hitchcock had cast him in *The Lady Vanishes*, and he had played David in Carol Reed's *The Stars Look Down*. Reed's film, adapted from A. J. Cronin's novel about a miner's son who leads a strike against a private coal company, was a great success when it was released that year of the Rice Krispies and the sirens, and it must have contributed to the growing demand among miners during and after the war for the coal industry to be nationalized. I saw the film for the first time when it was screened on British television one Sunday afternoon in January 1987, almost fifty years after it was made. I was watching it not long after the year-long strike of the National Union of Mineworkers, and I was struck by one scene in particular. An elderly miner is asking the middle-class anti-union butcher for some beef on credit. His wife is sick with pneumonia. The butcher abuses him and threatens to call the police. "Yes!" shouts the old miner. "You call the police as if you own them, you and your lot!"

"Michael Redgrave at Home," an article in *Picture Post*, one of the best photojournalism magazines of its time, appeared in 1940. In it, Michael talks about his interest in Equity, the actors' trade union, and what he hopes the theatre will be like after the war. "*All* theatre must be subsidized, that's the only way it will attract new audiences and new writers." There are photographs of Michael and Rachel singing at the piano; Rachel walking upstairs with a cup of tea; Michael, in a smart double-breasted suit, watering a pot of geraniums with his three-year-old daughter, Vanessa. But by the time the photographs appeared, the Blitz had begun and we were separated. Rachel, Nurse Dulcie, Corin, and I had sadly taken a taxi to Paddington Station, where enormous monster engines spouted columns of steam and smoke up into the arches and iron columns of the Great Western Railway terminal. Amid the soot, masses of people were packing into the railway carriages. Adhesive netting covered the windows to protect passengers in case bombs splintered the glass. We traveled via Rugby, changing trains at Worcester, and finally descended at Bromyard's small branch-line station.

A man in a peaked cap and navy-blue raincoat met us, and we climbed into a small car that smelled strongly of old leather and gasoline. We drove through the small market town and up a very steep hill and turned left through some white gates, coming to a halt before a large gray front door and a small elderly woman. "Ah! There you are, duckies!" cried Lucy Wedgwood Kempson, cousin of Grandpa Eric, welcoming us to her home, Whitegate. We went through a porch smelling of damp rubber galoshes and Wellington boots. Cousin Lucy showed us her barometer, an old aneroid instrument which she would tap whenever she passed it, to see whether the air pressure was rising or falling. As we stepped into the hall the scent of rose petals and toast greeted us, and a loose tile in the parquet floor "plocked." After tea we climbed a large staircase to the top floor of the house, where Corin, Nurse Dulcie, and I were to share a bedroom.

Cousin Lucy always called Rachel "Rachel-ducky," and Corin and I were "Corin-ducky" and "Vanessa-ducky." At first sight she seemed quite ugly, with a large mole on the side of her nose and thick spectacles over her pale blue eyes. But she was full of energy, always interesting, and always interested in us. Before her retirement she had been Warden of Bedford College in London and was one of the first women to have studied at London University.

It was summertime when we arrived in the countryside and still light in the evenings. But when autumn and then winter came, the large house was chilly and dark. To save electricity and help the blackout we used small wax night-lights on the stair landings and in our bedrooms. All the windows had regulation black blinds beneath the curtains, and the lights that we were allowed to use were very weak. Corin and I were frightened at night, so we were allowed to leave the night-light burning until Nurse Dulcie came to bed. When the wind blew from the west—it blew in from the Welsh mountains, which, on a clear day, we could see from our window—the blinds rattled and creaked and the night-light quivered, casting sinister shadows on the walls and ceiling.

Since Whitegate was at the top of a hill, an old engine in the basement was needed to pump water up. The age of the water system, combined with coal rationing, meant that both water and heat were in short supply. The basin taps provided only cold water, very slowly. Stone hot-water bottles were placed between the sheets when the weather grew cold, and a copper warming pan filled with hot cinders was put in our mother's bed when she came to stay. Rachel had gone back to London to be with Michael, and came to Bromyard to be with us probably more frequently than it seemed then. Time had only one meaning for us. When Rachel was away, the minutes went like hours. When she was there, the hours went like minutes.

It was in November of 1940 that I and some grown-ups looked out of a top-floor window and saw a fierce red glow on the southeast horizon. The city of Coventry was burning after a raid that killed more than two thousand people. In the early 1980s I read *A Man Called Intrepid,* about William Stephenson, the principal agent of the British secret service in America. It tells how a team working in Bletchley, England, had broken the Nazi Enigma machine code and learned of the plan to firebomb Coventry, and the date of the raid. On Churchill's instructions the city was not evacuated. The reason given in the book was that this would have told the Nazis that the Enigma code had been cracked. But what was the point of breaking the code if not to save lives? I had never felt fear of the war until that night. For years afterward I had nightmares. Fires started out of sight, miles away. When I raised the alarm, friends and relatives told me not to worry: "The fires will never reach us." But in the dreams the fires raced inexorably nearer until they engulfed our home.

Cousin Lucy would invite Corin and me into her sitting room every evening at five o'clock. She would read to us and teach us to play cards—Beggar My Neighbor, Happy Families, and Pelmanism—and after cards we would have a round of Snakes and Ladders. At five minutes to six, whatever the state of the game, she would turn on the wireless and we all sat silently listening to the weather forecast. "Attention, all shipping in Rockall, Fastnet, and Shannon. Winds slow to moderate, Force 2 rising Force 3. Winds east, veering to nor'-nor'east." The tones of the announcer were solemn and measured. The names of the shipping areas—Rockall . . . Malin . . . Faeroes . . . Hebrides . . . Cromarty—inspired pictures of unknown islands in unknown seas, surrounded by birds and shipwrecks. Rachel's brothers, Uncle Nicholas and Uncle Robin, were both in the navy, serving on armed merchant-cruisers protecting the supply convoys across the Atlantic. "Viking, Cromarty, Forth, Tyne . . . Winds moderate, rising to Gale Force 6 . . ." Our daddy, whom I barely knew and of whom Corin had no memory, was an ordinary seaman.

When I began to write this autobiography, Uncle Nicholas lent me a scrapbook that my grandmother Beanie, Rachel and Nicholas's mother, had kept to record Uncle Robin's career as an actor. There is a photograph of Robin lying in a field with some friends, picnicking. Under it she wrote one word: "Crisis." Then, just below, she added, "Sunday, September 3rd 1939, England and France declared war on Germany." There is a photograph of Robin's first ship, HMS *Salopian,* and near it are news articles about Dunkirk, where Robin assisted the evacuation of the British troops from Normandy. One report stated that HMS *Turquoise,* to which Robin had been transferred, had been hit.

Robin was wounded and suffered a nervous breakdown and shell shock. When he was given sick leave he came up to Cousin Lucy's to recover. I remember a tall man with blue eyes, a wide smile, and red hair, playing a hilarious game with us in the fields at the bottom of the garden, where there was a small hillock. "Get *down,* you dirty rascal!" Vigorous shoving followed, and the challenger either toppled the king or found herself rolling down the hillock. He was still at Whitegate when Michael and Rachel visited us for Christmas Day. It had snowed heavily and we had a huge Christmas tree in the hall.

Rachel dressed me in woolen trousers and gaiters and a pair of red Wellington boots, and we set off for a walk down the middle of a country road, deep in snow, to Birchyfields. Rooks were cawing in the trees that lined the drive leading to the house where Grandpa Eric had lived as a boy. He was then in Dartmouth, and I could tell that Rachel missed him. As we turned away she started singing to keep our spirits up:

Good King Wenceslas looked out
On the Feast of Stephen

Her voice was high and very sweet, quavering a little on the top notes when the page answers the king:

Sire, he lives a good league hence,
Underneath the mountain
Right against the forest fence
By St. Agnes' fou-n-tain.

I thought her courageous and gallant, singing as we tramped through the snow. I didn't want to go home. I wanted this walk and her singing to last forever, so I stumbled and fell. "Don't fall down again," she said, "or you'll be soaked through and we'll have to go home." She was so sweet and loving as she picked me up and brushed the snow off that I fell down twice more, deliberately. And yet the last thing I wanted was to go home. How can you explain such contradictory actions when you're very young? Rachel did not slap me; she never would. I am sure she was upset that our last moments together for a long while ended with my doing the opposite of what she and I wanted.

On Boxing Day morning, Rachel and Michael left, and soon after, Robin went to join the battleship HMS *Prince of Wales*. Grandmother Beanie continued to paste photos in her scrapbook, following Robin and the war. When the *Prince of Wales* was torpedoed off Malaya on December 10, 1941, the Admiralty sent a telegram written in pencil: "Very glad to state your son Lieutenant E. J. Kempson RNVR safe." But no more news was heard of Robin, and Beanie and Grandpa Eric lived in sorrow and suspense until one day in 1945, when a survivor, Stoker Farron, told them what had happened.

Robin had reached Singapore and had begun commando work behind Japanese lines, running motorboats through the mangrove swamps of Malaya to evacuate British soldiers. In mid-February 1942, he escaped from Singapore in a tugboat as the Japanese were advancing. Two Japanese destroyers spotted the tugboat and fired. Robin helped put the seriously wounded into a raft made with lifebelts, but there were not enough lifebelts for Robin and an army officer. They were fifteen miles from land, and since Robin had dislocated his shoulder some time before, his right arm was useless for swimming. Nevertheless, the two men struck out for land, Robin turning to wave and shout "Good-bye and good luck" to Stoker Farron, who had a lifebelt. Farron and a friend made it to shore and spent the rest of the war in a Japanese prisoner-of-war camp. Grandpa Eric had a small book printed in six copies to commemorate Robin. It has an epitaph from Homer's *Iliad:* "Hector, of all my sons the best beloved. Thou in thy life wert dear to the Gods and even in the doom of death they have shown care of thee."

Grandpa Eric inspired awe. He was extremely tall and wore a monocle in his left eye. Sometimes, when he sat in a chair looking at Corin and me rather gravely, he would suddenly lift his left eyebrow and out would fly the monocle. His grave face would crease with mirth and he laughed, more of a shout than a laugh, until he cried. "Do it again," we pleaded, even more fascinated to see how he could keep the monocle in place than how he made it fly out. I remember Grandpa Eric taking me out in a rowing boat down the river Dart in Devon at some point during those early years. He moored the boat on a sandy bank, made me hunt for twigs, put a kettle of river water on to boil, and made us both a cup of tea. He was famous for his skill with boats, especially the long, flat-bottomed punts. He and another old boatman, who had taught him, were the only two people in England who could take a punt up the rapids of the river Wye at Symonds Yat, Rachel told us. He called Corin "Bread and Butter" or "Towser," and took us for walks, which were runs for our short legs. Like all the Kempsons, he walked very fast and upright, never slowing his pace.

In the days when his family had lived at Birchyfields, Grandpa Eric's father had been bankrupted. So he left school and became a bank clerk, studying in his spare time for an engineering degree at Cambridge. He took jobs in a steelworks and a woolen mill, and for eight years he taught science at Rugby School. His favorite story from Rugby was about the housemaster's wife who used to order meat by telephone from the butcher's:

". . . and three pounds of your best mince, please."

"Three pounds, ma'am? For the boys?"

"Not for the boys, of course. For the dogs!"

Grandpa Eric served in World War I in Palestine, where he won the Military Cross, and then returned to teaching until, like many other teachers, he lost his job and had to take a post as a schools inspector. The salary was very low and there was hardly enough money to pay the rent for a tiny terraced house in Kew. He taught Rachel to drive a car, and at seventeen she left home to take a job as a companion to an elderly lady in Dorset. Then, in 1935, he got the post of headmaster at the Royal Naval College and moved to Dartmouth, in Devon.

Simple physical descriptions and memories cannot convey the sort of man he was. Rachel told us many stories about Eric, his life and his marriage, but I never felt I really knew him until Uncle Nicholas lent me a box of small books and albums, among which I found a loose page from the *Pottery Gazette and Glass Trade Review*, dated October 1943. Eric had given a talk on the BBC Radio Home Service, and the trade magazine had printed it.

From the standpoint of an educator, Eric saw British society with its rigid class system as "archconservative." And as a socialist he was acutely aware of the enormous contrast between the living conditions of the rich and the poor throughout the country. He realized that most working people were deprived of a formal education, while academics and industrialists, who knew nothing about labor at first hand, made decisions affecting the workers' lives.

Eric proposed a school curriculum in which half the time would be given to books and half the time to practical work: "The present one hour to art, one hour to music, one to carpentry is just so much time wasted, for it is a sham. What is done on the practical side must be taught by those who really know." He also proposed a compulsory period of National Service, "with pay, of not less than three years.

Labour by hand, or with machines, in factories, workshops, farms, mines, on the railways or at sea, to come between school and university . . ."

Eric was one of the last honest descendants of Robert Owen, the English utopian socialist of the 1840s.

Where would my proposals lead us? To this: instead of over-academic public servants handing out what they are pleased to consider benefits to the common man—we should have the work done and controlled by men and women who knew it from the ground up. Conditions of work would be good, not because some politicians had a conscience, but because the best men and women were in the work and knew what was wanted and how to get it. Men would be good citizens not because they had attended a course in Civics, but because their work was worth doing, was well done and had made them happy.

But the Labour government he voted for at the end of the war did not share his views, and devised an examination that streamed off the "bright kids," the "academic" ones, from the "nonacademic." The latter were given technical courses for manual labor, while their "academic" counterparts were groomed for college or university.

Thanks to Nurse Dulcie and Cousin Lucy I could read by the time I was four years old. My first book, *The Bird Talisman* by Henry Allen Wedgwood, was a gift, inscribed: "Vanessa, with Cousin Lucy's love, Xmas 1942." Lucy was a Wedgwood, and Henry Allen was a grandson of the original Josiah Wedgwood, the master potter of Etruria, Stoke-on-Trent. If I look at the book now I can hear Lucy's kindly, rasping voice, and I realize that her early influence on us as children, her books, her questions, and her answers, spurred me on subsequently as I struggled through the boring hours of Janet and John and their wretched cats on mats in my reading primer. Children would un-doubtedly learn to read much earlier, much faster, and with real pleasure if the subject matter was not limited to lambs, bad wolves, or three dreary little pigs.

In 1943 Corin and I and a new nurse, named Kathleen Randall, returned to London from Cousin Lucy's and Bromyard on the train. The worst of the Blitz was over, though bombing still continued, and

Rachel, who was pregnant, wanted us to be together. We had sandwiches for the journey, a thermos of tea, homemade biscuits, and, best of all, a new book, a present from Rachel. As the train started to move I opened my book and began the most enthralling story I had ever read—John Bunyan's *Pilgrim's Progress:*

> Then said Apollyon, "I am sure of thee now," and with that he had almost pressed him to death, so that Christian began to despair of life. But as God would have it, while Apollyon was fetching of his last blow, thereby to make a full end of this good man, Christian nimbly reached out his hand for his Sword and caught it, saying, "Rejoice not against me, O mine Enemy! When I fall I shall arise."

As children we never went to the cinema and did not have television. There were no entertainments like *Star Wars* to inspire us with mighty exploits. There was only war, and the reports of the war that we heard each day on the radio, with no explanation offered as to why we were at war or what fascism was. *Pilgrim's Progress* provided me with a perspective on the world of 1943, and a longing that the good—my father and my uncles—would triumph over the bad—Hitler and the fascists.

We came home to our parents' new flat in Putney, overlooking the Thames. The London sky was filled with great gray barrage balloons with ears like giant mice. At night the searchlights crisscrossed the sky on the other side of the river. We reached our flat on the sixth floor by lift. In the nursery Corin and I shared was a rocking horse with a real horsehair tail. Our next-door neighbor was a kind old lady who would occasionally beckon us into her flat for a tiny brick of delicious vanilla ice cream or a square of Cadbury's milk chocolate. But then, out of the blue, I fell ill.

"Have you got a mate?" asked a young girl's voice. I guessed she was about my age, six years old. Where was it coming from? I was alone in an isolation ward in the Middlesex Hospital, with scarlet fever. On March 8, my sister, Lynn, was born, and I looked forward to a visit, but no. "I'm afraid you might infect her," said the nurse, and it seemed my mother couldn't come for the same reason. The days were long and lonely, so the voice from the other side of the wall cheered me up. "What's a mate?" A friend, she explained, someone you can share everything with. She told me she was a real Cockney, born within the sound of Bow bells, and she taught me "Knees up, Mother Brown" and how to speak in Cockney rhyming slang. "Do you know any songs?" she asked. I sang a verse of "Good King Wenceslas." "Do you know this one?" she asked. Her clear, loud voice rang through the thin partition, Vera Lynn's song:

> There'll be blue birds over
> The white cliffs of Dover
> Tomorrow, just you wait and see.

And then she left. Just as I was about to go home, as I sat waiting on the edge of my bed with my suitcase packed, the matron looked at my face and said, "What's that?" She brought a doctor, who looked at my chest and told me to get undressed again. He was sorry to say I wouldn't be leaving for a few days yet. I had chicken pox.

The days seemed longer than ever, but one afternoon I heard a voice from the room behind my pillow. A man's voice. I was wildly excited, and now that my Cockney friend had taught me not to be afraid of talking to strangers, I lost no time in introducing myself. He was an airman. I sang him my new song, "The White Cliffs of Dover," and told him all about myself. I drew pictures for him and wrote him letters. "I wish you could see them." "That's no problem," he said. He made a gap of about two inches in the partition with his clasp knife so we could see each other and exchange drawings. He was dark and even more handsome than I had imagined. When his wife came to visit he showed her the gap and then closed it so that they could have some privacy. I was filled with jealousy and talked all through her visit. She was very kind and understanding and didn't lose patience even when I kept interrupting her with: "Are you going yet?" "Not yet." "Isn't it time for you to leave?" "Not yet."

One night the matron came into my room before we had time to close the gap. I knew that the thin line of light would give us away and I tried everything I knew to distract her attention. But she was not to be fooled. The panel was nailed up and the next day my airman was discharged. Later that afternoon, still covered in scabs, I was pronounced free of infection. My homecoming was worth waiting for. My baby sister was in her crib. That evening I watched, fascinated, as Rachel breast-fed her, amazed that a tiny creature could suck so strongly. Corin, at three years old, had been very put out by her arrival and still showed little or no interest in her. For a while he had hidden under the dining-room table in protest. At length he was persuaded to come out and cradle her in his arms. "Be careful," Nanny said. "You mustn't drop her." "Would it matter?" he asked.

Michael had bought me a two-storey doll's house and painted it himself, with hollyhocks and delphiniums round the front door and red and white roses trailing up beside the windows. The oil paints made the roses stand out, so that you could touch their petals.

Michael called me "Van" at this time. Later it was "Vanessa," or sometimes "V." At six I was already tall for my age, and my hair was long and straight, like Alice's in Tenniel's illustrations. I longed for those times when we could be together, he and I, reading, talking, or painting, which was our special hobby. But although he had been discharged from the navy with a wounded arm that wouldn't straighten properly, his work, on tour in the theatre, kept him away from home for long stretches of time. It was around then that Michael did something for me that established a close bond between us forever. One morning I was whining to Nanny Randall, "I'm bored. I've got nothing to do." "I'll teach you to be bored," said Nanny, who never stopped working from the moment she got up in the morning until she went to bed at night and didn't understand the word "bored." She picked me up, put me in my room, and shut the door. My father surreptitiously opened it a crack. Then he went to the piano and started to play some beautiful music. Nanny Randall must have had built-in radar. She stomped out of the kitchen and slammed my door shut, and I heard her scolding my father. I knew she was right to teach me a lesson, but none of that mattered now. I glowed with the music and the knowledge that Michael had played it for me. From then on I adored him.

I first saw him on the stage when I was five, in a melodrama, *The Duke in Darkness*. I cannot recall much of the story, but I vividly remember that at the end they threw Michael's dead body over a parapet. Michael took me backstage before the performance and showed me the mattresses he fell on so that I wouldn't be frightened.

I loved going to the theatre. For a treat one Christmas, Granny

Margaret, Michael's mother, promised to take us to a pantomime, and for months before the planned outing we lived in a charged state of excitement and anticipation. Granny Margaret had begun her career in pantomime in the chorus of *Babes in the Wood* at Aberdeen, though no one would have known it. She never appeared in public without a dead fox on her shoulders, and had a very deep, loud voice. She called Nanny "Nurse" and me "Van," the only person other than Michael to do so. But when she started life on the stage she was Daisy Scudamore.

Daisy Scudamore left her home in Portsmouth at the age of fifteen to try her luck in the theatre. Her mother wept, and her father, William Scudamore, a shipwright, cursed her and said, "Thank God you're no daughter of mine!" In London she went straight to see an agent in Maiden Lane, who took one look at her and said, "So *you* are little Scudie." He gave her the address of an actor-playwright-manager named Fortunatus Augustus Scudamore, William's cousin. "F.A." lived in Barnes, and when he saw Daisy on his doorstep he threw his arms around her neck and cried, "If you are not my daughter, then I don't know whose daughter you may be!" Daisy lived with F.A., his wife, and his actor son, Lionel, for some years. She became his leading lady and had some success at the theatre that he managed in Mile End in East London. But one day she made the mistake of siding with Lionel in an argument, and, worse still, she left the flat threatening she would not perform in F.A.'s play that night. Next morning she returned to make her peace. She had of course not kept her threat to miss the performance the night before, but she knew she had hurt the old man. She knocked for a while without getting an answer and, growing alarmed, called the caretaker. They found F.A. on the floor. He had died of a heart attack, having turned all her photographs to the wall, except one. To reach the last one he had needed a stepladder. His body lay at the foot of the ladder.

By the time Corin and I knew Granny Margaret she had become Mrs. J. P. Anderson, wife of a wealthy retired tea planter, although she was still a working actress. Michael never told her full story in print—probably because he wasn't entirely sure how much was truth and how much invention—but he often spoke of it to Corin and me.

When I was eight, Granny Margaret took us to see *Cinderella*. Evelyn Laye played Prince Charming in a dazzling white satin coat.

Suddenly a giant teacup descended from the flies with a song printed on it, and Prince Charming invited all the little girls to come up onto the stage and join her in the chorus. Cinderella asked for all the little boys. Corin was very brave and dashed down the aisle to be with Cinderella. I was longing to follow but I did not dare. Then we all sang the chorus, which was something like "Oh, I do like a nice cup of tea, oh, I do like a nice cup of tea!" In between the scenes a drop was lowered and a long stream of little boys and girls ran out in front of the footlights. The Terry Juveniles performed three numbers during the show. In one they were dressed as snowballs, tap dancing on the tea trays they carried on. Their finale was an amazing display of handsprings and double somersaults. At the end all the little Juveniles lined up in a series of backbends to form an arch, and the lead girl, after the customary tension-building drum roll, leapt over their ten bodies, landing with a somersault and a flourish on the other side. My hair stood on end with excitement and envy. I longed to be a Terry Juvenile.

Until my seventh birthday, I never thought that I might work in the theatre. Rachel gave me a book called *Curtain Up* by Noel Streatfield, which told the story of three children who were separated from their parents during the war and were sent to drama school. It had never occurred to me that there were schools where children could learn ballet, acting, and acrobatics. I found out there was one called the Italia Conti Stage School for Children, and it became my aim to enroll in it.

When the V-1 rockets started we had to queue up at Fulham town hall for our gas masks. For Lynn there was a gas cradle. She was laid inside and the lid was closed down over her, so that she resembled a miniature Snow White through the glass window. Corin had a gas mask that looked like Mickey Mouse. Nanny growled and prowled like a bear in her mask. Thinking it was very funny, we never asked what the masks were for. The V-1 rockets that Londoners called doodlebugs and the later V-2s thumped down day and night. We saw strange men with yellow diamonds sewn on the backs of their brown overalls clearing away the rubble in the streets. Nanny said they were "internees."

In 1944 Nanny took Corin, Lynn, and me away from London again and back to Herefordshire, this time to a small cottage in Bromyard that belonged to another Kempson, Cousin Joan. There was a wireless, and every afternoon at five o'clock we listened to a program called *Children's Hour*. Uncle Mac, David, and Elizabeth became almost as familiar to me as my own relations, and soon I had another ambition: to broadcast on *Children's Hour*. Not long after the war, Corin and I wrote to Uncle Mac at the *News Chronicle*, where he had a regular column, asking for an audition. He replied that he would be happy to see us. He was a nice old man—not unlike Grandpa Eric, except that he wore an eyepatch instead of a monocle—and his voice was so uncannily similar to that familiar voice on the wireless that it was like talking to a ventriloquist. He explained that he no longer broadcast himself, except on special occasions, but he arranged for us to audition for Uncle David. I read a piece in several languages and accents to show my versatility, but for some reason best known to themselves, *Children's Hour* never employed me, though they gave Corin a small part in a Christmas play.

During this second long visit to Bromyard we made friends with a ten-year-old boy, Stephen Croft. His parents had nothing to do with the theatre, but Stephen was even more stage-struck than I. He had a magnificent model theatre that he had made himself, with tiny electric lightbulbs for footlights and numerous different stage designs. He started our drama group. There were three members: Stephen, the dramatist and director; Corin and myself, the actors. Our first production was called *Shipwreck*. We rehearsed in the playroom on the top floor at Cousin Lucy's house and charged a halfpenny admission, all proceeds to be sent to the Merchant Navy Appeal Fund. My first entrance as a shipwrecked lady began with a long speech enumerating the possessions I had saved from the wreck. I stepped forward into the middle of the room, lost my nerve, forgot my list, and came to a dead halt. Stephen prompted me, but I was paralyzed before the dozen or so spectators sitting in rows a few feet away from me and looking me straight in the eye. Stephen stepped in front of me, furious. "Ladies and gentlemen, I must apologize to you. We must start the play all over again. Vanessa's gone and bished it all."

We met regularly to discuss further presentations, and eventually I claimed my right to take my turn as group dramatist. I wrote some scenes, which the boys obligingly rehearsed. I enjoyed this experience so much I wanted to prolong it. "The play's not finished yet. There are a few more scenes I forgot to tell you about. We'll rehearse them tomorrow." The next day we ran through my material very quickly, so I started to improvise the outline of what was to follow, but the boys had got my measure and told me firmly that enough was enough. Since Corin and I were dependent on plays as our main form of entertainment, I developed a passion for acting. When we didn't actually put on a play for an audience we rehearsed and performed for ourselves, but usually we would find some friends or relatives to watch us.

While we were staying at Cousin Joan's, Corin and I attended a class that included the sons and daughters of the local doctor, pharmacist, vicar, and grocer. The local parents had obtained a large schoolroom in a country house, about three miles outside Bromyard, to which Westminster School had been evacuated. Corin and I walked to the schoolroom every day, setting off from the cottage across fields, through some woods, and across a plank that spanned a narrow stream some six feet below. I was always frightened and Corin had to encourage me over to the other side. It is only now, as I write, that I recall Lillian Hellman's story about crossing the stream with her friend Julia. Corin was my Julia.

The governess who ran the class was a sadist. Her daily target, the doctor's eldest son, was a quiet, gentle, and rather plump boy. He suffered dreadfully from her bitchy sarcasm and occasional raps with a ruler. I had already read *Jane Eyre*, and this woman reminded me of the cruel Miss Scatcherd, who killed poor Helen by making her stand in the wind and rain at Lowood, the charity school.

In 1944 I read another terrible story, but this one was true. It appeared on the front page of Nanny's Sunday newspaper, the *News of the World*. First I saw the picture of two small boys, Neil and Terry, aged nine and seven. They were evacuees from London who worked in the fields for a farmer. He starved them, beat them, accused them of being lazy, then punished their "laziness" by locking them up at night in the pigsty. Desperate with hunger, they went into the fields and scraped up some of his turnips and ate them. The farmer found out and beat them with a strap so badly that Neil, the elder boy, died.

More than twenty years later, in 1970, I was reading to my daughters, Tasha and Joely, from a children's comic. One story was about a group of children who were evacuated to a farmer during the war and were forced to work in the fields. I realized that Neil and Terry were not so exceptional, and that many children like them must have been forced into labor gangs. Later still, in 1982, I was talking with a Glasgow bus driver about the Thatcher government's cheap labor scheme, the Youth Training Scheme for unemployed sixteen- and seventeen-year-olds. They were paid forty dollars for five to six days' hard labor at menial, unskilled work, and there was no job at the end of six months. Since the driver looked about forty-five years old, I asked him if he knew anything about child labor during the war. "Oh, yes," he said, and told me his story:

> I'll never forget it; it was scandalous. It happened to thousands of working-class children from the cities. It happened to me and my brother. We were evacuated from Clydeside. We were herded with loads of kids into a church hall. We were told to stand in lines. The farmers came in and went down the lines inspecting us, to select the boys they wanted to take on. One farmer came up to my brother and started pinching his arms and legs to feel his muscles. Then he opened his mouth and looked at his teeth. Then he said, "I'll have him." He said he didn't want me. I was too small. I began bawling and hollering because I didn't want to be separated from my brother. I made such a din, I wouldn't stop until he gave in, walked away, and chose another lad instead of my brother. All that was Ernest Bevin. He was in charge of that.

When Winston Churchill formed his wartime National Coalition government in 1940, he asked Ernest Bevin, chairman of the Trades Union Congress, to become Minister of Labour. Bevin and his Labour Party colleagues drew up special regulations. It became a crime for a trade unionist to call for a strike, or organize against the regulations covering hours, conditions, or wages. That didn't stop the strikes. But the conditions were harsh, basic democratic rights were denied, and some of those who organized went to prison. Many larger farmers and landowners made handsome profits from the conscripted labor, as did the coal owners and the steel and shipyard owners. That is the other side of the war, the history of these working-class families and their children. Many books have been written about the war, but I have yet to read one that tells their story.

One wet afternoon Corin and I walked with Nanny and Lynn, who was in her pram, down Bromyard High Street into the market square. It was raining hard. A van was parked with its back doors open and a huge crowd had gathered round. We went closer. Inside the van was what looked at first like a window. In the window, or beyond it, we could see more crowds. Suddenly, we saw a woman in a headscarf rush up to a soldier and embrace him. Then her face became very large and she turned her eyes in our direction and wiped away her tears. She waved at us. Corin and I waved back. Nanny laughed, and so did some of the others standing by. "It's a film," Nanny said. "There's nobody there. It's just a newsreel." The war was over, as was our stay in the country. We returned to London, and our parents.

CHAPTER 2

A n enormous heap of boxes, broken furniture, and planks was piled up in the middle of the road in front of our flat in Putney. At night the bonfire was lit, sending sparks and smoke flying past our sixth-floor windows, while down below small figures ran to and fro, clapped their hands, and threw more fuel on the flames. No more searchlights crisscrossing the skies, no more sirens, no more bombs. Down in the subway stations three-tiered wooden bunks still lined the platforms. Posters in the stations, trains, and other public places warned against spies—BEWARE OF IDLE TALK. But in the narrow back streets of Putney, white cotton banners were strung across the roads from house to house—WELCOME HOME, BILL. WELCOME HOME, TED.

I read the front-page headline on Nanny's *Daily Mail:* HIMMLER SUICIDE. So it was April 1945. Nanny grabbed the newspaper and stuffed it beneath the cushions of her armchair in our nursery. When she left the room I pulled the paper out and read the forbidden report. The chief of the Nazi Gestapo had been captured, but he had bitten on a cyanide capsule concealed in his teeth and had died in a few minutes.

Then later came the first reports and photographs of the concentration camps that had been liberated: Auschwitz, Belsen, and Dachau; thousands of starving men, women, and children; tens of thousands of corpses, withered bodies with open eyes that seemed to say, "Find out how this happened to us." Rooms full of the spectacles, shoes, and hair of all the human beings who had been gassed and burned in the Nazi crematoria. Did I read then or was I told that six million Jews had been deliberately slaughtered by the Nazis? A world of horror, a real world beyond my little world of the nursery, where an illustrated map of a fairy kingdom included a child with a candle as a head. "How many miles to Babylon? Three score miles and ten. Shall I get there by candlelight? Yes, and back again."

The Polish artist Felix Topolski visited my parents and showed us his drawings of the people of Leningrad and Moscow. I learned of the nine-hundred-day Nazi siege of Leningrad, and of the terrible hunger and amazing fortitude of the Soviet men, women, and teenagers, who had eaten wood and paper to stay alive and fight the Nazis.

Nanny took us to Putney Bridge to join the crowds and wave to Churchill. He drove past, standing up in his boiler suit in an open car, giving the V-for-victory sign with his right hand. A general election was announced. Nanny's *Daily Mail* said Churchill's leadership had won the war, and a grateful nation must reward him and the Conservative Party with a victory vote.

"How are you voting?" a woman in a blue-and-white floral dress demanded of Rachel as we were about to get into a taxi to go to the Putney town hall and cast Rachel's vote. "Labour," replied Rachel firmly. I clutched my mother's hand as the woman argued with her fiercely, her face becoming redder, her frizzled hair whiter, producing, with her blue rosette and floral dress, a startling patriotic red, white, and blue. I wanted my mother to give in and agree to vote Conservative, since to say the word "Labour" was clearly distasteful and alarming to the red, white, and blue antagonist.

I realized at that moment that Rachel and Michael were not voting for Churchill. Neither did the returning soldiers and their working-class families. They remembered the general strike of 1926. They remembered the mass unemployment and lockouts of the 1930s. They had fought fascism for a democratic way of life; for a national health service; for a free and decent education for all children; for housing; and for the right to organize in trade unions for jobs, better wages, adequate living standards, and decent pensions for the retired.

As I discerned much later, neither the Conservatives nor the Labour, Liberal, or Communist Party leaders had wanted a general election at all. Palme Dutt, the Communist Party's leading theoretician, proposed in April 1945 that Churchill's Coalition government should continue to rule "in the transition years following victory in Europe." The fact that there *was* a general election is testimony to the organic urge for social, civic, and democratic rights that swept the whole of Europe, India, Africa, Asia, and the United States after the defeat of fascism. This movement was related to the historic truth that the Third Reich was defeated by the citizens and soldiers of the Soviet Union *in spite of* the policies and totalitarian rule of Stalin and the Soviet Communist Party. Stalin's historians called this "the great patriotic war," mimicking the slogans and politics of the *Daily Mail* and the other right-wing media of Western governments, most of whose leaders had applauded Hitler's fascist state in the 1930s as a bulwark against Bolshevism.

The Labour Party won 396 seats out of 640. My father recorded a commentary for a film documentary, *Diary for Timothy*, which itself was a small but significant contribution to this victory.

Michael never talked about politics with me or Corin until the last years of his life. But he must have noticed how heavily influenced I was by the Tory press—the *Daily Mail*, the *News of the World*, and the *Sunday Empire News*—and he attempted to interrupt this process. "Have you read this?" he asked one morning, thrusting a copy of the liberal *News Chronicle* at me. "Try this for a change." At other times, when I would thoughtlessly echo some snobbery or prejudice I'd picked up from a schoolfriend's Tory parents, he would stare at me and say rather sharply, "What do you mean, uneducated people? Why haven't they been educated?" And once, to my horror, after I had made some particularly obnoxious remark, he pushed his plate away and declared he would not sit with me if I really meant what I had just said. In his library were several pamphlets by Lenin, and one in particular, *Socialism and War*, had been heavily underlined and annotated. One day, Corin and I were looking through his collection of phonograph records and we came across a 78-rpm recording labeled "Workers' Music Association, 'A New World Will Be Born'—Michael Redgrave." His singing was strong and clear and beautifully phrased, but it was the song and its chorus—about the new world, which would see the end of exploitation and suffering—that puzzled and amused us. We must have played it for the fourth time, very loudly, when Rachel came in and asked us to turn it off. "Don't play that, for Heaven's sake. It'll upset Daddy." "Why?" "Don't ask him. It'll only upset him."

Why would he be upset? I couldn't understand why he should not want to talk about it. I often wanted to ask him, but I remembered what Rachel had said and I didn't. We talked about everything under the sun, but not that. Later, when I joined the Campaign for Nuclear Disarmament in the 1960s, I couldn't understand why he wouldn't discuss this, or why he began to tremble as he urged me, slowly and quietly, to concentrate on my acting. Only in the last years of his life, after his long struggle with Parkinson's disease had finally forced him to give up full-time work in the theatre, so that he could start again the autobiography he had left unfinished years before, only then did he begin to speak about his political experiences. The reasons for his silence and his fears, as he explained them, were of central importance in shaping his life, and mine.

Like so many artists of his generation, Michael's political horizons were dominated by the menace of fascism, the defeat of the Spanish revolution, and the horrors of Nazi Germany. At university in Cambridge, many of his friends were members or supporters of the Communist Party. Guy Burgess designed the set for Michael's production of J. M. Barrie's *The Admirable Crichton*. Anthony Blunt, then a postgraduate art historian, was his coeditor on a literary journal, *The Venture*. Though he never joined the Communist Party, he saw the party as the main political force to defeat fascism. Once, reading through a book of his and Rachel's press cuttings from the prewar period, I found an interview in which he called himself a "red-hot socialist." No doubt the expression was the interviewer's, not Michael's. But he was certainly a socialist.

In September 1940, while Michael was waiting for his call-up papers, he was sent a manifesto, "The People's Convention for a

People's Government," that had been published in the *Daily Worker*, the newspaper of the British Communist Party. The manifesto presented a six-point program:

1. Defense of the people's living standards
2. Defense of the people's democratic and trade-union rights
3. Adequate air-raid precaution, deep bomb-proof shelters, rehousing and relief of victims
4. Friendship with the Soviet Union
5. A people's government, truly representative of the whole people and able to inspire the confidence of the working people of the world
6. A people's peace that gets rid of the causes of war

Michael thought this "a good socialist document" and signed it. The first three demands of the petition were very popular. No attempt had been made by the wartime Chamberlain government to provide public shelters against the bombing raids. It was only after this petition that the order was given for people to take shelter from air raids, and later to sleep, in the Underground stations. Friendship with the Soviet Union, and a democratically elected government, rather than the National (all-party) government, he approved of. The sixth point appeared to be absolutely reasonable. Who could object to getting rid of the causes of war? These demands seemed in accord with his hopes, as a socialist, for the kind of world that might be built after the war. Michael was not a pacifist or a conscientious objector, like his good friend the actor David Markham. For Michael the issue was not whether to fight, the issue was *how* fascism could be defeated. His generation had lived through the nonintervention policy of Britain and France and the United States, which had denied arms to the Spanish Republicans, and thereby assisted the victory of General Franco's fascist Falange in 1939. He had seen Prime Minister Chamberlain return from Munich in September 1938, having consigned virtually half of Czechoslovakia, and the Skoda armaments factories, to Reichsführer Hitler. Then six months later the Nazis invaded the Czech republic, and the British and French governments took no action to defend the Czech people and their government from fascist rule.

On September 1, 1939, when Reichswehr forces invaded Poland, Chamberlain was forced to declare that Britain was at war with Nazi Germany, but no military aid of any kind was sent in the following months to defend Poland. In April 1940 Denmark and Norway were occupied by the Nazis, who then rolled the Panzer divisions into Belgium, Holland, and France. The policy of appeasement of fascism logically proceeded from the British and French governments' policy that Bolshevism and the USSR were a far greater evil than fascism. It was throughout this period that the BBC deliberately suppressed reports of the Nazis' persecution and planned extermination of the Jews of Europe, as we in England learned only in the summer of 1993.

On May 9, 1940, at a series of behind-the-door all-party meetings in London, it had been agreed to replace Chamberlain as leader of the Conservative Party, and to select Winston Churchill as leader of a National government. This meant that the pro-Nazi political circles in Britain had been defeated. It also meant that the Conservative Party stayed in power, while sharing posts in the wartime cabinet with Labour and Liberal leaders. (In France the pro-fascist Daladier government fell and was replaced by the Reynaud government, which still included pro-fascists.) When Michael signed the "People's Convention for a People's Government" petition, he, like many others—intellectuals and workers, Communist Party members or not—believed that only a newly elected People's government could defeat fascism.

Michael, accompanied loyally by Rachel, attended many People's Convention meetings. It was at this time that he recorded "A New World Will Be Born," which became the campaign song for the People's Convention. Two more demands were added to the program: the nationalization of the banks and basic industries, and national independence for India. Michael wholeheartedly supported both.

In the last week of February 1941, he received a letter from the BBC asking him to come to Broadcasting House for an interview. A senior executive and a lawyer told him that the BBC governors had decided that those who supported the People's Convention should not be employed by the BBC. Michael wrote a letter to the *News Chronicle* explaining what had happened. "They asked me if I would write a letter to the organisers of the Convention withdrawing my support and send a copy to the BBC. I replied that my personal views were none of their business," he wrote in the March 5 *News Chronicle.* "Of course I didn't write any such letter. I asked them directly if this meant that I should not receive another BBC contract and they replied that this was so."

The news of this blacklist, which also included twelve other people, outraged many artists and intellectuals. Leslie Howard and a number of actors working, like Michael, at Denham Film Studios signed a resolution denouncing the BBC's ultimatum. A number of public protest meetings were held. One of them, called by the Council for Civil Liberties, was attended by Edith Evans and E. M. Forster, who announced that he was immediately canceling two BBC contracts for radio talks in protest against the ban. The composer Ralph Vaughan Williams wrote to the BBC withdrawing permission for his music to be performed as long as the BBC refused to play music by Alan Bush, one of the blacklisted artists.

The BBC was unmoved: "The policy of the BBC is not to invite any person to the microphone whose views are opposed to the national war effort." But the protest against the blacklist was so vehement and so widespread that Winston Churchill made a statement to the House of Commons on March 20, announcing that the BBC had withdrawn its ban on Michael and his cosignatories.

Michael was profoundly shaken, not so much by the ban, nor by threats that his film contract might also be terminated. His chief concern was the nature and purpose of the People's Convention program. "The more I thought about the People's Convention, the more ambiguous it seemed. What was its attitude to the war? What would it advocate, supposing we were invaded by Germany? How could we answer the charge that it was a Communist Party front, on orders from Moscow, following the line of the Molotov-Ribbentrop pact?"

The People's Convention program was in fact equivocal. There was a poisonous sting in the political tail of the sixth point, "A people's peace . . ." These words of peace were a cover for the Stalin-Hitler nonaggression pact, signed in Moscow on August 23, 1939. Stalin undertook to provide huge quantities of raw materials for the Nazi war machine, in return for a promise of nonintervention in Finland and the Baltic states and a treaty for the partition of Poland.

German fascism was greatly fortified by the pact, militarily and politically. The Soviet Union was terribly weakened. Stalin's confidence that the treaty would protect the Soviet Union against attack proved to be criminally light-minded. Communist parties everywhere were completely compromised. Obedient to Moscow's orders, they opposed the war with Germany, while still appealing to the instincts of those, like Michael, who wanted to fight capitalism and fascism.

One of Michael's friends who was a member of the Labour Party told him that the Communist Party leaders would drop the People's Convention like a hot potato the moment they had no use for it. Michael sought reassurance from a friend in the CP. Would they do such a thing? "Probably," said his friend, "and so what? Why shouldn't they?" News of his worries and his questions must have reached the CP leadership, and a meeting was arranged with D. N. Pritt at his country house outside Reading. Pritt was a successful barrister, a king's counsel, and a well-known apologist for Stalin's regime in the Soviet Union. He had reported the Moscow trials for the Labour weekly *New Statesman,* describing them as an impeccable model of socialist justice. He was charming, relaxed, talkative. The dean of Canterbury, he said, had also had his doubts, but was "still staunch." Probably, when all this commotion had "blown over," Michael would be awarded the Order of Lenin. As to Michael's fear that the CP would drop the People's Convention when it seemed opportune to do so, he too replied, "Well, so what?"

The *Daily Worker* published a reply to Michael's letter: "The People's Convention is not a 'stop the war' movement. It is not a movement for a deal with Hitler or for 'peace at any price.' All supporters of the People's Convention are irreconcilably opposed to Fascism or to any victory of Fascism." The last sentence was true. Yet the statement as a whole was a lie. The People's Convention was *based* upon a deal with Hitler. Its raison d'être was the Stalin-Hitler pact; and it was clear that the Communist Party was *not* calling for the defeat of fascism.

On March 16 Michael wrote in his diary:

To the Royal Hotel for Convention. A long depressing day, full of disappointment and dismay. I can see very well why the movement is charged with revolutionary defeatism. Everyone who speaks, airs a grievance. . . . I long several times to get up and say, "But what about the War? What is our attitude to the possibility of defeat? Friendship with the USSR certainly—but England must do better than that."

Politically, Michael was completely undermined. The program of the People's Convention was a parody of revolutionary defeatism, the policy first advanced by Lenin and the Bolsheviks in World War I. Lenin and the Bolsheviks opposed those socialists who called on workers to support their fatherland, join the army, become cannon fodder for the capitalists, and, after the war, turn their attention once again to a socialist program. Lenin and the Bolsheviks said that this was a war waged by capitalist states for the redivision and reconquest of territories, raw materials, and peoples in the interests of private profit. The workers' war is the war against capitalism. The workers' only enemy is the capitalist system and the capitalist political power that protects the private profit of a privileged class and is prepared to go to war to do so. For all workers in every country, the main enemy is at home.

The Bolsheviks called for peace; the capitalists and their socialist allies called for war. The Bolsheviks answered, "Very well, this is now a civil war between workers and peasants who want peace, bread, and land, and a system and state that brings war and destruction. Take state power, establish the workers' ownership and political control over basic industry, restore land to the peasants, and declare peace!"

This is the essential content of revolutionary defeatism—the political struggle to unite all workers in all countries to overthrow a system of production that destroys generation after generation of workers through exploitation, economic slump, political oppression, and war. In the twenties and thirties Stalin's theory of "socialism in a single country" led inexorably to domestic and foreign policies of economic and political disaster and betrayal, to the conversion of the Communist Party into a state bureaucratic apparatus of totalitarian terror, and to the rise of fascism in Germany, Italy, and Spain.

The People's Convention was a political fraud. On June 21, 1941, Hitler launched Operation Barbarossa, his long-planned invasion of the Soviet Union across a two-thousand-mile front. From that day on, the British Communist Party dropped the People's Convention and began mobilizing support for Churchill's National government, which a few weeks earlier they had insisted must go. Now British workers who fought for their trade unions, basic democratic rights, and decent working conditions were denounced as Trotskyists who were "sabotaging the war effort."

When Stalin, Churchill, and Roosevelt met in Yalta, they agreed on a division of countries and spheres of influence. This was why the British Communist Party favored the continuation of the Churchill National government and opposed those who called for the election of a 100 percent Labour government. Michael and Rachel were among the millions who voted for that Labour government, but although Michael voted Labour to the end of his life, he never spoke on a public platform for socialism again.

CHAPTER 3

A year after the war's end, in 1946, we moved from the flat in Putney to Bedford House on Chiswick Mall, the first house our parents ever owned. The Mall, as its inhabitants called it, was a long road lined with beautiful eighteenth-century houses overlooking the Thames. Swans swam down it at high tide in the spring and autumn, when the river overflowed its banks and flooded over the road, the front gardens, and down into the basements of the houses. Tugboats plied up and down the river, towing long lines of barges loaded with coal or steel girders, and there were pleasure boats in the summer. From our nursery window we could hear the commentary of the guide, through his loudspeaker, pointing out the house where "Michael Redgrave, the film star," lived.

Round the corner from the Mall was the Cherry Blossom shoe-polish factory, and when the hooter went off at half past four, scores of women in factory-blue overalls and headscarves ran out of the gates and home down Devonshire Lane, where little children played in the gutter in bare feet. At the other end of the Mall was Miller's Bakery, where men in white hats, their faces whitened with flour, lounged against the wall during lunch breaks in summertime, whistling at any girl who passed by. Further up the road, beyond the Upper Mall, was the Bemax factory, and at the bottom of our garden was the Griffin brewery of Fuller, Smith, and Turner. The smell of hops poured over the garden from the brewery funnels, reminding me of the Herefordshire hop fields, where we stood in the long lines of pickers every summer, giving a "helping hand" for a few days.

Chiswick after the war was a Labour constituency. But Chiswick Mall, where I spent my childhood and teenage years, was home for well-to-do people in the arts and professions. Mr. Edwards, at Red Lion House, was the curator of the Victoria and Albert Museum. Next door were the Trevelyans; beyond, the Lousadas, Anthony Lousada and Jocelyn Herbert, the theatre designer; and at the further end of the Upper Mall, George and Sophie Devine. The world of my parents and their friends, that of the theatre, painting, and music, dominated my early childhood, and the only hints of a world beyond were given to me by the Home Service on the radio, the *Daily Mail*, and our governess, Miss Glascot.

For a year after we moved to Bedford House, Corin and I walked a mile or so to the state primary school in Sutton Court Road. I was neither happy nor unhappy there, simply a fish out of water. I was far ahead of my class in reading and way behind in mathematics, and although I and my classmates tried, we found we had little in common. What I read and thought about struck no chord with them, and though at first it seemed that having a film star for a father might help, their interest waned when they realized I had seen no films to speak of and had no autographs of my own to exchange with theirs. I was lost and out of my depth. So Miss Glascot was found.

"School" became the vicarage, next door but one to our house. Now our classroom consisted of two tables placed end to end in a back room on the ground floor. Round the tables sat Corin and I, Matthew Guinness, Alec Guinness's son, the vicar's two sons, the Lousadas' two daughters, Caroline Westmacott, and at the head of the table, Miss Glascot of the Parents' National Education Union. Why this handle, with its initials PNEU, should have stuck in my mind I have no idea, except that Miss Glascot made it sound impressive when she mentioned it from time to time by way of a credential.

Whatever it was, it had in her a formidable exemplar. She taught us everything—English, French, history, mathematics, natural history, art, and scripture.

Our history lessons in 1947 were based on an out-of-date illustrated textbook, *Our Island Story*. We read about a fortunate island, Britain, whose history was made almost exclusively by its kings and queens, their generals, and latterly, to a degree, by their prime ministers. The task of the historian, and his illustrator, was to distinguish between the Good, the Bad, and the Ugly. There was Brave Boadicea, defying the Romans (neither Good nor Bad), and scything the legs of legionnaires not nimble enough to leap out of the way of her chariot. Courageous Richard the Lionheart, the Bad or Wicked King John. Great Queen Elizabeth, Unwise and Autocratic King Charles I, Tyrannical Oliver Cromwell, and Merry King Charles II. Young Queen Victoria, we noted, promised to be Good. Early in her reign there were some signs of autocracy, but they were soon curbed by Prince Albert. Queen Victoria knocked at her husband's bedroom door one night, demanding entry. "Who's there?" asked the Prince Consort. "The Queen." "Who?" asked the Prince again. "The Queen!" This exchange was repeated many times, with the Prince stubbornly refusing to open the door until at last she repented and said, "Vicky." Thereafter all was well. History consisted of stories such as these, punctuated by an occasional visit to a museum to look at the clothes, furniture, weapons, and transport of the times we were studying.

But when it came to the Napoleonic wars, Miss Glascot cast aside the textbook and told the story in her own terms, which were dramatically different from those in *Our Island Story*. You would have expected her to revel in the victory of Nelson at Trafalgar, and of the "Iron" Duke of Wellington at Waterloo. Quite the contrary. She was heart and soul pro-Napoleon. She made us weep with her description of Bonaparte going among his troops before a battle, fraternizing with them, calling them by their first names, astounding them by his memory of each one, his family and his problems. How different from the brutal disciplinarian Wellington, whose troops were "the scum of the earth"! Waterloo, in Wellington's words, was "a damn close-run thing." In Miss Glascot's version it was a tragedy. How this neat, kind, punctilious, patriotic spinster came to cast aside her patriotism and embrace the cause of Napoleon and France we never knew, or thought to ask. Perhaps she had once fallen in love with a Frenchman. Perhaps some earlier generation in her family had shared Byron and Shelley's love for Napoleon in his revolutionary days. For the whole term devoted to her hero, we ceased, temporarily, to think as Little Englanders.

There were long nature walks, gathering specimens of yellow ragwort, campion, and rose willow beside the sidewalks on the grounds of Chiswick Park. She taught us to take a blade of grass and, holding it between our thumbs, cup our hands and whistle through it. We learned how to draw a profile and then a three-quarter profile and, one thrilling day, how to mix a flesh-colored tint with the waterpaints to make the painting of a face more lifelike.

Books were expensive and we didn't know about lending libraries. An elderly friend of Michael's gave me twenty-five massive bound volumes of her favorite magazine, *Little Folks,* dating from about 1880. There were long serial stories, competitions with prizes promised and long since awarded, scientific tidbits and—always—news and stories about the crowned heads of Europe and their families. I was so hungry for reading I devoured them, burying myself in them day in and day out. In my thoughts I lived at the turn of the century. "Bookworm," my brother called me. "If you don't stop poring over that book you'll wear your eyes out," said our nanny. In fact, I already had. As a result of reading so much, often in bad light, by flashlight under my blankets at night and in the early mornings, I was already badly shortsighted.

Our nanny during this time was Nanny Randall, who had come to us in Bromyard in 1943 and would live with us until she retired in 1961.

> Kathleen Randall
> Ran around the candle
> and couldn't find the handle.

She was born in the village of Mattishall near East Dereham in Norfolk, where her father, George, had been a small farmer, and this is where she lived again when she retired. I never went to Norfolk until I stayed with her in her bungalow after her retirement, but long before that I had become more familiar with the names of its towns and villages from her stories than with those of any other county in England. Her stories unfolded gradually, in episodes told many times over, until we knew them by heart and loved them all the more for that.

When we had colds, flu, or bronchitis, she would smash an onion with a spoon to extract the juice until her eyes poured with tears; then she mixed glycerine of thymol and some sugar into the juice and gave us a teaspoonful. She had false teeth, top and bottom, and was proud of them. Her teeth had been perfect until at twenty-one she went to the dentist and had a tooth drilled without an injection. "I told him never again," she said, and asked the dentist to remove all her teeth. She had a misshapen big toe, which she had broken in an accident on a staircase. It had not been set properly and made her other toes bend, causing corns, and her shoes hurt every time she put them on.

Nanny Randall's first job had been as a nursery maid to a Norfolk gentleman who would wait on a landing on the back stairs and waylay all the maids. She told him she would "soon put a stop to that," and resisted him so fiercely that he did stop. But he disgusted her so much that it had put her off marriage forever. Her greatest day came with another family when she nursed four children back to health after an epidemic of diphtheria. She was still a nursery maid but the family doctor had told her employer, "This one should be your head nurse," and she was promoted to be in charge of the nursery. She loved all her children, especially those who were naughty and rebellious, but best of all she loved a boy born with Down's syndrome, and her saddest day was when he was taken away from her at the age of ten to be put in a home.

Much later, when I saw Shakespeare's *Henry IV, Part I,* I recognized Nanny Randall in the extraordinary character of Falstaff, and again in Hotspur's furious description of a "certain Lord." She had absolute hatred and contempt for snobbery, for anyone who gave himself airs and graces. "Who does he think he is? Lord Muck?" On the subject of any strike she would mutter through clenched teeth, "I'd put them up against a wall and shoot the lot of them," echoing the political sentiments of the gentry she had worked for all her young life. She sang when she was contented and clenched her teeth and looked extremely grim when she was upset. If we did not hear "K-K-K-Katy, beautiful Katy, you're the only g-g-g-girl that I adore" as she scrubbed the washing or made the beds, we knew she was troubled. She made skirts, knitted stockings and sweaters for us, mended and darned. She made us say the Lord's Prayer on our knees before we got into bed, with a "God bless" for all our relations and a "please make me a good girl, amen," but she never went to church herself, except at Christmas. "I don't need some vicar to tell me how to pray," she would say, and "What makes him think he's better than I am?" She could not tolerate being "bossed about," and had long feuds with every female member of her family, as well as with her best and oldest friend, who was also a nanny. During these feuds she would not speak to or see the relative or friend until an apology was offered, which it usually was, because she was implacable. "That'll teach them to keep their nose out of *my* business."

Once a week she had a night off to go to the local whist game. She won many prizes—tea sets, trays, tablecloths—and these were all kept in trunks for the day when she would retire to a bungalow. Her legs and painful feet had been up and down stairs every day of her working life, and they longed never to climb stairs again.

Since our parents were often away, for much of our childhood Nanny was mother and father to us. She loved us all and was scrupulously fair with her favors and punishments, but she loved Lynn best, because she nursed her through her early illnesses and because, as the youngest, she missed her parents most and needed the most love.

When she retired to her bungalow we promised to visit her often, but "often," as it often does, meant sometimes. Once I was making a film near Yarmouth, and when I realized how near I must be to Mattishall, I took a taxi and knocked on her door, unannounced. She opened the door and for a second or two we didn't recognize each other. Her hair had lost all its perm, which she hated, and I realized she could no longer afford a perm except for special occasions.

She had a stroke and partly lost her memory, and in the hospital in Norwich they would sometimes find her in the corridor at night looking for Lynn. Lynn was then married and living outside Dublin with her husband, John Clark, and they found a hospital run by nuns, who looked after Nanny until she died, two days after her seventy-ninth birthday. I will never forget her, especially her hands, and if I picture her hands now, I want to cry and laugh. Cry, because they were so cracked and worn with hard work, and laugh because her big hands were so gentle and comforting.

Our first winter at Bedford House, 1946–1947, was the coldest that anyone could remember. The newspapers called it the Big Freeze— and blamed the Labour government for the fuel shortages and the rationing of clothes and food. In reality there was a measure of social justice in rationing, except that the rich could buy their way out of it through the black market. Michael had bought a little prewar Morris 8 saloon car. He refused to drive himself—had never driven, in fact, since the first day of his marriage—but Rachel was a fine, confident driver. And then the squat brown little Morris that Corin and I were so proud of disappeared and was replaced by a great, black gleaming Rolls-Royce, vintage 1936, with a window between the back seats and the front and a telephone to communicate with the driver. Off we drove to Richmond Park, scattering the sheep as the speedometer swept past sixty miles an hour and up into the nineties. Rachel was now in the passenger seat. The driver was Kenneth, the new chauffeur.

At a time when cinema audiences were larger than ever before, or since, Michael was making two or three films a year, earning a lot of money, saving none of it, and employing—besides Kenneth—Birdie, the cook, Ella and Mary, the housemaids, and Mr. Owers, the gardener, all of them living at Bedford House. In 1947, Michael, with Rachel following shortly afterward, went to Hollywood, and we children stayed in England and continued our lessons with Miss Glascot. Our life settled into a routine, a word I shall always associate with childhood, where sometimes routine is comforting but more often it means waking in the morning with an awful foreboding that nothing will ever change. Lessons at the vicarage, walks to Chiswick Park, hair washed once a week.

Lynn is six years younger than I and nearly four years younger than Corin. As a small child she was very anaemic and suffered from many attacks of bronchitis, which made her breathless and unable to walk far. Her frailty combined with the gap between our ages meant that she could not share in the games Corin and I played together, or more truthfully, that we seldom wanted her to share. My most abiding memory of Lynny as a child is of the little girl who trailed behind us crying "Wait for me." Only when she too became a professional actress and had her second baby at the same time as I had my last did we transcend the gap and become close friends.

The vicar's sons were fun to play with, but we had no other friends, so Corin and I were dependent on each other's company for long hours of the day, and for entertainment we put on plays or invented our own games. There was one in particular, our favorite, which we called The Game. We had begun it in Bromyard, during a long convalescence from measles. We lay in bed for days on end, with the curtains drawn, forbidden to read. There was nothing to do except look forward to the meal brought up by Nanny on a tray, and a teaspoonful of Dr. Lewis's sticky pink medicine. Somehow the news on the radio about the American heavyweight world boxing champion, Joe Louis, the "Brown Bomber," and his forthcoming fight with Bruce Woodcock, the British champion, filtered up to our room. This may have been because Nanny followed sports news with interest. One of her former "babies" was the British ice-skating hope.

Corin and I developed a long saga, in which Corin, the son of Joe Louis, and I, the son (not daughter!) of Bruce Woodcock, swapped inventive stories about the lives of our fathers in the boxing world for hours on end, day after day. Perhaps these imaginary fathers made up for our own father's absence or perhaps it was an expression of the wartime alliance between British and American troops that we had heard so much about on the wireless. At any rate, The Game lasted until 1947, when a real fight took place, a match for the world title, between Woodcock and the American heavyweight Joe Baksi. The *Daily Mail* and all the other papers were blowing the trumpet for the British contender, "our" Bruce, and we confidently expected him to win, though we knew it would be a hard fight. But Baksi pounded Woodcock into a terrible defeat, knocking him out in the seventh round. Worse still, we read the next day that Woodcock, who had boxed very bravely but was heavily outpunched, had suffered a broken jaw, probably in the fifth round, and had fought the last two rounds in agony. So boxing was out. We could no longer be the imaginary offspring of champions.

We created a new scenario, in which I was the president of the United States, and Corin the vice-president. At any spare moment, in the garden, or on a walk, or at nighttime in the bedroom we still shared, long and complicated adventures unfolded, with endless twists and turns. It makes me laugh now to wonder why on earth we selected such characters. Neither of us wanted to be these people, or knew anything at all about the lives of U.S. presidents; if we had, we probably wouldn't have wanted to play the game at all. I guess we chose them because by assuming their identities we could fly all over the world and meet whomever we wanted to meet. Like the producers and writers of *Dynasty, Falcon Crest,* or *Sins,* we wanted a social milieu where we could be on a ranch one minute and in New York the next, or could suddenly fly to Paris or Rome, run a newspaper, or ride our own horses and win the Derby.

When Corin went away to boarding school in Malvern Wells at the age of eight we were separated for the first time. He hated the school and a year later Dad took him back, but meanwhile I had started at a girls' day school called Miss Spalding's in Queen's Gate. "Your husband, Michael," Miss Spalding told Rachel, "is one of the intelligentsia." But whatever the intelligentsia was in Miss Spalding's vision, it was not to be hoped that any of her pupils would ever join it. We were back in a routine I remembered well from the two terms I had spent at Putney High School during the war, in between our stays in the country. The piano thumped, "How many flowers are there that grow"; we had prayers every morning and a hymn. In the afternoon we lined up two by two into a "crocodile," as English schoolchildren call it, and walked up Queen's Gate to Kensington Gardens for netball and lacrosse in the winter, and "rounders" and tennis in the summer. Queen's Gate, like most schools, had a yearly school play. Since I had always put on plays with Corin, particularly when we were in Herefordshire, I had a lot of time throughout my childhood and teens to work at acting for the sheer fun of it, with plenty of encouragement and without any pressure to succeed. I played the Tin Man in *The Wizard of Oz* when I was twelve, and Mole in *Toad of Toad Hall* when I was thirteen.

My best friend was a girl whose grandfather had been the foremost Persian scholar of his time. Maria Browne and her parents lived in the nineteenth rather than the twentieth century. Her books were the books of her parents and grandparents. She talked their language and shared the ideas and used the vocabulary of the public school boys in Rudyard Kipling's *Stalky and Co.* She used the same expression of contempt—Foo!—and said "nothin'," "somethin'," and "anythin'," without sounding the *g*. Her parents' house was still and quiet, with heavy curtains, silver candlesticks, and volume upon volume of books, including every edition of *Punch* back to the 1860s, and all the stories of E. Nesbit.

Maria and I read E. Nesbit together, and passed our weekends building temples of heavy volumes of the *Encyclopaedia Britannica*, with silver candlesticks for pillars. She had read Samuel Butler's *Erewhon* and most of Walter Scott, and regularly got A's on her history, English, Italian, and French tests, always coming first or second in the class. She left school after the school certificate exams to have special tutoring for her entrance examination to Oxford.

Tasha Kallin, my other friend, was the daughter of a Russian aristocrat. Her father, an artist, had been killed in the war. Her mother, Princess Xenia Galitzine, survived on a small pension derived from a trust that had been set up for Tasha. They lived in a bed-sitting-room near Queen's Gate when Tasha first came to the school. Tasha, like Maria, was brilliant academically. I adored her, and when Maria left she became my best friend until I left school, a year before she did, in 1954. Tasha introduced me to Tolstoy, and together we read *War and Peace* and *Anna Karenina*. Then she and her mother moved into a friend's house, where the son of the house had a treasure trove of American comics, and where food parcels would arrive containing peanut butter, something I had never tasted before. We thought ourselves very "advanced." When our turn came to stand as candidates in the sixth form mock elections, we chose to stand as communists and quoted *Das Kapital* in our election address. We thought our lessons very boring, as indeed they mostly were. The English literature class for us fifteen-year-olds included a sadly and badly abbreviated version of Dickens's *David Copperfield*, plus *Kidnapped* by Robert Louis Stevenson, and the obligatory Shakespeare play, in this case *Macbeth*.

Things livened up a bit when Miss Hodgkins suggested we take parts in the reading. "Now, who can do a Scottish accent?" she inquired. My hand shot up. Hours spent listening to the radio serial *Dick Barton, Special Agent* had tuned my ear to Dick's assistant, who was Scots (and imaginatively named Scottie). So I read the part of Macbeth over the interminable months spent preparing for the General Certificate examinations. When it came to our abbreviated version of *David Copperfield,* Miss Hodgkins inquired, "Now, who can do a rough accent?" Dad had taken us to see David Lean's film *Oliver Twist,* so I could copy the London Cockney of Kay Walsh and Robert Newton.

Clothes were a problem. When I was fourteen Nanny stopped knitting brown wool knee-length socks (worn with garters), and I graduated to brown cotton lisle stockings. Nanny made two woolen skirts for Lynn and me for winter and knitted us two sweaters each. We had itchy woolen vests and large knickers with elastic. In the summer there were ugly cotton-print dresses. At fourteen Tasha and I longed for boyfriends. We both had pen-friendships with boys we had met in the summer holidays, she in Biarritz, I in Bromyard. At about that time a beautiful French actress from the Comédie Française was cast by Laurence Olivier in a play with Rachel at the St. James's Theatre. Geneviève Page wore a beret angled smartly over her eyes and the most silky of silk stockings. As she sat cross-legged on our sofa, her delicate fingers stroked up and down her silky legs in a slow seductive way. I thought this gesture was the ultimate in sophistication. Tasha and I howled and rolled on the floor with laughter as we tried to stroke our wrinkled brown stockings.

Together we went in search of life and adventure to a dance at the French Lycée, round the corner from our school. I wore a dress that a friend of my father's had sent from America—a blue-and-green silk skirt, a blue velvet bodice, and a blue-and-green stole. Tasha borrowed a skirt from her mother. I thought my dress was beautiful, and we came into the hall full of hope. A band was playing bebop, and we looked aghast at the girls, all in sweaters and tight skirts, all bebopping and jiving. I stood at the side of the room, and no one asked me to dance all evening. Tasha, who was dressed in a gray sweater and ordinary wool skirt, got one very good dance.

It was 1950, and I was attending classes at the Ballet Rambert four times a week. My father had taken me to meet Madame Rambert when I was ten. He expected that I would want to act sooner or later, and he knew that I would be very tall, so he wanted me to learn ballet. I had seen Margot Fonteyn dance the Sleeping Beauty and wanted, more than anything else, to be a ballerina. Now, at thirteen, I could graduate to Madame Rambert's own Saturday-morning class. I worked extremely hard. I could dance well, although I failed to do good work with the point shoes. Madame Rambert encouraged me and raged at others, but I soon realized that she raged most at the student who was most promising. One day she was so furious with our stupidity she tore her green bead necklace off and threw it on the floor. The beads rolled everywhere and the boys ran to pick them up. I loved her for it. I admired and worshiped her angry, passionate fight for high standards, her emotive explanations of the content of the music and the gesture. She would make us repeat and repeat an exercise until we were exhausted, and then repeat it again.

Thanks to her training I became aware of the significance of physical movement and physical space, of extension and the relations of bodies in space. Aware also of tempo, and that while the music may have a certain regular beat, the form of the movement sometimes takes a different, longer tempo than the beat that sustains it. While in my daily life I was round-shouldered and stooping, so much taller than my friends and self-conscious about my height, in class I stretched upward and ceased to think about myself. One day Madame Rambert said, "You are a tight little rosebud, but you are beginning to open."

I thought I knew what she meant. I was beginning to be able to give myself over to the music and movements. I was filling with life. I had been almost entirely introspective and more interested in dreams of the past than the present. In early adolescence I was still very much in my own world, leaving it only when I thought about the boys I might meet and fall in love with. One Saturday morning after class we were chatting in the changing room, wiping down sweaty feet and pushing lamb's wool in between our toes to protect them from blisters in new, hard point shoes. A new girl had joined the class. She had a part in a film, someone said. I looked along the bench, jealous, admiring, and excited. She had large dark eyes and a wonderful big mouth with a beautiful smile. "That's Audrey Hepburn," my neighbor whispered. I went to see *The Lavender Hill Mob*, a marvelously funny film with Alec Guinness. There she was, in a scene about two minutes long, with one line of dialogue. A lovely girl with a tray, selling cigarettes: Audrey Hepburn's first appearance in a film.

At the age of fourteen I was as tall as my father when I stood on points, and he was taller than any of his friends. For some time I had resigned all hopes of becoming a prima ballerina assoluta, like my idol, Fonteyn. What male dancer could possibly lift my 5 feet 11 inches above his head, or catch my 133 pounds? For a little longer I clung to the hope that with a neatly regimented line, as in the vanguard of the Grenadiers when on parade, I might still pass muster at the end of the back row of the corps de ballet. But that hope was soon extinguished. Overgrown, as my nanny used to say. Too tall for anything. Too tall for Walt Disney. Not that Disney himself had objected. He had sent for my photograph for a film he was planning about Lewis Carroll's Alice, and I had made sure to put my height on the back so he wouldn't be disappointed when he saw me. But apparently he approved, and asked my parents to send me to Hollywood for a test. I was ready and eager to go, but it never happened because at about that time I started to have blackouts and fainting fits, and also alarmed my parents by sleepwalking. Dr. Mary Nelson next door, a dear friend of Michael and Rachel, said it was because I had grown too fast and needed time to "grow into" my height. No Hollywood. And now, no ballet. I should have to be an actress.

Michael and Rachel often came to see me in school plays, but the first time I remember being aware of them in the audience was when I was fourteen and played Saint Joan. My parents loved my long Alice in Wonderland hair, but I had finally persuaded them to let me have it cut quite short. I had my picture taken for a magazine article by the celebrated photographer Angus McBean in Saint Joan's trial costume with my newly cut hair. We did three performances of *Saint Joan*, and my schoolfriends loved it. They sent me bouquets and little notes. The morning after our last performance the headmistress gave a sermon at prayers saying that while we should all be very glad at success, there must not be any lionizing of particular pupils. Although I glowed at being, in her words, "lionized," I don't remember thinking until many years later, when I was appearing with Michael in *A Touch of the Sun* in 1959, that I really could act.

CHAPTER 4

I n 1951 Michael went to Stratford-upon-Avon to play Richard II, Hotspur in *Henry IV, Part I,* the Chorus in *Henry V,* and Prospero in *The Tempest.* Besides playing these four parts, he directed *Henry IV, Part II.* It must have been hard and often exhausting work, but Michael was exhilarated. I think he was happier during that season than at any other time.

Rachel, Corin, and I went to join him for the opening of the season in April. It was the spring school holiday and we were to spend a whole week at Stratford. We began preparing for the visit months before, polishing our bicycles, which were to be sent up to Stratford by train, and fitting them with lights in case we needed to cycle home at night after the theatre. We saved our pocket money, making one purchase only—a map, one inch to a mile, on which we marked every village within a twenty-mile radius of Stratford.

We drove to Stratford in Rachel's Hillman Minx with its canvas hood that howled in the wind when you went at any speed. There were no motorways or bypasses then, so the journey seemed interminable. Rachel stopped our boredom by telling us about her first season at Stratford, before the war, when she had played Juliet.

"Who was Romeo?"

"John Wyse. I adored him."

"Did he adore you?"

"Not at all. He paid no attention to me. But I adored him just the same."

And there was another actor she adored, a legendary barnstormer called Anew McMaster, who told her: "You're very good in your tin-pot way, but remember, it's me they want to see!"

Rachel, like all the Kempsons, has a loud infectious laugh, and we laughed so much on that drive and were so giddy with exhilaration at the prospect of Stratford and seeing Michael that night in the dress rehearsal of *Richard II* that I pulled Corin's cap off his head and flung it out of the window. It caught the wind and sailed away, coming to rest, forlornly and incongruously, a bright green school cap with a red Maltese cross, in the middle of the highway a hundred yards behind us. "*What* did you do that for?" asked Rachel crossly, slamming on the brakes. She was hardly ever cross.

But nothing could dim my excitement. The Memorial Theatre smelled exactly as I thought a theatre should smell. There was no curtain. Tanya Moiseivitch's wooden-beamed set, with side stairs, a balcony, and rushes on the floor of the stage, was the setting for the whole cycle. Leslie Bridgewater's theatre band struck up what sounded like a medieval march—it was in fact the overture from Bizet's *L'Arlésienne*—the doors at the back of the stage opened, courtiers and soldiers came on, and when the lights went up, Richard was seated on his throne:

> Old John of Gaunt, time-honoured Lancaster,
> Hast thou, according to thine oath and bond,
> Brought hither Henry Hereford, thy bold son . . .

The plot of *Richard II* does not thicken. It is thick from the very outset, clarifying and simplifying as the play progresses. But at the beginning there is a mass of allusions and a tangled web of intrigue surrounding Woodstock's murder, at the center of which stands Richard, charming, cruel, and despotic. Michael's appearance was startling. He glistened, like a golden sovereign—golden hair, golden beard. When he banished first Mowbray and then Bolingbroke you didn't know whether to laugh at the brilliance of his trickery or to cry at the certainty that he would be caught by it himself. Not many Richards make you believe that in boyhood they confronted Wat Tyler, tricked him into abandoning his rebellion, and then slaughtered the rebels, but Michael's did. Counting that first dress rehearsal the night we arrived, I must have seen *Richard II* at the least half a dozen times, usually standing at the back of the stalls for half a crown. Fourteen is an impressionable age. But years later I stood at the side of the stage at Liverpool Playhouse and watched Michael play the great central scene, Act III, scene ii, of Richard's return from Ireland. He was seventy-four. Illness had made his voice quieter, though it still had an extraordinary range and flexibility. He said that when he came to play Richard he used some of John Gielgud's phrasing: "To this day I can see no way of improving on the dazzling virtuosity of phrasing and breathing which was Gielgud's." I could see no way of improving on Michael's playing of that scene. Richard's sudden wild flights of optimism, his violent spasms of rage against the favorites he thinks have betrayed him, his horrified contrition when he learns they have been executed, all were grounded not only in my father's imagination, which included a vivid sense of the reality of betrayal, but in his historical sense of the period in which the absolute monarchy was coming to an end.

We returned to Stratford in the summer holidays. Every afternoon we played tennis, or hired a boat to row on the Avon. We played endless sets of tennis with the actors William Peacock, David King, and Robert Shaw. Bob Shaw invariably strove to win every point. He was intensely ambitious to succeed in everything he did, and his straightforward, nonactorish voice and the aggressive, clenched-teethed manner with which he spat his words out brought a note of reality and freshness to every part he played, whether it was Dunois in *Saint Joan*, or later, when to many people's surprise, though not to mine, he became a very popular film star playing parts like Quint in *Jaws*. I liked him very much, and *Cato Street*, which he wrote for me in 1970, and which we both produced, is one of the best plays I ever read. Robert Shaw never got the leading part at Stratford in the 1950s. He should have, and he would have played it superbly. I suspect this was because he did not fit into the stereotype of the Shakespearean hero: a BBC "gentleman's" accent, and tall, rather docile physique.

This was finally changed during Peter Hall's and Trevor Nunn's directorships of Stratford.

We went to the Memorial Theatre every evening. Richard Burton was playing Prince Hal and Henry V, and I, like all my generation, became a passionate fan. He was the only actor I have ever seen whose voice and eyes literally compelled the audience to listen and observe his every move. When he turned his deep, steady gaze upon the audience his eyes seemed to search you out, so that even in the furthest row of the stalls or the back row of the circle you felt close to him. His raw, resonant Welsh voice, sorrowful and sometimes harsh, his physical stillness, and that steady piercing gaze were unique. I longed to meet him, and only managed it once, by chance, as I was leaving the stage door with Rachel and he came running in. He stopped and looked at us, as though he thought he should recognize us, and I found his face, which was heavily pockmarked, even more attractive than I had remembered it onstage. "You must be Rachel," he said, and leaned forward to whisper in her ear. "What did he say?" asked Corin as we drove back to the flat Michael had rented in director Anthony Quayle's house on the banks of the Avon. Rachel seemed not to notice. "What did he say?" Corin persisted. Once he had decided to ask something he would not be put off until he had the answer. "He said, 'You're so beautiful I could eat you,'" Rachel said, laughing.

We went back to Stratford again, two years later, in 1953. It became part of our young life, as much loved and longed for as Cousin Lucy's in Herefordshire, or the farm of our cousins Ralph and Sylvia Carr in Northumberland. Rachel was in the company that season. She played Elizabeth Woodville in *Richard III*, Octavia in *Antony and Cleopatra*, and Regan in *King Lear*. She loved acting, and especially loved acting with Michael. She taught us to punt, which she had learned from Grandpa Eric, showing us how to trail the pole behind in the water so it would act as a rudder and stop the boat careering helplessly from bank to bank. She took us to tea at the Lygon Arms in Broadway, told us about the deer in Charlecote Park, which Shakespeare was said to have poached, and seemed as happy as I had ever seen her.

As with all actresses, Rachel's career had been interrupted by having children. She had played the Princess of France in *Love's*

Labour's Lost, the first production of the first season she and Michael were at the Old Vic. But when I was born she had to leave the company. Then she had Corin in 1939 and Lynn in 1943. Although she was always in demand, playing with Olivier at the St. James's and with Peggy Ashcroft in the famous production of *Hedda Gabler* at the Lyric, Hammersmith, and was a founder-member of the English Stage Company in their first season at the Royal Court, she did not really come into her own until television in the 1960s brought her a range of parts that no theatrical producer had ever had the foresight to offer her. Perhaps they would have if they had seen her in Shaw's *Saint Joan* in 1954 at the tiny "Q" Theatre, where she played Joan opposite Robert Shaw's Dunois. She was brave, eager, direct, and very moving. In Chicago in 1977 I watched my sister, Lynn, play Joan with the same brave directness. Lynn must have been eleven years old when Rachel played Saint Joan, old enough for the experience to affect her own performance years later, just as Rachel's performance was surely affected by her memory of Sybil Thorndike in the first production of the play that Rachel saw, as a schoolgirl of fourteen.

Michael, when he had a large part to play in the evening, seldom enjoyed company or talked much. It was not that he "lived" the part during the daytime hours, rather that he kept himself in readiness mentally, like a boxer before a big fight, or an athlete before the race. And because he was never satisfied to repeat what he had done the night before, he was often distracted and sometimes irritable. There were other troubles that season, though we knew nothing of them at the time. Bailiffs were hounding him for unpaid bills. Corin and I watched the dress rehearsal for *Antony and Cleopatra*, aghast. He seemed to forget every other line, and yet the next night he was triumphant. His best and most creative work was done that season, as Antony, Lear, and Shylock. He revised the lectures he had given the year before at Bristol University for a book, *An Actor's Ways and Means*, which was published in 1953, and began work for the Italian producer Filippo Del Guidice on a film script for *Antony and Cleopatra*.

His Shylock was fierce, funny, anguished, and awe-inspiring, combining a real ferocity in fighting for his rights under the laws of Venice with the pride and burning anguish of the Jewish patriarch, isolated in the ghetto. Forbidden to trade, Shylock is forced into money-lending by the laws of the rich mercantile state, whose merchants despised the Jews with the racist contempt and envy of the newly and fabulously rich. The play has not been fashionable for many years, and that is understandable. But I did not think the play anti-Semitic then, and I do not now. Robbed of his daughter and mocked by the anti-Semitic yuppies of Venice, Shylock loses his mind with grief. The pound of flesh, a bitter joke against the merchant Antonio, becomes a symbol for Shylock of those rights under law which he, as a Jew, has been denied. Many of the productions I have seen, including that one at Stratford, idealize the merchant society of Venice. But Michael's Shylock transcended this. His speech "Hath not a Jew eyes?" was a furious denunciation of anti-Semitism, and he wore the Star of David—"the badge of all our tribe"—on his cloak with defiant pride.

I was fifteen and almost dying with excitement when I went abroad for the first time. Tasha and I, with four other schoolfriends, set off by train to Italy, with "Mademoiselle" Eleanor Tassarty. I had a new gray flannel suit, two berets, cherry pink and gray, and a red blouse and blue skirt I had made myself in the dressmaking class. We crossed the Channel at Newhaven and were sick.

At Paris we changed stations, and sat in a French café, eating croissants and drinking French coffee. "I'm in Heaven," I thought. I was half asleep, half awake at the frontier station of Domodossola when Italian customs men came on the train to inspect our passports. Standing in the corridor, looking out of the windows, I talked to an Italian soldier. He kissed me and I felt an electric shock run through me. When he left the train I told Tasha, glowing with pride and silly with excitement. We got out at Florence and gasped—we had never seen such beauty—the glowing terra-cotta tiles on the roofs, the Duomo, the bridge across the Arno, the slopes of the hills up to Fiesole, covered with olive orchards. We strap-hung in the long buses, tramped up the 350-odd steps to the top of the Duomo, and giggled whenever our bottoms were pinched. We saw Botticelli's *Birth of Venus* and the originals of all the reproductions on the walls of our school.

On to Rome, and then Bologna and Ravenna. Here we ate with Mademoiselle Tassarty's family friends and I sat next to the son, Franco. Our knees touched under the table. He passed me some sweet wine and said, "Sweets for the sweet." He was the first man I'd ever met who wore cologne. It was Pino Silvestre, and it smelled marvelous. I gave him my address and he told me he would be coming to England for an English course to help him with his commercial studies. I noticed his hair was going thin on top, and when Tasha teased me, I became very tight-lipped and refused to talk to her. I was fifteen, but I said I was sixteen and sweated with fear in case my lie should be discovered. We were English girls, nourished on overboiled cabbage, watery boiled potatoes, and tough, tasteless meat, and like countless English girls before us, we had fallen head over heels in love with Italy, its life, its noise, its warmth, its color, and the beauty of its cities.

My last year at school, 1954, consisted of study, arguments, and endless games of racing demon. I shared a small study with my three closest friends, Tasha, Sue, and Sarah. We were the first girls at Queen's Gate to sit for and pass A-level examinations. Others, like Maria, whose parents had set their hearts on a university education, had left school for special tutoring before going on to Oxford. But we wanted to stay and study together, so we demanded and received tutoring for A-level history, French, Italian, and English, with art and Spanish as "extras." We argued for hours over the meaning of T. S. Eliot and Ezra Pound and the French symbolists that Sue was studying. Our mission was to love life, and we were told to praise poetry that "affirmed" or "enhanced" life. Our senior-year literary contributions to the school magazine, however, were steeped in sorrow, old age, and death. "Falling, the ground that met him was a grave," Sue wrote that summer in a poem called "Dissolution." One of the lines in Sarah's "Release" went "Blindly he stares ahead, but his heart drags back through the wake, and his young eyes are clouded already with age-old regret." Both were very superior to my own contribution: "As the sun disappears, its last glow fading from the villa, I see Death appear, embodied in this house." We were all seventeen years old. I finished school at the end of the summer term, proudly listing the twenty-four plays, ballets, and concerts I had attended.

That summer, Dad paid for me to spend two months staying and studying with an Italian family, the Minettis, in Tuscany. As a young man he had been sent by his stepfather to study in Heidelberg, and he knew that this was the most enjoyable way to learn a language. But he must also have known from his own experience, and certainly deduced from my ecstatic postcards, that it might be the surest way to learn absolutely nothing. After one wonderful month at the old villa in Tuscany with four generations of the Minetti family, I received a postcard from him: "I very much want to hear when you have started your lessons. Your ever devoted Dad."

Stung into action, I found a teacher in the nearby town and immersed myself in selected cantos from Dante's *Inferno*. I learned most of Machiavelli's *Il principe* by heart. I walked with Carlo Levi through the poverty-stricken villages of Catania in his classic *Cristo si è fermato a Eboli,* and disappeared for hours on end into the lives and times of Franco Maironi and his wife, Lucia, in Antonio Fogazzaro's *Piccolo mondo antico.* That "little, ancient world" slowly became as real to me as the hot sun, the cicadas, and the hospitable, happy Minettis. Set in 1852, when Italy was under the political, military, and economic occupation of the Austrian Empire, the book opened a window onto the lives of Italian men and women who lived under constant surveillance by the secret police and the threat of arrest and imprisonment. These were the years of reaction, following the defeat of the revolutions that swept across Europe in two weeks in 1848. I remember every small incident in the lives of Don Franco and his wife as vividly as I recall my own early life, and as intimately as if I had lived every moment of domestic and social detail. The wind and rain of Lake Como lashed my face. I wept with Lucia when her little girl was drowned. I shared that last solemn, silent moment with Franco and Lucia in their hotel room in Turin, and walked with them to the steamboat that would take Franco and his young friends to the battlefield to fight the Austrians. "These young men spoke of fighting with enthusiasm, but without boasting; they spoke of the future of Italy with a good deal of silliness, but one felt they didn't think their lives were worth a dried fig unless they could liberate this great old country."

From the moment I first learned to read I had always retreated into my books and lived long hours in my imagination. But what stirred me in Fogazzaro's novel connected with my world in 1954 and made me look at it more closely. On May 7, 1954, after a fifty-five-day siege, the army of the Vietnamese League of Independence had finally routed the French army, backed since 1945 by the American government. The French military chiefs and government were forced to the negotiating table. On May 8, for only the second time in my life, I read a political news story from beginning to end, on the fall of Dien Bien Phu. I was ignorant of the history of French imperialism in Indochina, but I knew immediately that I was very glad to read in the *Daily Mail* that the Viet Minh had won. As I read the history of the long Italian struggle to liberate and unify their country, moving on from *Piccolo mondo antico* to Silvio Pellico's *Le mie prigioni* (*My Prisons*), I learned how a national liberation movement suffered, and thought I knew all I needed to know about the Vietnamese struggle for liberation. The French were defeated, the Vietnamese League of Independence had won, and the war, on July 21, was officially declared to have ended. I thought it was the end of that cruel period.

Three years later, in 1957, Michael was in Saigon filming Graham Greene's novel *The Quiet American*. Vietnam had been partitioned. Two countries, North and South Vietnam, had been artificially created as the result of an international "peace" conference whose cochairmen represented Britain and the Soviet Union. A puppet regime, backed by American money and the CIA, had been installed in the South. One evening the American film crew was shooting scenes of the Indochinese New Year in the streets of Saigon. It was a religious demonstration. Suddenly the Vietnamese interpreter began shouting at the cameraman and gesturing at the placards carried aloft in the procession.

"What's he saying?" asked the director, Joe Mankiewicz. "He says we should cut," yelled the cameraman, Robert Krasker. "He says they're anti-American slogans." "What the hell," said Mankiewicz. "No one'll know what they mean."

When Michael arrived in Rome to film the interior scenes for *The Quiet American* at the Cinecittà studios, I was on holiday before my last term at drama school, renting a room in a small *pensione,* and I saw him every day. He showed me some sixty black-and-white photographs he had taken from the window of a Dakota flying from Saigon to Cambodia. A knot gathers painfully in my stomach when I look at those photographs. The year before, at the Edinburgh film festival, he had seen some of the very earliest film shot by the Lumière brothers. "Somehow it's awfully touching," he wrote, "when you see a moving picture of a small boy running across the road in 1890, to think that if he's still alive he must be a very old gentleman." Dad's black-and-white photos are curled round at the edges from being kept rolled up in a plastic band. He was a keen photographer and often pasted his snapshots into a book. But I suppose he never found the time to paste these up, and I never have. Far, far below the plane, almost beyond the range of the Leica lens, are rice fields, small roads, woods, and villages. Somewhere along those roads small boys are running to their friends or their families. A little, ancient world where life was not worth living unless that great old country could be liberated from the Deuxième Bureau, the Paris Bourse, Wall Street, the CIA.

In Tuscany in 1954 I knew no more of Vietnam than I could imagine and interpret from my studies of the Risorgimento led by Garibaldi. Then I knew America as the country that sent delicious food parcels to us in England, the country of Hollywood and the hilarious Danny Kaye, the buxom Betty Grable, and the astounding Ethel Merman, whose records I had listened to again and again. In 1953, however, I had learned that Julius and Ethel Rosenberg had been executed in the electric chair. They were communists and were said to have given the secret of the atomic bomb to the Soviet Union. Whether this was true or not, it seemed preposterous and impossible that the primitive drawing that was published in the newspapers could have explained the complicated equations of nuclear fission. In any case, capital punishment and the electric chair were positively medieval.

Paul Robeson, the great black American singer and actor, was also a communist. His passport and right to travel were taken away from him in 1949. Michael and Rachel had records of all his songs, and Corin, Lynn, and I played them over and over again on the wind-up phonograph that had been a wedding present for Rachel. We learned the words of "Let My People Go!," "My Curly-headed Baby," and "Ol' Man River" at the same time as we learned the words of the song Jiminy Cricket sings in Walt Disney's *Pinocchio*: "When you wish upon a star . . ."

It seemed the United States government was afraid of Paul Robeson and his songs, since they would not let him sing them abroad. I feel it was thanks to artists like Robeson that I did not blindly accept the anti-Communist hysteria and witch-hunting of the Eisenhower years; nor the terrible lies published about the Kenyan Mau Mau liberation movement leader Jomo Kenyatta in the British press. The truth about the British concentration camps in Kenya, such as the infamous Hola Hola camp, came out later: Africans dying in ditches they had been forced to dig themselves. What the press ignored in their coverage of the acts of revenge against white Kenyan settlers was the extreme racism and oppression of the black majority by the colonial British government and settlers of Kenya.

Finally there was Garibaldi. On the mantelpiece above the fire in Bedford House stood the six-inch-high porcelain figure of Il Generale, mass-produced in the Staffordshire potteries when Garibaldi came to England in 1864 and was welcomed by some noble families and tens of thousands of British workers. "I am not a soldier," he said at the Crystal Palace to an Italian delegation who presented him with a sword, "and I do not like the soldier's trade. I saw my father's house filled with robbers and snatched a weapon to drive them out. I am a working man, I come from the working people, and I am proud of it."

It was the reliable Dottore Sambalino, Dida Minetti's grandfather, who advised me to buy the memoirs of the Russian exile Alexander Herzen, *Passato e Pensieri*, that hot summer of 1954 in Tuscany. Through Herzen I learned about Garibaldi and read the details about his meeting with Mazzini, the founder of the Italian liberation struggle and its first illegal movement, the Carbonari. In 1864 Mazzini lived in retirement in Teddington, two and a half miles downriver from our house in Chiswick, at a time when London was a place where all the political exiles and asylum seekers in Europe could find refuge and basic democratic rights.

All the poorer classes of Teddington had crowded round the railings of our house waiting from early morning for Garibaldi. When we drove up, the crowd rushed to greet him in ecstasy, pressed his hands, shouted "God bless you Garibaldi!" Women caught at his hand and kissed it, kissed the hem of his cloak—I saw this with my own eyes—lifted their children up to him and wept. Suddenly, an old Italian, an emigrant from days long past, a poor fellow who made ice cream, burst through, caught Garibaldi by the skirt of his coat and stopped him, burst into tears and said, "Well, now I can die. I have seen him, I have seen him!"

An Italian novel, some black-and-white photographs, some phonograph records, a porcelain figure, and the diaries in Italian of a
Russian exile who died in London in 1870—these few and varied
mementos of history guided my attitude to the political struggles of
the 1950s. In spite of the fact that my father did not wish to talk. In
spite of the fact that my school was thoroughly conventional and
taught Italian art of the Renaissance and not the art and history of my
times. In spite of the propaganda on the radio and in the widely
available press. These small seeds, all that remained of great struggles
for democratic rights of long ago, required only a new time of
struggles for liberation and democratic rights in order to germinate.

Twenty-three years later, in 1977, I stood in the refugee camps in
Lebanon and saw Palestinian and Lebanese women lift their baby
sons to greet Yasser Arafat. "Allah bless you, Abu Ammar!" they
called to the leader of the Palestine Liberation Organization, just as
the Italian emigrants and British workers had greeted General Giuseppe Garibaldi in 1864, a few years before the liberation of Italy from
Austrian rule, and Italian unification.

CHAPTER 5

I passed the Italian exam with distinction and my father glowed with pride when I told him that the oral examiner, a lady in her sixties, had offered to recommend me for an interpreter's job.

Throughout the autumn of 1954, while studying, I had taken a bus twice a week up Abbey Road for singing lessons with Jani Strasser. Jani and his wife, Irene, were Hungarian and very close friends of my parents'. Michael met Jani when he needed coaching for the role of Macheath in *The Beggar's Opera*, which he performed at the Haymarket in March 1940. Jani was a superb singing coach and developed Michael's light baritone into a very good voice. He was on the teaching staff of the Young Vic Theatre School formed by Michel Saint-Denis and George Devine, and later went to the Glyndebourne Opera House.

Jani sat before the grand piano in the teaching room, the light dim because of the heavy wet trees outside and the sixty-watt electric lightbulb inside. All the surfaces in the room were covered with pictures and small silver objects he and Irene had brought with them to London from Hungary. I knew so little history when I met Jani that I never asked him about his early life or how he left Hungary because of the Nazis. His enormous intelligent eyes shone with vigor behind thick spectacles, and I have never forgotten what he taught me. He gave me a number of physical exercises to loosen and strengthen the muscles around the small of the back and the ribs. We worked up and down the scale on da's and mm's with sung phrases.

"Winter, summer, autumn, spring! All the little birds are on the wing." (Chord up a semitone.)

"You must feel as if you have diarrhea."

"Stop listening to yourself! Stop listening to the sounds you make! If you listen to the sound you start correcting the sound. You have a lot of little poodles, you see. If you keep them on a lead and keep pulling at it they can never do anything on their own. They are very clever little poodles. But if you keep pulling at them they can only do what you tell them. You must only think of what you are singing about, why you are singing, what your feelings are. Singing is just the same as speaking, only your feelings are so strong you just have to sing."

Whenever an actor asks me to listen to a reading of a line, I want to explain about the poodles. I believed what Jani said, because he spoke with the kind of authority I trusted absolutely, but it took me years to understand fully why he was right, and to let my own poodles go free, never to plan how I would say a line, only to think of the situation, and listen to the other actors. The pressures of film and TV schedules are intense. Directors get nervous if they don't see and hear something that "works," or, on the contrary, if they see and hear something that they are not expecting and that does not accord with the sounds they think they ought to be hearing. So actors get nervous and start checking and controlling. Skillful actors acquire great expertise, and the greater the expertise, the more difficult it becomes to give Jani's poodles a free rein.

His advice stays with me and has been invaluable throughout my professional life as an actress. Acting means working to be alive and alert to the incident and the moment, to the director, the other actors, and the script. What is hard, and really has to be worked at, is being able to go with whatever comes up from other actors or the director at each moment of a performance and not to try to force a repetition of something that went well the day before. I love reading around a

My father's mother, Daisy Scudamore (*above*), left home when she was a young girl to try her luck in the theatre. *Above right*: Roy Redgrave, my father's father, starred in Australian silent films. *Right*: My parents, Rachel and Michael, in 1940. He was by then the most popular film star in Britain and had just joined the navy. *Below right*: My mother's parents, Eric and Beatrice Kempson, at Dartmouth in 1939, with me and my brother, Corin.

Above left: With my father in the garden of our house in St. John's Wood, August 1940. *Above right*: Cousin Lucy Kempson. *Center*: The family at Bedford House, 1950. *Inset*: Michael filming *The Quiet American* in Saigon in 1957.

Playing my father's
Bechstein at Bedford
House, 1950.

With my best friends, Sue, Sarah, and Tasha, on
the balcony at Queen's Gate School, 1954.

Above: With Claudio in Italy in 1954. *Below*: Corin
and Lynn in Rome in 1957.

On the lake at Wilks Water (*top*), my mother's cottage in Hampshire. Corin and I are rowing Rachel and Barney, her Labrador. Michael and Lynn are on shore with Lynn's pony, Rosalinda. *Bottom*: Rosalinda with Rachel, Lynn, and me.

Playing Colin in *Mother Goose*, the Christmas pantomime at Leatherhead Theatre, 1958, with Nyree Dawn Porter (*right*); with Tony Britton in *Behind the Mask*, my first film, 1958 (*below, left*); with Michael in *A Touch of the Sun* at the Saville Theatre, 1958, my first part in a West End play (*below, right*).

Opposite, top: With Derek Godfrey, Bill Travers, and Peter Hall at the opening of the Royal Shakespeare Company's season in 1962.
Far left: As Rosalind in *As You Like It*, with Rosalind Knight as Celia, 1961.
Near left: As Katharina, with Derek Godfrey as Petruchio, in *The Taming of the Shrew* in 1962.
Above: Michael and Rachel's silver wedding anniversary, 1960; and as Nina in *The Seagull*, with Rachel as Polina, 1964 (*right*).

As Rosalind in Michael
Elliott's production of
As You Like It at
Stratford-upon-Avon, 1961.

role—finding out about the times when the writer wrote a play, the social conditions, the literature, and the culture. It is exciting to make discoveries through reading, and while this takes time, particularly when you are married and have children, I don't regard it as hard work. The real work of acting is letting go and unleashing Jani's poodles.

At home, every Sunday afternoon, Michael would sit down at the piano. He played well, both classical music and American songs with a syncopated rhythm. He and Rachel sang through *The Beggar's Opera,* Schubert—especially the dramatic "Erlkönig"—Benjamin Britten's setting of "Little Sir William," Noël Coward, Jerome Kern's *Show Boat,* and, a regular favorite, Judy Garland's "The Trolley Song," which Corin, Lynn, and I sang with gusto. "Clang-clang-clang went the trolley! Ding-ding-ding went the bell! Zing-zing-zing went my heart strings . . ." The exhilarating tempo, the words tumbling, pouring out, caught us breathless, scrambling to keep pace with that wonderful trolley. Michael had made me learn ballet before I grew too tall; now he wanted me to train for musical comedy. He urged me not to go to drama school but to concentrate on singing and modern dancing. He told me about Noël Coward's star, Gertrude Lawrence, saying that an actress who could sing and dance would have a big career. He paid for me to take tap lessons at Buddy Bradley's school in Denman Street, Soho, just behind the famous "we never close" Windmill Theatre, where the showgirls played five or six performances every afternoon and evening.

Buddy Bradley, whose very name conjured up the lights of that mysterious, glamorous, faraway place in New York called Broadway, did not teach beginners. In fact I never saw him. Twice a week I joined seven or eight other novices, and we tapped up and down the rotting floorboards behind an agile instructor who never took his eyes off his reflection in the big mirror. Bradley was being squeezed out of his premises in Denman Street by his landlord. Hence the rotting boards. Soho, the center of pimping, prostitutes, and crime, was also the location of Wardour Street, the offices of all the major film studios, desperate independents, sleazy agents, and most of the West End theatres. The delicious aromas of fresh Italian bread, French patisserie, and Algerian coffee on Old Compton Street mingled with the smells of urine, sweat, and stale whiskey. The tiny dirty name-plates of film companies in Wardour Street were not alluring, only frightening.

If there had been a brilliant modern dance teacher in London, I would probably have taken Michael's advice and pursued musical comedy. As there was not, my admiration and yearning for the lights of Stratford-upon-Avon, the plays of Shakespeare, and Peggy Ashcroft remained steadfast. I doubted if the Memorial Theatre would ever invite a musical comedy actress to join the company, so I told my father I wanted to go to drama school, and I attended an audition and interview with Gwyneth Thurburn, the principal of the Central School of Speech and Drama.

Gwyneth Thurburn looked at me over the top of her desk, and told me not to expect anything noteworthy in the way of employment in the theatre until I was well into my thirties. My height, she said, was a handicap I would not overcome until the onset of middle age. I was neither alarmed nor discouraged by her view. I accepted it as my fate. To make matters worse, although at the age of fourteen I could still play tennis without spectacles, by now I had to wear them all the time. Rachel was very sensitive and always knew when I was depressed and discouraged, and she would exclaim, "Oh! my beautiful daughter!" with such total conviction that for a moment I believed her. My morale was also sustained by Ellen Terry, that great Shakespearean actress who had written in her autobiography that her main ambition was always to be a useful actress. If that was good enough for Ellen Terry, it was good enough for me.

On January 11, 1955, I took the Underground to Gloucester Road station, ascended the stairs that I had climbed every morning for six years to go to school, and walked up Queen's Gate to the Royal Albert Hall. The Central School had its theatre, main rehearsal room, and a registrar's office in a section of the vast corridors that ran round the enormous circular concert hall. For my first day I bought black tights, a leotard, a copy of Miss Thurburn's book, *Voice and Speech,* and a one-inch-long piece of whalebone with a groove at either end. In my bag was *The Oxford Book of English Verse* (a required textbook), a towel, soap, and a hairbrush. I was handed a typewritten page of Elizabethan prologue. For the spring term we would concentrate on

voice, mime, movement, verse-speaking, and the delivery of a prologue from Elizabethan drama.

Speech therapy was one of the courses provided at Central. We
did hours of consonant and vowel practice with the whalebone between our front teeth. But I found concentrating entirely on technique limiting. Weeks spent listening to sounds and correcting them,
with no work on a scene or situation from a play, on subject or
character, made me nervous. My voice strangled with self-conscious-
ness. I compared this with Jani's method, but I could not analyze what
was going wrong. And the mime classes were not much better. They
were of the old school, "pretend you have a teacup and saucer in
your hand." But in my delight at being a student I was not in a critical
frame of mind and accepted on trust that I was getting the best
training possible.

Four years earlier the Young Vic Theatre School, run in conjunc-
tion with the Young Vic Theatre by the great French director Michel
Saint-Denis, Glen Byam-Shaw, and George Devine—all close colleagues of Michael and Rachel—had been closed down. The Treasury refused funds to the organization, which at that time included
the Old Vic Theatre Company. The Arts Council drama director,
Llewellyn Rees, was hostile to the exercises he saw the students
working on. "I went into a class of Saint-Denis's," said Rees, "and
these boys and girls were all being animals; it was like going into a
lunatic asylum." When Michel Saint-Denis took my father round the
school for the last time he was crying.

Before the Young Vic, Michel Saint-Denis had run another school,
the London Theatre Centre, for four years. And he had persuaded
Litz Pisk to join him. A brilliant young Viennese woman who had
fled from the Nazi Anschluss in 1938, Litz was working at Dartington
with Michael Chekhov, Anton Chekhov's nephew, when Michel
found her. As a young girl in Vienna she had studied painting, design,
and movement from the most advanced generation of artists. At
Dartington she taught movement and painting. When I worked with
her later in the 1960s, she told me that one of the tasks she set her
students at Dartington was to find a hundred different shades of red
in various textures, and make a collage of them. The challenge and
excitement of such a project took my breath away. Animal mime,

clown techniques, music hall, Noh masks, improvisation, the work of Isadora Duncan, Meyerhold, Stanislavsky, Picasso, Cocteau—all were embodied in the approach and the concepts of Saint-Denis and George Devine. When they were denied funds and resigned on a point of principle, this work was brought to a halt.

Thinking back now, I can understand why my father urged me not to go to drama school. No reverberation of this kind of work and these great cultural achievements existed in the training at the Central School. But when I went there in 1955, I failed to recognize either the depths of English middle-class philistinism or the extraordinary creativity of the European, Soviet, and American artists my parents and their colleagues admired so much. I was amazed when an Israeli student bitterly and angrily criticized the training at Central. I could not understand what he thought was missing.

This may have been why Michael gave me two tickets for a production by a new company in the East End of London. Theatre Workshop was presenting *Richard II* at the Theatre Royal, Stratford East, directed by Joan Littlewood. The company had toured all over England for a few years and, thanks to Peggy Ashcroft and many of her friends, including my father, they now had a permanent home for the first time. I sat in shock through the performance. The stage was gray and black. Richard was accompanied by a group of sycophants, liars, and careerists, and he was clearly a man of similar character. He spoke like an ordinary man. Bolingbroke spoke with an accent—in fact none of the nobles spoke or behaved like either actors or aristocrats. The old theatre was dingy and threadbare. My shock turned into pompous effrontery. I took the Underground train home elated with indignation. My father was waiting for me and invited me to sit down and eat some scrambled eggs with him.

"Well, tell me about it," he said.

"Oh, it was dreadful—well, interesting—but dreadful." I took a deep breath and let out a tirade of prejudice and ignorance. When I had stopped to breathe and take another mouthful of scrambled eggs, I looked up at my father. He looked back in silence with grave, troubled eyes. He did not speak for quite a while. Then he said, quietly, his voice deep and tremulous with emotion: "Never, never speak like that. Never, never go to a production with your head full of what you like, and then come away full of what you don't like. You must always begin with what is the aim of the production. Then you can speak about what the production achieved, and only then can you speak about what it failed to achieve, what the mistakes may have been."

He said more than this, but that is what I remember, and will never forget. I was shocked and chagrined. I was made to think.

I went back for the next production—*Edward II*—with Amos, the Israeli student. My prejudices had been rocked by my father's criticism and a feeling that Amos knew a lot about life that I did not. This time I understood more about Joan Littlewood's company and their approach. The courts, the church, and society of these medieval monarchs were cruel, vicious, and criminal. They and their barons were basically feudal families fighting ruthlessly for absolute power. They were not supermen appointed by God. Neither were the churchmen, who were weak, greedy, and treacherous. The more poetic their language, the more it served to cover up their actual deeds and ambitions.

That summer Michael asked Joan Littlewood if Corin and I could watch rehearsals of a Ben Jonson play, *Volpone*. We watched the energetic, forthright Joan working on improvisations with her company, stripping away every cliché that even *her* actors sometimes fell into: "No, let's get rid of that crap!" Her actors treated her familiarly and directly; there was no false diplomacy and no egotism. The play was staged in semi-Elizabethan costume but included a variety of hilarious anachronisms. Mosca, Volpone's pimp, fleeing through Venice from his pursuers, swam down the Grand Canal, indicated by the small orchestra pit, with a snorkel tube and flippers.

Michael introduced us to Sean O'Casey's plays. I remember vividly sitting on hard benches in a room in Notting Hill Gate called the New Lindsey Theatre. At the other end of the room, with no curtains and no effects, a group of actors opened our eyes, ears, and minds to the tragic stories of the Irish struggle for self-determination. The performances were so powerful that we forgot who we were and where we were.

That July, in 1955, Michael opened in the Jean Giraudoux play *Tiger at the Gates,* directed by Harold Clurman. Corin and I watched all the rehearsals, thanks to Clurman's kindness. Robert Shaw played a sailor; Diane Cilento, later Sean Connery's wife, was Helen of

Troy. The theme of the play, written in the 1930s, was antiwar. Its original title was *La guerre de Troie n'aura pas lieu* (*The Trojan War Shall Not Take Place*). Hector, played by Michael, was doing everything in his power to prevent Troy from going to war with Greece. For the first time Greek and Trojan history came to life before our eyes; we had both plodded through pages of Homer's *Iliad* at school without excitement. Diane Cilento, with her Australian accent, was beautiful and sexy, and Harold Clurman cast her knowing the play would transfer to Broadway if it succeeded. An English director would never have cast her, and she was perfect. She had an extraordinary speech in which she foresaw her own future, old and wrinkled, covered with makeup, eating sweets by the fireplace.

Harold Clurman was a founding member of the Group Theatre of the 1930s in the United States. He had often visited the Soviet Union, where he had met the great Russian actor/director Konstantin Stanislavsky and had been inspired, like many other Americans, by the extraordinary work of the Moscow Arts Theatre Company. The vigor, precision, and energy of his direction, and his attention to detail during rehearsals, were thrilling. The production was a big success. It was taken to Broadway, and that Christmas my father paid for me to join him in New York for three weeks.

I saw Arthur Miller's *A View from the Bridge*, with Van Heflin; Shirley Booth in *Come Back, Little Sheba;* Julie Harris in Anouilh's *The Lark;* and *A Hatful of Rain*, with Shelley Winters, Ben Gazzara, and Tony Franciosa, developed from improvisations at Lee Strasberg's famous Actors Studio, which I was allowed to attend every morning for a week. Here I saw professional actors working on scenes, which they then analyzed with Strasberg and their fellow actors. The Actors Studio had become world famous because many of the greatest American actors—Marlon Brando, Julie Harris, and Eli Wallach—worked there, and studied "the Method," based on Stanislavsky's teachings. It was housed in an old church hall, with wooden benches ranged in tiers around an acting area. Strasberg sat in the center, by a table, sometimes taking notes. After a scene had been played or improvised, a discussion would begin, with Strasberg and other members putting questions to the actors. His comments were often fascinating. On Shakespeare's Richard III: "His deformity is basically a spiritual degeneration, something inside the man. He exaggerates its physical effects to win sympathy or strike fear in his opponents. Probably his hunchback is not actually very noticeable physically. Look at pictures of David Garrick in the role and you will see; he hardly padded his costume at all." Then, "You must be very careful with illusion onstage. For instance, if the scene is set in an unswept, untidy room, like this [he gestured at the studio, and we all laughed, because it was], and you beat a carpet or a cushion and real dust comes out, the whole audience will sneeze and you'll stop the performance."

Watching one scene, I thought there was a problem. Unlike the method of Stanislavsky, where the actor must start from the given circumstances of the play, the Actors Studio started from the "feelings" of the individual actor. An actress was having difficulty; I felt she had decided to concentrate on her feelings of cold, fear, and so on, and had forgotten the situation her character was in. So I asked Strasberg about this. Strasberg said it was not the issue. The truth of her feelings and her own conviction were the task at hand. I was not convinced; I felt that both would develop from her consciousness of the given circumstances. But I admired him and his colleagues for recognizing that acting is not a question of sufficient practice; it is first of all a question of what outlook or approach is guiding the work, and that continuous and serious analysis is required to overcome problems. Without this an actor's craft will degenerate into repetition of effects that "work," or, as Stanislavsky said, "empty stencils."

That Christmas I also saw Strasberg's daughter Susan in *The Diary of Anne Frank*. I cried and cried, marveling again at the total conviction of Susan, Joseph Schildkraut, and the rest of the cast. One of the members of the Actors Studio, Fred Sadoff, had become a close friend of Dad's. I had long discussions with him about the Method, and watched him work on a scene with another actress. One day we were in the Actors Studio when an actor said to Fred, "Look, there's Eva Marie. Isn't it great how beautiful she looks now she has a job." It was Eva Marie Saint, who played Marlon Brando's girlfriend in *On the Waterfront*.

In New York I experienced the glitter of the city's thousands of lights in the skyscrapers and in the expensive stores. But I also saw the actors' world, always treading between unemployment and hunger and the "big success," with ovations at Sardi's restaurant. The actor who spoke about Eva Marie Saint was excited and proud that one more hungry actor had got through, and I knew what he meant when he said she was "looking great" because she had a job.

I got back to England in January 1956 crammed with impressions of what I had seen. I had been given a new perspective on the actor's work, so different from everything I had been taught at Central School, and I longed to share it with others.

CHAPTER 6

Clive Goodwin, a student in the third year at Central School, listened to my description of my experiences in New York. The more we talked, the more we convinced ourselves that we should publish a magazine where work of the kind I had seen at the Actors Studio could be discussed. Neither of us had any knowledge or experience of writing, still less of editing or publishing a magazine of this kind. But neither, for that matter, did anyone else. There was no magazine or periodical at that time in England that seriously discussed and criticized work in the theatre. So *Encore*, which began as a quarterly in the mid-fifties and soon became a monthly, found quite a substantial readership.

What had invigorated and excited me so much in New York was not really new. It had begun with the Russian Revolution, which had profoundly affected a generation of writers, actors, and directors in the American theatre of the 1930s. But it seemed new to me, and suddenly this new life was springing up in London too. At the Royal Court Theatre in Sloane Square in 1956 George Devine formed the English Stage Company, dedicated to the work of writers and play-wrights such as Bertolt Brecht, whose work had hardly been performed in London. Rachel was a founder-member, and the company included George Devine himself, Rosalie Crutchley, Kenneth Haigh, Alan Bates, Michael Gwynn, and Robert Stephens. The top salary, earned by four members of the company, was £30 a week. Four were on £20, four on £15, and another four on £10. The assistant stage managers, who were students, were paid £1. That was the wage Granny Margaret had earned and had just survived on, provided she walked to work, when she joined Sarah Bernhardt's company in London as a lady-in-waiting and an extra in *Hamlet* and *La Dame aux Camélias*. In those days, she complained, the London theatre was hidebound in snobbery and outworn tradition. So it seemed to most young English and American writers, until the English Stage Company began its first season.

At the Royal Court one morning when *Look Back in Anger* was in the third week of rehearsal I saw Tony Richardson, a tall, thin young man who was the director of the play. He had come to see Rachel two years before, to ask her to join the cast of a BBC TV play he was directing. "He's just down from Oxford," George Devine told her, "and he's very clever." Tony Richardson had exasperated the BBC by insisting on casting a black West Indian actor as Othello. He hated the BBC program chiefs, thought they were hopeless philistines, and left the BBC as soon as he could. *Look Back in Anger* was to open in a few days and the company was nervous. The future of the English Stage Company, and opportunities for new writing, were at stake in this production.

The play opened on May 8, 1956, and was greeted with a nearly unanimous howl of scorn and abuse from the drama critics in the daily papers. One of them used the phrase "kitchen sink," meaning that here there were no maids or butlers, and the penniless young men and women who lived in bed-sitting-rooms washed their own teacups. But that was the whole point, as I saw it; that was how most of my fellow drama students, and thousands of young people all over the country, lived.

Sunday came, and Kenneth Tynan, the drama critic of *The Observer*, said he doubted he could fall in love with anyone who didn't like *Look Back in Anger*. Harold Hobson, the elderly and much respected critic of *The Sunday Times*, declared that he had seen the play a second time and had changed his mind: it was a masterpiece.

I don't think of John Osborne's play as a masterpiece. I loved it because its principal character, Jimmy Porter, was funny and defiant, utterly scornful of middle-class society, its values, its hypocrisy. Arthur Miller's *The Crucible,* which was the second play the English Stage Company performed, fully deserved that praise. I was enthralled by it, though I didn't recognize its greatness, nor its contemporary significance. I knew of Senator McCarthy, and the House Un-American Activities Committee. I knew that Miller himself had been interrogated and cited for contempt for his refusal to name names; that all Paul Robeson's records had been removed from shops and libraries; and that hundreds of American artists and writers had been blacklisted. But Senator McCarthy's star was on the wane, or so we were told. He was to die a year later, and *The Times,* in one of its most pontifical and elegant obituaries, remarked that the passing of such a vulgar, unscrupulous demagogue would hardly occasion much mourning. What the obituary didn't mention was that those who had been ruined by the McCarthyite witch-hunts remained blacklisted, or were forced to work at a fraction of their former salaries under assumed names. Nor did any of the obituaries point out that the specter of communism that had haunted America in the 1940s and 1950s had also haunted Britain.

Samuel Beckett's *Waiting for Godot* was performed at this time, directed by Peter Hall. Once again it was Kenneth Tynan and Harold Hobson who went against the damning tide of press reviews. *Godot* played at the Arts Theatre for one week and at the Criterion Theatre for eight months. Both plays are now classics of the contemporary theatre.

When the autumn term began at Central, my class was to perform Angus Wilson's *The Mulberry Bush,* which had opened the season at the Royal Court that spring. I was given the part of Rose Padley, the elderly matriarch of a family of Fabian socialists. I knew that I could never understand this woman and her family from within the limits of my imagination. She was modeled on Beatrice Webb, so I borrowed every book by the Webbs that I could lay my hands on, read George Bernard Shaw's diaries, found a reference there to Eleanor Rathbone, the Labour MP, and then, in a biography of Miss Rathbone, found to my delight a reference to our dear old cousin Lucy Kempson. Now Rose Padley began to come to life. In her lines I could hear Cousin Lucy's characteristic flat vowels and the forth-right, emphatic rhythms of her speech. Our director, James Roose Evans, encouraged us to improvise and to analyze and discuss our characters. One night he organized a dinner party for us at his flat. Each of us had to arrive "in character" and stay in our role until we left, some hours later. Jimmy was a breath of fresh air. We began to think that our training was making progress.

When the Bolshoi ballet made their first visit to London in 1956, a group of us slept all night under the back portico at Covent Garden in order to be first in line in the morning for gallery tickets. Nowhere, not even in New York, had I seen a stage filled with such life and dramatic conviction as the Bolshoi presented in *Swan Lake, The Fountains of Bakshisarai,* and *Romeo and Juliet.* The legendary Ulanova danced Juliet. She was said to be fifty. When she ran across the stage to meet Romeo in Friar Laurence's cell, there was the kind of silence in the audience I had never known before. I became one with Ulanova, knowing or rediscovering what it was to be sixteen and desperately in love in a hostile world. She transcended her years, the centuries, and the limits of the stage itself.

When I got home I pasted the ticket stub for *Romeo and Juliet* in my scrapbook. When I married Tony Richardson, seven years later, that scrapbook, together with boxes full of cuttings, old photographs, and every copy of *Encore,* were gleefully chucked on a rubbish heap by my husband. "What did you do that for?" I wailed, half in admiration of such a radical solution to the problem of clutter. "Those are my memories, for when I'm old." "If that's all you'll have when you're old I feel sorry for you," Tony said. So I lit a match under them. But I still have—or rather I have my eye on, since it belongs to Rachel—Ulanova's ballet shoe. It was presented to Michael at the Soviet embassy in London, from Ulanova, in honor of the first visit to Moscow by the Shakespeare Memorial Theatre Company.

The press notices were unanimous in admiration of the Bolshoi, and we students were aglow with love for the Russians and their artistry. We hoped and believed fervently that this cultural exchange would bring about a closer understanding between people in England and the Soviet Union. We were convinced that great art like the Bolshoi's would not only overcome barriers but break them down.

We did not know, as we went home that Saturday night, that the Hungarian revolution had begun.

On Tuesday, October 23, the Petofi Circle, a group of Hungarian writers and poets, had demanded freedom of the press, free elections, and changes in the government. Ten thousand students had demonstrated at the Kossuth Memorial in Budapest and marched to the radio station demanding that it broadcast a seventeen-point manifesto. Workers from the giant Csepel factory joined them, and soon one hundred thousand workers and students had gathered. The secret police fired on the demonstrators. Stalin's statue was pulled off its pedestal, and detachments in the army handed out arms to units of the workers and students. The first secretary of the Hungarian Communist Party called officially for troops to be sent from the Soviet Union, but when the first regiment arrived they began to fraternize with the Hungarian workers' units, and soon a general strike had spread throughout the country. Workers' councils were formed and demanded the immediate disbandment of the secret police and the withdrawal of Soviet troops.

On Thursday, November 1, I woke early and rushed to the door as usual to pick up my dad's copy of *The Guardian*, together with Nanny's *Daily Mail*, eager to get the news from Hungary before the papers disappeared on my dad's breakfast tray. But to my surprise the front-page story was not from Budapest. Prime Minister Anthony Eden had ordered the RAF to bomb Port Said, Suez, and Cairo, and the Canal Zone was being invaded by British troops. There had been many civilian casualties.

Three months earlier, President Gamal Abdel Nasser had nationalized the Suez Canal to finance the Aswan Dam project, which would provide electricity for the whole of Egypt. The British and American governments and the International Bank for Reconstruction and Development had reneged on an earlier promise of a loan for the project, and Israel had stepped up raids into the Egyptian-controlled Gaza Strip. All year, but crucially since the nationalization, the British press had been whipping up war fever. Editorial writers recalled Eden's prewar resignation in protest against Chamberlain's appeasement of Hitler, and now racist cartoons appeared depicting Nasser with a huge hooked nose.

The press proprietors, of course, all have close connections with the British military and security services, so they knew Eden's cabinet was secretly preparing for war. No doubt they also knew about the MI6 plot to assassinate Nasser. According to Peter Wright, the former MI5 officer who wrote *Spycatcher* and who bugged the Egyptian embassy in London, Eden initially approved the murder operation and called it off only when the French and Israeli governments agreed to a joint attack on Suez.

The Israeli army launched a full-scale invasion of the Sinai. The Egyptian army counterattacked to protect their territory. This was the prearranged cue for the British and French governments to issue an ultimatum that they knew must be rejected: Egyptian troops must withdraw ten miles from the Canal Zone, allowing British and French troops to occupy Port Said, Suez, and Ismailia, "to separate the belligerents." To maintain this fraud, the ultimatum was simultaneously conveyed to the Israeli government, which of course accepted it. It had already been agreed that the Israeli army would halt its invasion outside the ten-mile "exclusion zone" so that it could accept the ultimatum and hold its troops at the ready.

When I read of these events I was horrified, not only at the unlawful invasion and the bombing of civilians just because they were Arabs, but also because it was now obvious that the British and French governments, who had condemned the entry of Soviet troops into Hungary, would not answer President Nagy's appeal for help. With the European troops engaged in Suez, it followed automatically that Khrushchev and the Soviet government must have known there would be no European opposition if new tanks rolled into Budapest. This happened on November 1, and these new troops did not fraternize; they shot, believing what they had been told, that fascists were trying to take over Soviet Hungary.

Why was the Soviet Union crushing the Hungarian political revolution—a workers' revolution that sought workers' power for socialism through workers' councils—and yet supporting Nasser and the Egyptian Arab revolution? I could not understand this contradiction, and no one I knew could explain and clarify these events. That weekend I walked for miles through the Odiham woods near my mother's house in Hampshire, questions tumbling in my mind. I did not believe for one moment the official Soviet explanation. Neither did I believe Anthony Eden's lies. I knew that the old colonialist whip was out again, and I knew neither Britain, France, nor Israel had the right to control one yard of Egyptian territory. I knew nothing about the Palestinians at this time, but I did know that Israel had joined the British and French governments in an attack that bore all the hallmarks of the old pre–World War I imperialist looters. Why did the United States oppose the British/French invasion of Egypt yet refuse Imre Nagy's appeal for help against the Soviet invasion of Hungary? Had not the United States spent millions of dollars in opposing the totalitarian rule of Stalin, and then Khrushchev?

I began writing to Cousin Lucy, asking her help with the history of social reformers so I could better understand the history of my character in *The Mulberry Bush*. But neither she nor I could think of anything else but Hungary. I read a letter in *The Guardian* from a Hungarian organization in Ladbroke Grove, which appealed for volunteers to help sort and pack clothes for the refugees who were pouring across the Austrian border. I told my parents I must leave Central at once. It was the start of my final year, but Gwyneth Thurburn was understanding and said I could still come back in the spring term if I wanted to.

A red, white, and green Hungarian flag hung over the front door of the Ladbroke Grove offices of the relief organization. I was shown upstairs to a room full of clothes and was told to sort them into piles—trousers, skirts, shoes, coats, gloves, children's clothes—and put them into cloth sacks. I worked with the other volunteers from first thing in the morning until late at night, with a plate of goulash for dinner at midday. Every morning, before catching the bus, I would pore over the newspapers. The Hungarian workers were forming councils, which in effect were soviets. A letter in *The Times* confirmed that real authority in Hungary for the past few weeks was "in the hands of the workers' councils, now outlawed by a regime which is supported by nobody except the invading Soviet forces." I went along to my first political rally, at the Albert Hall. It was a huge gathering, very subdued, and I remember nothing of what was said, nor even the names of the speakers, only the freedom fighters who came onto the platform, wearing black hoods to prevent identification.

"One feels quite desperate at being so helpless," wrote Cousin

Lucy, "but one must cling to the fact that we *are* doing what lies in our power, little as that is, and I think the Hungarians know it. It is for *Europe* to pull together and that is exactly what they are *not* doing. Then there might be a solid body of opinion to which even Russia might pay some attention." After signing herself "your loving old cousin," she added a comforting postscript: "And I *do* think you are doing all you can to help."

But it was no comfort, though it was kindly meant. I had no wish to disparage my work, nor my fellow volunteers, who worked every bit as hard as I. But surely it could not be all that could be done? The Christmas lights and decorations in the shops around Knightsbridge and Kensington seemed grotesque. Training to be an actress and planning a career seemed utterly secondary, of little or no importance. Reality, in the form of the Hungarian political revolution, had burst through the limits of my student life and my ambitions. Worse still, it confronted me with the poverty of my knowledge. I sorted clothes and I copied maps for students who were driving trucks to Hungary, but I could do nothing more. The Hungarian revolution was crushed, the British and French troops withdrew from Suez, and I could not understand what could be done politically because no one could explain the contradictions.

Dear old Cousin Lucy, aged eighty, the most knowledgeable and thoughtful of all my relatives and friends, was typical of the caring liberals of her day. Her remarks about Europe pulling together and Russia bowing to public opinion reminded me of the nineteenth-century cartoons in her old bound *Punch* albums. What I needed was someone who could have explained to me the contradictions, origins, causes, and consequences of Stalinism. The inability to analyze objective contradictions runs like an open sore through the whole history of English philosophy. Shakespeare had a good laugh, I believe, as he wrote the scene where the superstitious Macbeth believes he sees Burnham Wood moving up the hillside to his castle. Shakespeare was something of a materialist, like his contemporary the scientist Francis Bacon, and something of a dialectician. Those who cannot understand that all contradictions have an objective historical source are doomed either to ignore them and be defeated by them or to become skeptical about any possible solution and empirically jump from day to day doing "what they can." Unable to answer any of the most important questions in my life, I jumped unhappily back into the daily routine of a final-year drama student. Get on with the things you know about, I told myself. Leave politics to the politicians.

CHAPTER 7

A bout two dozen students, including Judi Dench and myself, graduated from Central School on June 4, 1957, at a public matinee at Wyndham's Theatre in the Charing Cross Road. Our teachers had selected roles and scenes for us to perform before an audience of producers and their assistants, directors and their wives, casting directors and their secretaries, and, of course, several hundred mums and dads, sisters, cousins, and aunts.

What a strange ordeal. It seems incredible now that our three years of training and our prospects for a career in the profession we had chosen should be summed up in one hot afternoon's performance in June. But we were so conditioned to accept that our profession was a lottery in which the odds were heavily stacked against us that I doubt whether any of us thought what a wretched waste of training and of talent it was to be thrust out upon the world in this way. In one respect at least we were more fortunate than those who came after us. At that time, if you were lucky enough to get the offer of a job when you left drama school, you could take it, wherever the job might be. Four years later, British Actors' Equity introduced a policy known as "restricted entry," which meant that only a small quota of jobs was available to students leaving drama school. The West End theatres, and many other areas besides, were out of bounds to anyone who did not already have a union card and previous experience. It was an iniquitous policy, discriminating against the young, those who were trying to enter the profession, supposedly to the advantage of those who were already in it.

Each of us had sat for a portrait photograph and had it copied, postcard size, to send to every management agency in the country. Mine was by Paul Tanqueray, who had a little studio in his flat in Thurloe Square. He had taken pictures of Mum and Dad, and Uncle Robin, who had started acting not long before he joined the navy and was killed at Singapore. Paul Tanqueray's friends called him Tank—a most unsuitable nickname since he was slight and gentle. He flitted and fluttered around his camera, changing the setting and changing it back again. I tried to look thoughtful and serious, capable of playing the "older woman," which I was sure I was destined for. I was twenty, and my main role in the public matinee was that of a forty-five-year-old society mother. I was disappointed with the part but well prepared to swallow the lump in my throat and do my best.

Strangely, I cannot remember the play from which my scene was taken, or anything about the other characters, or even the name of the character I was playing. I must have played many such parts in my last year at Central and in my memory now they have merged into one. I thought I knew all about how to make up for such roles using the fat, hard sticks of Leichner greasepaint that were the tools of the trade. How to use the palm of the hand as a palette, smeared with a dab of Crowe's Cremine, which the warmth of the hand melted. Rubbing the sticks of No. 9 and No. 5 into the greasy palm made a flesh tint. A touch of No. 3 and a dab of one of the slender carmines brought a blush to the cheeks. For the lips, carmine mixed with white No. 20 produced a pink suitable for Shakespeare. For modern parts you used vermilion, or a real lipstick if you could afford it. To curl or wave our hair we used bobby pins or pipe cleaners. There were no electric tongs or heated rollers then, although I did possess three giant American metal clip rollers that I had brought back from my trip to New York.

For the older woman, as a rule, I used a generous sprinkling of Johnson's baby powder for my hair. But since this was our final show, we who played the older parts were allowed to rent wigs. I chose an absolutely white wig with a blue rinse, short and waved. My own mother was forty-five, and if she had any white hairs one never noticed them. But I drew no conclusion from that. If I were to convince an audience that I was a society woman of forty-five, I had first of all to convince myself, and that meant a white wig.

I looked at myself in the mirror. The woman who looked back was satisfyingly different from myself, and certainly considerably older. I patted my blue-rinsed white wig from behind with the palm of my hand. Society women have their hair dressed every day. They make such gestures, half unconsciously, reassuring themselves that every hair is in place. But still there was something about that woman in the mirror, my reflection, that was disconcertingly like myself. Of course—my glasses! My wretched, pebble-thick glasses. If I took them off, all that remained in the mirror was an indistinguishable blur. It would be many years before I acquired contact lenses and could finally see my reflection unadorned with glasses, could apply makeup without a hand mirror a few inches away from my face, and, most important of all, could see the other actors on stage.

Half an hour still to go before my scene. In another hour it would all be over, my three years' training at Central. In those three years I had played scenes from Shakespeare, Beaumont and Fletcher (Jacobean), Wycherley, Congreve, and Farquhar (Restoration), George Bernard Shaw and Ibsen (Modern Classics), J. B. Priestley (Modern), and several plays you could forget as soon as look at them because "that's the kind of play you'll be doing in weekly rep." Nothing by Tennessee Williams, or Arthur Miller, or Eugene O'Neill. No French drama, except Anouilh's *Ring Round the Moon,* in which Judi Dench had been wonderful, and no German drama at all. In other words we had been trained for the English theatre as it was.

In the summer of our first year we had performed scenes from *The Merchant of Venice.* I was allotted Act I, scene ii, of Portia, Judi Dench the final scene, coming home to Belmont. We wore the same costume, which made us laugh for a lifetime—she is just one inch over five feet. The wardrobe mistress, Mrs. Fox, who was still in wardrobe when my daughter Natasha went to Central twenty-three years later, did a brilliant job with a false hem. For my scene I copied Peggy Ashcroft and Richard Burton alternately. I loved Peggy's work and her spontaneous joy as she performed. I hated my voice, which didn't sound right, because I didn't sound like her or Burton. I was nervous and self-conscious and my throat tightened hard when I came to speak onstage. I looked at Judi and was both admiring and jealous. She was confident enough to speak in her own voice; she skipped and hopped with pleasure and excitement up the stairs, down the corridors, and onto the stage. She wore jeans, the only girl who had them, a polo-neck sweater, and ballet slippers that flopped and flapped as she bounded around. When I came back after the Easter holiday that first year and joined the crowd round the notice board with the plays and cast lists, another student had turned to me: "Oh you. You haven't changed." My heart sank like a stone. I wanted to change. I felt unattractive and old-fashioned. My hair wasn't sleek like Judi's. It crinkled and fuzzed in the damp air. I screwed it round into a sausage roll and clamped the coil onto my head with bobby pins.

There had been one chance to do something different, and I had seized it. In our second year we were invited to submit proposals for a student production. I asked my father's friend Fred Sadoff for advice, and he suggested Federico García Lorca's *Blood Wedding*. I read it and was astounded. Why had no one at Central ever mentioned this great poet? Obviously, because they had never heard of him. Fred explained that Lorca had been murdered by the fascists in Spain because he was in sympathy with the revolution, and also because he was homosexual. I was wrong. The Central staff had heard of Lorca, and what was more, they accepted my proposal and told me to go ahead.

Every night after school I sat up late and then rose at five in the morning to copy the refrains of Andalusian peasant songs from a book I had found in the local library and to plot the physical positions and movements of the characters with figures I had made from plasticine. I looked everywhere for books and photographs of Spain at the turn of the century. I knew that Lorca's poetry had to be grounded in the physical representation of a hardworking, superstitious peasantry. The bride's family sat stiffly and formally on four black, wooden high-backed chairs in an empty pink room dominated by a large, black wooden door center stage. The bride was dressed to meet her husband in a tight, corseted black satin bodice with long sleeves and a high collar and a long black skirt.

"And why did you dress the bride in *black?*" It was the day after the performance and we were getting our "crits" from a member of the drama staff, seated in a circle of chairs while he methodically ticked off each note in his pad. Days and weeks of study, argument, hope, and frustration were ticked off one by one in his notepad; our enthusiasm was draining away as he talked and ticked, without a hint of excitement in his eyes and voice. Spain at the turn of the century, the civil war in which Lorca wrote and died, all faded away, and we were back within the familiar prison of the English Southern Counties. "And why did you dress the bride in black?" He hardly paused for an answer, and even if he had, I no longer had the heart to tell him how I had discovered that the bride in a Spanish peasant family wore a magnificent black, not white, dress, which she would wear again and often, because she had only one wedding but there would be many funerals. And when the song in the text referred to "the bride, the white bride," it meant that she had lovely white skin and was a virgin, not that she wore a white wedding dress. But he wasn't interested in knowing the answer, and I was furious that he assumed so dogmatically that there could be no valid reason for dressing her in black.

All the while our teacher was ticking off his notes I could see my Israeli friend Amos grinning at me, as if to say, "What did I tell you? Now do you believe me?" I had often listened to his bitter, passionate criticism of our training at Central, and of the standards of playwriting and acting in the London theatre. He was much more knowledgeable, thoughtful, and critical than I was, with my English disposition to be fair-minded and see the other person's point of view. Amos had done his military service in the Negev desert. I listened uncomfortably to his stories of ambushes and patrols, and I noticed that when he spoke of the Arabs, it was as if they were an alien, even inferior, race, in much the same way as I had heard some English people talk about the Jews. He never talked of the Palestinians, only Arabs, and I, knowing nothing of these people at that time, hid behind my lack of knowledge and deliberately forbore to ask Amos any questions in case his answers might disturb me and make us disagree.

≡

Now there was a quarter of an hour to go before my graduation performance. Butterflies were chasing each other in my tummy, and my legs began to feel as though they belonged to someone else. I lay down on the floor of the dressing room, resting my head on a towel to protect my wig, and propped my feet up on a chair. It's an old trick, but quite effective. Having your feet above your head increases the circulation of the blood to the brain and makes you feel more clearheaded. Then I got up and jogged a little from foot to foot, letting my arms and head go limp like a rag doll.

These were techniques I had learned from Maître Harmer Brown, who taught us acrobatics and fencing. He had his own school somewhere in Pimlico, Salle Harmer Brown. French is the language of fencing. The parries are prime, seconde, terce, quarte, quinte, sixte, septime, and octave. All except the last two are pronounced in an uncompromisingly English accent. *Quinte*, for example is "kwint," like the dead manservant in Henry James's *The Turn of the Screw*. At least, so it was pronounced by Maître Harmer Brown, who was totally English, and since he was a very good teacher, we all copied him. He had taught Corin, who had won the All-England Schools Sabre championship, and would go on to fence for Cambridge before giving it up for study and for acting. Maître Harmer Brown was very rueful about Corin, saying that he had lost his best pupil, who could have fought for England at the 1960 Rome Olympics if he had dedicated himself to the sport.

I was only passably good at fencing, but I thought it was an excellent training for actors as well as an exciting sport. You had to be very alert and watch your opponent the whole time in order to anticipate what he would do next. This sharpened your reflexes. I was never very good at acrobatics, but I shall always be grateful to Maître Harmer Brown for what he taught us, and for one trick especially. He showed us how, if you keep your legs perfectly straight, and your spine straight, you can bend at the waist and fall backwards on your bum without hurting yourself. I tried it, aged fifty-two, when I played Lady Torrance in Tennessee Williams's *Orpheus Descending*, and it worked.

≡

I stood in the backstage darkness in my long green satin moiré dress and white evening gloves borrowed from my mother. The dress had been made for her by Victor Stiebel and seemed just right for my part. I wished she could have been there in the audience, and my dad too, but he was in Rome working on *The Quiet American.* Rachel had spoken to Olive Harding at MCA, which was a big theatrical agency in those days, and Olive had said that Kenneth Carten would be there. And maybe, somewhere in the audience, was a producer who would have room for me in his next season. None of us had a job to go to, except Judi Dench, who had already been cast to play the Virgin in the cycle of mystery plays at York Minster.

I looked down at my hands, which were trembling slightly, and concentrated all my attention on smoothing my gloves over each finger, and then along my wrists. Stanislavsky describes how in an agony of nerves before an entrance he saw some nails on the stage and bent down to pick them up. One small physical action, kneeling down to pick up some nails, concentrated his attention outside himself, calmed him, and enabled him to think.

I had discovered Stanislavsky's great textbook on acting, *An Actor Prepares,* for myself. No one had recommended it to me, not even my father, who was, says Professor Jean Benedetti in his biography of Stanislavsky, "perhaps the only major English actor of the twentieth century to have applied the system consistently." Well, my father had written about Stanislavsky in his book *An Actor's Ways and Means,* so perhaps I should have taken the hint, but I hadn't. No member of the staff at Central had ever mentioned him, or said that here, in *An Actor Prepares,* was the first serious study of acting as a process, the first analysis of a method of work with which an actor can overcome the problems that arise in the course of developing a part. So I discovered him for myself on my father's bookshelves.

The simple introduction penetrated the bewildering and jumbled empirical experiences that were the sum of my knowledge, like a map on a dark, rainy night in the streets of London.

Since the modern theatre came into existence, something like three centuries ago, conventions have accumulated, outlived their usefulness, and become hardened, so that they stand in the way of fresh art and sincere emotion on the stage. For forty years the effort of the Moscow Art Company has been to get rid of what has become artificial, and therefore an impediment, and to prepare the actor to present the externals of life and their inner repercussions with convincing psychological truthfulness.

I disappeared into my chair. Chapter 2, "When Acting Is an Art":

Because the very best that can happen is to have the actor completely carried away by the play. Then regardless of his own will he lives the part, not noticing *how* he feels, not thinking about *what* he does, and it all moves of its own accord, subconsciously and intuitively.

The next lines had been marked with a red pen:

Salvini said: "The great actor should be full of feeling, and especially he should feel the thing he is portraying. He must feel an emotion not only once or twice while he is studying his part but to a greater or lesser degree every time he plays it, no matter whether it is the first or the thousandth time."

My heart was beating with the excitement of discovery: *"Moreover, and this is of primary importance, the organic bases of the laws of nature on which our art is founded will protect you in the future from going down the wrong path."*

I read on and on, unable to put the book down. Surely this was what every actor wanted, to analyze problems from the standpoint of the natural processes of life? Why on earth was this book, a real handbook, unknown at Central? It was the third term of my second year, and no one had even mentioned it. It was not as if there were no provision in our curriculum for history and theory. We studied the history of the theatre from Greece to modern times, its architecture, and its methods of staging. So why didn't we study Stanislavsky's unique contribution, on the basic processes of the art of acting? I was so impatient to get to Central and tell them all this that I could hardly sleep that night.

As it happened we had a student-staff meeting the next day. I sat among the students, tapping my feet and quivering with impatience.

Why were we all floundering about, sometimes getting it right, and all too often getting it wrong? At the first opportunity I jumped to my feet. "It's all here! IT'S ALL HERE!" I shouted, waving the book at them. Some students looked amused, others bored, or as if their tolerance was strained to the limit. The staff's response was discouraging. Of course they had read it and felt it might certainly be of interest to students, but we should remember that there is room for all kinds of methods or none at all. If it worked for Vanessa, fine, but each individual must decide for himself. No one suggested a reading or a group discussion, and I was too deflated to suggest one myself. It was my first real encounter with ingrained English eclecticism, and I was astonished and maddened by it. I little realized then that this open-minded acceptance of the equal validity of all methods concealed a real hostility to any method in particular, and especially to such a method as Stanislavsky's, which based itself upon objective processes in nature and society as the source for all development in art. Nor did I understand the social roots of such an outlook. But my eyes were beginning to open.

It was about this time, 1956, that I attended a Sunday-night meeting at the Royal Court Theatre organized by George Devine, on the theme "What Is Wrong with the English Theatre?" The audience was made up mainly of young writers, directors, and designers. Marilyn Monroe, whom I knew attended the Actors Studio in New York and studied with Lee Strasberg, was also there. Her husband, Arthur Miller, was one of the speakers. Miller's *A View from the Bridge* had just avoided the Lord Chamberlain's censorship by being presented for "club members" at the Comedy Theatre. Quietly and very clearly, Miller explained that the problem with the English theatre was that its themes and characters were all based upon the narrow prejudices of English middle-class life and a total evasion of all the problems in society as a whole.

≡

I took a deep breath and concentrated on my character's self-satisfaction with her elegant appearance in her brilliant green dress and blue-rinsed white coiffure. I boldly seized the door handle, shouted my entrance line, and strode onto the brightly lit stage of the Wyndham's Theatre.

I won the Sybil Thorndike prize and began to search for a job. Directors held auditions each summer at the Dinely Studios in Marylebone Road. I prepared monologues and managed to get two auditions, but these turned into interviews, so I had no chance to show how I could act. In response to my letters to every repertory theatre in the country I received three polite rejections at my parents' flat in Hans Crescent. (Michael had sold Bedford House in 1957 to pay income tax bills.) Then a small brown envelope containing a letter dated June 4, 1957, from Peter Hoar at the Frinton Summer Theatre arrived in the letterbox.

> Dear Miss Redgrave
>   I was unfortunately not able to come to Wyndham's this afternoon, but my wife came and enjoyed your performance. We should very much like you to come to Frinton. I could offer you a salary of £7 a week. The season opens on July 11th, and rehearsals start on the 4th.
>
> > Yours sincerely.
> > Peter Hoar.

I ran into my mother's bedroom shouting, "I've got a job!" and telephoned Peter Hoar, full of gratitude. It never entered my head to wonder whether £7 a week would be enough, or to think that I might ask for more. I went to work at a coffee bar in the King's Road, Chelsea, hoping to save enough in the four weeks before rehearsals began to buy myself some clothes, which I knew I should have to provide for a ten-week season of modern plays. Espresso coffee had just arrived, and the coffee bar had the first Gaggia machines to be imported from Italy. I earned a pound a day, plus tips, and was entirely happy, dreaming about the season to come.

CHAPTER 8

Frinton-upon-Sea, a front-rank seaside town for the retired on the coast of Suffolk, did not have a front-rank repertory theatre. Some seaside towns, such as Worthing, had theatres that played all the year round. When we opened there in July 1957 Frinton had to be content with a summer season program of ten plays in ten weeks, which meant about five days' rehearsal for each play. Thursday morning would be the first read-through, and all the moves had to be plotted by Saturday lunchtime. On Sunday we learned our lines. Monday and Tuesday were run-throughs, Wednesday afternoon was the dress rehearsal, and Wednesday night was the first night. That way, or so it was hoped, the holidaymaker who spent a week in Frinton might see *Dial M for Murder* on Tuesday and *Witness for the Prosecution* on Thursday. This was probably wishful thinking, since Frinton's town council appeared determined to discourage holidaymakers by putting every possible obstacle in their way. Buses, for example, were made to park on the outskirts of the town, so that no day-trippers would disturb the residents' peace. There were no noisy fights between Mods and Rockers in this very quiet English resort. But it was a job, and I was so thrilled to have it, so proud to be a professional actress paying her own way, that I saw nothing to complain at.

I soon found out that surviving on £7 a week was only just possible. Mrs. Branch, my landlady, charged £4 a week for a room and a large breakfast. That left £3 a week for food and everything else, which included makeup and clothes for the plays. Each member of the cast was responsible for all his or her costumes. Every Sunday the company met at the theatre for a communal lunch, a great cauldron of spaghetti Bolognese, which filled us up for the rest of the day and most of Monday. I think the leading man and leading lady were paid £10 a week; we were all in much the same boat. Equity, the actors' union, which we had all joined, had been in existence for just over a quarter of a century, but it would be another thirteen years before the "living wage" campaign secured a basic minimum salary of £30 a week.

Halfway through the season, Corin came down to visit me. I was playing Miss Pringle, an amiably loony lady botanist in her sixties who offered learned and useless advice to anyone within earshot. In the play the leading man's father has apparently gone berserk, tearing off his clothes and alarming the neighbors. "What can I do?" asks his son. Slight pause while the other characters scratch their heads in bewilderment. "You could try blowing up his nose," suggests Miss Pringle. I got a big laugh from the audience on that line, though I think I was much helped by our leading man, Gawn Grainger, who did a long, slow "take" when I said it. Miss Pringle goes on to explain that she discovered this particular piece of lore on her last safari to Africa when a native porter recommended it as the best way to deal with a maddened rhino. The leading man looks incredulous. "Yes, yes," insists Miss Pringle. She is about to launch into a breathless account of how she faced the charging rhino when the upstage door bursts open and on comes the father in his underclothes, brandishing a poker. The leading man offers a silent prayer, tries to blow up his father's nose, and is nearly decapitated with the poker. "Not like that!" says Miss Pringle, and proceeds to demonstrate, holding the old man's face very close to her own before applying her lips to his nose. The old man's expression changes from apoplectic fury to moonstruck adoration. He flings his arms around Miss Pringle, who sighs beatifically and swoons. Curtain.

Corin was very proud that I had made the audience laugh so much. I don't think it had occurred to either of us that I could be funny. Certainly I had plenty of practice in my ten weeks at Frinton. In our opening play, *The Reluctant Debutante,* I played the heroine's spotty friend, and after that a long line of parts, aged between fifty and seventy, for which my experience with Johnson's baby powder came in very handy. I was never a quick study, but none of my parts were long, and I don't recall having to struggle hard to learn them. Pauline Murch, our leading lady, and Gawn Grainger performed wonders every week in order to be word perfect on the first night, somehow managing to look different in each part, and always well dressed.

The last play was John Osborne's *Look Back in Anger,* a surprisingly adventurous choice for Frinton, and a wise one: every seat was sold. Halfway through the season Geoffrey Edwards, our director, had promised me the part of Helena, the actress, and I began to study it there and then. I knew my father would come down to see me in it, and more than anything else in the world, I wanted to show him what I could do. He had first seen me act at Queen's Gate School when I was fourteen, in Shaw's *Saint Joan.* As we drove home that night he told me that his mother, Margaret Scudamore, had been a favorite actress of Shaw's and later he showed me a postcard Shaw had written to her in 1938 from Ayot St. Lawrence: "What!!! So Michael is *your son?* I must rewrite Coriolanus for the two of you."

He came by train on Friday, for the second performance, and I met him at the station. He had finished shooting *The Quiet American.* Glen Byam-Shaw, director of the Memorial Theatre at Stratford, had been to stay with him to persuade him to play Hamlet, and Benedick in *Much Ado About Nothing,* for the next season. "Oh, you must, you must," I pleaded. "That's what I thought," said Michael, taking me by the arm. "So will you?" I asked. He could be very teasing sometimes. "I shall be fifty next birthday," he replied. "What does that matter?" "Just what I said myself." "So, will you?" I persisted. "Reckon so."

After the performance he said very little, and I began to fear that he had not been impressed. He had somehow persuaded the hotel he was staying in to keep a late supper for us. As we sat eating, I talked without a pause—until I ran out of words and sat miserably looking at my plate. For what seemed a quarter of an hour, my father looked out of the window, or at the space above my head, and drank whisky. Eventually he sighed, wiped his mouth with his napkin, and said, "Brian Desmond Hurst wants me to do a film about a surgeon. I was thinking of suggesting you for my daughter."

I met Hurst, the director of *Behind the Mask,* and the producer, George More O'Ferrall, in a mews flat in Kinnerton Street, Belgravia. All the furniture was covered in velvet and silk; everything looked expensive, and I immediately felt out of my depth. The film test, the following day, was a nightmare. I had nothing to do except arrange flowers in a vase, look left, look right, turn toward the camera, and smile. The cameraman was kind and helpful, and everyone wanted to put me at my ease, but I was frozen with fear and felt stupid and ungainly. Three days later a script arrived with a contract for £500. My part, Pamela, was what Stanislavsky would have called "a stencil." When she wasn't arranging flowers she was pouring cups of tea. Invariably polite, Pamela was worried about her engagement to an up-and-coming surgeon, her father's chief critic and rival at St. Dominic's hospital. But it was a film part, and it never occurred to me to say I couldn't play it, although I knew I lacked the experience or the nerve to carry it off.

Pamela was no different from half a dozen other parts in half a dozen English films that year. There were two stereotypes of womanhood on the British screen in the late fifties. One was the English rose, in a tailored suit, with a handbag and gloves to match. The other was the peroxide-blond bombshell. I fitted neither category. Too tall and too large for an English rose, and certainly no bombshell. Pamela was the English rose, and since I had accepted the part, I had to try and look it. My father sent me to Dr. Goller, a dietician in Harley Street, who put me on a diet of lemon juice, four cups of liquid a day, four ounces of meat or fish, and any quantity of tomatoes or hard-boiled eggs. Fruit was forbidden "because it turns to alcohol in the stomach," and alcohol was forbidden because of its sugar content. Pills were provided in case the patient's kidneys should rebel at the prospect of four cups of liquid a day.

"Some people have big bones," our old nanny used to say. "They *can't* get thin." With this theory she stoutly defended my 156 pounds against all criticism. But my father was very obstinate, and I was determined not to let him down in that respect at least. Nanny's theory proved wrong. I went down to 119 pounds. My bust, which was not large in the first place, shrank commensurably, so the wardrobe compensated by giving me a padded bra, and makeup gave me a big, bright red bow for a mouth. I was so nervous I couldn't smile naturally, and when I was told to smile, one side of my mouth went up and the other went down. I was told to flick my eyes from right to left when I looked at my partner in close-up. "Flick your eyes, dear, otherwise they look dead." I was probably staring out of sheer fright, but having to concentrate on flicking my eyes from side to side drove all other thoughts out of my head, and ruined whatever slim chance was left of identifying with my character. A photomagazine, the *Illustrated London News,* published an article about the film for prepublicity. There was a picture of a canvas chair with my name on it, and underneath it a caption: "Vanessa's seat—will it be too hot for her?" I thought it a very fair question.

Michael's next job was a play by N. C. Hunter, *A Touch of the Sun,* and again he put me up for the part of his daughter. This time Caroline Lester was a character I could identify with completely, the daughter of a hardworking underpaid schoolmaster, whose family is invited for a holiday with rich relations in the South of France. My heart lifted. I forgot all about lemon juice and four cups of liquid a day, ate what I wanted, and threw myself into work I knew how to do. I saw very little of my dad after rehearsals, although I still lived at the flat in Hans Crescent. By a sort of unspoken agreement, neither of us would wait for the other at the end of a day's work. In any case, when he was working and happy with the work, he led a kind of solitary, bachelor existence, eating alone at a club and calling on his friends, always unannounced, late in the evening, and then talking till one-thirty in the morning.

One day, during rehearsals, we did walk home together. "I felt dreadful today," I said. "Yes, and you let everyone know it." Rather chastened, because I didn't think it had been that obvious, I tried to explain why I felt so bad. I didn't think my character, Caroline, would do such and such, or say such and such. "Why?" he asked. "I wouldn't in that situation." "But you're not Caroline," he said. "Your job is to play *her.*" Because I so respected my father, I accepted what he said and didn't argue. But I cannot say I wholly believed him at the time. It was my first lesson in subjective idealism, though my father didn't call it that, and I was far from absorbing it completely. We are so conditioned to start from ourselves that all too often, when we consider a character in a play, we proceed from a word here or a phrase there, and instead of considering the character and the given circumstances that make them act in the way they do, we are in reality only considering our hastily assembled impressions of the character and ourselves. But in good drama, it is those given circumstances, and especially the unexpected changes in their given circumstances, that make people act in a way that is *not* typical of them, not expected by others, and least of all by themselves.

A Touch of the Sun opened in Blackpool in November 1957. I had a room in a house that was so cold and damp with the November air that when I got up in the morning my woolen vest steamed as I held it in front of the gas fire, fed with a shilling in the meter. I shared digs with Thelma Holt, who was the assistant stage manager and understudy. We shared the excitement and our problems, and years later, when she took over as artistic director of the Round House Theatre in Chalk Farm, we renewed our friendship and have worked together a great deal ever since. The first night started well. When the curtain rose on the second act, on a huge apparently stone staircase leading up through Riviera palm trees to a wide stone balcony, the audience clapped. Ronnie Squire, a superb comedian who played my father's elderly uncle, was seated in a deck chair, dozing. Ronnie had been a famously handsome actor in his youth, playing all the romantic parts. He told me that the theatre was so competitive in those days that if an actor was jealous of an up-and-coming rival—and evidently many of them were jealous of Ronnie—he would hire someone to sit in the balcony on the first night and boo the rival off the stage. "What did you do?" I asked. "Hired myself a tough," said Ronnie. "At the first sign of a disturbance in the balcony, there was a loud clunk. My fellow had walloped him on the jaw and he was out for the count." Then Ronnie had performed in at least three theatres a night, leaping into a horse-drawn cab, from Act I in Wyndham's to Act II of another play at the Prince's, perhaps ending up at the Coliseum in a sketch at the end of a variety bill.

Ronnie had a much younger wife, Ursula. All through rehearsals he had looked perfect, with his balding pate, skin that was mottled with age, and a mournful mustache, which he tugged ruminatively to "point" a line. But when the first-night curtain rose on the Riviera, Ronnie was wearing a toupee and quite a lot of makeup, and his lips were slightly but definitely pink. The cast looked at one another, amazed and rather horrified. Michael spoke to our producer, Hugh Beaumont. Ronnie must be persuaded not to wear his toupee. "Binkie" Beaumont spoke to Ursula, who proved herself to be the thoroughly nice, calm, tactful woman she had seemed. "Don't worry," she said. "It's going to blow out of the window." Whether it did, or whether she spoke to Ronnie, we never knew, but the next evening he came onstage without the toupee and the makeup, and no one said a word about it.

We toured Leeds, Liverpool, Manchester, and finally Brighton for the last week before playing at London's Saville Theatre. In Liverpool I had a room just round the corner from Falkner Street, where, young and in love, Michael and Rachel had shared their first digs while playing at the Liverpool Playhouse. Like theirs, my bedroom had a real grate, and my landlady lit a coal fire every evening before I came back from the theatre. I had a brass bed and a lumpy, faded eiderdown. The furniture was dark brown and on the walls were reproductions of allegorical maidens in Greek tunics. The fire flickered, sending shadows across the walls and ceiling. I thought of my parents in 1935, and of my Granny Margaret—Daisy Scudamore— who had spent most of her professional life touring week by week around the country, until she met and eventually married her second husband, J. P. Anderson, Grandpa Andy.

Twenty-seven years later, in November 1985, I caught a sleeper from Euston after a performance of *The Seagull* at the Queen's Theatre and rang a doorbell in another street, just around the corner from these digs. My daughter Joely had her first job, playing *Miss Julie* at the Liverpool Playhouse. She was tired and wound up, and we hugged each other tight for many minutes in her bedroom. The next day we went to the Walker Art Gallery and into the Playhouse to see the set, still in construction, and her dressing room. Of all the things I had ever dreamed about or hoped for, I had never imagined the pleasure of seeing both my daughters on the stage. Seeing Joely in Liverpool, I knew how my father must have felt when I went on tour with him in *A Touch of the Sun*.

Dad played in *A Touch of the Sun* for three months at the Saville

Theatre, now a cinema, in the upper end of Shaftesbury Avenue, before leaving to play Hamlet in the 1958 Stratford season. Rachel was also going to Stratford, to play Lady Capulet, and Ursula in *Much Ado*. Michael's part in *A Touch of the Sun* was taken over by Michael Gwynn. In April that year, Corin, who had won an open scholarship in classics at King's College, Cambridge, went to stay with a family in Versailles to learn French before he went up to university.

Lynn and I were the only ones left at home that summer in the flat in Hans Crescent. Lynn was in her last year at Queen's Gate School. She said nothing about wanting to act, although I think she secretly did, and I'm certain that if I'd been more sensitive at this time I might have picked up signals and encouraged her. The next year, 1959, she came to Stratford to see me in *A Midsummer Night's Dream,* and when she returned to London she told Rachel, "That's what I want to do."

I had fallen in love with the actor playing my brother in *A Touch of the Sun*. One afternoon I learned it would come to nothing: he was already embroiled with someone else. Before that, however, we had some wonderful times. He had bought an old car, a convertible Jaguar, I think, the hood patched together with adhesive tape, and when it rained we got thoroughly wet. One fine morning in May 1958 he put the hood down and we drove together to Stansted Airport in Essex. The Russians were arriving, the very first visit by the Moscow Arts Theatre to London, and the Foreign Office and the Civil Aviation Authority between them had cooked up a reason to route them to Stansted instead of Heathrow. It was said that their Tupolev plane was "too big" for Heathrow. The news went round the theatres that no reception or welcoming party had been provided. We were horrified. Thanks to Diana Wynyard, who had found out what was happening and telephoned everyone she knew, there were about fifty of us at the airport, and when the Russians finally landed we cheered, clapped, and gave them flowers.

I booked tickets for every Wednesday matinee at the Sadlers Wells Theatre. The Moscow Arts brought three productions—*The Cherry Orchard, The Three Sisters,* and *Uncle Vanya.* I thought the acting was the best I had ever seen. After *The Three Sisters* I went backstage and for a few moments was able to speak with the actress playing Masha. I asked whether the moment when she watches the humming top on the floor and recites Pushkin's "The Oak Tree" was created afresh for this production, or whether it was copied from previous productions. She said there had been some changes, but basically this production had been in their repertoire for some time. I didn't think to ask her why the company had brought no new work with them. To see great acting is an inspiration. By that I mean not so much the work of a great actor, exciting as that is, but the collective work of a company. For the rest of that week and the week that followed, when they played *Uncle Vanya,* I thought about the Moscow Arts Theatre and longed to work in such a company. On Sunday I caught the train to Leamington, and then a bus to Stratford, arriving just in time for the start of the technical run of *Hamlet.*

The Sunday technical rehearsal at Stratford was an endurance test for everyone in the company. It was the first rehearsal on the set, and too little time was allowed for scene changes, lighting cues, music cues, timing of exits and entrances. One does not go to a technical rehearsal expecting to see a performance, nor anything more than the semblance of the production as a whole. Every few moments a voice will call out from the auditorium and the actors will halt, find a light, take a new move, or wait for some scenery that has been mistimed or jammed. The actors' costumes still feel alien to them. The wig is too tight or too loose, the sleeves too long or too short. The set is totally baffling. Countless technical problems must be and will be overcome in the long hours into the early morning. At Stratford in 1958 time was desperately short. Four weeks' rehearsal; Saturday morning, the dress parade; Sunday, lighting and technical rehearsal; Monday afternoon, a semi-dress rehearsal; Monday evening, a full-dress run before an audience of friends and relatives; Tuesday evening, the one and only preview; and Wednesday night, the first night with the drama critics from the national press.

My father loathed and feared "opening cold" at Stratford, without previews or the chance to take the play on tour before showing it to the critics. In his autobiography he claimed to be "a notoriously slow starter," but this time, amazingly for a technical rehearsal, the first five scenes ran continuously, without a hitch. My father listened to the ghost's speech as if the most terrible crime had been committed and his own beloved father had been killed. Agony poured out of him when the ghost had disappeared. "My fate cries out" was delivered at full power, as if his lungs and heart were strained to breaking point.

There were, and are, many fine voices in the English theatre. My father's favorite actor was Henry Ainley, whose voice was legendary, and after Ainley, Robert Loraine, neither of whom I ever saw. But I never heard an actor, other than Michael, who could speak at full volume without producing an "effect," a special register. It was awesome, and made the hair rise at the back of my neck, giving me the same tingling feeling that I have when I hear Placido Domingo sing Puccini's "*Che gelida manina.*"

The drama critics in England, led by James Agate, had decided that my father was an "intellectual" actor. And after Agate, Ken Tynan, at whose side the ghost of Agate sometimes seemed to walk. Tynan could be very generous and very perceptive, but he swallowed Agate's opinion hook, line, and sinker, as if being an intellectual actor were some kind of handicap or defect. For my part, I never saw any actor, except perhaps in the Moscow Arts Theatre Company, who possessed such capacity for emotion, and the appropriate form of that emotion. Michael was unequaled in *Hamlet, King Lear,* and *Antony and Cleopatra.* Perhaps it never occurred to those critics that only an actor who can think can also feel to the extent demanded by Shakespeare's tragedies and histories, and moreover without any distortion to Shakespeare's blank verse, and with the form and content of the play so deeply assimilated that Shakespeare's words spring from his mouth with complete spontaneity, as if they had been born in him and were his own.

Later that year Michael and Rachel went to Moscow and Leningrad with the Stratford Company—the first English company to visit the Soviet Union since the war. I have some photographs of Michael, still in his Hamlet costume, moving toward the great smiling figure of Paul Robeson in the corridor of the Moscow Theatre. In another photograph they are hugging each other closely and with great emotion. I found these photos in a trunk I opened the night before I flew to Moscow in January 1985, and I called out to my new friend, Paul's granddaughter, Susan Robeson, who was staying in my house in London, trying to find the ways and means to make a feature film about her grandfather. Then we drove over to show my dad the photos. His eyes shone when he saw them.

That year, 1958, ended with my playing Colin, the principal boy in *Mother Goose,* the Christmas pantomime at Leatherhead Theatre in

Surrey. There were no Terry Juveniles, and no variety acts, as in the big London pantomimes I had seen as a child with Granny Margaret, just the traditional ingredients of a repertory pantomime: the dame, the pastry-cook scene, the pantomime horse, and dialogue like: "It's a lovely day, Jill!" "Yes, isn't it, Colin." Cue for a song. It had been my ambition for as long as I could remember to play the principal boy, if possible Peter Pan, in the annual festival at the Scala Theatre. That I never achieved. But Colin in *Mother Goose* was a good second-best.

CHAPTER 9

I n 1959, not long after he had met my father in Moscow, Paul
Robeson came to Stratford to play Othello. I was a fairly junior
member of the company that season. I walked on in *Othello,* one of the
crowd in the Cyprus scenes; played Valeria in *Coriolanus,* and Helena
in *A Midsummer Night's Dream.* Denne Gilkes, who taught singing at
the theatre, had a studio flat at 18 High Street, which I rented for the
season. To be working at Stratford, where I had come almost every
summer since I was fourteen, was as exciting as getting my first job
at Frinton. Stratford was the center of the world's theatre, or so it
seemed, and this was an exceptional season, even by Stratford's
standards. Robeson was playing Othello, Olivier was Coriolanus with
Edith Evans as Volumnia, Tyrone Guthrie was directing *All's Well
That Ends Well*—it seemed the most amazing good fortune to be
working there, in such a company.

Robeson had a commanding presence, and his great bass voice
came effortlessly as if from the depth of his whole being. His famous
line "Put up your bright swords, for the dew will rust them" was
spoken with such majestic resonance that the whole theatre and the
banks of the river beyond seemed to reverberate. He was sixty-one

and had been ill, spending two weeks in hospital in the Kremlin before his arrival at Stratford. He was under constant surveillance by the CIA, and every speech he made that summer in Britain was reported back to J. Edgar Hoover and the State Department. Glen Byam-Shaw, Stratford's artistic director, asked him if he was still a communist. "Yes, and proud to be," replied Robeson. When he first arrived in the Soviet Union he had acknowledged it as the first country to banish the evil of racism, but his political ideals, for which he joined the Communist Party, were undermined and betrayed by Stalinism. He felt he could not speak against Stalin without betraying the Soviet Union, however, and inwardly, as I learned later, he was in despair. I count it a great privilege to have known him, even from a distance.

There was a general election in June, which the Tories won with Macmillan's slogan "You've never had it so good." I didn't vote. I hardly read a newspaper all summer. I rehearsed my understudy parts, especially Desdemona, with Julian Glover understudying Othello, never hoping especially to go on, but longing for the chance to show our director, Tony Richardson, what I could do. I rode my bicycle down the country lanes Corin and I had explored, every inch, eight years before. On Sundays I was part of Sam Wanamaker's baseball team. In August and September, when most of the plays were on, we would play softball with American airmen at one of the Oxfordshire bases. They welcomed us with great hospitality, offering a more bewildering choice of food in their canteens than I had seen even in Stratford's best hotel. They told us about the excitement of flying jet aircraft, which had ten times more power than even the most versatile propellor-driven plane, they said. On their brightly colored flying jackets they had stitched badges—dragons breathing fire, sharks with mouths gaping, flying tigers—with the caption "Aggressor Beware!"

Then in the autumn H. M. Tennant sent me the script of a new play by Robert Bolt. Would I be interested in the part of Stella Dean? My dad wrote a day or so later, hoping I would take the part. It meant I should be playing his daughter again, and perhaps I had other ideas, but—Bolt's play was special, and that happens only a few times in a career. Bolt's title, *The Tiger and the Horse,* was taken from the *Proverbs of Hell* by William Blake: "The tigers of wrath are wiser than the horses of instruction." Stella Dean's father, a brilliant astronomer, turned to writing philosophy when he married. Stella's boyfriend, Louis, a young lecturer at the university where Dean is a senior don, says: "They're beautifully written, lousy books! Don't commit yourself! Examine your umbilicus! Breathe deeply; turn round in circles and quietly, quietly disappear up your own imagination! He's dangerous, he's off the ground—oh yes he is; when your father walks across the quad you can see light under his boots. That's why your mother's off her head."

Louis is taking a petition for unilateral nuclear disarmament round the university. Stella's mother says she will sign: "Largely it's the unborn. The unborn. Radioactivity stimulates mutation; and the chances are astronomically against a mutation being favourable. In other words it produces monsters. Babies that are monsters. I shall certainly sign the petition." As I reread these words I think of the article in a women's magazine I read recently in the doctor's waiting room, about jelly babies, products of a nuclear bomb exploded in the Pacific in 1954. Jelly babies have no heads, no arms and no legs, and they die soon after birth. An islander told a conference in London that she had given birth to seven jelly babies. She and her teenage friends were covered with radioactive ash after the explosion. They danced in it and rubbed it over their bodies like sand. All the islanders were removed from the island about ten years later. Then they were returned, and were told the island was free from radiation. Some time after that they were sent instructions not to eat fish taken from the northern shores. They had been fishing and eating from those shores for years.

In the summer of 1958 I had argued long and hard with an actor in the cast of *A Touch of the Sun*. He supported the case for nuclear disarmament and tried to convince me. But since the Hungarian revolution had been smashed by tanks, and Port Said in Egypt reduced to rubble by RAF bombers using conventional high-explosive bombs, I could not see that nuclear weapons were the main issue. Also, I could not accept that marching to or from Aldermaston every Easter would force the British government to halt the production and stockpiling of nuclear weapons.

The Tiger and the Horse, and Robert Bolt himself, influenced me immensely. He attended all the rehearsals, never intervening in the direction of the play but talking seriously and deliberately about its ideas. He was a socialist. I started reading the newspapers again and saw that everything indicated an increasing threat of nuclear war.

It reminds me uncomfortably of the thirties, when, as you remember, the younger dons talked like election agents, and the undergraduates to all appearances regarded their time up here as an extended leave from the Spanish Civil War. They're getting agitated again.

The Tiger and the Horse opened in August 1960. After four months, I was released to join Glen Byam-Shaw's production of Ibsen's *The Lady from the Sea,* which came into the Queen's Theatre in 1961 as soon as *The Tiger and the Horse* had closed after a six-month run, the extent of my father's contract. The cast was led by Margaret Leighton playing Ellida, Andrew Cruickshank as Dr. Wangel, and John Neville as the Stranger. I played Dr. Wangel's eldest daughter, Bolette, and made close friends with Joanna Dunham, who played Hilde. Esmond Knight, who had been a comrade at sea of my uncle Robin, played Ballestad.

The newspapers reported that Bertrand Russell had split from Canon Collins and the Campaign for Nuclear Disarmament on the issue of a civil disobedience campaign to force the government into unilateral nuclear disarmament. The Committee of 100 was formed, and a number of respected artists and intellectuals put their names down to take collective responsibility for its campaign—among them Robert Bolt, Arnold Wesker, and Sir Herbert Read.

I read that a demonstration was planned to go to the U.S. Embassy in Grosvenor Square. I decided I must join them, telling no one in the theatre company, or at home. The police blocked the street leading to the embassy. Orders to disperse were given by the commissioner in charge. I looked around me to see what we would do. Some of the demonstrators started to sit down in the street; then we all sat down. Vans came, the police picked us up and put us into them, and we were taken to a magistrates' court and fined. I paid my fine and went straight back to the Queen's Theatre, where I talked to John Neville. Two weeks later, Neville and I joined another demonstration in Whitehall. Again we were ordered to disperse;

again we refused and sat down. This time we were arrested. We were taken to Vine Street police station, locked up in a small room, and then taken to court, where we paid our fines and left to go back to the theatre.

≡

It was spring 1961. I had my own flat now, off Gloucester Road, on the ground floor, with a door that led down some iron steps into a communal garden. The telephone rang and Peter Hall asked me to come to Stratford to play Rosalind in *As You Like It*. Over the next weeks I studied and learned all my lines. I tramped along the soggy, springing paths in the woods around Wilks Water, the cottage in Hampshire given to my mother by Cousin Lucy, thinking over the play. Before going up for rehearsals I listened to an old recording of Dame Edith Evans and Michael playing one of the love scenes. Rosalind has long, incredibly quick-thinking, quick-witted speeches. Like a driver about to set off on a complicated cross-country drive to an unknown destination, I needed a really good map. Dame Edith, one might say, had recorded an Ordnance Survey of the Forest of Arden, if only for one scene. Her tempo, her phrasing, her through line on the dialogue, were superb. I copied everything I could, and committed it to memory. Next, I read every piece of Elizabethan prose I could lay my hands on, including the short stories of the time, particularly the story of Dick Whittington. I have never dared tell a journalist that I prepared for Shakespeare's *As You Like It* by reading legends about Dick Whittington, but that is exactly what I did. The prose, which was the nearest window into the actual vocabulary and style of speaking in everyday life in the late sixteenth century, made it possible for me to understand how a lively, interesting man or woman might talk.

Michael Elliott, our director, took me to lunch on the day of the first night. We had rehearsed for six weeks. I was nervous and keyed up, anxious about the performance but looking forward to it. Michael was looking at me with the same grave eyes as my father. I thought he was going to thank me for my hard work, offer me words of encouragement. What he said shocked me: "Vanessa, the whole production is going to be a failure. You won't give yourself up to the play and to what is happening. You are refusing to give *yourself* over; you are holding back. You've held back all through rehearsals, and if you don't go onstage tonight and give *all* of yourself to the play, the actors, and the audience, we will have failed totally."

The grilled plaice turned to sticky cotton wool in my mouth. My jaws continued to munch, but the saliva had stopped totally and I couldn't swallow. I was terrified. Then he said: "That's all I have to say: if you can't do that, there's no meaning to the play."

John Barton, Peter Hall's codirector, gave me one of his notorious massages. Since I was so tense, his fingers felt like steel rods punching away at my shoulders, back, and neck. My mind was racing. I wanted to run after Michael and say, "Why now? Why do you tell me all this now, after six weeks?" But I couldn't. I respected Michael and trusted his direction of the play absolutely. Rosalind, which is one of the longest and most complex of Shakespeare's parts for an actress—longer than Cleopatra—had been making me more nervous than I realized. I was cautiously trying to control my performance, to get it right. With Michael's words burned into my brain I realized that I had absolutely nothing to lose and everything to gain by going with the immediacy of the moment and the audience. It goes back to Jani Strasser's advice: If you keep controlling your poodles they can do so much and no more; you've got to let them off the leash. This isn't something you can suddenly do, unless somebody gives you a very big jolt, as Michael did.

I dressed, went down to the wings, and took a leap into the unknown. All mental control and calculation vanished, all precautions, all thought of *how* I do this, *how* I say that. I threw myself into the moment of Rosalind's life, into Orlando's eyes, into the Forest of Arden. Around the giant oak in the dapple clearing we danced in a chain, four men and four women, celebrating their love for each other. With *As You Like It* I rediscovered on a new level and in a different way the same sheer enjoyment and living of my part that I'd felt in *A Touch of the Sun,* and that alertness and immediacy has stayed with me in my acting to this day.

I doubt whether any other director would have had the courage, or the wisdom, to speak to me as Michael Elliott did only hours before the first performance. Only a director who had won the total confidence of his actors could have said such things, and only a man who cared so deeply about his work would have dared to take such a risk. There are people who will be important to work with throughout a career, but if you are lucky enough to work with them at just the right moment in your development, it can be crucial. Michael was the same person with everybody; he loved his work and respected the theatre. He combined a conviction and thoughtfulness in trying to bring out what he saw in *As You Like It* that I found absolutely inspiring. He was very direct, but when he gave advice or encouragement I trusted it completely. I certainly could not have played the part as I did without him. A great Italian actress once said to me about the director who found her and cast her in three of his films: "He is my husband, my lover, my father, my son, and my brother." I felt that way about Michael Elliott, with whom I worked three times. He changed my life.

As You Like It was praised beyond praise. Michael Elliott's production struck a deep, responsive chord with audiences and critics, for there was not a shadow of cynicism in it, and that was already rare among directors of his generation. The word was that "upstairs," in the offices of the administration, the production was thought too sentimental. It was not in the least sentimental. Michael had understood the essence of the play. The dream of Orlando's older brother, which changes him, is the allegorical form of the story for all the characters, who discover their essential, true human nature, at odds with the inhuman world of the Court and Frederick, the usurper. Ian Bannen played Orlando, and I was, as every Rosalind becomes with her Orlando, in love with him.

Peter Hall told me that *As You Like It* would transfer to the Aldwych, which at that time was the London home of the Stratford company, and asked me to play Katharina in *The Taming of the Shrew*. The BBC wanted to televise our production. Newspapers and magazines besieged me for interviews. I was almost saturated with kindness and praise, which might have choked me forever if I hadn't known that Michael Elliott would be watching our performance once or twice a week, and I wanted his notes and his opinion more than any praise. Having the chance to continue as Rosalind in *As You Like It* in London, then play her again on film, was exceptional, since it meant that I could change and develop the part, add small touches. With classics—whether by Tennessee Williams, Ibsen, or Shakespeare—I find it very necessary to be able to play the part more than once, which is rarely possible today since there is no longer a proper repertory system and rehearsal time is very short.

≡

I had made a leap as an actress, and now I took an irrevocable decision to make a leap into political life as well. Bertrand Russell and members of the Committee of 100 had been arrested and charged with incitement to break the law when they spoke at a rally in Hyde Park in September 1961. John Morris, a member and organizer of the committee, rang and asked if I would join them, taking the place of those who had been arrested. I agreed.

During that autumn and winter, I wrote to my father in New York. A large part of this letter describes my feelings at this point in my life.

My Darling Poppa . . . I go back to London on Sunday to take part in a discussion 'whether artists should involve themselves directly in politics' which is being televised in the new programme of Ken Tynan's on ABC TV called 'Tempo'. Similar to 'Monitor'. Lindsay Anderson and I versus Auberon Waugh and Noni Jabavu, a coloured woman who is editor of the 'New Strand' magazine.

Generally speaking I think that an artist has the same responsibility for thinking and acting politically as any other human being, but of course there are many qualifications to this statement. . . . It is said that if Beethoven had joined the army during the Napoleonic wars he would never have written some of his most marvellous work, and the world would be poorer for it. That's true: But Beethoven lived at a time when it was possible to live and work more or less normally whatever wars or upheavals were going on around you. Conquerors needed music and drama in the capitals they occupied. It's a wonderful thing that art has this kind of Red Cross immunity. But Beethoven knew that life would be carrying on centuries after his death. *Anything* we create or work for in our ordinary lives can only be done for each other in the present. The only thing we can do for the future is to do all we can to make sure there is a future.

I want to act as well and as continuously as possible all my life, no holds barred; I want to play Imogen next year, and maybe St Joan the year after that, to play Rosalind all my life! But in the present situation I have to realise that there may not *be* another season at Stratford; it sounds fantastic and incredible; I can't really believe that I haven't necessarily got forty-odd more years of life, but I should be deluding myself if I was sure that I *had*.

Anyway, all this apart, I just can't help myself. The more I think, the more I read (arguments on both sides) the more convinced I am that unilateral disarmament for Britain is a *must—must, must*. And is the only minute hope we can have for a *beginning* which could conceivably make possible an ultimate world disarmament.

But darling, I won't go into details of why I think this.

I can promise you that my present actions concerned with the Committee of 100 are in no way reducing my capacity, will and concentration for acting. You told me that Dame Edith once said approximately: 'One must never let one's life outside the theatre become more important or demanding than one's imaginary life in the theatre' or one's work would suffer. I agreed with this at the time. Because if this does happen, it tends to make the theatre and acting seem too 'unreal' to be gone on with. There is this danger, and I have several times sensed it.

But the last two weeks or so have proved to me that on the contrary my work in the theatre and 'real life' have now marvellously become one. I am more aware and awake in my work and everyday life.

When I play at night I not only feel happy, as I always have done, because I enjoy acting; I've always been far too self-indulgent in this as you probably know; but I feel a far greater joy, a longing to share everything with the audience, to give them all I can. I feel almost in love with them.

I used to feel tired and even slightly irritable if I had to do more than two different things during the day—such as writing letters, seeing and talking to someone I didn't particularly want to—I used to feel rather peevishly 'I do like having the day to *myself*'. You may be horrified but it was true. During the week up to and just after the Sunday sit-down not only did I have a first night, but I saw and talked to at least five reporters, interviewers, Committee people etc. etc. a day, and wrote all the letters I could, answered questions of any kind as fully as I could, made countless telephone calls (which I am paying for) and answered countless calls; I am reading and thinking and living. Does this sound very silly? Most other people have done this all their lives but it's new for me. Now *no* amount of work can dismay me!

Last of all. I expect you have read a general account of what happened in the Square so I won't tell you in detail. I didn't get hurt as some people did. Shelagh [Delaney] and I, and some other girls, spent Sunday night in a cell of a police station in Ealing, of all places. We were sent there in a Black Maria, each sitting in a little upturned coffin-cupboard with the door closed. I was lucky to be with Shelagh throughout all this as we could keep each other's pecker up by joking and chattering. We were very cold that night on the floor of the cell, and very tired and dirty the next day. We waited until 4 o'clock at Marlborough Street [the magistrates' court], sitting in the corridors. None of it was really unpleasant, but being tired and hungry and dirty completely saps one of feelings, clear thoughts, or anything. The first thing I did when I got home was to have a bath and ring Mum up. Six of the organisers on the Committee were charged with the 1936 Incitement Act and will almost for sure get three months; but they are fighting the case as they were particularly charged with inciting people to charge or break the police barriers. And this is just not true. It is completely against the policy of the Committee for any such thing to be done. And besides we can all give evidence that this was not true.

Bob Bolt is in an open prison with the rest, Wesker, Michael Randle, Christopher Logue among others. And they are treated extremely well. But the prison authorities refuse to allow Bob, alone of all the others, to write, and I hear he is very het-up and worried as he must finish the Lawrence of Arabia script by tomorrow or probably be sued by Spiegel who is furious. He even applied to the Home Office and all he can get out of them is that if he would sign an agreement to keep the peace then he could write or leave prison or anything. Why he has been picked upon no one knows.

I'm so happy to hear rehearsals are going so well, hurray. Please give much love to Freddie and thank him for his nice letters. I can't write just yet as I have a mass of other stuff, letters, the discussion, a speech and a poetry reading Max and I are going to do this month.

Fondest, fondest love my dearest— Take care of yourself—

Your loving V.

My father kept all my letters. Alas, I have not kept all his, and I have not preserved his reply to my letter. But reply he did, and evidently he was even more worried than before. He had never fully recovered from his wartime experience with the People's Convention, and I am certain he feared I was being used, as he had been used for purposes and a cause he could not believe in. I, on the other hand, could see nothing wrong in being used, provided I understood and believed in the cause for which one was used, which I did.

Monday

Darling, your letter, Express, came this morning, and I will answer it as best I can—

Firstly, I should explain that I have been on a Sub-Committee for arranging the Public Forum the Committee are holding next Sunday. Five speakers are dealing in specific detail with the aims and beliefs of the Committee of 100, and will be explaining why we feel it necessary to commit civil disobedience. The public will then be able to ask questions, and finally Russell will speak. This was an idea of mine, which I am very glad to have carried out, and is probably the most positive contribution I could ever make.

The reason I think this Forum is very important is that most people do not know exactly what we stand and hope for. This is partly due to misrepresentation of us by the political leaders and particularly the Press who are only interested in the sensational aspect, the sit-downs and arrests. *Also* many supporters are not clear in their heads either, and there is a definite tendency to be far more interested in sitting down than the reason why we sit down—I won't go into detail but you yourself probably don't know that many, not all of us, but many supporters and Lord Russell himself advocate a policy of neutralism for England—not to save our own skins but for many practical reasons, thought out in terms of practical politics.

However most people think we are just making a cri-de-coeur, or that we naively and stupidly want the West to renounce nuclear warfare, leaving Russia a monopoly on the Bomb. Until we can let everyone know exactly what we are sitting down for, we can't possibly expect them to join us or even sympathise.

I have read your last letter to me carefully to see what point in it I had not answered. I found your two main points and I feel that I answered them at great length, however I probably interpreted them differently so I will try and answer them again, and more specifically.

You say—

1) That I have a divine gift, which is more important than heroism, and that I must do nothing to jeopardise or paralyse this gift.

2) That I have made my point, and proved I am committed.

Answer to Number 1: I mainly interpreted this in terms of doing nothing to *paralyse* this gift, which is why I tried to explain that my awareness of all the life around me, political, personal, natural or theatrical, and my love for that life which is *why* I act after all, had been doubly *increased* since becoming more aware and involved with the present political situation. As I see it, very clearly, one's desire to act, and the juice, energy and feelings that prompt this desire, *could* be diminished by falling headlong into politics, Bomb, and Committee of 100. But they are not diminished and can never be. However, if one thinks of *jeopardise,* then there are several things to be clear about and beware of, I know.

Firstly, as I proved for myself last week, if I tag along to any or all of the various small demonstrations, the night previous to a Stratford performance, I am very tired the next day, and in fact the performances the next day were not good. This was very wrong of me, and if I did it again, I would not only jeopardise one performance but certainly my work in general and my career in future. I talked to Corin about this, whose judgment and love I respect enormously as you do, and he cleared my mind on this point; but if I hadn't (however foolishly or wrongly) done this just once, I could not have realised so fully for *myself* how wrong and stupid I was.

Lord, I want to act and go on acting more than I can, or need say. Don't imagine there aren't many moments when I long for the personal comforts of body and mind that I could enjoy if I forgot about everything nuclear etc.; I believe I could contribute a good deal to the theatre; and that the theatre contributes something valuable to people; but having become really aware, intellectually as well as emotionally, of the present situation—I can never go back—*How* I go forward is something I must work out bit by bit for myself, as I said earlier.

I could go on writing forever at this rate! But it's probably better that it should be by letter than a personal talk, for which there is never enough time, and when we might get too emotional!

I must stop now darling. I do hope I've been able to calm a few of your fears; though as I now realise that you disapprove of the civil disobedience campaign, I also realise that nothing short of me steering clear of the whole thing could completely reassure you. But don't worry about my ever becoming a crank. With my darling Corin, and sensible marvellous friends like Bob Bolt, and you, last but not least, there are enough people for me to discuss matters with to prevent me ever becoming the wild woman of Grenville Place!

Most enormous good luck for the next few days and for your opening. And always all love—V.

Dad was in New York playing in Graham Greene's *The Complaisant Lover*. He had been asked by Olivier to play in *Uncle Vanya* that summer at the new Chichester Festival Theatre. Everyone had been sworn to secrecy, but it was understood that Chichester was to be the trial run for the launching of the National Theatre Company. Just before Christmas 1961 I wrote to Dad again from Wilks Water, trying to calm his fears about my commitment to the Committee of 100.

I came here on Wednesday and shan't leave until first thing Sunday. I got another cold and was feeling a bit nervous and depressed, so I cancelled everything and joined Mum here. A few days of walks and music and patchwork in the evenings have already made me feel peaceful and longing to start rehearsals again for 'As You'.

I was wanting to write you a proper letter for a long time. Particularly now. You may not have heard this but whether you haven't or will I want to tell you. I was in a bit of a state last Saturday—the 9th—when I was feeling very upset, and also feeling that I *must* go on the demonstration which would have meant missing two performances. This will shock you terribly and shocks me now I am clearer. I can only explain that I had to for two reasons:

1) If I couldn't make this sacrifice for something I feel to be terribly important, how could I ever ask anyone else to; and how could I any longer believe there was a small hope of our success sometime in the future?

2) None of the other 'names' were going for various reasons. Of course as soon as I'd had a talk with Peter and John Roberts to get this off my chest, I realised that I couldn't dream of breaking my contract. So I didn't go, and the 'Sunday Times' asked me for an interview, which I gave them, hoping to get across to them that I felt the demonstration had *not* been a flop as the Minister of Home Affairs called it. The reporter was mainly interested in why I hadn't gone. We discussed responsibilities etc; and I said that you and I had always felt that under no circumstances *whatever* should one ever break a promise or contract, or irresponsibly avoid one's duty to the theatre. But that while actors and actresses of your genera-tion would feel that under no circumstances *whatever* should one break a contract, I felt that there were certain conditions under which I would, albeit against every instinct and wish in me. How-ever, this came out in the paper very differently 'my father has always urged me to never miss a performance or break a contract. But people of that generation would feel that way.' I felt terrible at the thought that you would read this, or anybody else, and think I meant such a thing. Well it was my own fault for giving an interview and I shan't again, but darling I just want to tell you not only that I never felt or said such a thing but that I do see now that I can be of far more use to the Committee if I continue to work as hard as I can in the theatre; and that it is important and more right for me if I do. There is no question of what I *want* to do. To put everything into the theatre for the rest of my life. It is just that for one thing I do not feel at all convinced that there will be all my life ahead of me, or ahead of *us;* and that believing in unilateral disarmament etc. etc., I could not be at peace with myself if I didn't join with other people to do something according to my beliefs. Anyway darling, please believe that I love and respect what you are and what you think, and that I love the theatre. Mum says you

may be coming back in April and that you have been asked to go to Chichester. I'm so glad, and I'm longing to see you again.

Very much love my dearest and a happy happy Christmas.

Your loving Vanessa.

P.S. Bernard Levin has now taken me out twice, and red roses on the last night of 'The Shrew!' and is escorting me to Covent Garden on Saturday to see 'A Midsummer Night's Dream'. He is a very interesting person to talk to and I've enjoyed myself thoroughly, but alas! my heart is elsewhere engaged. So we'll have to have a splendid Shaw-Terry relationship.

Alas for Bernard Levin (whose heart is now safely engaged elsewhere, and who probably thanks his maker a thousand times for saving him from a fate worse than death, if indeed he so much as spares a thought for his youthful folly), my heart, and soon my hand, was engaged to Tony Richardson. When he came to see *As You Like It* one night at the Aldwych he said I was the only actress who could play Shakespeare's heroines, and drove me off to supper in his red Ford Thunderbird.

CHAPTER 10

Toward the end of 1961, Tony was in the middle of rehearsals for *A Midsummer Night's Dream* at the Royal Court, with Lynn as Helena and Corin as Lysander. I'd received a letter from Lynny a month earlier up at Stratford telling me that Tony had offered her the part. She was in her final year at Central and I think Dad had told her she should not accept the offer but should finish school. So she was unsure what to do and not confident she could take it on. I told her how Tony had auditioned me for the film of *Look Back in Anger* in 1958 and had turned me down. "He must be quite certain you can do this or he'd never have offered you Helena. I think you should say yes and leave Central."

That summer Corin had left Cambridge with an honors degree and joined the Royal Court as assistant director. At the end of a long day of auditions Tony asked him, "By the way, can you act?" Corin launched into Hotspur's speech "My liege, I did deny no prisoners," and Tony stopped him after a few lines, saying, "Okay, you can play Lysander." Lynny was eighteen years old and Corin was twenty-one. Rita Tushingham played Hermia. She was also eighteen and had been chosen by Tony for the film of *A Taste of Honey* the previous year. David Warner and James Bolam had just left drama school; Alfred Lynch had come from a very successful production by Joan Littlewood of Brendan Behan's *The Hostage*. Samantha Eggar was twenty-five and had been in one film. Nicol Williamson was still virtually unknown, as was Ronnie Barker.

I thought the production was wonderful; I can still hear Lynn and Rita in the scene between the two schoolgirls when they have a fight, and I doubt that Bottom the Weaver and his village friends have ever been so real and so funny. But the critics who only five years before had ridiculed the Royal Court for introducing the kitchen sink into the hallowed halls of English drama were now equally incensed that the home of the kitchen sink should open its doors to Shakespeare's fairies and their mischievous magic. Tony and his young cast were castigated without mercy. Tony was absolutely indifferent to his own success or failure, but he loved his actors. He persuaded George Devine to direct them all in a Sunday-night performance of *Twelfth Night* to take their minds off the bad notices.

The snow fell on New Year's Eve and I ran from the Aldwych Theatre at the top of the Strand to my parents' flat in Knightsbridge to join Tony, Rachel, and Michael before midnight struck. Later I went back to Eaton Mews South, to a flat Tony had rented with John Osborne, who was living with the writer Penelope Gilliatt. When Tony flung open the door of the fridge in the morning the shelves were full of oranges, Dom Pérignon champagne, and Fernet Branca. Penelope had the whitest skin and the reddest of real red hair. The Elizabethan poets would have written another five hundred sonnets about her. John, whom I had last met at Stratford in 1959 with Mary Ure, was very merry and sardonic. He and Tony were taking judo classes with a wrestler called Joe Robinson, and in the evenings they practiced throwing each other to the floor of the sitting room. Penelope, who wrote film reviews for *The Observer*, was distraught because Roger, her former husband, was very unhappy, and she sat on our bed while we all tried to comfort her.

Tony was thirty-four years old. My first vivid memory of him went back to a Sunday morning in Stratford-upon-Avon when he and Mary appeared to fly into the house on a March wind, both laughing and laughing, unable to stop. He always wore sneakers and an open shirt with a loose sweater, and I had the impression of a marvelous merry bird that knew more about everything than anyone I knew, even Corin. I was immediately attracted by his political views, his scorn for the prudery and cruelty of philistine England, his love for his friends George Devine and the designer Jocelyn Herbert, his lack of propriety and reverence for any tradition, and his careless attitude to his own success, which was phenomenal. There is a short BBC interview with him, filmed behind the Memorial Theatre in 1959, when *Look Back in Anger* had just opened in the cinemas, and he was rehearsing *Othello.* "Do you really believe there should be no censorship at all?" inquired the incredulous journalist behind the camera. "Absolutely none. There is absolutely nothing that shouldn't be shown in the cinema." At this time the film censorship board and the Lord Chamberlain's office exerted an iron control over film and theatre texts and production. When Peter Hall directed *Waiting for Godot* at the Arts Theatre in 1955 the Lord Chamberlain insisted that Fartov should become Popov, and that Pozzo had "warts" and not "clap."

Tony had had endless problems with the film censor over *Look Back in Anger,* and in 1961 the government prosecuted Penguin Publishers, asserting that *Lady Chatterley's Lover* by D. H. Lawrence was an offense under the Obscene Publications Act. Thirty years later the English press summoned to their sides everyone they could to attack the BBC TV film series of *Lady Chatterley,* which starred Tony's daughter Joely. The grounds of the attack were D. H. Lawrence's celebration of physical love, and his attack on sexual relations that are based on and dominated by money. When Rita Tushingham flung her arms wide on the Salford skyline in *A Taste of Honey* and announced, "I'm a very considerable person," Tony was celebrating the defiance and innocence of the sixteen-year-old pregnant schoolgirl, who was, in a way, the Connie Chatterley of 1961.

Tony was the first English filmmaker to shoot feature films on real locations, rather than in a studio. He was the first director to show England as it was, from top to bottom, at the end of the 1950s. He was the first to show the racism of the petty Labour council officers toward the Asian shopkeepers. When we were living together in Eaton Mews South he was preparing and then filming Alan Sillitoe's *Loneliness of the Long Distance Runner,* the story of a boy sent to Borstal Prison for a petty theft. Tony cast a new young actor, Tom Courtenay, as the boy, and he cast my father as the prison governor. The locations were found in London, and in an unused army barracks in Hampshire. The genius cameraman, who was also camera operator, was Walter Lassally.

I watched all the filming I could in between rehearsals of *The Taming of the Shrew*. At night Tony came back exhausted after a long day's work, laid his head in my lap, and closed his eyes. I think I decided at that moment that I wanted to look after him more than anything else in the world. *The Taming of the Shrew* opened in Stratford, and Tony came up for the first night. After the performance, while we were having a drink in my old studio in front of the tortoise stove, he asked me to marry him. We fell asleep and he drove back to London early the next morning in his Thunderbird. I slept some more and then made some coffee. I wondered if I had dreamed his proposal. I rang his London office in Curzon Street. "Did you ask me to marry you?" "Yes, darling," he said. "Do you want to?" "Yes I do. Yes! Yes!"

He organized our wedding two weeks later at the register office in Hammersmith town hall, since officially he still lived in the flat on the river there at Lower Mall where George Devine had lived. George was deeply in love with Jocelyn Herbert, and they were our best man and best woman on April 28, 1962. We four giggled all the way through the legal ceremony and then drove back to Eaton Mews South for champagne with Rachel, Michael, Corin, and Lynn. I did two last performances of *As You Like It* at the Aldwych, and the next morning Tony and I caught a plane to Athens.

That evening we sat in a sidewalk café on Constitution Square and discussed what names we wanted for our first baby. We discovered our favorite book ever was Tolstoy's *War and Peace*. We discussed the chapter where Natasha goes to her first ball at the age of thirteen. We looked at each other. "It's Natasha!" If the baby was a boy, he would be Tom, after the hero of Fielding's novel *Tom Jones*, which Tony would start filming in Somerset in a month's time.

We flew on to Corfu, still a small, almost deserted town, and stayed in an old white house on top of a hillside rented out by a Greek Anglophile. We went for long walks and one afternoon stopped above a small bay to watch a wooden fishing boat chug across the water to a landing stage. Tony's bright brown eyes lit up and he started laughing. Without explaining why, he ran down the hillside, looking rather like Garibaldi, I thought, in his red shirt and blue jeans. Still laughing, he ran up to the boat, where a couple of perspiring men prepared to hitch the rope to a stake on the shore. Off the boat came Albert Finney and Peter Bull, who were taking a holiday together before filming *Tom Jones.*

By July I was pregnant, playing Imogen in *Cymbeline* at Stratford, and speeding with Jan, Tony's Polish driver, down to Dorset and Somerset on my days off. I have memories of white roses everywhere, farmyard animals everywhere, horses everywhere, a helicopter swoop over the downs the day before Tony filmed the hunting scene, and suppers in strange old houses, rented to the film crew by impoverished landowners, one of whom lived in a tree. We supped for some weeks beneath moldering bullet-torn flags, which proved to be trophies of the Boer War, as a clock ticked and boomed through the night. In one house I made friends with the son of one of these mad country gentlemen, who gave me a fascinating account of a journey he had made to Aldermaston, the main atomic energy plant in England. He was a watercolor painter, in the mystic tradition of William Blake, and he had begun to paint the weird nuclear plant out there in the countryside. He was suddenly surrounded and seized by military police, who drove him into the plant and made him turn out his pockets. They were particularly interested in some crumbs he turned out of a pocket lining. "What are these?" they demanded fiercely. They did not believe the young painter when he told them the crumbs were the remains of a digestive biscuit. They confiscated his painting and released him the following morning. He showed me the painting. I could dimly perceive why they were convinced they had trapped a Russian agent, even though he spoke with an impeccable public-school accent—or perhaps, remembering Philby, *because* he spoke with a public-school accent.

I have two particular recollections of the filming of *Tom Jones* that indicate Tony's approach to cinema:

Dame Edith Evans stood in the middle of the farmyard, in full eighteenth-century dress, lecturing Albert Finney as Tom, who was riding by on a donkey. Albert and the donkey jogged accidentally through a mucky puddle and splashed dirt all over the front of Dame Edith's lovely dress. She stopped short in mid-speech and clutched her dress skirts with a look of absolute horror and disdain. Tony kept that shot in the film.

Another day rain stopped filming. We sat in the caravans, and Tony was impatient to find some way of using the rain and not losing a day's shoot. We ploughed around the wet gardens and fields and came across a farmyard pond covered with water lilies. "Albert! We've got a new scene for you! You jump into the pond in the rain and you get a water lily and you give it to Susannah." That idea did not thrill Albie or Susannah, but half an hour later they were jumping up and down in the pond in the rain, while the crew rigged up hoses in front of the camera to ensure the rain would "read" and Tony clapped his hands with encouragement. "That's absolutely wonderful, my dahlings. MORE RAIN!" The scene *was* wonderful and was included in the editing of a montage of Tom Jones and Sophia falling in love. This was the first time in British or American cinema that a montage with music was used to tell a love story.

All of George and Tony's friends were in the movie. George himself played Squire Allworthy, Tom's adoptive father, Rachel played his sister, and Lynn played an innkeeper's daughter who ran through the inn crying "Rape! Rape!" when she found Tom in bed with a lady. Wilfrid Lawson played the old gamekeeper, Peter Bull a huntin' squire. Joan Greenwood was an exquisite London countess, and Joyce Redman was the delectable lady who eats her way through a seven-course meal before making love with Tom.

The film opened in London in June the following year. Over coffee, Tony and I sat reading the reviews, which were absolutely scathing and contemptuous without one exception. Then the film opened in France. The French press went mad with excitement. The film was an enormous hit, and this persuaded United Artists to keep it in the British theatres and plan a wide general release in the United States. The following March, 1964, Tony and the film won countless Oscars and *Tom Jones* was the film of the year. When the American press invented the phrase "Swinging London" and the "Swinging Sixties," I always thought of the uphill battle it actually was then to achieve anything in London, in film especially, or in the theatre.

≡

From late 1961 to 1962 I had been fully participating in the daily meetings of the Committee of 100 in their offices at Finsbury Park. We had planned a mass civil-disobedience action around the entrances to the U.S. Air Force base at Wethersfield in Essex. The leaflet we printed had a map of the base, showing the entrances and feeder roads. This brought a Special Branch raid on the committee offices. Returning to Rachel and Michael's flat after a performance at the Aldwych, I found two plainclothes policemen waiting for me. "Special Branch, Miss Redgrave. May we have a word with you?" They questioned me for two hours or so in my father's study. Had I seen the map of Wethersfield air base before? Had I agreed to the demonstration? Had I been present at meetings on such and such a date? I did not know it was my right to ask for a lawyer to be present before I answered questions, nor did they tell me. I wanted to answer their questions as points of principle in any case.

All the committee members, including myself, were completely taken by surprise. We had not anticipated Special Branch intervention, and neither I nor anyone else at the committee had sought, or been given, any legal advice. Eager to assert my moral coresponsibility and commitment to the demonstration, I gave a firm "yes" to all the questions related to my own involvement in the decisions and the planning, and evaded questions concerning other committee members. I rang the committee later and went over to the offices the next day. Michael Randle, the secretary, George Clark, Helen Allegranza, Pat Pottle, and two other members were charged with offenses under the Official Secrets Act. I was not charged, even though I and other members wrote to the attorney general declaring that we were equally responsible with our friends. The trial took place at the Old Bailey. Many of us gave evidence as witnesses in our friends' behalf. Our testimony, mistakenly, I later thought, was centered entirely on the moral grounds for the demonstration, rather than contesting the permissibility of prosecuting the committee members under the Official Secrets Act. I remember we were all excited when a radar scientist gave evidence on the possibilities and dangers of misreading radar air-warning signals. None of his evidence, however, could challenge the issues of the Official Secrets Act.

Michael, George, Helen, and others all received prison sentences. Helen was in Holloway. On a cold, rainy day a year later she came out of the gates and we greeted her with flowers, hugs, and a strong cup of tea. I saw her once after that, and months later I learned that she had committed suicide.

Bertrand Russell and his secretary, Ralph Schoenmann, came to many of the meetings of the committee, and I saw them frequently. I was surprised that other members did not appear to listen to him closely, nor agree with his views. Russell told me one day that he'd had a dream in which God told him, "Bertie, I will give you whatever you want. Make one wish and you shall have it." I expected him to have replied that he wanted all nuclear power put out of action by the Divine Power he did not believe in. Instead he told the Eternal Father that he wanted a piece of Noah's Ark. I believe that year was his ninetieth birthday. His grandson, the Duke of Bedford, organized a meeting and recital at the Royal Festival Hall, and I read a poem and presented a book to him.

I considered myself a pacifist, became a subscriber to *Peace News,* and was asked by the founder, Vera Brittain, to become chairman. I refused, feeling I was not knowledgeable enough, but I agreed to become honorary treasurer for the Movement for Colonial Freedom. I felt dissatisfied, however, with the process of repeatedly organizing and participating in protest activities that had no perspective beyond the next date for an action. Furthermore, I could find no satisfactory answer to the repeated question posed after a civil-disobedience action: Would I pay the fine or not? If I refused to pay I would be choosing an automatic prison sentence. If I went to prison I would lose performances and be fired. If I was fired I would not be hired again, my reputation as an actress would decline, and the press would not listen to what I had to say. I noticed the press never printed what I or Russell or anyone said anyway.

One Sunday at lunch I had a long talk with Tony, George, and Jocelyn. I had been offered a lot of money to advertise Weston Biscuits. They even said they would pay the money to the Campaign for Nuclear Disarmament if I wished. I wanted to accept. George told me I must do no such thing. If I could be paid to put my name to biscuits, then I could be paid to put my name to anything. The value of my name was based on my integrity, the fact that I could not be bought by anyone for anything. I was convinced George was right, and Jocelyn and Tony agreed. But what could stop nuclear war? It could never be that an increasing number of moral people would finally outvote the immoral leaders who would stop at nothing to achieve their political interests. I read a lot about Mahatma Gandhi's civil-disobedience movement and I was very impressed with his moral example, the correctness of the demands for rights for the poor workers and peasants of India.

≡

That autumn Tony and I went to New York. I was at first intoxicated by the lights of Manhattan and the sharp, funny, and informed discussions of the New Yorkers. In the daytime Tony had rehearsals. *Luther,* by John Osborne, had recently opened, and now Tony was rehearsing Brecht's *Resistible Rise of Arturo Ui* with Christopher Plummer and Lionel Stander. The production of the play, based on the history of the rise to power of Hitler, coincided with the publication of Simone de Beauvoir's second book of memoirs, *La Force de l'âge* (*The Prime of Life*). Her life with Sartre and the political events they were involved in were engrossing. The book opened new political horizons for me. Until then I had been constrained by the religious and pacifist connections and influences of the nuclear-disarmament movement. De Beauvoir was telling me of a whole period of history I was ignorant of—the 1930s, the Spanish revolution, and the Nazi occupation of France. I learned a little about the French Communist Party and a great deal about the philosophical and political discussions between Sartre and his French colleagues. Then I read *L'Invitée* and *Les Mandarins,* alternating between the French and English versions to improve my French.

One paragraph from *L'Invitée* stuck in my mind. Nadine is taken to Portugal by Henri for a holiday. They stand on a hill looking at the lights of the town below, able to drink real coffee and eat fresh oranges once again. Henri is full of excitement at the sunset, the view, and the good food. Nadine says she can think only of the actual life of the workers, unable to drink real coffee or participate in the kind of life that makes possible the luxury of enjoying a beautiful view. She tells him she finds the beautiful view and the enjoyment of it obscene.

Tony loved New York and said it recharged his batteries. I liked it too, but found I was looking at it through Nadine's eyes. The rounds of expensive meals paid for by United Artists, which was going to distribute *Tom Jones* and perhaps finance Tony's next film, the vast quantities of food and alcohol—whiskies first and then French wines—and endless discussions of film budgets running to millions of dollars began to drive me up the wall. I was restless and, not for the first time, made a resolution: I must work. So I took singing lessons. My teacher was highly recommended by Tammy Grimes, star of *The Unsinkable Molly Brown*. He insisted that his pupils suck in their breath, "Hee-hee-hee!" It was a far cry from Jani Strasser and his poodles. A friend of Tony's found me another teacher up on the East Side in a brownstone full of antiques. I went there every morning for a lesson and then spent the rest of the day in the New York Public Library.

There in the library I felt Simone de Beauvoir was at my side. Okay, it was New York, not the Sorbonne, but I was awed and excited by the vast, quiet library, and by the rules and facilities that permitted an English visitor to see any book and any microfiche on request. I felt a deep need to know more about my own history as an English radical, and the idea came to me of devising a program for a Sunday-night performance at the Royal Court Theatre. I took for a beginning the slogan of John Ball, the peasant leader of the English Peasants' Revolt of 1381: "When Adam delved and Eve span, who was then the gentleman?" I found my way empirically through the history without a guide. Cromwell's revolution of 1642 against the absolute monarchy, with the issue of property as the decisive qualification for the vote. Tom Paine, *The Rights of Man*, and the French Revolution against the absolute monarchy in 1789. The Irish revolution against British rule led by Wolfe Tone and inspired by the revolution in France. The struggle for the right to organize in trade unions for jobs and better wages, and the savage repressions of the 1820s. Easter 1916 and the uprising against the British occupation of Ireland. The EOKA uprisings in Cyprus against British rule, and the shooting of schoolchildren by the British armed forces. I ended the program with Socrates' last speech to the Athenians before he was forced to take poison. I named the program "In the Interests of the State: A Historical Guide for the Modern Agitator." George Devine made a Sunday shortly before Christmas available, and I directed the program, lucky to have Robert Stephens and Jack McGinnan and George joining me as my cast.

Before returning to England, however, Tony and I went to Cuba. He had been invited by ICAIC, the Cuban film industry, established three years before, when the Batista dictatorship was overthrown. We went first for a few days' holiday in Jamaica since Tony was exhausted from two theatre productions in a row and needed a rest before all the interviews and lectures he would be giving to Cuban filmmakers. The island was more beautiful than anything I could have imagined, but the poverty of the shacks where Jamaicans lived was stark and very apparent. When we drove in a taxicab through the country roads or village streets, the people looked at our taxi and at us, as tourists, with undisguised hostility. The hotel at Ocho Rios was extremely luxurious. The Jamaicans who swept the white sands of the private beach were called "boys" by the management, although they were adult men. It was sickening and obscene. We moved on to Acapulco in Mexico. Vast billboards by the roadside, PEPSI-COLA, NADA MAS. Water sprinklers whirred round softly, keeping the hotel grass green. One hundred yards across from the brand-new hotel, with its cabanas, its piña coladas, its tourist shop full of beautiful embroidered Mexican smocks and papier-mâché bracelets, were small shacks surrounded by fences and dust, lacking both water and electricity. I hated to be living the life of a rich tourist at these people's expense, served and waited upon in the hotel, in restaurants, and in the port by Mexicans who could not even afford to buy meat for their children. Those children had nothing at all. I felt guilty because I knew Tony needed this rest, but I did not feel at all grateful for any of the luxury he was paying for.

We went to Mexico City to line up for our visas to Cuba. A few yards from the American hotel we saw the same poverty as in Acapulco. The U.S. government had broken diplomatic relations with Castro's Cuba, and already severe penalties had been announced to stop Americans from going there.

Havana was rain-soaked when we arrived. We walked down the long deserted promenade by the gray sea. Out near the skyline, about three and a half miles away, was a huge destroyer, the *Monroe*, its guns within reach of Havana. In Cuba, too, there were giant billboards, but instead of urging us to drink Pepsi-Cola, the advertisements exhorted everyone, "Learn to read." There were appeals to learn about hygiene and health for the children: "The mother, too, has her place in the revolution." We were taken by the young filmmakers to the Hilton Hotel, which had been the pride of Batista's Havana. Food was rationed, and the Hilton had two items on the menu, frogs' legs and hot chocolate. Cuba was under the economic blockade of the United States. The government could not borrow money from the American banks, and could not buy urgently needed industrial machinery, tools, or spare parts.

At the Cuban film institute we were shown the first Cuban feature film, *Las Doce Sillas* (*The Twelve Chairs*). Before the revolution only the worst American films had been shown in Cuba, and there had been no Cuban film industry. We saw several documentaries: *Playa Giron*, about the defeat of the Bay of Pigs invasion, and *The Year of the Pencil*, which showed us the literacy campaign—trains and trucks full of young students going into the villages with books, pencils, and paper to teach reading and writing. In one of the editing rooms, technicians were improvising with ingenuity but no tools to set up projectors sent out from Czechoslovakia.

Our companions were young filmmakers in their mid-twenties. They took us to the former country club of Havana, whose golf course was now a building site for a new university, planned on the scale and in the form of a medieval forum in Italy. The former villas of rich Cubans and American businessmen had been converted into orphanages and schools, with housemothers and -fathers who were young students also. The chief goal was to provide primary and secondary education for children and young people. The textbooks and readers were beautifully illustrated, and Cuban writers had written special stories and poems for the children about the before-and-after of the revolution.

The young filmmakers who drove us around all took part in volunteer brigades at weekends to help cut the sugar cane, Cuba's only source of income. They told us the history of the United Fruit Company, the transformation of Cuban agriculture into a one-crop economy, and the transformation of Cuba into a virtual colony of the United States. They were all members of the street militia and took turns patrolling with rifles, for there were continuous attacks from

small CIA-trained teams from Miami. The Cuban people were virtu-
ally under siege from the Wall Street banks, the Pentagon, and the
CIA. On the southern tip of the island was a large U.S. air base,
Guantanamo.

Fernando and Manuela, a young Cuban filmmaker and his wife,
drove us up through the rain-sodden country roads and woods to
Ernest Hemingway's house, which had been left to the Cuban people
in his will. It was kept open as a museum, just as Hemingway had left
it. The caretaker, a tall black Cuban, had looked after the house for
the Hemingways. The rooms were clean and quiet; everything was
in place—his desk, his books and photographs. The bathroom had
scales, and he had charted his weight day by day with small pencil
notes up the side of the bathroom door. Today, as I write this, I think
of Tennessee Williams's beloved home in Key West. It was sold in
1992 because no American institution or philanthropist would save
this great playwright's house so that future generations could see
where he lived and worked and met with some of America's most
extraordinary and gifted intellectuals. En avant! as Tennessee said.

Tony gave a few question-and-answer sessions to the filmmakers,
and he agreed to send them some of his films and arrange for one of
the young directors to come to London and work as an assistant on
his next film. We went to Fernando and Manuela's flat and had a rum.
She was pregnant, as I was. "What are you calling your child?" I
asked. "If she's a girl, and she will be a girl, I know, I am calling her
Viridiana after the film of Luis Buñuel." Manuela and Fernando said
that a lot of their friends had left Cuba, including her mother. Life
was hard, and the blockade prevented them from seeing any films
except those from Eastern Europe and the Soviet Union. "Sometimes
I would give anything to see Dracula," she said, mocking herself.

This visit to Cuba fundamentally transformed my political outlook. I had seen a society that had carried out a revolution to end the
police terror of a U.S.-backed dictatorship, the poverty and squalor
and illiteracy of capitalist exploitation, and the domination of international finance capital. These people were being punished by the
United States government for this. While Stalinist-style one-party
rule was not their idea of how their society should be run, they did
not accept that the United States should impose its own political and
economic interests upon Cuba and the rest of Latin America. The

revolution had opened the way for a socialist Cuba, even though what the people were living under was definitely not a socialist state. The bureaucratic dictatorship of Castro's regime prevented the social revolution from advancing. Isolated and under economic blockade, the Cuban people could not progress economically or politically.

Nevertheless, Cuba showed how the rest of the Caribbean and Latin America might liberate millions from the starvation and poverty of the "free market" system, controlled and policed from the giant skyscrapers of Wall Street, the domes of Washington, and the sprawling military bases. Pacifism was now out of the question. The Cuban people had to maintain their militias and army, and they needed all the political support possible. Otherwise the "Yanquis" would certainly send destroyers and bombers to reimpose a regime of wealthy Cuban jet-set exiles and torturers. I hated President Kennedy for ordering the invasion of the Bay of Pigs, and now I realized why Castro had asked for missiles to protect Cuba from invasion.

Tony and I came back to London in November 1962, full of enthusiasm, and longing to share our Cuban experience with our friends. George and Jocelyn and Alan Sillitoe were excited and wanted to hear everything. But we were appalled by the blank disinterest of some of our English friends. They quite simply did not know and did not want to know, unlike the Americans we met, who were always eager to know anything they did not know.

The house in St. Peter's Square we had bought in the summer but never lived in was now ready for us. Tony and I had played canasta on every plane trip to decide who would decorate which room. He won all the games but conceded the nursery to me. I now bought a wicker cradle-cot on wheels and a pine chest of drawers, and I put my one-and-only possession, a Victorian armchair, into the nursery because it would be comfortable for breast-feeding. I had a chicken run built at the bottom of the garden and ordered a cockerel and a dozen chickens. Tony had enormous birdcages built and brought over his tropical birds from Lower Mall and all his books. The house cost £12,000 and I suppose we spent about £2,000 on new carpets, a large sofa, a large chair, a double bed, and bookshelves. Terence Conran, not then famous or rich, worked out kitchen units. I framed our Cuban posters and hung them. The house was uncluttered and rather bare—Tony fought to keep it that way, and I was entirely happy it should be so.

I was now directing rehearsals of "In the Interests of the State," the program I had devised while doing research in the New York Public Library on radicalism. We had our Sunday performance at the Royal Court in March 1963. Our baby was due in May. I remember George Devine standing on a box with an umbrella as George V reviewing British troops in Dublin, and Robert Stephens delivering Lord Byron's maiden speech in the House of Lords denouncing the notorious Judge Jeffries and the suppressing of the English workers who had taken part in an uprising to end their misery. I delivered a complacent speech given by Elizabeth II at Christmas and counterposed this with transcripts from radio reports of schoolchildren's demonstrations against British troops in Cyprus.

Tony's parents, Cecil and Elsie, came down to London from Morecombe to stay with us for a few days. Cecil was delighted about the coming baby. "Oh yes, so the baby will be born in May, the merry month of May." They gave us a wonderful wedding present, a heavy mortar and pestle and a number of brown jars from Cecil's pharmacy filled with spices and useful home remedies like bicarbonate of soda. I marveled to see this quiet and very contained Yorkshire couple. How had their brilliant and fascinating son come from them? Tony's father unbuttoned a little to tell me how Tony had tamed the wild owls in the woods outside the town of Shipley when he was a boy. "He 'ud go out at night and 'ud call to these owls, and they 'ud answer him and come to him and take food from his hands." I think I knew then what a changeling was, a baby who didn't fit into the parents' mold or their way of life.

Tony's father gave me a photograph of Tony at six, large for his age, smiling at the camera from beneath the neat brushed pudding-basin haircut. This was the Tony his father and mother wanted. Who would have guessed the inner thoughts of this passive-looking child, who was longing to break out of the stifling confines of Shipley. His parents must have been astounded when he chose theatre and university. He certainly astounded Bradford when he and his girlfriend, a dancer called Doreen Whitfield, decided to put on a production of

Milton's *Comus,* a seventeenth-century play that had never been performed anywhere since the time when it was written.

It was May. The lilac trees flowered in the London square, and our small garden was full of lilies of the valley. The three small ponds were full of Tony's tree frogs, who croaked in the warm nights, causing phone calls from irate neighbors, who dozed fitfully and then woke again with a start when my cockerel started crowing at six in the morning. In the last four weeks of my pregnancy I had a passion for pizza, and Tony would drive off to the nearest pizza house, far away in Knightsbridge, and bring me back big slices of pizza. Corin had fallen in love with a merry and beautiful girl called Deirdre and had moved into my old flat in Grenville Place. Lynn was in love for the first time, with a young painter, and had joined Olivier's National Theatre Company, playing the daughter in *Mother Courage.*

I drove with Rachel to her cottage, Wilks Water, on Friday, May 10. When we arrived I released Marvellous, the little Yorkshire terrier, my first present from Tony, and she scampered off through the fresh green spring grass. That night the nightingales were singing in the ancient Odiham woods, and I didn't want to sleep. The next morning I would be picked up by some Labour Party members to officially open a new museum of trade union history. On Sunday Tony would drive down to Hampshire and join Rachel, me, Corin, Deirdre, and Lynny for a Sunday roast lamb lunch. At the bottom of the bed lay a small wicker case with baby's nightdresses, which I had sewn by hand that spring in Norfolk, staying with Nanny Randall, who had taught me how to cut the pattern and how to make different embroidery stitches.

I heard an owl in the woods. Deep down inside my belly I felt a small pain, as if I were getting my period. It disappeared almost immediately and I fell asleep listening to the nightingale and the owl. "Tu-whit, tu-who—a merry note, while greasy Joan doth keel the pot."

I woke again with the tiny brief pain. Some time went by, and I felt it again. I switched on the light and looked at the clock. It was four in the morning. I left the light on. About twenty minutes later I felt the twinge of pain again. "It's wishful thinking," I said to myself, and switched the light off. "But, look, the morn, in russet mantle clad . . ." I opened the curtains. It was six o'clock. The evening star shone above the sweet woods, and the air through the window smelled clean and fresh with new leaves and grass and pear blossom and lilac. The twinges came regularly, every fifteen minutes. I ran to Rachel, who got up and made us both a tea tray, and I sat in her bed as we both crowed with delight. Rachel and I rang Tony, who said he would telephone Jan, his driver, and tell him to come down and take me back to London and the Welbeck nursing home, where I was booked in for the birth.

I rang my trade union friends, explained I had begun labor, and dictated a message of good luck for the new museum. Then I dressed and went out for a walk round the small lake and woods. Marvellous scampered along, sniffing the air, her long hair ruffling as she raced. I picked a small bunch of primroses and violets to take to the nursing home. Jan's Mercedes screeched down the gravel lane through the woods. "Okay, Mrs. Richardson, we're off." I offered him some coffee, but like most men, he was nervous, imagining the baby might be born any minute, so I kissed and hugged Mum and we drove back to London at breakneck speed.

CHAPTER 11

I had signed up some months before the birth with a Mrs. Betty
Parsons, who was recommended by the National Childbirth Trust.
"Pains," said Betty, "are in fact contractions, preceding and following
the breaking of the waters, which open the neck of the womb."
Contractions came in waves, short and shallow at first, with intervals
between, later in almost continuous waves. I must breathe and pant
in rhythm with the waves. Then my baby would have plenty of
oxygen in her blood, and I wouldn't tense up and fight against the
contractions. Only fear, and ignorance of the natural processes of our
own bodies, made us fight what we had been taught to believe was
unbearable pain, and so prolong our labors and tire ourselves out.
"Give me your wrist." Betty grasped my wrist in both hands, twisting
it in opposite directions, giving me the Chinese burn. "That's pain,"
she said. "That's me hurting your body. That's destructive and painful. But contractions are creative, and they're *not* painful. Every
contraction is opening the neck of your womb so that the baby can
get out."

   She warned me that the Harley Street gynecologist I was attending would not approve of the natural childbirth technique. She was

right. He thought it a harmless eccentricity, something to be humored. I was twenty-eight pounds overweight, owing to my craving for pizza and salty biscuits followed by glasses of cold milk, but the gynecologist had never been concerned about this; he had simply advised me to rub baby oil onto my stomach to relieve the itching caused by the stretching skin.

I asked myself why, in the third quarter of the twentieth century, despite all the advances in natural science, attitudes to childbirth and to children should be so primitive and even downright inhuman? Tony had insisted that our baby be born in a nursing home instead of at home because he imagined they would provide advanced obstetrical methods for a safe delivery. On the contrary. My pubic hair was shaved and I was given an enema. Tony went off for a drink at the office, having been told, "It will be some hours yet." But he came back very soon and held my hand. This was wonderful, because I wanted his support. The nurses and the doctor were kind and gentle people, but they'd been trained to believe that giving birth is one of the most painful experiences a human being can undergo, and that their job was to administer gas and other anesthetics to lessen or stop the pain and get the whole business over as quickly as possible. In America in the 1960s virtually all women in labor were given injections to paralyze them from the waist down, which almost always meant forceps and pain for the baby, and sometimes damage.

Today in England official reports say that 60 percent of the babies in private clinics and hospitals are delivered by caesarean operations. Were the women in their twenties in the 1990s, the children of my generation, all born with dwarf-sized pelvises? If so, what caused this? The answer is that they and their husbands have been brainwashed into believing what the private hospitals tell them: "A caesarean would be safer." It so happens, you will not be surprised to hear, that a caesarean birth costs more; that is to say, the hospital earns more, which was the aim of the Conservative government's reorganization of health and hospital care in the 1990s. This simple fact demonstrates once again the significance of the capitalist system's essential need to put profit before people.

More than half my energy during labor was spent telling the nurses that I did not need or want any painkilling injection or gas. "Now, how about a little injection to make it easier for you, Mrs.

Richardson?" "Puff—puff—puff—no thank you." (I remember in a flash the advice from Betty Parsons—don't get panicked when the nurses keep insisting you need a painkiller.) "How *very* kind of you—puff—puff—puff—but I assure you—puff—puff—I can manage—puff—puff—perfectly well—puff—puff." I closed my eyes, held Tony's hand, shut the nurses out, remembered Marvellous panting through the wet spring grass that morning, and panted in rhythm with her running and the waves of contractions.

> Everyone suddenly burst out singing,
> And I was filled with such delight
> As prisoned birds must find in freedom,
> Winging wildly across the white
> Orchards and dark green fields,
> On—on—and out of sight.

I told the nurses I wanted to push, and they helped me roll over onto my back. I pushed my knees up, took hold of the bottom of my thighs, held my breath, and went with the calls of my muscles, and our baby. I asked Tony, "Can you see it yet?" Suddenly with a whoosh the baby spurted out into the hands of the doctor. They rushed her away, telling Tony and me, "It's a girl," and brought her back washed and wrapped in a cotton blanket and put her in my arms. It was five o'clock on a Saturday afternoon in May. The sun poured through the window. Rachel came in soon, and she and Tony and I gazed and gazed at Natasha and kissed her and kissed her. From the crown of her head, spirals of fine hair like a gossamer solar system stirred as she breathed. Natasha Jane became Tasha as soon as she was born. She smiled at five days old. Mothers are told, "Newborn babies don't smile—it's only gas." When babies have gas they don't smile, they cry and whimper. When Joely was born eighteen months later, and Carlo five years after that, I knew that a breast-fed baby, born without drugs, cuddled and kept clean and carried around, is happy and does smile.

I breast-fed Tasha, fortified by a bottle of Guinness a day, and battled with the nurse who was hired by Tony. I advertised for an Italian girl to come and help me, since I rejected the staid English nursing approach to babies: "Speak roughly to your little boy and beat him when he sneezes." I got Viola, who had come to England from Italy in answer to an advertisement for girls to work in a stocking factory. Viola came from the north of Italy, and she had vehement prejudices against the south, especially against Sicilians. For her, the color bar began once you left Rome. Sicilians were the same as Africans, almost black, and people she wanted to keep well away from. She herself had jet-black hair, which made her views all the more curious. She believed, furthermore, that northerners were industrious and southerners were lazy and corrupt. When I tried to question this view, she looked at me with amazement. She was in every other way, however, a very sweet woman.

Tony took Tasha, Viola, and me to the south of France for a month, and we had a holiday such as dreams are made of. A swimming pool, lavender, sun in the day, and stars and fireflies at night. The lavender was steamed into oil in a vast hubble-bubble iron cauldron with a long pipe that jerked in various directions.

Tony read at least one book a day, was writing a film script, and was preparing a Broadway production and a play for London. We had lots of his friends to stay, and when Lynny arrived she and I did cabaret turns in the evenings after supper, singing the main songs from *Gypsy*, including our all-time favorite, "Everything's Coming Up Roses."

Tasha got whirled around, hugged, kissed, and the whole repertoire of *Gypsy* all for herself. It was the first time since the early days at Wilks Water that Lynny and I had spent time together, and she made us laugh and laugh with her stories about the National Theatre. She had a devastating mind and ear for a theatrical sketch and improvised brilliantly, embellishing real anecdotes with flights of her own observation and imagination. She had graduated from walk-on parts to leading roles at the National. Noël Coward directed her in his production of *Hay Fever* with Dame Edith Evans and Maggie Smith; he admired her so much that he wrote his first and only television play for her.

≡

Back in London I began to read the newspapers again. Nelson Mandela, Walter Sisulu, and the leaders of the African National Congress were on trial for their lives in Rivonia, South Africa. The leaders of the Labour Party denounced apartheid fiercely in their speeches. I thought that meant that they would boycott South Africa if they came to power in the next election. I wrote a song, "Hanging on a Tree," and sang it in Trafalgar Square. I recorded it, together with a poem by Paul Éluard, "Liberté, j'écris ton nom," which I had seen pasted to a wall in Havana. The words of "Hanging on a Tree" were published in *The Observer*, and a day or so after it appeared someone told me that a group of businessmen headed by Sir Jock Campbell, whom I had never met, had paid for an advertisement in *The Financial Times*, using my song as a text, to appeal for sanctions against South Africa. Even in those less inflationary days a full-page advertisement in *The Financial Times* cost a sizable sum, and I think I may have wondered if there was not some more practical or better use to which the money might be put. If so, I could have spared myself the worry, because to everyone's surprise, not least Sir Jock Campbell's, *The Financial Times* refused to print it.

> From: Sir Jock Campbell
> Bucklebury House
> London EC4
> 23rd January 1964

Dear Miss Redgrave,

I think you may have heard from David Astor that, having been deeply moved and impressed by the words of your song published in *The Observer*, I decided to try to get them published, in the form of an advertisement in *The Financial Times*. Businessmen being usually more romantic it occurred to me that they might be influenced by your poem in a way which they are not by factual reporting from South Africa. Hence my choice of *The Financial Times*. The whole thing has failed because, even after going so far as sending me a proof, and the Advertising Department having obtained editorial approval, somebody decided that the advertisement should not be accepted. I am very disappointed. I enclose a copy of the proof as a monument to the attempt! I sent all the facts to John Freeman, and I think he may say something about it in this week's *New Statesman*.

Don't bother to reply to this,

> Yours sincerely,
> Jock Campbell

Peter Finch and his Jamaican wife, Yolande, joined me on the steps of St. Martin-in-the-Fields for a protest against the terrible massacre of Africans in Sharpeville. Tony cast Peter as Trigorin in the first play of our season at the Queen's Theatre, Chekhov's *The Seagull*. Peggy Ashcroft played Arkadina, I played Nina, Rachel played Polina, and George Devine was persuaded to take Dr. Dorn. The play begins with the rehearsal of a new play on a summer night by a lake—a play that, like Beckett's *Waiting for Godot* or *Happy Days*, breaks with all the stale theatrical conventions and stereotypes of Russian theatre in 1894. Nina, in love with the young writer Constantin, falls out of love with him when his mother, a famous actress, ridicules his remarkable play in front of her lover, a popular novelist.

I would listen every night to George as Dr. Dorn, kindly trying to encourage Constantin to believe in himself and his writing, in spite of his mother's cruelty and her lover's indifference. George and Tony were perfect partners. George, with his great knowledge and experience of European drama, was totally dedicated to encouraging new young writers, directors, and actors. He had a personal gusto for every new look at life, and for combat against suffocating reaction, in life as in the theatre. George's opinion mattered more to Peggy, to my father, and to Tony, than anyone else's. Tony asked George to play Dorn because George, like Chekhov, understood what a young man was trying to reach for, and understood why the young and their new ideas frightened some of the older theatre people.

Rehearsals of *The Seagull* seemed effortless, and I felt just like Tony, who wrote me a note on the first night: "Working with you has been all I ever dreamed it would be." Peter and I enjoyed our Act 2 scene very much. Tony gave us carte blanche during the run to change our moves and to surprise each other. Peter entered from a different side of the stage every night and strolled around with a croquet mallet, once even going right off the stage in the middle of his longest speech. This, in my view, is how acting should be approached. It requires the greatest trust between actors and the director. Tony always said, "Moves don't matter at all—it's what the scene is *about*, what people are thinking and feeling, that matters. If that isn't right, no physical move is right; if that *is* right, then any physical move is right." (This of course applies to two actors, and a text by Anton Chekhov.)

Tony went to New York and wrote to me about our next production, Brecht's *Saint Joan of the Stockyards*. "What is so fascinating about Brecht," Tony wrote, "is that he makes each and every actor see what they themselves really are." There is so much truth in that. I did a lot of reading in preparation for this play, which became a source for the development of my political consciousness. The microcosm of the Chicago stockyards of the 1930s taught me for the first time how capitalism operates, and how the morality of Christian ideology actively assists the exploitation of the poorest of the poor. That is not to deny the great bravery and courage of church leaders in South Africa like Bishop Desmond Tutu, or of Archbishop Romero, who was gunned down by the Salvadoran death squads for preaching against the dictatorship. But by showing *how* and *why* capitalism works, not just its cruelties and injustices, Brecht's play taught me that a morality that appeals for charity from the oppressor and patience from the oppressed is utterly utopian and reactionary. Thinking back to the "romantic" instincts of businessmen, which my unknown friend Sir Jock Campbell had vouched for and I myself had subscribed to, I thought I had much to learn from that.

Donald Sutherland, a young Canadian actor, joined the cast and Lionel Stander came from New York to play the Chicago meat baron. With only four weeks to rehearse, and some of the cast, like myself, still playing in *The Seagull* eight times a week, Tony enlisted the help of Lindsay Anderson and Anthony Page, both then Royal Court directors, and soon every bar, lobby, and corridor was filled with actors rehearsing in triple shifts. Tony always turned to his colleagues—directors, writers, designers, actors—for advice, and always listened to what they said. Theatre is a collective art, and a collective approach to problems is always the best way. It was Tony's way, and he never felt that his ego was under threat from listening to others. In this he is almost unique among British directors.

It was hard and difficult work. In order to grasp what freezing cold and gnawing hunger do to human beings we had much detailed, physical work to do to break free from our "stencils"—"Please, sir, I want some more?" I was pregnant again, and congratulating myself on the extra energy that pregnancy seems to provide, when suddenly I started to hemorrhage. I stopped work for three days and had an injection, and the bleeding stopped. George helped me by preparing a script with special notes and divisions to clarify Joan's development. As soon as I went back to work, however, the bleeding started again. Tony and I both wanted our second baby, so there was never a doubt for either of us. I had to come out of the play. Siobhan McKenna flew in to take over Joan, and I went to bed for two weeks, and our baby was saved.

I waited a few more weeks and then flew to Los Angeles to join Tony, who was preparing to film Evelyn Waugh's *The Loved One*, with a screenplay by Terry Southern and Christopher Isherwood. Waugh had written the novel in 1947, but what Jessica Mitford called the American Way of Death was still in business and doing a prosperous trade in 1964. Terry Southern, who scripted the film with Tony, took me to Forest Lawn. It wasn't called a cemetery; it was a "resting place." There, for a small fortune, the remains of the Loved One could be laid to rest amid porphyry statues of Philosophy, Wisdom, and Love, watched over by Michelangelo's *David* or Phidias's *Discobolos*, in a copy of Annie Laurie's wee kirk or trysting bower. Or, if the relatives preferred, the ashes of the Loved One could be sealed in an amphora and placed in a marble niche in a marble mausoleum, lulled in perpetual sleep by piped music. For a suitable consideration they could provide an eternal flame, or, for a slightly reduced fee, a semieternal flame, a gas jet in an iron holder which would be turned on and lit by one of the "guardians." Terry told our guide that we were married and wished to book a resting place for my English mother. We were shown the coffins, ranging from the Imperial, lined with purple satin and costing three thousand dollars, to the Commodore, a modest but sturdy oak. We met the chief mortician. I was astonished. Waugh had exaggerated nothing. My mother would be embalmed so perfectly that with makeup, hair tongs, and the mortician's expertise, she would look in death ten years younger than in life—forever. It was astounding to find that the funeral rites practiced in Egypt three thousand years ago were still alive in the age of the computer and fast food.

I became firm friends with the cameraman, Haskell Wexler, and his wife, Marion, and through them I enrolled for a summer course at the University of California, Los Angeles. I chose political science, and for the next eight weeks I buried my nose in books or sat in lectures with our course teacher from the Rand Institute. I was twenty-seven, a few years older than most of my fellow students, and felt alternately like Mrs. Rip Van Winkle and a callow fifteen-year-old ignoramus. The other students were much better read than I, yet in discussion a narrow, conservative outlook prevailed. They seemed to accept everything they read in the papers or heard on the radio. This was soon put to the test. Early in August 1964 the Gulf of Tonkin incident hit the headlines, and almost to a man my fellow students believed the government and the newspapers' version of the affair. I couldn't. It was all too clear that this was a deliberate provocation. A U.S. destroyer entered the twelve-mile zone of North Vietnamese waters deliberately, Vietnamese patrol boats fired warning shots to drive the ship out of their waters, and President Johnson declared that this was an act of war against the United States. He demanded and won a vote from Congress for an enormous increase in funds, and tens of thousands of troops began to land on Vietnamese soil. A dictatorship as rotten, cruel, and corrupt as the Batista regime in Cuba was to be kept in power by the American army, without even the prospect of free elections. I studied every press report I could lay my hands on, amazed that editors and reporters without exception fell for the provocation and swallowed the State Department's explanations. Despite everything, I still believed that the duty of the press was to report the truth, and that by and large they did. I wanted to protest, and wrote an article saying that Johnson and the Pentagon were dragging America into full-scale war against Vietnam and had created a provocation to justify it. I wanted to send it to an American paper, but each day's reading chipped away at my faith in their objectivity, so I sent it to *Peace News* instead.

In the early mornings, while the dew was still on the grass, and not even Tony was awake, Tasha, aged fifteen months, and I bathed in the shallow end of the pool. Tony had heard of a young woman called Jann Stevens who could teach babies to swim, and soon she came every day with her eighteen-month-old daughter, Jolie. She explained to me that a baby's most natural environment for the first year of its life is water. The water had to be warmer than blood temperature, like a very warm bath. I watched Jann's daughter blowing bubbles, kicking, and swimming underwater with her eyes open. She wore tiny flippers to give her the propulsion her legs were not yet strong enough to provide. "What happens if Tash falls in off the side by mistake?" I asked. "Once she's confident and accustomed to the pool she won't be frightened," Jann said. "She'll just come up and hold on to the side. There'll be plenty of time for you to reach her. Just be sure you don't show her you're frightened. She'll soon learn how to climb out of the pool. We'll show her." Jann was right. The pool was filled to within an inch of the brim, and in no time at all Tasha could climb out on her own. Jann became my firm friend, and before I left California I invited her to come to London. She had given me an idea for a school where every child would learn to swim as soon as it learned to walk. Jann's idea was so simple and so demonstrably right that I was sure it would be accepted wherever it was shown. Teachers like Jann, who extend our ideas of what children can do, and who can teach them to do it, should be honored everywhere.

I finished my thesis for the political science course and received a poor mark, a C. I don't even remember the particular subject, although I was generally concerned with "war games theory" and the drive to war. In the last weeks of filming *The Loved One,* Tony rented a house right on Trancas beach, where enormous waves crashed on the shore. I used to hurl myself into the surf and get picked up and rolled over and over under the water, with our baby inside me. I felt terrific getting hurled about, and I think the baby must have felt it was in a washing machine. I reasoned that the surf would make me strong and healthy, which must be good for a baby. Tony asked Chris Isherwood's painter friend and lover, Don Bachardy, to draw me. I used to fall asleep sitting for him in the Mexican smock Tony had bought me back in the Acapulco days.

≡

I flew to London with Natasha and Viola for a television play, and a general election was called. With Tony's encouragement I decided to stay in London and help the Labour Party campaign that October. I ran the constituency office in Hammersmith and asked what they would like me to do. My front room became the canvassing center for the local ward. The party sent canvassers, I enlisted all my friends and fellow actors in the area who supported the Labour Party, and we worked night and day, pasting up cards and sending out election addresses. I knocked on doors from nine in the morning until nine at night.

Labour's campaign song for that election was "Thirteen Wasted Years"—the Conservatives had been in power since 1951. I thought it rather tame, and despite my faith in Labour and what they would do, I wondered why they chose to promote themselves as the party of efficiency rather than the party of socialism. Nevertheless I fervently wanted Labour to win and was puzzled by the large numbers of housewives and old-age pensioners in the council flats who told me wearily and politely that the election of a Labour government would bring nothing they needed. "It won't change anything," they said. "We'll still be living like this. Labour don't care any more than the Tories." "Oh, they *do*, I'm sure they do," I protested, convinced I was speaking the truth. But as I listened to the Labour leaders on the platforms I was invited to share with them, I began to have my doubts. They said nothing to reassure housewives and pensioners about prices, the state of their flats, or their pensions. Nor did these politicians speak of unilateral nuclear disarmament or Vietnam. They spoke brightly, cheerfully, energetically, but in generalities. Perhaps, I thought, they were just not very good speakers and would say more if they could.

So I buried my doubts and worked nonstop. At the count in the town hall we had a majority for Ivor Richards, our Labour candidate, of just over a thousand votes; we cheered him to the echo. I was invited to a postelection reception at the Labour Party headquarters. I danced with James Callaghan and George Brown. Prime Minister Harold Wilson made a speech thanking us all, and we cheered again until our throats were hoarse.

Tony was delighted at the result of the election and proud of my campaigning. We celebrated Thanksgiving in Los Angeles with my first turkey-and-sweet-potato dinner and a long session of bridge from midday to midnight with Neil Hartley, producer for Woodfall Films, Tony's production company. Then he persuaded the American producers, John Calley and Martin Ransohoff, to let him edit *The Loved One* in London so we could be back in our house for Christmas and the baby's birth. I saw a rough cut of some of *The Loved One*, footage of John Gielgud playing an expatriate British actor sitting by an empty swimming pool covered with dead vines and weeds, shaking a cocktail courteously and hoping the telephone would ring with a summons from a film studio.

The doctor said that I should go into the nursing home, and that our baby ought to be induced for safety, since I had nearly had a miscarriage early on. So on January 9 I went back into the Welbeck Street clinic and was given an injection to start the birth. The gas fire hummed and popped, and I sat on my bed with my guitar, practicing chords, singing the baby songs to give it courage; it seemed to me that an injection must cause it great discomfort. Tony joined me at the end of the long afternoon, which was a difficult one, as the induction disturbed all the natural rhythms and contractions. The curtains were drawn, it was dark outside, and if Tony had not been with me I think this time I would have given in and asked for a painkiller. But Tony did something much better than the doctor's drugs. He murmured to me, "You look absolutely beautiful, darling, just like Monica Vitti." I knew he thought Monica was fabulous, and so did I, so my morale soared instantly. His back-rubbing was not so good, and the labor was very long, but he talked to me and kept me from getting discouraged.

At last the second stage began, and this was very quick. Tony had his Leica camera and took pictures of the baby just as she came out onto the mattress between my legs, covered with the white protective grease of the womb like a cross-Channel swimmer. I heard a nurse muttering. She sounded shocked that he was taking pictures, but he didn't give a damn and neither did I. I didn't let the nurses take the little girl away, and I put her immediately to my breast. Her mouth opened instantly and she took my nipple in her gums and her lips started to suck. The crumpled, wrinkled red face began to fill out and smooth over, and the tiny, delicate, tendril-like fingers began to open up from the fist, like a sea anemone. Joely Kim had arrived on January 9, 1965.

f I set aside my early stumbling efforts as Pamela in *Behind the Mask* in 1958, about which the less said the better, *Morgan—A Suitable Case for Treatment*, was my first feature film, in the summer of 1965. "What must I do?" I asked Tony. "You must listen to what Karel says, and try to do everything he asks you," Tony said. "Remember, in the theatre everyone has eyes and can watch what they like. But in the cinema only the director has eyes, and they are the camera. What communicates through the camera is a *different substance* from that of the theatre."

Karel Reisz and Tony had first met when they were making documentaries in the late fifties. "Free Cinema," the manifesto they wrote with Lindsay Anderson, emphasized the subjects and technique of the kind of moviemaking they believed in. Betsy Blair, Karel's wife, was one of the generation of artists who had left America because of the McCarthy witch-hunts. Karel had left Czechoslovakia after the Communist Party took power. Both of them were immensely well read and thoughtful, and set the pace for me politically. Karel taught me that in film acting, unlike the theatre, the moment is all-important. One must never enter the scene with the mood of the previous scene or the previous day. It is wrong to imagine that acting before the camera should be in a lower key just because the camera is closer than the audience in the theatre. There has to be just as much energy and spontaneity as in life. The basic difference between film acting and stage acting is that more than half of the film is *made* in the editing. Both the director and the actors can find, on viewing a rough cut of a film, that some point they all thought needed to be brought out and explained in a sequence of scenes is already contained in one scene, and so the additional material is immediately cut away. Film acting is a process that demands the utmost understanding of the fact that any moment in life will contain more in it than any single person involved in it is conscious of, and the actor or actress has to accept and use this all the time. It may be that a scene that did not seem very significant in the actual filming appears in the rough cut and editing to be the *key* scene in the whole film. While everyone participating in the filming is playing their part, a strange thing happens—independently of them the story and all their work takes on a life of its own.

The rules of formal logic that are often and detrimentally applied to acting in the theatre become intolerable and damaging in filmmaking. Michael described this to me once when he was telling me about a particular scene in the film of *The Quiet American* where he had thought he would approach it quietly and develop it into its emotional climax. Joseph Mankiewicz, the director, chose the opposite direction, wanting him to start the scene at the emotional climax and end it quietly. In film you often go against, even invert, what might appear to be the normal shape of a scene. Just as life does not happen in a logical progression, so trying to impose such an order in filmmaking has a totally lethal effect.

When making a film you have to play every scene as if it were the only scene. I find this approach helpful in the theatre, where we are all, directors, writers, and actors, subjected to the ludicrous time limit of four weeks of rehearsal. This short period strengthens the director's tendency to make up a plan and impose it on all the actors, and also for the actors themselves to rush too quickly for results, for "what works." If you are rigidly improving and controlling what you do according to the plan in your head, sooner or later you will be fighting against the life that emerges in the process of interaction between the play and the actors and directors and that develops *independently* of each individual's consciousness and schema. The very nature of filmmaking, especially as understood by Tony and Karel Reisz and all the "greats," encourages these processes. In the theatre the old notions of empirical craft and formal logic still prevail, with deadening and deadly effect.

Long before *Morgan* was released I began to get calls from producers and directors, and life seemed crammed with opportunity. Federico Fellini sent a photographer to take pictures of me, looking mysterious among the cedars and statues in Chiswick Park. It was about this time that I received an invitation for lunch with a journalist from the Democratic Republic of Vietnam and met him, his wife, and a colleague of theirs in their flat in North London. U.S. troops and weapons, officially known as U.S. advice and support missions, were pouring into Vietnam. In February 1965 the U.S. Air Force began bombing strategic targets—bridges, roads, and railways—and all the civilians who lived and worked in those areas. About twenty-five thousand U.S. Army and Marine Corps soldiers were fighting with the South Vietnamese Army units. On June 19, Air Vice-Marshal Nguyen Cao Ky seized power in a coup, the fourth in six months, and the United States had the man they wanted.

The Vietnamese journalist asked me if I would be willing to go to Vietnam and see the destruction caused by the U.S. bombing. I would then be able to report back to the people and the press in Britain. But I was afraid to go, and told him so. I thought I would lose all prospects of a career in films, just when life seemed so promising. "And if that were to happen," I rationalized, "I should be no use to you at all." I had torn up my Labour Party card because the leadership under Wilson was backing Johnson's Vietnam policy all the way, but there were no mass organizations or protests against the war yet, and I knew that if I went I would be fiercely attacked in the press. I wanted victory for the Vietnamese National Liberation Front, which of course was a very different thing from wanting "peace"—everybody wanted peace—and I thought that if I went to Vietnam I would have to say so. I trusted neither the Labour Party nor the Communist Party, nor the clergymen, however sincere they were, and so I clung to my profession, feeling ashamed that I could not do what was asked of me, and that I was on unsteady ground both politically and in my personal life.

In 1965 Tony was to film Jean Genet's *Mademoiselle* in a village called Le Rat in the Corrèze, a poor, depopulated, densely wooded region in France. He found a small house above a river, surrounded by woods, and rented it. "You'll hate it, darling. It's very, very *simple*." On the train from Paris with my two little girls, Natasha, now two years old, and Joely, four months, I sat opposite a plump and formidable French woman who talked for two hours to her male companion about business, the currency markets, strikes, and the fate of La République. As the train neared Limoges she concluded triumphantly, in the tones of Sarah Bernhardt: "Ainsi, je dirai à mon fils, 'Mon fils! La bataille a commencé et nous—nous devons nous préparer!' " ("So, I shall tell my son, 'My son! The war has already begun and we—we must get ready for it!' ") I was riveted to my seat by the force of the implacable class-consciousness of this French bourgeoise, and I made a note in my diary immediately and planned to tell Tony.

Tony had fallen in love with his star, Jeanne Moreau. I thought this completely understandable, for she was enchanting. In fact, we had both fallen in love with her when we went for a weekend to Paris to see *Jules et Jim* just before we got married. The crew, the cast, the entire village of Le Rat were in love with her. Monsieur Le Bonnet, our chef, who produced extraordinary soups, roast rabbits, and wild ducks from the damp cellar where Tony had installed a large stove, became lyrical with his sauces when Jeanne came over for dinner.

David Mercer, who had written the screenplay for *Mademoiselle* as well as the script of *Morgan*, provided a gloomy contrast. He came to stay with his girlfriend, Kika Markham, whose wistful face told me, without any words, that David had fallen out of love with her, just as Tony had with me. At the time I cried bitterly. Not because Tony loved Jeanne, only because he didn't love me anymore. "It's a tragedy!" I wept one evening as we talked. "It's not a tragedy, it's life," he replied simply. His objectivity, combined with his passionate feeling for life, always amazed and inspired me.

I passed the days with Tasha and Joely, trundling the stroller through the old forest to pick wild strawberries, and splashing with

Tasha in the shallow river, inventing long stories for her delight and mine. Some days Tony took us off into the wet woods to catch baby frogs for the grass snake that he was keeping for a scene in the film. On Bastille Day we hung the trees with tricolor flags, and Monsieur Le Bonnet prepared a feast for the trestle tables in front of the house. There were some happy days and happy hours, but Tony and I slept in different rooms, and it seemed neither of us knew what to do for the other. If I had not been so self-centered I would have known, but I was consumed by my own feelings and my own pain, and these became a wall of glass between the two of us.

We moved late that summer to a villa on the Appia Antica in Rome, and Tony began preproduction for his second film with Jeanne, *The Sailor from Gibraltar*. He offered me a good small part in it, which I immediately accepted. Meanwhile I was off to China for a month as a member of the first English delegation of artists and writers to be invited there since 1948. One of the delegation was Robert Bolt. I had studied Chinese for three months, and, carrying a Leica and a tape recorder, I got on board a Czech airliner from Rome to Moscow. There I discovered I had no transit visa, which meant I must stay in a transit hotel for one night while the Chinese embassy sorted out my permit so I could set off to Peking the following afternoon. I was enchanted when I learned from the young Chinese representative that the embassy was in the Sparrow Hills, which were just outside Moscow in Tolstoy's day and are now a part of the city suburbs.

I fell asleep in the six-foot cubicle of the transit hotel and next morning sat down at the small table to write a letter to Tony: apologies, expressions of love, promises to be different, less egocentric, more understanding. By midday, having written and torn up page after page, with tears all over my cheeks and the writing paper, I had convinced myself that I could successfully prove to him that I loved him by returning immediately to Rome. "My marriage is over if I don't go back," I told myself, hiccuping with deep emotion. "If he believes I love him, then he'll love me." If we could only learn how mistaken is this logic that starts with "me." "I must save our marriage!" My tears flowed again and I lurched off with my enormous trunk to the airport. How to use the telephone? A kind Russian lent me five kopeks, put the pieces in the machine, dialed the number I wrote down for him, and handed me the receiver. The young Chinese attaché came on the line and received the following story: "I'm sorry, I'm so sorry, I can't go to China. I have problems, personal problems, my husband, my children. I am so very sorry, I must go back to them—gulp—gulp—gulp." The puzzled attaché promised to meet me in a hour.

I ran all over the airport to find a plane back to Rome. Air India had a flight to London in the early evening, so I changed my ticket, running to the other side of the airport for an Aeroflot endorsement, and then to greet the attaché, tearfully apologizing and shaking his hand. He left me. I swapped a five-dollar bill with a passerby for a few rubles, reckless of the exchange value, bought a piece of bread with red caviar and a cup of black tea, and took a deep breath, feeling suddenly elated. By teatime the next day I would be back in Rome with Tasha and Joely, Tony would laugh and clap his hands, and we would make a fresh start.

In London the next morning I phoned the Society for Anglo-Chinese understanding, who had organized our delegation, feeling in my bones that my oblique references to family problems were beyond all human understanding, Anglo or Chinese. Back in Rome I took a taxi back down the Appia Antica to the old medieval house, and shouting, "I'm back! Darlings, I'm back!," I ran through the door of the villa into the room where Tasha and Joely were having their tea with the temporary English nurse. They were happy to see me. Tony, when he came back from the studios, was not. "It would have been much better if you'd kept to your plans and gone to China. I'm going on a holiday with John [Osborne] on a yacht to Greece."

"Can't you cancel your holiday? Or can't we go on another yacht or something?"

"No, we can't. I'm going to Greece. It's all arranged."

So I stayed the next two weeks on the Appia with Tasha and Joely, driving frequently to the beach at the Ostia Lido, listening to the jukebox on the sands, and enjoying a good cry over my favorite love songs.

We started filming three weeks later in Agropoli, on the coast above Naples, near ancient Paestum and its Greek temples. The first day of shooting was on the sand dunes. The man, Ian Bannen, tells his English girlfriend, Sheila, he doesn't love her anymore. Ian and

I had played Orlando and Rosalind in *As You Like It* in 1961 and 1962. We also knew and trusted each other. Tony and his cinematographer placed the camera on a track in the sand so we could play the whole scene in a master shot. We did a couple of really good takes, one or two of short cover close-ups. I knew I'd done good work. I knew Tony was pleased, and the crew. I had told myself before we began this film that I would put the work we had agreed to do before anything else. I completely trusted that Tony would be truly friendly and professional, and it was up to me to be the same. This decision had been made, and everything fell into place. Besides, I really liked my role and the story.

We moved to Florence. The makeup department was in two small rooms at the top of a house near the Duomo. Early every morning I could see the swallows diving up and over and round the red-tiled roofs and cupolas, restless before their long journey to Africa. I love that hour in the makeup room before the first setup, a time for testing out the opinions of those you are working with, hearing and discussing their problems and your own. I love the communal life and the collective work of filmmaking, and that hour in Florence, with a paper cup of espresso from the bar below, a cigarette, a newspaper, and Maria the hairdresser, was the most welcome time of the day. Maria was very good to me, and extremely good at her job. She watched my work, and one morning gave me a tip. I was standing close to the camera for the shot, and Maria told me to look up to the sky, slightly away from the camera. I remembered how Lynn had told me that James Mason, after they had been working together for some weeks, gave her a tip. Always look into an arc lamp, he told her, just before a take. Your pupils will contract, and that's good for the camera. Tony had spotted Maria talking to me, and later that day he looked at me and thanked me for working so well. "The film crew are impressed," he said. "They like you. They don't often bother to give actors advice."

When my filming was over I was proud I had passed the most important test of my life. I knew also that whatever happened, Tony and I would have a lifelong friendship. I flew back to Athens about eight weeks later when the principal photography on *Sailor* was finished. Tony and I had a great weekend. I remember one thing he said to me about this time: "The thing is, Vanessa, you're simply wonderful in an emergency, but life in between, with all the small humdrum details, is just as important. If you could only be reliable in small things you would be amazing. But that's exactly what you don't care about."

We were thankful to find we were still friends and still respected each other. We made the decision in due course to divorce, but for the moment we were in no hurry to decide our future. We went back to London, and I found a Montessori nursery school for Tasha. I had been impressed by a book about Maria Montessori's life, which explained her practical and tactile method of instructing very young children. I also read an extraordinary book by an American child specialist, Glenn Doman. Seriously concerned about the lack of an educational program for children with brain damage, he had developed a program of teaching these children to read. With Tony's help I sent off for his instruction book and the full set of his giant letters and reading cards. There were two main issues: First, a child's eyes, still not fully coordinated, require very large letters. Second, reading should be built up from learning small *words* first, and not individual letters. Children see cartons, jars, and tins from an early age. Cut out the "Kellogg's" logo from a box of cornflakes, cut out the word "Krispies," repeat the words, and play with the cutouts. Seeing the different shapes of the large letters and cards, as well as the lower-case letters, would train the child's eyes to perceive irregular shapes and spaces, and at the same time establish the connection between the word and the actual object the word represented. Soon our sitting room was covered with white cards. One of our chairs had a foot-long white card in front of it that said CHAIR. The kitchen had six cereal cartons with the logos missing. There were groups of milk bottles, with milk and without, covered by the MILK card.

In the new year, 1966, Tasha was almost three. My favorite picture of her from that time is one Tony took of her on her new rocking horse, his Christmas present to her. I had a new play to rehearse, *The Prime of Miss Jean Brodie*, based on the novel by Muriel Spark. The girls had a new nanny, Christine Newman, who was very young, very sweet and serious. She stayed with us until she left to found a Montessori nursery school in Hawaii in the summer of 1969.

When Peter Wood, our brilliant young director, began rehearsals with us, every omen seemed good, and we also had a brilliant group of schoolgirls, including Hillary Turner and Olivia Hussey. I started our long pre-London tour with a tweed suit, a bobbed wig, and a genteel Morningside Edinburgh accent, assuming that Jean Brodie, the schoolmistress, would look like an ordinary teacher of her time and situation, only neater and prettier than most. I played her for two weeks like that, and both Peter and I knew we weren't "there." John and Penelope Osborne came to a matinee in Brighton and, when I told them my doubts, suggested that I drop the Scots accent for a while. No sooner had I done so that evening than I suddenly realized what was wrong. I stared at myself in the dressing-room mirror—that was not Jean Brodie. Jean Brodie was determined to mold her girls, her world, in the shape of her fantasies—the Duce, her hero; D'Annunzio, the poet-airman; General Franco; The Lady of Shalott—and so she would shape herself to fit her fantasies. She would dye her hair Titian-red, like that of her adored Pre-Raphaelite heroines, and loop it over her ears the way Anna Pavlova, her idol, did. Within the limits of her small teacher's salary she would wear clothes with a "medieval" line. Peter and our producer, Donald Albery, understood what I was after, and ordered a new wig and costumes. Now I could restore the Morningside accent, and now Brodie had arrived. Our notices were splendid—for the play, the production, and the actors. That night I looked at an evening newspaper for the first time in weeks. I was on the front page, photographed at our first-night party the night before. Next to my photograph was a report of a new U.S. bombing offensive against Vietnam.

Michelangelo Antonioni came to see the play and asked me to be in his new film, *Blow-Up*. I began filming by day while playing every night at Wyndham's, with two matinees a week. Antonioni asked me to dye my hair black and shave an inch from my hairline to give me a higher forehead. With Michelangelo the camera angle, its movement, the frame, the objects in the frame, their color, position, and movement, whether human or inanimate, told his story. The dialogue was of no great significance, or certainly of secondary importance. Trained as a dancer, I was able to appreciate this. I learned to look sharply and precisely at the shapes and colors around me. Exact positions, angles of the body, the head and shoulders, exact tempo of movement, were vital to him. I had never encountered such an eye in the cinema. In English and American films, colors and shapes were part of the decoration, appropriate, but only as background to the action. In Michelangelo's films they *were* the action. *Blow-Up* was about the unity and difference of essence and phenomena, the conflict between what *is*, objectively, and what is seen, heard, or grasped by the individual. Much later, when I saw Joely in Peter Greenaway's film *Drowning by Numbers*, I thought he too was a director for whom everything, every shape and every object on the screen, told his story. I would only add that Michelangelo's ear, not for dialogue but for the sounds of nature and normally inanimate objects, was as subtle as his eye. The sound of the leaves rustling in *Blow-Up* and of the wind blowing cords against metal poles in *The Eclipse* are unforgettable.

On location, one day, I heard hoots, shouts, and laughs, and Claude Watson, our first assistant, came running across the grass to me in Greenwich Park with a glass of champagne. "You've won the Cannes Film Festival prize for the best actress." It was for *Morgan*, and from that moment everything seemed to go mad. I was photographed, interviewed, and invited to a nonstop round of parties and nightclubs. At Leslie Caron's one night I was warned by her secretary that a newsreel team from France was there to film "a swinging London party." Since I had always secretly considered myself rather out of the swim, for which I blamed my conventional middle-class education, I was hopelessly flattered and thrilled to think that, to the French at any rate, I was part of the "swinging" set.

Tony had a new film project. He, Lindsay Anderson, and Peter Brook were each going to make a thirty-minute film for United Artists, and all three would be distributed together. His film, *Red and Blue*, concerned a singer in a small club who told her story through seven songs. The songs were by Serge Bassiak, who had written Jeanne's songs in *Jules et Jim.* Julian More and Kirsty Norman turned the French lyrics into English and arranged the music.

Jeanne couldn't do the film, which had been devised for her to star in, so now Tony offered the film to me. It was June and he had taken a house in the woods of the Ardèche about thirty minutes from Saint-Tropez. On Saturday nights or early Sunday mornings I caught a plane with Julian More to Nice, and Jan drove us like the wind down to the house. We discussed the script, and especially the songs, and found ourselves one Sunday morning knocking on doors in Saint-Tropez, asking if anyone had a piano. Then at midday Monday

I boarded a tiny plane in a field and flew for a thrilling twenty minutes to Nice, to catch a plane, hop in a cab, and get to Wyndham's stage door in time to make up as Jean Brodie.

One night, as I waited for my entrance into my classroom, schoolbooks under my arm, the other hand on the doorknob, ready to walk onto the stage with the famous lines "Good morrrning, little girrrls!" "Good morning, Miss Brodie!"—I wondered, How is it, why is it, that I actually know every word I am going to say? As soon as this thought entered my mind, which frightened me into quickly thinking through the lines of my first speech at the blackboard, the whole scene and Miss Brodie became unfamiliar and alien to me. I experienced a wave of panic. I recorded what I felt in my diary:

Through another performance and then the next day, all day, with a shaking stomach and trembling spine. I had a sleep on the divan in my dressing room which made me feel better, stronger that is, so that I was able to control my nerves. Tony rang me and told me to improvise or sing a song if I forgot my words, which made me laugh, and feel more determined to go on and *play*. Also, I forgot, dear Corin rang up, and he was helpful and reminded me to think of the situation and what I was after, rather than *words*, which of course is really good advice.

Wednesday, 7th September.
Panic all Tuesday as never before in my life. I was trembling all over with the effort to remember and keep going and the strain of feeling all this would crack up suddenly and I would go berserk on stage and have to leave or something. This morning I stayed in bed until 12 and went to John Henderson who gave me a shot of B12 and some Librium and promised me that by Saturday all would be well. Robin Fox, my agent, met me at Sheekey's and I couldn't eat I was so frightened. He had a ticket for the show, and all was well in fact, because I had a note from a father who had bought a ticket for his daughter's fifteenth birthday and wanted to bring her round to meet me. I sent a note saying of course, and felt better, thinking I just couldn't go mad and forget, or run away when it was someone's special treat . . .

It is easy enough, looking back, to diagnose the cause of my panic. I had hardly thought about Brodie since our first night. Throughout the run I had been filming, first in *Blow-Up,* then with Tony in *Red and Blue* (which had also involved recording sessions of the songs). Work in the theatre, especially in the London West End theatre with eight performances a week, must be re-created every night, and replenished as often as possible with notes and sometimes rehearsal. With no time, and little energy, to do otherwise, I was relying on memory to carry me through, and my crisis was a kind of inner rebellion against this. In fact I never did forget my lines, though for the rest of that run I felt that I was never more than one syllable away from a yawning abyss. Muscles in the face, lips, and tongue have a "memory," and when they have repeated certain sounds and movements a sufficient number of times, *they* don't forget, even though the mind disclaims all knowledge of what comes next. But to stand upon a stage and to feel your lips forming words and your throat making sounds with no knowledge of them is, in Kierkegaard's famous phrase, a "crisis in the life of an actress."

Every retreat exacts its own price, even if the bill is presented later. Given the invitation to go to Vietnam, I had clung to my profession as an actress. I had rationalized my decision at the time, and my fear of the consequences to my career, by saying that I could serve causes like Vietnam only if I maintained my position as an actress, and to do that I must follow my career. That was my father's argument, in those anxious letters he sent me when I joined the Committee of 100, and it was persuasive. Indeed its logic, on its own terms, was irrefutable. But it was wrong. The source of all development in art is in nature, which art reflects, mirrors, and criticizes. That was why Aeschylus insisted that his epitaph should mention nothing except that he fought at the battle of Marathon. I had walled myself off from the source of my development, but I didn't know that and had no method for understanding it, except an empirical grasping for something that would make me feel stronger. "A man who has no nature beyond himself," Karl Marx wrote, "is not a natural man." And an actress who uses her profession, as I did, to shield herself from reality, runs the risk of finding that what she is doing seems totally unreal.

≡

Joshua Logan, who had directed a lot of wonderful movies, including *Bus Stop* with Marilyn Monroe, came to see *Brodie* and offered me *Camelot*, which would be filmed by Warner Bros. in Hollywood. I nearly turned it down because Richard Lester had offered me *Petulia* and I had longed to work with him ever since I had seen *The Knack*. Luckily, I turned to Tony for advice, and he said, "Darling, you must be mad, of course you must do *Camelot*. When you've done that you will be able to do anything you want."

So I set off to Los Angeles with Tasha, Joely, Christine, our new nanny, and my secretary, Ruth. I rented a little wooden house belonging to Gladys Cooper, with a large wooden verandah and a tiny swimming pool. I found a Montessori school for Tasha, and I engaged the cook who had prepared the delicious Thanksgiving supper for Tony and me in 1964. I was driven down to Burbank Studios and taken onto the back lot, where hundreds of daffodils and dozens of apple trees had been planted to blossom in October for "The Lusty Month of May." Joshua Logan had engaged the designer John Truscott, and everything was to look like *Tom Jones*. I was taken for measurements and fittings into the building where the cutters, fitters, seamstresses, embroiderers, worked—about one hundred skilled men and women. I saw the wedding dress being made for Guinevere, hundreds of finely crocheted woolen spiderwebs sewed together, with tiny red shells sewed into the center of each web, and bleached melon seeds instead of pearls hanging from each corner. In the makeup department they were preparing the wig for Merlin, who would wear opaque contact lenses that reflected strange colors. They were practicing the work with latex to transform Lionel Jeffries into an ancient knight. In the property department they were carving wood for medieval chairs and screens and twisting iron for jousting weapons, spears, and candlesticks.

Camelot was the last film Warner Bros. made as a studio product. The Burbank studios went "four walls" after that, which meant that television companies and Warner-financed films rented the space and hired their crews and personnel on a temporary basis. Carpenters, plasterers, and painters in the scene dock, joiners and painters in the props department, tailors and cutters, seamstresses and embroiderers in the wardrobe block—all were fired. Generations of craftsmanship were destroyed, because craftsmanship requires continuity, and continuity meant trade union organization, union rates, wages, sickness pay, and holiday benefits. Of course there remained many highly skilled individuals whose skills were prized. But high craftsmanship and standards require time, and time is money, and the businesses that own and control television production care little or nothing about standards unless they can get them for nothing.

Richard Harris was generous, funny, and, I thought, perfect casting as the idealistic Arthur. It was very easy to be in love with him. Franco Nero had come back from three months of filming in Spain, where all the scenes of Lancelot's exploits against the giants, and his main song, "C'est Moi," had been filmed. He wasn't at all impressed by me. In fact he told me later that he had got quite cross when he first saw me. "Why have I got this ugly, shortsighted Englishwoman for my Guinevere?" He had blue eyes and a sweet, kind, open, trusting face and heart, the perfect Lancelot, I thought. He was on his guard. "The English are the most treacherous people in the world. You kiss, you say 'darling,' but you are insincere. You think Italians are always embracing? When they meet, yes. When they part, sometimes, but they are sincere. You English, you promise everything but you never keep your word."

We became great friends, especially when he learned that I wanted to go fishing and enjoyed learning to shoot clay pigeons. Two of his friends, Mr. and Mrs. Guglielmo Donati, took us under their wing, fed us pasta, and let us sleep together in front of their fire. I contrasted Franco, who was totally naïve, totally straightforward, and totally a man, with the other film stars I met. Some of them were nice, brilliant actors, much more successful, and very intelligent. However, none of them loved, really loved and needed, the ordinary basic things of life, and none of them had Franco's idealism and honesty.

Lynny was married in New York to a young actor who had starred in my favorite radio series during the war, *Just William.* Rachel and I flew into New York and went up to the first-floor bedroom in Sidney and Gail Lumet's house on Lexington Avenue. Lynny was getting dressed in her short white sixties organdy dress and looking absolutely beautiful. She and John were married in front of Sydney's mantelpiece by an American priest, surrounded by flowers and our friends. She was starring on Broadway in *Black Comedy,* by Peter Shaffer, and had won the Golden Globe Award for her new film, *Georgy Girl.*

Lynn and I were both nominated for Oscars that year, I for *Morgan* and she for *Georgy Girl.* I thought Lynny would certainly win the Oscar. She was so comic and so vulnerable, and so totally surprising in every scene she played. However, Elizabeth Taylor had also given an extraordinary performance in *Who's Afraid of Virginia Woolf?* and she got the Academy Award. The press had a whale of a time playing Lynn and me against each other. Actually, I know that if either one of us had won, we would have been pleased. I certainly was really excited and happy to see how my little sister, who had always been treated as an "also ran" while a child and young teenager, had proved once again my strongest belief—that every child, given even half a chance in life, and however unlikely it may seem superficially, has an enormous and totally individual potential to be "a very considerable person." Lynny had truly proved herself before *Georgy Girl,* in *Mother Courage,* and in *Hay Fever* at the National. In *Georgy Girl* she captured for all people the agony and the comic side of being a lumpy, awkward teenager who can and will become someone very special.

The last scene of *Camelot,* the joust, was finished. It was April. The girls had left with Christine to join Tony for Easter. Franco and I got a plane to Paris and the chestnut trees, and then on to Rome, and then to Cannes for the Festival, where *Blow-Up* was showing. Here Franco told me he loved me and gave me a golden bracelet with a little disk: "Francesco e Vanessa—per sempre."

CHAPTER 13

Franco Nero was born on November 23, 1941, in a northern Italian village near the city of Parma. His father, Gabriele Sparanero, migrated from the south in the thirties. With his wife Ninetta he had five children—Guglielmo, who died as a baby, Franco, Rafaele, Rosa, and Patrizia. In 1967, when Franco took me to meet his family, they all lived in a flat in Parma. Ninetta brought a big bowl of *capelletti in brodo* to the table. Her other speciality, almond cake, was ready for us on the sideboard. Gabriele produced two bottles of his own wine to celebrate. All the tenants in the block had the use of a small cellar in the basement, and every September Gabriele went round the markets, chose his grapes, and crushed and fermented them in the cellar. The wine was purple, "with beaded bubbles winking at the brim," and was delicious. Some years later, Franco bought his parents a small villa covered with wisteria on the slopes of Velletri, in the hills outside Rome. Gabrielle spent the last years of his life fulfilling his greatest ambition: digging, hoeing, spraying, and pruning an acre or so of grape vines, working the earth and enjoying the produce of his labor.

Franco and I met the film director Elio Petri and agreed to act in his film *A Quiet Place in the Country*. Franco played a successful abstract artist who is driven mad by the commercialization of his art and plans to murder his mistress, an art dealer. We filmed in a huge deserted villa about twenty miles from Vicenza and Padua. Franco and I rented a wing of the Casa Veronese, a villa surrounded by a farm, from two elderly spinsters, the Misses Veronese, and we spent about two months there, in May and June 1967. For Tasha's fourth birthday on May 11 we organized a farmhouse feast, with two baby goats roasted over the wood embers of the gigantic kitchen hearth. Tasha ran all over the villa exclaiming, "I am so excited I'm going to burst into bits!" Christine, Joely, Tasha, and I made giant scarecrows with faces and hats, and Franco and I made seesaws and created obstacles for an obstacle race across the grass of the small courtyard. The peasants' children thought we were lunatics but accepted us with kindness, invited Tasha and Joely into their homes, and taught them games and rhyming songs, and how to count in Italian.

Franco and I had some thunderous rows, and some wonderfully happy days with the children. Happiness was driving through the country roads in our white Mercedes with Tasha and Joely at the end of the day's filming, singing songs from *The Sound of Music*—"Do, a deer, a female deer"—and songs from Peter, Paul and Mary—"Oh, once I had a little frog" and "If I had a hammer, I'd hammer in the morning, I'd hammer in the evening, all over this land. I'd hammer out danger! I'd hammer out warning! I'd hammer out love between my brothers and my sisters, all over this land." I got the tapes of Joan Baez songs. Tony and I had been to one of her concerts in Saint-Tropez the year before. I learned all Sergio Endrigo's ballads and the songs of Celentano, and I learned to play bocce outside the dusty bar at the bottom of our farm road. Franco played bocce and the pinball machine and table tennis with awesome intensity, as if his life depended on winning. I learned never to console him if he lost—he so seldom did lose that it was a nasty shock to him. "It's only a *game*," he would growl. "Yes, but I'm sorry you lost." "What did I tell you? It's ONLY A GAME!"

Our rows blew up from nowhere like a storm in the Adriatic. I was thankful sometimes for the many rooms in Casa Veronese. There was always somewhere for him to hide, or me. How obstinate and pigheaded he is, I thought, and I congratulated myself that I had not married him. However, the next minute I would see how kind he was with the girls, or he would make me laugh, and I knew I really loved him. He passionately wanted us to have a baby, and I was all for it. We both agreed we didn't want to marry, however, and we both had exciting prospects for films that year.

A Quiet Place in the Country, which had proved far from quiet and always to be treasured, ended, and the girls and I piled into the Mercedes, which dropped us off at the airport and continued, with our luggage and the five white doves we'd won shooting in a fairground, back to London and down to Hampshire. Tony was waiting for us to join his film *The Charge of the Light Brigade.* He and his crew, led by the extraordinary cameraman David Watkin, had just returned from Turkey, where they had filmed all the Crimean War scenes. Corin, who played one of the Light Brigade officers, had a fund of stories to tell about their adventures. Now the London scenes began, with John Gielgud's extraordinary General Raglan waving his hands as he gave a dramatic picture of "poor little Turkey, desperate, damned in distress, raped by the Russian bear! Chivalry demands we come to the poor maiden's assistance!"

Tony and David insisted that the women wear no makeup, not even mascara, and they really meant it. The makeup artists spent most of the day chasing the actresses, who were sneaking in mascara brushes, desperately trying to apply black to their lashes. In daylight and in candlelight (one scene was lit *only* by candles) the women's faces came alive on screen in the most unexpected and unusual way. Every face became unique, every skin tone particular, and the eyes acquired a special quality.

I played Clarissa, the wife of Captain Morris, one of Cardigan's officers in the Light Brigade, who falls in love with Morris's best friend, Nolan, although she remains devoted to her husband. We shot Clarissa's scenes in the garden of the hunting lodge near Rachel's cottage. At the bottom of this garden was a lake, which Rachel and her dear friend John Fowler, the owner of the lodge, had restored, and beyond it was the Basingstoke canal, half choked with waterweed and rushes. Roger, the film's location caterer, parked his kitchen-wagon in the trees beside John Fowler's drive. Bernie, one of the "sparks," wearing nothing but his heavy-duty gloves and a minute pair of denim shorts, waddled to and fro, cursing obscenely and dissolving Fowler into helpless gurgles of laughter. They, and many others, all reappeared in Charles Wood's play about the film, *Veterans.* I doubt if any director other than Tony had two plays written about him in his lifetime: Charles Wood's affectionate tribute, and John Osborne's *Hotel in Amsterdam,* which was malicious. I am certain that few directors have been so badly misjudged by the critics of their day.

I find it astonishing. *The Charge of the Light Brigade* was met with the same caviling, carping, patronizing dismissal that had greeted *Tom Jones* and *The Loved One.* I saw the film again recently on the wide screen. I think it a real masterpiece—script, photography, casting, design. The acting is superlative, from John Gielgud, Trevor Howard, and David Hemmings, who played the hero, Captain Nolan, down to the tiniest part. The film was introduced by black-and-white cartoons especially designed in the style of the 1850s *Punch* cartoons by Richard Williams. These cartoons, which gave a sense of the political, social, and military views of the ruling class of this period, were counterposed to the terse and sometimes tender scenes of Queen Victoria's England. In one scene Tony drained the gentle greens and blues away behind the pregnant Clarissa, dancing when she received the news of the fall of Sebastopol. Her dancing figure acquired a manic, surreal quality as myriads of cartoon ladies waltzed their men to war, never to return to England.

In August, Tasha, Joely, Christine, and I, accompanied by Litz Pisk and Anthony Bowles, went for three weeks to Cogolin, near Saint-Tropez. Every day for five hours Litz, Anthony, and I prepared the dances for *Isadora,* which Karel Reisz would direct for Universal. My friend Jann Stevens joined us with little Jolie. Both my daughters, who had learned to swim perfectly at the ages of three and one and a half in Los Angeles during *Camelot,* were soon developing an excellent underwater crawl.

We filmed almost all of *Isadora* in Yugoslavia. Opatija and the Istrian coast, in 1967, looked like Nice and the Promenade des Anglais in 1927, forty years earlier. We worked very hard. In the evenings, when we had "wrapped" on the day's shoot, Litz, Anthony, and I retired to a rehearsal room and worked another three or four hours on the dances. I felt lucky, however, because, even if only for fifteen minutes, I had Joely on my knee, or had a twenty-minute swim in the lunch break with Tasha. The girls were welcomed by the hair and makeup department, who took turns telling them stories or playing with their Barbie dolls. Joely was very shy; she had a sad, pensive look in her periwinkle-blue eyes that touched me to the quick and made me want to keep hugging and stroking her back. Then, just as I was looking at her, wondering what her sad thoughts might be, she would start being really funny and would set Tasha and me laughing until we cried.

Isadora was ambitious. Imagine—the story of an American dancer who broke with the limitations of classical ballet to invent a new kind of dance, in which the dancer would not be miming and dancing to music, but would dance the music itself. A romantic communist, Isadora denounced the greed and philistinism of Wall Street and went to Moscow at the invitation of the Bolshevik government, at a time when famine was knocking at the door of every family, to build a new school of dance for Soviet children. This is a scenario that no producer or studio would contemplate financing today. Not everything succeeded. We could not do justice to Essenin, one of the greatest poets of the twentieth century, largely because Madame Furtseva of the USSR Ministry of Culture refused to let Oleg Tabakov join us to play the role. Tabakov was one of the artists who were opposing Furtseva in just about everything, especially her censorship of the theatre, so the lady paid him back by making sure he was refused a visa. (For the best account of Furtseva at this time, I recommend reading Yevgeny Yevtushenko on the subject.)

≡

The Vietnam War marked a political awakening for many of my generation. In 1967 I organized a full-page advertisement in *The Times* of London demanding a halt to the bombing of North Vietnam, and peace talks with the National Liberation Front. Peter Brook had signed it, along with a number of scientists and bishops. James Cameron, the journalist, had also signed. He had just published a series of reports in the London *Evening Standard,* the first articles in the British press to expose the sheer savagery of the U.S. government's war against the Vietnamese. Cameron was the only journalist in Britain at that time to challenge our 100 percent pro–United States press coverage, and the Wilson government's total support for the U.S. invasion of Vietnam.

In January 1968 *The Times* published a letter in which I pointed out how America's refusal to stop the bombing and talk to Hanoi and the National Liberation Front (despite repeated invitations to do so), and their disingenuous semantic arguments, showed that they had not given up blindly hoping for a military solution, despite protestations to the contrary. I also wrote a letter about My Lai. An entire village was wantonly massacred in front of eyewitnesses, yet every British newspaper referred, if at all, to the My Lai "allegations," not "massacre."

Above the entrance gate at Dachau near Munich you can still read the words *Arbeit Macht Frei*, "Work makes you free." The architects of Dachau chose these words with sadistic, deliberate irony, for indeed, work that enables us to develop our skills and our talents *is* liberating. The Nazis knew this, just as they knew that slave labor, which was the purpose of their concentration camps, destroyed its victims by devouring their human identity. In Vietnam, General Westmoreland and the U.S. forces turned whole villages into concentration camps, and called them "pacification zones." In the name of "pacification" the most terrible atrocities were committed against the Vietnamese people. One of the most horrible was what was inflicted by the "butterfly," an anti-personnel bomb with scores of razor-sharp blades that "fly" when the bomb explodes. No surgery in the world can restore the human being who has been sliced in the head or the stomach by those steel slivers. During the Israeli invasion of Lebanon in 1982, the "butterflies" left over from the Vietnam War and sold to Israel flew again over the Palestinians and Lebanese, along with the "clusters" and the phosphorus.

Camelot opened in Paris on March 13, 1968. Tariq Ali, a student member of the London-based Vietnam Solidarity Campaign, telephoned me. At the premiere, would I wear a white headband, as the Vietnamese did when in mourning for their dead? It seemed to me an inadequate gesture of protest, even disrespectful, so I refused. But I did agree to lead the Vietnam Solidarity Campaign march to the U.S. Embassy in Grosvenor Square on March 17.

About twenty thousand people came to the demonstration. The

big Grosvenor Square hotels such as the Europa were doing a thriving business. Tourists and businessmen booked rooms and ordered champagne lunches so that they could enjoy a grandstand view. When we arrived we were surprised that the police let us into the square. When most of the demonstrators were inside, the police put up cordons so that the exits were effectively blocked. Mounted police then charged with batons, and large numbers of the marchers were badly hurt by blows on the head or by the horses' hooves. That night, and all the next day, the press and the television had a field day. The "poor" horses were the favorite theme, with endless footage of policemen grooming them and old ladies and children bringing carrots. Glass marbles, said to be offensive weapons, were produced. I was asked if I would appear on television to be interviewed by Ludovic Kennedy, a member of the Liberal Party and a notable campaigner for victims of injustice. He was in no doubt on this occasion who the victims were. The police and the horses. At least, that was the line he put to me. I tried to explain as precisely and calmly as possible what had actually happened.

A few weeks later President Johnson announced that he would not be running for reelection and would call for a reduction in U.S. bombing raids. I received a rather surprising telegram from the actor Robert Morley, congratulating me "for the results of your efforts." I certainly hadn't seen a connection between our demonstrations and the president's announcement, and although I did not feel as optimistic as Robert, I was immensely grateful for his encouragement.

On April 4, 1968, Martin Luther King was assassinated. Some months earlier he had been at the Grosvenor Hotel in London for a television interview. I had wanted to ask about his mass civil disobedience marches for civil rights for the black American people and his protest rallies against the Vietnam War. He answered my telephone call and said he was sorry there would not be time to see me; he was leaving for the United States in a few hours. His voice was strong and warm. We wished each other well and hoped we would meet soon. We never did.

King was under surveillance from the very beginning. But as his work developed he became a target not only for individual racists, but for the U.S. government. On March 28, 1968, he was in Memphis, Tennessee, marching in support of striking garbage collectors, both black and white. He had mobilized the masses of black America, and for the first time called on them to join their struggles with those of poor and low-paid white Americans. King had become politically dangerous, but exactly who was responsible for his assassination is not clear. We now know that the CIA was responsible for Nelson Mandela's capture in 1961. It was their agents who gave the South African security police the information that enabled them to arrest him. Someday we shall know the truth about King's murder.

It was at this time that I realized how futile it was to continue demanding that the Wilson government protest against the U.S. invasion of Vietnam. The Labour government had completely tied itself, both politically and economically, to United States policy. At a mass rally in Trafalgar Square I rejected the slogans put forward by Tariq Ali and his Vietnam Solidarity Campaign (VSC). In my speech I called for the victory of the NLF and General Giap's armed forces, and the immediate withdrawal of American troops. I denounced the Wilson government and said we could not vote for them again.

I was never asked to speak at a VSC rally again. The British Communist Party's policy was for an end to the bombing and for peace talks, but on the basis of maintaining the North-South division that had been agreed upon by the Americans, French, and British at the Geneva Conference in 1955. Tariq Ali's International Marxist Group, which had initiated the Vietnam Solidarity Campaign, preferred an unprincipled solidarity with the British Communist Party and the Labour and trade union centrists to principled support for the right of self-determination of the Vietnamese people, which would mean an end to the American puppet state of South Vietnam and victory for the Vietnamese over the United States government armed forces. So the "solidarity" of the VSC embraced any group prepared to swallow the line of the British Communist Party, but it most emphatically excluded anyone who shared my position. I could find no political party or group that shared my support for the Vietnamese national liberation struggle. I did not know where to go or what to do. I did not know that the Socialist Labour League, a political party of Trotskyists, was calling for victory for the Vietnamese National Liberation Front. The SLL called for the defeat of the Wilson Labour government and a general election to elect a Labour government pledged to socialist policies.

I read the news reports from France, where hundreds of thousands of workers and students went on strike in May 1968, occupying universities and factories and offices. On June 4 the French Treasury borrowed $745 million from the International Monetary Fund. At the end of the month, President Johnson announced U.S. participation in an international "paper-gold" plan and appealed to Americans to "Buy American" and save the dollar. The United States government had an international crisis of enormous proportions on its hands. But I was unable to grasp the interconnections between this and all the political developments I read about, so I retreated and took refuge again in my professional work.

When I packed my bags and flew with Tasha and Joely to Sweden to play Nina in a film of Chekhov's *The Seagull*, directed by Sidney Lumet, I shut my mind to all that was taking place in the world. Sidney, his wife, Gail, and their children were in Stockholm with Simone Signoret, James Mason, David Warner, and his girlfriend. Harry Andrews, Ronald Radd, and our Russian adviser, Baroness Moura Budberg, Tony Walton, our designer, his girlfriend, Jenny, and his daughter from his marriage to Julie Andrews, six-year-old Emma, were also there. I felt as if for the first time in my life I was part of a community of real, true friends. It was idyllic. We shared our work, our free time, our thoughts, our meals, our children. We were isolated, as if in a time warp, dated August 1968.

Soviet tanks invaded Czechoslovakia. We discussed the invasion, watched it on television, and then forgot what we had seen. Only the house by the lake existed for us, and the lives of Councillor Sorin's household—the torments of Constantin, the jealousy of Arkadina. All of us were working for less pay than we had received for any film we could remember, but we were so happy with our choice, and with those ten weeks, that when the journalists who arrived to interview us asked, "What made you choose this part?," we burst out laughing and replied: "We did it for the money!"

The script, director, and crew were all superb, and for an entire Swedish summer we had the luxury of escaping the distractions of daily life, and could concentrate entirely on what we were doing, and on each other. None of us wanted to leave or to see anyone from outside. We wanted to forget the countless problems we must all face soon. I read in Maria St. Just's book *Five O'Clock Angel* that Tennessee

Williams was asked: "What is happiness?" He answered, "Insensitivity, I guess." Yes, that summer we were all happy, insensitive to everything except ourselves and our enjoyment. Later this became a stern reminder of the price others must pay if artists seek happiness by retreating from the problems of the world. "Life, liberty, and the pursuit of happiness," says the American Declaration of Independence. Certainly the pursuit of happiness is a noble aim, and one that Benjamin Franklin and the founding fathers must have intended as a counterblow to the awful New Testament morality of suffering that served the British ruling class so well. But life and liberty come first.

When I finally watched the film of *The Seagull* I found it exemplified for me the difference between film acting and theatre acting. Strangely, although I can't fault any of the component parts—the acting, atmosphere, lighting, camera work, and direction are excellent—it remains a filmed theatre performance, a recorded piece of theatre, even though it was filmed on location. A filmed theatre performance can be enthralling to watch and tremendously exciting, like the Olivier/Redgrave production of *Uncle Vanya* in 1964, which I still watch on video for Michael's extraordinary performance, but it does not set out to be a film. Theatre and cinema are so different that a recorded piece of theatre does not become a film simply by being captured on celluloid. The independent life of the story does not come through, and that is where *The Seagull* falls short as a film.

In the autumn, Simone and I flew to Paris, dropped our luggage at her little apartment in the Sixteenth Arrondissement, and went straight to the famous Olympia to hear a recital by her husband, Yves Montand. The Olympia was packed. For the first time I heard the song of the Italian partisans, "Bella, Ciao":

> I woke up one morning,
> Good-bye, beauty, my beauty, my beauty, good-bye,
> I woke up one morning,
> My country was invaded.
>
> Oh, Partisans, get me away!
>
> Good-bye, beauty, my beauty, my beauty, good-bye,
> Oh, Partisans! Take me away!
> For now I'm going to die.

On October 16 I sat with Simone and Yves in their sitting room and drafted the text for a telegram to the Soviet ambassador in Paris. Five Soviet intellectuals were on trial in the USSR for protesting in Red Square against the Soviet invasion of Czechoslovakia. We rang Alain Resnais, the film director, and Jorge Semprun, the Spanish writer, close friends of the Montands'. They came over and added their signatures. This is my translation of the French text; copies were also sent to the French news agency, Agence France Press, and to United Press International.

> Gathered together today, we decided to send you this telegram, Monsieur Ambassador. Please convey our warmest congratulations to the Soviet people you represent here. It is with great encouragement that we realize there are still people in your country who have the courage to be heirs of the traditions that have amazed the world since 1905; legions of men and women, in opposition to the regiments of sheep in the world. We are referring of course to Pavel Litvinov, Larissa Daniel, Constantin Babitsky, Vladimir Delaunay, Vadim Dremliouga. It is very fortunate for the people of the Soviet Union that these five exist and that they are citizens of the Soviet Union. As it is fortunate for the American people that the Nine of Baltimore: Daniel Berrigan, Philip Berrigan, David Darst, John Hogan, Thomas Lewis, Marjorie Melville, Thomas Melville, George Mische, Mary Moylan, and also Dr. Spock, were born on American soil. As it is fortunate for France that Gabriel Peri d'Estienne d'Orves, Manouchian l'Armenien, Henri Martin, and Maurice Audin were French.
>
> We are sending a copy of this telegram to the newspapers so that, whether for bad or good motives, it will be published. That it should be published is the only thing that is important to us.
>
> Signed: Yves Montand, Alain Resnais, Jorge Semprun, Vanessa Redgrave, Simone Signoret.

The nine Americans had been sentenced to prison for inciting young men to resist the Vietnam draft. Peri d'Orves and Manouchian were executed by the Nazis. Martin was imprisoned for refusing to fight the Viet Minh in Indochina. Audin was imprisoned and murdered for denouncing French atrocities in Algeria.

All the French newspapers except the French Communist Party's *L'Humanité* published the statement. The *International Herald Tribune* published the first half but cut the paragraph referring to the anti-Vietnam resisters and to the French martyrs of the Nazis and the war for Algerian independence. After Simone rang the chief editor he published the full text, followed by an apology. And in England? Blackout. *The Times* made a brief reference to the telegram. I protested to the editor but received no answer. I could not understand why *The Times* would not print our letter, since they more than any other paper had publicized the case of the Jewish dissidents who were imprisoned in the Soviet Union. And the names of the five signatories were surely of some weight, one way or another. *Le Figaro* published the text in full, and I concluded that British imperialism was more gravely threatened by opposition to the Vietnam War than their French allies were. It never occurred to me that *Le Figaro* was glad to publish anything they deemed anticommunist because of the political significance of the French Communist Party.

I loved and admired Simone and Yves. Simone was the most beautiful woman I had ever met, warmhearted, loving, and amusing. She was everything I had imagined her to be since I first saw her, as a girl, in *Casque d'Or*. Yves was the star of the most outstanding French film made since the war, Clouzot's *The Wages of Fear*. I envied them because they were not isolated, as I felt myself to be. French intellectuals in the cinema and theatre had been involved in political struggles for years, alongside writers like Simone de Beauvoir and her friends. During the May/June struggles in France in 1968, the Cannes Film Festival was brought to a halt by François Truffaut, Louis Malle, Jean-Luc Godard, and Roman Polanski. Truffaut and Godard were then at the height of their international fame. Since 1961, not one English intellectual of note had participated publicly in any rally or demonstration. Even in 1961, I remember, two well-known English theatre directors wavered for a week before they could bring themselves to join the disarmament rally. Peter Finch was the only famous actor besides myself who, to my knowledge, made a public protest after the Soweto massacre in South Africa. None of the British filmmakers had made films like *Z, State of Siege,* or *The Confession* by Costa-Gavras. Northern Ireland has been occupied by the British Army since 1969, but no filmmaker in Britain has

made a feature film taking the side of the Irish Republican movement, as Pontecorvo did when he supported the Algerians in *The
Battle of Algiers.*

I had felt inspired when I read *My Life* by Isadora Duncan. In
preparing for the film I read everything about her and by her, including her passionate statement about the Russian Revolution and her
commitment to the USSR, quoted in Gordon McVay's *Isadora and
Esenin:*

> For the second time in the world's history a great force has arisen
> to give capitalism, which stands for monstrous greed and villainy,
> one great blow. The dragon, man-eating, labour-exploiting, has
> here received his death-stroke. What matters it that in his final
> throes he has cast destruction about him? The valiant hero who
> smote him still lives, though enfeebled from the deadly struggle,
> and from him will be born a new world.

What had happened between 1921 and 1968? Why did the Communist
Parties in Moscow, Britain, and France refuse to call for the victory
of the Vietnamese and the Algerians? Why had the Russian Communist Party degenerated so far as to order the invasion of Czechoslovakia, and the brutal repression of the 1968 reforms led by Dubček, and
the persecution and repression of its own intellectuals when they
protested? Some people could tell me *what* had happened; none
could explain *why.*

I left Yves Montand and Simone Signoret in Paris and returned to
London in October 1968, once more conscious of my need for political struggle. Inspired by Litvinov, Daniel, and their comrades, and
glimpsing an international connection in our struggle, I wrote to Jane
Fonda. I had read about the antiwar work she was leading with
Donald Sutherland in the United States and decided I must initiate
a similar campaign in Britain with the American GIs stationed on the
giant USAF bases in East Anglia.

A return of political confidence, and the will to struggle. Perhaps
my short stay in Paris with Simone and Yves and the sense of
political hope I now found gave me the courage to work again in the
theatre. Connections are never so simple and straightforward, but

they are there nonetheless. Certainly the fact that Michael Elliott was directing *Daniel Deronda* encouraged me to take a step I had not dared to take since *The Prime of Miss Jean Brodie*. He, Caspar Wrede, and Braham Murray had begun work in Manchester in a makeshift theatre while funds were being raised and plans drawn up for what would become a theatre in the Royal Exchange, the center of Manchester's cotton trade in the nineteenth century. Michael's friend and colleague, the actor James Maxwell, had adapted *Daniel Deronda*, and I played Gwendolyn Harleth. I made a copy of the first page of George Eliot's manuscript and kept it with me for protection. Her writing is small, neat, and entirely legible, as clear as her mind. There are four or five corrections on the page, all certainly made in the course of composition, not as afterthoughts or revision. It is fascinating to look at that first page, the confident start of a process that would unravel through two thousand such pages. If I felt that I was stepping near the awful abyss that had confronted me each night in *The Prime of Miss Jean Brodie*, I looked at George Eliot's handwriting and it steadied my nerves.

While in *Daniel Deronda* I took a large flat, with seven other members of the company, and cooked for them each night. Franco was working in Italy, and, to my great joy, I found I was pregnant. The baby we had both wanted was on its way. All in all I got through, and simply getting through was, in its way, a triumph. I would never feel the same fear of the stage again.

When our five-week run in Manchester was over I packed my bags and headed straight for the farmhouse in Italy at Brendola and the Misses Veronese. Tasha was now six years old and Joely four.

On the morning of July 21, 1969, Tasha and Joely came downstairs early with me to the kitchen. We made some breakfast and joined the elder Miss Veronese in front of her black-and-white television set. We half closed the wooden shutters to keep out the strong sunlight and saw Neil Armstrong step out into the black sky onto the soft white powder of the moon. We watched, amazed. It was impossible, yet it was true. Outside, in the burning sunshine, the peasants Beppe, Angelo, and Giovanni were moving the wagons off the fields. Their families didn't eat meat even once a week. Angelo's wife was my age, thirty-two years old, and she was missing four teeth. And out there in the black space beyond the earth, Neil Armstrong was speaking to us as he climbed down a small ladder from the space module onto the moon.

The girls and I spent hours by the washing pool, where the wives washed the clothes in cold water with bars of soap and wooden scrubbing boards, or in the courtyard, where the sweet corn was winnowed from the maize, the husks laid out to dry for fuel for the cooking stoves. We played games in the barns and, when we were thirsty, walked through the field to the stream where a spring of cool, sweet water fell just above the waterwheel that drove the millstone to crush the maize into polenta flour. In the cool evening we danced to music from our portable record player as the sun set. Corin came to stay, and Bob Regester, a dear friend with whom I shared some of my happiest and unhappiest times.

One afternoon, Tasha and Joely came and sat on my bed and asked why I didn't live with their father. They sobbed when I explained that we didn't love each other anymore, but we loved them. I assured them that both of us would always love them. I had convinced myself that children can face and understand such problems as long as parents don't try to maintain a false and unhappy relationship by lying to conceal their unhappiness. How is it possible to tell children to speak the truth, however difficult, if the parents are living a lie? And yet the explanation, even as I said it, seemed to me inadequate. How could children accept the truth? They knew Tony and I still worked together, laughed together, and respected each other. We dried our tears and went out and sprayed each other with the garden hose.

When Franco and my father joined us we traveled by busboat to Padua, down the ancient Brenta canal to Venice, Franco's favorite city, and saw the liquid glass twisting and twirling at Murano. One evening we heard an anguished cry from Michael. He had risen from a sofa and his legs had given way as he crossed the room. Franco took a photo of him that evening as we sat in the garden, and later Corin chose it for the front cover of Michael's autobiography, *In My Mind's Eye*, published in 1983. When I look at that photograph I see in Michael's eyes fear of the disease (Parkinson's) that, as yet unknown to him, had already attacked him.

We all flew home about six weeks before the baby was due. I had booked a midwife on the National Health Service through my doctor. I rang her at about six o'clock on the morning of September 16, 1969. Linda, our new nanny, drove Tasha and Joely across the river to Barnes to spend the day with Lynn and her family until the baby was born. Franco booked a flight to Rome immediately and fled from the house. I set to work with my doctor and the midwife, and the baby was born about four hours later. Immediately I rang Lynn and told her the news, and she drove right over. The girls came running up to my bedroom. I rang Franco to tell him we had a boy. He booked the next flight back to London, burst upstairs, opened the baby's nappy, and kissed his little balls.

Betsy Reisz gave me a small album with gold letters stamped on the cover: THE DAY CARLO SPARANERO WAS BORN. Inside she had collected headlines from newspapers and magazines, all published on that day, September 16, 1969. These included:

ANGER IN U.S. OVER NIXON'S ORDER TO RESUME BOMBING

AMERICANS TO PULL OUT 40,000 MORE TROOPS IN VIETNAM

TWO MILLION INDUSTRIAL WORKERS TO GO ON STRIKE IN ITALY
   THIS WEEK

VICTORY TO MRS. GANDHI IN CALCUTTA

EVE OF ELECTION STRIKES ROCK WEST GERMANY

BAZOOKA MEN HIT ISRAELI VILLAGE

CHEERS FOR DUBCEK . . .

Next to these I pasted Franco's photographs of the new baby with Tasha and Joely, cuddled in the bed next to their fat, happy mum. I published our boy's birth in *The Times*'s birth column: "Vanessa Redgrave and Franco Nero are happy to announce the birth of a baby boy." The following Sunday the editor of *The Observer*, David Astor, denounced me for immorality. What was particularly immoral was that I was happy and unwed. My agent, Robin Fox, and his wife, Angela, were upset. They suggested that Robin and I should go to see David Astor at *The Observer* and ask for an apology in print. I don't remember the details of this meeting, but Robin must have said something acute and to the point, because the following Sunday another editorial expressed apologies for any distress and stated there had been a misunderstanding.

Carlo was five days old when I put him into a woven basket with handles and flew to Toledo, where Franco was filming with Luis Buñuel. I arrived with the Moses basket and Carlo to watch Buñuel shoot a scene at a railway station. Normally it takes a matter of seconds to spot the film director on location. I looked and looked. Everything was quiet; everyone was getting the lights and the actors, Franco and Catherine Deneuve, into their positions. I heard a quiet voice say "Accion!" and I still couldn't spot Buñuel. After the scene, Franco came over and introduced me to one of the Spanish crew, looking like all the rest, with brown cap, brown jacket, and brown trousers, a little worn, a little shabby. "Luis, this is Vanessa," said Franco. We ate supper together and Luis told me he slept on the floor in his hotel, instead of in a bed. He had slept on the floor for about ten years. In his view it was good for the lungs and the back.

Carlo was three weeks old when I laid him on the floor in his basket as I squatted with two students at the Royal College of Art, painting a large canvas as a carpet for Yehudi Menuhin and Ravi Shankar, whom I had asked to play together for the Gandhi Centenary Memorial Concert in October 1969. I got to know Louis Mountbatten very well at this time. We worked together organizing the concert. Then Tasha, Joely, and Linda flew with baby Carlo to Rome for Carnevale and Carlo's christening. Franco was a Catholic, although he shared Nanny Randall's fiercely Protestant view that your beliefs are a private matter between you and God. He wanted Carlo to be blessed by his friend Friar Borromeo, who ran a boys' orphanage in the hills below Tivoli. Franco then, and to this day, entirely finances this orphanage through his fund-raising football matches in the winter season.

We took the girls to Rinascente to choose their dresses, which were to double for Carnevale and Carlo's christening. Tasha chose a purple satin dress with a golden crown and white mock-fur trimmings. Joely chose a white gauze dress and bonnet sprigged with little blue flowers and looked like a little Jane Austen. Carlo looked happily up at the priest as he dabbed the baby's head with oil, and then we all adjourned for a feast at the long table in the refectory.

I didn't work at all until Carlo was about one year old, and I breast-fed him for nine months. So for about a year I was a mum, and stayed at home with my three children. We spent another summer at Casa Veronese. This was the first and last year that I spent entirely with the children, to the exclusion of everything else, except my plans for building a nursery school where three- to five-year-olds could learn to swim. Joely was five years old and Tasha seven years old, and they both attended the French Lycée because Tony wanted to make sure they knew French fluently as a second language. He had bought some semi-ruined farmhouses in the Ardèche forests above Saint-Tropez, and the girls set off on every school holiday to join him.

The first film I made after this period was *The Trojan Women,* which was a high point for the simple and wonderful reason that Katharine Hepburn starred as Queen Hecuba. She took me under her wing during our filming in the mountains above Ronda and cooked me lunch every day in her little house. When she was not filming she went for long walks on the bare mountains, collecting seashells, which were scattered everywhere as a result of a colossal earthquake in the Atlantic some millions of years earlier.

CHAPTER 14

Writing your own history is an exacting and fascinating test. There is a strong inclination to bend the facts to fit what you like to remember and want to have happened. Memory, for this reason, is absolutely unreliable. I have had to check all my dates rigorously, and when I have done this I have found plentiful shocks and surprises and a lot of real contradictions. Life definitely does not proceed in a formally logical way.

This checking of dates and documents, diaries, letters, and newspapers starts a process whereby the eclectic jumble of "good" and "bad" memories is stirred. Subjective predilections dissolve and then the objective record stirs thoughts and a new perspective emerges.

I found I was pregnant with Franco's second child while filming *The Trojan Women* in the summer of 1970, and I should have remembered how I had nearly lost Joely, and that I was now four years older. Then in November I began filming *The Devils* with Ken Russell, in an extraordinary set of a seventeenth-century French town, designed by Derek Jarman. Towering walls and chilly corridors of shiny white ceramic tiles instead of brown medieval brick. I rank *The Devils* with

The Charge of the Light Brigade as the two chief works of genius in the postwar British cinema.

During the filming, I organized a meeting of our cast to discuss the Conservative government's industrial relations bill. A congregation of white-robed nuns shivered around two electric heaters in a tent on the Pinewood Studios back lot. Our union, Equity, had circulated a document called "Our Profession in Peril," protesting against the clauses in the bill that would remove the trade unions' right to a closed shop. A closed shop allows a union to maintain national minimum-wage contracts and acceptable working conditions by insisting that all the workers in their trade join the union. Unlike some of the craft unions, ours over recent years had created many divisions by keeping young people out of the union even when they got offers of employment. This obnoxious deformation of basic democratic rights had also been given the name "closed shop." So we nuns had a good discussion, wrote out a resolution calling for a special general meeting of British Actors' Equity to discuss a one-day strike, obtained forty signatures, and felt we had done two good days' work in the course of a freezing winter's day.

On Sunday, my day off, I lay in bed, feeling terribly tired and in pain. The telephone by my bed, and the special general meeting the next weekend drove me to make a call to Robert Morley, to ask him to be sure to come. I had read a letter he had sent to a newspaper protesting against the bill, and I knew he would be a strong advocate. Robert wished me luck and said he wasn't sure about a strike, but he would be there. The pains in the pit of my stomach got worse, and then I knew I was having a miscarriage. The little dead baby came out into my bed, and would have been a boy. I rang Franco in Rome, who was heartbroken, and that made me cry even more bitterly. At dawn I got up and took the little body and buried it under a bush that would flower in the spring. I phoned Kathleen, the doctor who had delivered Carlo just over a year before. She came by a couple of hours later and soothed me, explaining gently that the miscarriage was nature's method for preventing the birth of deformed or disabled babies. She took me to the Samaritans Hospital to have the afterbirth removed by surgery and I stayed there until Corin came to fetch me for the special general meeting at the Adelphi.

Our resolution was heavily defeated. The union's officers—Gerald Croasdell, the general secretary, and the Council—were vehemently opposed to a strike, and argued that Equity should plead with the government for a special dispensation to permit it to keep a closed shop. Many of the members were sympathetic but didn't believe that a one-day strike would be sufficient to deter the Heath government. But, by a large majority, they voted that the meeting had been necessary. And a few months later Corin was voted onto the Council.

In June I began filming *Mary, Queen of Scots* for producer Hal Wallis. Timothy Dalton played Darnley. "Let me not to the marriage of true minds admit impediment," Shakespeare wrote. Franco and I had quarreled that Easter because he did not wish me to take Carlo to France to join Tony and the girls. There was no way I could agree to this decree, so I went to France, knowing that this meant I would not see Franco again for a long time.

From the moment I met Timothy Dalton we could agree on only one thing consistently, and that was fishing. Regular quarrels are not the steady basis for a marriage of true minds, but there always remained the possibility of reconciliation with the three men I have really loved. One of the first arguments Timothy and I ever had was about a speech from *Hamlet*—"To be, or not to be . . ." He asked me, "What do you think this means?" I told him, and we argued for about six hours. Although we should have had a discussion rather than a row, it is nevertheless extremely stimulating to talk with another actor who wants so passionately to find out what a playwright means in a particular passage. It can also be extremely exasperating, but Tim made me think, and over the years, as we acted a great deal together, in the film of *Agatha* and in *The Taming of the Shrew* and *Antony and Cleopatra* in 1986, and *A Touch of the Poet* in 1988, the keynote of our professional life has been our volatility and directness.

As time goes by, I find fewer and fewer people, even friends, or especially friends, who will spend time discussing and analyzing a production or performance, whether mine or someone else's. So I always valued the fact that Tim cared enough to talk for hours, giving me strong criticism of my own work and explaining what he thought was wrong. While this too would usually end in an argument, I did know that *if* he had praise, then I really had hit the bull's-eye. His own stage performances, as Petruchio in the *Shrew,* and especially as Con Melody in O'Neill's *Touch of the Poet*, were remarkable.

It was Tim who taught me to use a rod and line, first in rivers and the sea, coarse fishing, and later with the fly. Fishing, a sport that usually enables men to seize a few hours of solitude away from their wives, brought us together. Over the years we have spent many hours along riverbanks in Derbyshire, Suffolk, and Kent, many more on the loughs and strands of Ireland, and some unforgettable days on the wooden fishing boat of Ralph Comacho as he scoured the banks off Antigua. When I saw *A River Runs Through It*, the film exactly captured the obsession and joy that seizes you as you cast that fly again and again, fingers gentle on the line as it carries round in an arc over the pool, and suddenly—the take!

Back in June 1971, when we were filming *Mary, Queen of Scots*, the Upper Clyde ship workers occupied the four shipyards that provided work for the whole of the Clyde and its surrounding communities. The Edward Heath government rejected the request for £6 million to save the yards from bankruptcy on the weekend of June 11, and the following Monday, Upper Clyde Ship Builders was officially put into liquidation. The men called for support for their occupation, and I ran around the Pinewood Studio canteens collecting money in the lunch hours.

In the autumn, I flew to Los Angeles for some concert performances of Berlioz's *Beatrice and Benedict* with the Los Angeles Symphony Orchestra. During rehearsals I was invited to a beach house in Malibu for a fund-raiser for the anti–Vietnam War movement. I had met Jane Fonda back in the sixties when she was married to Roger Vadim and I had been demonstrating in London against apartheid and against the Vietnam War. Now she was involved, and she had called her daughter Vanessa after me, a compliment I really cherished.

Ronald Reagan was governor of California, and the schoolteachers were on strike. They were demanding not better wages but above all more funds for such basic requirements as textbooks for the public schools. The funding of these schools was horrifyingly inadequate, especially given the riches in California. I was invited to attend meetings of the striking teachers, and I listened carefully to their demands, which were urgent and clearly explained. I promised to give some special lectures on English drama to the teenagers, and I did.

Beatrice and Benedict, conducted by Zubin Mehta, was fun, and a great success. On the second night there was an antiwar street performance outside the Los Angeles Music Center. I was requested by the protestors to draw the audience's attention to their performance. I asked Zubin's permission to give a short announcement to this effect after we had taken our bows at the end of the concert. He agreed. Some of the wealthy music patrons were not pleased, but antiwar feeling ran high in Hollywood. The majority of the intellectuals, writers, filmmakers, and producers were totally opposed to Governor Reagan and to President Nixon. Many were Jewish, and had been abused and attacked, and blacklisted in the McCarthy period. They were appalled by the war and the increase in censorship, surveillance, and phone-tapping, the whole repressive and corrupt apparatus that was exposed officially in the Watergate hearings in 1973.

With two English friends, and some American Rhodes scholar graduate students at Cambridge, I began to organize a GI antiwar newspaper, *PEACE.* The acronym stood for PEople Against Corrupt Establishments. We built up contacts with a considerable number of GIs at Mildenhall and Bentwaters, the two biggest USAF bases in Britain. We held meetings, leafleted the air bases, and printed a small pamphlet, *A Guide to Military Rights.* This gave detailed advice on how to file complaints against unjust disciplinary measures of any kind, including illegal seizure of a serviceman's mail or personal possessions, and how to obtain deferments from posting overseas and also discharges. I began to receive many letters from soldiers in Vietnam encouraging and supporting my antiwar protests.

Meetings with the GIs took place once a week, and I organized a benefit for them at the Lyceum Theatre in London, which was filmed by Harlech Television, an independent company, and televised. Jane Fonda sent a taped message that we played to the audience before the GIs themselves came up onto the stage:

Show your solidarity with the long-suffering people of Vietnam by inundating the American army bases throughout Great Britain. There is one in Lakenheath in Suffolk and the other in Brize

Norton in Oxfordshire. Hold out your hands in friendship and support to those Americans thousands of miles from home who need your assistance to organize effectively against the war.

Many of the GIs who came to the Lyceum were interviewed that day on the radio. They spoke of commanders who completely ignored intelligence reports and sent their men to certain death. Those who voiced criticism were sent to mental hospitals. One explained how desertion rates had soared to over seven thousand a year by 1968. The poverty of the Vietnamese came as a shock to many of the soldiers. According to one GI, there were over seventy underground GI newspapers, with a total circulation of over seven hundred thousand. Dissenters were punished in the most cruel and brutal way. A GI could "draw six months in the stockade for refusing a haircut after he'd had three haircuts that week." I still have a lot of tapes with the interviews.

In the summer of 1971 a sturdy group of U.S. airmen presented a petition to the embassy in Grosvenor Square, calling for an end to the war in Vietnam. In the afternoon we held a concert for them in Victoria Park, Hackney. Mia Farrow took part in this. Jane had sent me the texts of some sketches she and Donald Sutherland had used in their antiwar concerts. Gerald Scarfe, the political cartoonist, made some papier-mâché heads of the president and his wife, Pat.

PAT: Dick! Dick! Who are all those nasty men on the lawn waving cards at us? Can't you do something?
NIXON: I don't know what I can do, Pat.
PAT: Send in the army and clear them off my lawn!
NIXON: Pat, they *are* the army.

I met a small, neat, pretty Vietnamese lady who had come to London to explain to some of the Labour Party MPs the process and objectives of the National Liberation Front in the Geneva peace talks, which proceeded, on and off, through these years. I found it difficult to understand how she could bring herself to talk at all about peace to the political representatives of governments who were still slaughtering her people. If I, who lived in England, had terrible dreams about napalm and Agent Orange, what must it be like for her?

"I have to try to get peace for my people. They are suffering too much. So I have to sit down and try to get peace for them."

Under the American Freedom of Information Act, which was passed some years later, after Watergate, I applied in 1990 to the CIA and FBI for my files. Many pages were withheld, but I have a large number, heavily scored and obliterated with a black felt pen, which date back to 1964. Clearly I was watched and informed on while I was in America, and also while I was in England. I was categorized as a "subversive." Having studied my own files, and read plenty about J. Edgar Hoover, I can easily see why, after that demonstration of U.S. airmen, I got few major film offers and, when I did, was refused a visa.

I went to the U.S. Embassy for an interview with regard to my visa application. On the desk, in front of the CIA station officer, was a file. The officer made a point of letting me see that it was *my* file, and it was a very big one. In late 1974, the Ahmanson Theatre in Los Angeles invited me to play Lady Macbeth with Charlton Heston. As this was a prestigious American theatre, and since this was after Nixon had resigned and Attorney General John Mitchell had gone to prison, the officer told me he would grant me a visa "when we hear from Frankfurt." "Does that mean I may not get a visa?" "I can't tell you that. A waiver has been requested for you. When I hear from Frankfurt we will notify you!"

I can only speculate as to the reason why "Frankfurt" came into the picture. I did get a visa, strictly limited to the period of the Ahmanson contract. I had to apply to the embassy every time I wanted to go to the States, even to visit my daughter Joely. I did not get a multiple-entry visa until 1985. Even when I came to New York in December 1990 for Natasha's wedding, the coded letters on my visa made the immigration officer at Kennedy Airport tell me to wait. "Did you do something ever? There's a letter and number on your visa that tell me something happened," she said with genuine surprise. "I protested against the war in Vietnam and I had some problems." She was too young to know about the Vietnam War, so she just smiled and shrugged and stamped my entry.

But we are back in late 1971, and I was taking singing lessons and tap lessons to play Polly Peachum in Tony's production of Brecht's *Threepenny Opera*, which would run at the Prince of Wales Theatre. Tony was in top inventive and inspiring form. We had Annie Ross as Jenny, and little Barbara Windsor and I had a great duet together. My nursery school was nearly ready to open at last. I had put all my money from *Camelot* and *Isadora* into this building. Jann Stevens and her family were living round the corner in a small house I bought for them so they could give children swimming lessons and we could prove to the Inner London Education Authority the unique value of a nursery swimming school. I had moved from No. 30 St. Peter's Square, which Tony had sold for £17,000, into No. 18, which Franco had bought me for £20,000 and I had bought back from him when we separated.

Lynny and John Clark had moved to Dublin—to be precise to the seacoast outside Dublin at Howth. I wanted to buy a house near them and move to join them, but there would be too many complications for the children and their fathers if I moved, so I never did, although Dublin has always struck me as a very fair city, and the small villages near the coast, with their "victuallers," their bars, the wild rocks and long beaches, make me feel at home as nowhere else.

On my birthday, January 30, 1972, I was invited to fly to Londonderry to take part in a civil rights protest march against the Conservative government's policy of internment. Men and boys were being arrested in their houses and kept in jail without trial. Bernadette Devlin had spent six months in prison the previous year, charged with inciting riots. In April 1969 she had become member of Parliament for Mid-Ulster, with a huge vote from the Catholic working class, at the age of twenty-one. Her maiden speech, which by House of Commons tradition should have been on a noncontroversial subject, followed by polite applause from MPs of all parties, had Tory and Unionist MPs baying for her blood and Labour members sitting in shocked silence. In 1969 the Labour government had sent the British army into Northern Ireland, ostensibly to keep the peace and protect the Catholic population from loyalist violence. In reality, they were there to make war on the Irish Republican movement.

I knew "Derry" quite well. I'd been there several times while the "Free Derry" banners flew over the city and the armored British saracens clattered around the housing estates. But I did not go that "Bloody Sunday" of January 30. A bout of flu and eight performances a week of *The Threepenny Opera* made me cancel my visit, thinking I'd go next time. So I was not there that Sunday when thirteen civilians, eight of them boys under twenty-one years of age, were shot down in cold blood by the British paratroopers. All were innocent victims of a calculated plan by British army High Command to provoke the IRA into battle on the streets of Derry and then wipe them out.

I flew to Newry the following weekend, to take part in a protest against the Bloody Sunday massacre. Bernadette Devlin and Eamonn McCann met me. We waited in a small bungalow until it was time to assemble for the march. Reports came in continually that leaders of the various political groups involved in the march were trying hard to stop a massive turnout and limit the numbers to a small show of silent protest. The *Sunday Press* carried a front-page article, headlined NEWRY WANTS NO HOOLIGANS, saying: "Last-minute orders issued by the organisers of today's Civil Rights March in Newry were 'Hooligans Out—Civil Rights In—Stop at the Barricades.' There is to be no chanting, no singing, no hurling of words of abuse at the steel ring of British troops which now surrounds the town." I thought this an insult to the dead of Bloody Sunday and to all the men and boys who defied the British troops, their racism, and their brutality.

Helicopters buzzed overhead. Army officers shouted orders to disperse. The march was illegal and anyone taking part could be prosecuted and sent to jail for six months. No one knew what the army might do, though we guessed that the large numbers of members of Parliament and clergymen would prevent a shoot-out. We marched and dispersed at the army barricades. The organizers claimed a victory because it was a peaceful march. But Bloody Sunday was a peaceful march until the British army, on orders from Whitehall, opened fire on innocent, unarmed men and boys.

After interviews with press and television journalists from all over the world, Bernadette and I sat down with some other women, exhausted and drained. We talked about the politics of the different parties who had participated in the march. She was mistrustful and very critical of them. "Why don't you tell everyone what you know, that these other groups are not to be trusted?" I asked her. Bernadette herself, unlike virtually all other Irish leaders, spoke frequently and publicly of the need to unite Catholic and Protestant workers. This was not a popular line, but it was absolutely right. And because Bernadette had real courage, and was unafraid to speak out against the British government and army, she had immense support from the

Irish people. On the other hand she did not believe, and neither did I at that time, that the English working class would ever support the liberation of the Irish.

On March 24, 1972, Edward Heath suspended the parliament in Stormont, and a police-military dictatorship was established in Northern Ireland. I offered to stand bail for a young man, Sean O'Toole, who had been arrested and charged with incitement to riot in Whitehall during a February demonstration in London. Detective-Sergeant Ian Will opposed my surety in the court: "She is passionately involved in demonstrations and civil disturbances and would not be acceptable as surety." I felt cold and worn out and did not know what could be done politically. I did not support terrorism against civilians. I did support the Irish people's right to self-determination and their right to fight the British army and choose their own methods. I could see no political road forward. I felt there was no party or group I could really trust, because none I had worked with or talked with had a perspective beyond protest or terrorism.

I had for a couple of years known the leader of one of the black political groups in Britain. C. L. R. James was a cultivated and intelligent man who had been a member of Trotsky's party in the United States until 1939, when he had joined a faction and subsequently rejected Trotsky's perspectives. He was in his seventies when I met him. His book *Black Jacobins,* about the Haitian revolutionary Toussaint L'Ouverture, is world famous. He also wrote about cricket, very well indeed, I believe. A close friend of his was the great Trinidad cricketer Learie Constantine. He loved and studied Shakespeare as did no Englishman I have ever met other than Tony. One evening he enthralled a group of writers and actors at my house with a two-hour lecture on *King Lear.* He said very little about his days as a comrade of Leon Trotsky. I recall a meeting in Ladbroke Grove when he said that he and Trotsky had disagreed about "the Negro question." He, James, had argued for separate political organizations for black Americans, much as the Jewish Bund workers had disagreed with Lenin on a similar issue in 1903.

Lenin and Trotsky, as I realized later, were right. The Bund workers who split from the Bolsheviks and the black intellectuals with James who split from the Fourth International made a big mistake. Both political streams finally had no confidence in the prospects of uniting workers of all nationalities in the same international party to end racist and class oppression. At the bottom line they were nationalists.

As far as James was concerned, the Soviet Union was a state capitalist system, ruled by a bureaucracy that had become an exploiting class. He blamed Lenin and the Bolshevik party for this. Leninism had produced Stalinism, and that was the end of all analysis. I did think to myself that you could just as well say that Jesus Christ was responsible for the Spanish Inquisition, and with as little foundation. James gave me and several others lessons on *Das Kapital,* and because of James, though not on his advice, I went up to Collets bookshop and bought Lenin's *The State and Revolution.* However, James's political influence meant that when I saw and felt the frustration of political forces in Ireland fighting each other, with no program or perspective for political struggle together to end the British dictatorship, I did not know how to go forward and therefore dropped out of politics altogether. I reached for the "practical solution" to the contradictions. I told myself: If all good intentions and just causes become compromised because all political leaders and political parties become compromised, then, my dear, stay out of politics! Do something you can do, within the limits of your own individual life. Finish your nursery school.

The architect Rodney Fitch, a professor in education from Brunel University, Jann and Bob Stevens, and I worked hard down to the last details, nonslip paint for the pool area and a plentiful supply of flippers for the children. On September 16, 1973, the Vanessa Redgrave Nursery School was officially handed over to be a state nursery school under the control of the Inner London Education Authority (ILEA). Jann Stevens had a two-year contract with ILEA to teach the kids swimming. Carlo was four years old on September 15, and he spent his first year as a schoolboy at the Vanessa school.

That year Allende's democratically elected socialist government in Chile was overthrown in a military coup by the army led by General Pinochet. Castro had officially visited Chile and inspected the armed forces there. How had it been possible to successfully and brutally destroy the Allende government? I felt a real urgent personal need to know the answer to this question. Corin, who had joined the Socialist Labour League in 1971, gave me a careful and precise analysis of any question I put to him. I noted his answers and contrasted them with C. L. R. James's explanations, which failed to satisfy. When James had seen that his answers were not convincing me, and when he heard that my brother had joined the SLL, he darkly warned me off: "Don't go near that outfit. It is run by Gerry Healy; he's a Stalinist."

For quite a while this did frighten me off. I certainly didn't want to get involved with a Stalinist. I also found that Corin's explanations posed further questions, which I didn't really want to deal with because they challenged some fixed political ideas I had. When I didn't want to deal with these I turned to the wine bottle to forget. In congratulating myself that I was an individual with an individual point of view who would not fall sucker to someone else's political perspective, let alone join a party led by a Stalinist, I did not realize that I was treading a very well beaten path, down which hundreds of thousands had stumbled, blindly and sometimes drunkenly, convinced that they were upholding freedom of thought and the rights of the individual to have an independent point of view. No Bolshevism, thank you very much!

The political and economic situation in Britain went from bad to worse. Prime Minister Heath and his chancellor of the exchequer had led a "dash for growth" that had promoted inflation and the crash of a number of banks. Britain was heading for a colossal slump. On March 8, 1973, a wave of car bombs blasted off outside New Scotland Yard in Victoria Street, London, and, shortly afterward, outside the Old Bailey. Bombs shattered windows and injured ordinary civilian passersby in the street. The police and press claimed this terrorism was the responsibility of the IRA. I thought: If this *is* the IRA they are crazy. What was being done to the Irish was not the responsibility of ordinary British people. The Tory government was attacking British as well as Irish workers. Could the bombings be a deliberate provocation? I knew that the police, army, and secret services had been involved in several bombings, and in preparations for a coup in Italy in 1964 and again in 1969. Could there be a political connection?

A group of Irish youths were arrested, taken to Ealing police station, and refused permission to see solicitors. I knew they could be badly beaten, interrogated, and forced to sign false confessions before solicitors were allowed near them. I telephoned anyone I could think of who would have sufficient weight to demand entry into the police cells. I rang Laurie Pavitt, a Labour MP. He said they were terrorists, and he would not go. I rang Lord Soper, the leader of the Methodist Church and a Labour man, who had always opposed British colonial atrocities in Kenya and Malaya. He also refused. In desperation I turned to the Church of England. The Bishop of Southwark, Mervyn Stockwood. No. The Roman Catholic Church. No. I tried my local vicar. No. I pulled out the directory and found a small Catholic priory near Ealing. The priest who answered my call was very sympathetic. He said he would have to get permission from his superior, but he was prepared to go. When he went to the Ealing police station he was told to come back later. He did, and was at last permitted to see the youths. He rang me and said they were in not too bad a state and had been relieved to see him. I was telephoned and asked if I would go to the magistrates' court in Bow Street and offer bail for one of the girls. I said I would. Edna O'Brien was there too. Our offer of bail was refused.

I drew the curtains, took the phone off the hook, lay on my bed. I stayed like that for a day and a night. Thoughts raced, and halted. But I *had* to think, and I took no wine. These young Irish were in a political blind alley through no fault of their own. British workers were not to blame for the atrocities of the British military dictatorship. The military dictatorship in Northern Ireland was as dangerous for the British trade unions and posed as great a threat to basic democratic rights in Britain as in Ireland. Military and police intelligence would have a field day with terrorist groups. Terror played right into their hands because they needed terror to get agreement from the opposition in Parliament for new repressive powers against the trade unions.

My thoughts turned to Robert Shaw's play *Cato Street*, which I had coproduced, researched, and performed in as Susan Thistlewood in November 1971 at the Young Vic Theatre in Waterloo. It was about a group of radicals, led by a craftsman, Arthur Thistlewood, which was infiltrated by a secret agent working for the Home Office of the Tory government of 1819. The agent, Edwardes, working under orders from Lord Sidmouth, the home secretary, proposed a plan to assassinate the Tory cabinet and provided the money to collect arms and ammunition for the attack. *Cato Street* told how the Home Office

With Michael in *Behind the Mask*. The portrait of Rachel by Anthony Devas is now in my flat in Chiswick. *Right*: Almost my favorite picture of Michael, leaving Shepperton Studios after a day's shooting on *Behind the Mask*.

Tony and me leaving for our honeymoon, June 1962. *Above right*: Natasha, just after she was born, May 11, 1963; Tony took the picture. *Right*: Tasha and Joely, ages four and three. I took this one.

On holiday with Tony in Mexico, 1963 (*right*); and (*below*) Joely trying on my glasses, California, 1966. Luckily all my children have good eyesight.

Top: Filming *Red and Blue* with Tony Richardson in 1967. *Right*: With Richard Attenborough on the set of *Oh What a Lovely War* at Brighton pier in 1968. I played Sylvia Pankhurst. *Above*: Sidney Lumet directing me as Nina in his film of *The Seagull*, Stockholm, 1968.

Jean Brodie and her "little girls," Olivia Hussey and Vickery Turner, Wyndham's Theatre, London, 1966 (*top*); with David Hemmings in *Blow-Up*, 1966 (*center*); and with Jane Manning, Daniel Barenboim, and Zubin Mehta (*bottom*) rehearsing *Pierrot Lunaire* at the Queen Elizabeth Hall, 1969. I was pregnant with Carlo.

When I was filming *Camelot* in 1966, Victor Skrebneski took this photograph, which was used to promote *The Loves of Isadora*.
Below left: As Michelangelo Antonioni's mysterious lady in *Blow-Up*, 1966; and (*bottom right*) playing Leonie in *Morgan!*, for which I received the Best Actress Award at the 1966 Cannes Film Festival.

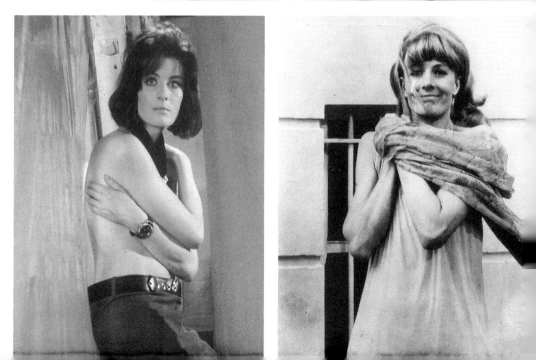

Franco Nero and me in
A Quiet Place in the Country,
directed by Elio Petri,
1967 (*left*); with Franco,
Tasha, and Joely at the
Cannes Film Festival, 1968
(*center*).

Franco in *Carmen*, 1967.
Vittorio Storaro was the
cameraman.

Natasha, Joely, and Carlo join Franco and me in 1970 during the filming of *Drop Out* in London, directed by Tinto Brass (*above*); Lynn's daughter, Kelly, a few days old, and Carlo at four months, in January 1970 (*left*); Carlo and me in 1977, the year after *Bugsy Malone*, at the Young Socialists Summer Fair.

placed a notice in *The Times* stating that the entire Tory cabinet would be dining at a house in Grosvenor Square on Wednesday evening, February 23. This was a fake, published so that the agent, Edwardes, could bring arms to Cato Street and encourage Thistlewood's group to attack. Troops were alerted. They surrounded the house, arrested the group, and seized the arms. All members of the group were hanged, and a savage round of repression, arrests, and hangings ensued. The Whigs, the Liberal parliamentary opposition, muttered but agreed. The Home Office operation, known as the Cato Street conspiracy, had achieved its objective.

Robert Shaw wrote his play with ringing precision and hatred for Tory class oppression. Susan Thistlewood's words, based on the trial records and execution speeches of Thistlewood and his comrades, returned to my ears: "One generation passeth away and another generation cometh. Do you not identify at all with us, my friends? Are we strangers to you?"

I realized at that moment that I had no other way to live except in a political struggle with a party that knew that a serious study of history is necessary if we are to gain understanding and prevent a recurrence of repression. I rang Corin and asked him to come to my home then and there. He came, and I told him I wanted to apply immediately to become a Trotskyist and a member of the Socialist Labour League.

CHAPTER 15

I remember so clearly that day in 1973 when I sat down with Corin at the table of my sitting room in 18 St. Peter's Square. He gave me a Socialist Labour League pamphlet and a large brown volume from Lenin's collected works, volume 38, the *Philosophical Notebooks*.

In that edition, which I still have, there is a photograph of the reading room in the Berne Library in Switzerland, where Lenin studied Hegel and made his notes in the last two years of his second period of exile, before the Russian Revolution of 1917. In the preface by the editors, from the Institute of Marxism-Leninism of the Central Committee of the CPSU, there is an important observation:

It is no coincidence that Lenin devoted so much attention to philosophy, and above all, to Marxist dialectics, precisely during the First World War, a period in which all the contradictions of capitalism became extremely acute and a revolutionary crisis matured. Only materialist dialectics provided the basis for making a Marxist analysis of the contradictions of imperialism, revealing the imperialist character of the First World War, exposing the opportunism and social chauvinism of the leaders of the Second

International and working out the strategy and tactics of the struggle of the proletariat.

Nothing is said in that preface about the postrevolutionary history of Lenin's philosophical notebooks, and about the fact that they remained unpublished in the Soviet Union until after Stalin's death. This is also, as the editors of my edition would say, "no coincidence." Stalin suppressed them, just as he suppressed the last notes and letters dictated by Lenin, which came to be known as Lenin's Testament, because, even more than the latter, they would have revealed the whole character of Stalin's tyranny. Consequently, there was no English translation of Volume 38 until 1961, eight years after Stalin's death. Only then could Gerry Healy, the founder of the Socialist Labour League, begin to study them. Now, Corin told me, all party members studied them, and he promised that in a few days' time we would read them together. I felt uncertain, and as I flicked through the pages I was awestruck. "Logic," I read, "resembles grammar, being one thing for the beginner, and another thing for one who knows the language (and languages) and the spirit of language." And then a quotation from Hegel: "It is one thing to him who approaches logic and the sciences in general for the first time and another thing for him who comes back from the sciences to logic." Next to this Lenin had written in the margin, "Subtle and profound!" Yes, no doubt, but I was most certainly one who was approaching logic, not to speak of the sciences in general, for the first time, and I felt inadequate; I had had no education whatsoever either in the sciences or in philosophy.

The other book, or rather pamphlet, which Corin gave me was *A Marxist Analysis of the Crisis,* and I fell on it as soon as he left. I must have read it through at least three times that day. It explained the connection between the economic crisis of 1971–1972 and the postwar policies of the Bretton Woods Agreement of 1944; it discussed the connection between the dollar, no longer backed by gold, and the massive inflation in advanced capitalist countries. The capitalist countries were in a crisis that was driving them to seek the same solutions as German capital had sought after the Wall Street crash of 1929—the destruction of the trade unions, racism, and war.

I read and reread the paragraph on "The USSR, China, and

Eastern Europe." This explained why Trotsky had founded the Left Opposition in 1926: to lead the political revolution against the Stalinist bureaucratic apparatus. Lenin had devoted the last two years of his life to analyzing and opposing that same bureaucracy and its usurpation of the workers' power. Despite Trotsky's assassination by a GPU agent in August 1940, despite Stalin's terror purges and gulags, Soviet citizens and the Red Army had defeated fascism. The East German uprising in 1953, Khrushchev's secret speech on the crimes of Stalin at the Twentieth Party Congress in 1956, and the Hungarian revolution later that year, the "Prague Spring" in 1968, the strikes in Poland in 1970 . . . all were expressions of a developing political revolution against Stalinist bureaucracy. Here was a party, the Socialist Labour League, that defended the fundamental gains of the October Revolution, the social ownership of the means of production, against the Stalinist totalitarian bureaucratic rule, and, in spite of Stalinism, against imperialism. I did not understand this fully until I read Trotsky's *Revolution Betrayed*, published in 1936 in the United States. However, I understood the main issue: Stalinism was not socialism nor communism.

The Socialist Labour League stood for the right to self-determination of all nationalities, including those in the USSR, the Irish, and the Palestinians. The SLL absolutely opposed terrorism, individual acts of terror against civilians. I was to read later Trotsky's passionate defense of the young Jew Grynzspan, who assassinated the Nazi ambassador to Paris after Kristallnacht. He did not support this act of terror, but he blamed the politics of the Communist Parties, which had led to the taking of power by the Nazis, and to Grynzspan's despair, and he called for workers' organizations to campaign for the release of Grynzspan. Terrorism was different from the right of an oppressed people to wage a war against an army of occupation. Consequently, like Trotsky and Lenin and Marx, the Socialist Labour League consistently opposed the politics of terrorism while upholding the right of the IRA and the PLO to have an army and wage political and military struggles against the armies occupying their countries.

I had always supported the goal of a united socialist Ireland, first proclaimed by Padraic Pearse. Connie Marciewicz was one of my heroines, as was Sylvia Pankhurst. When I first joined the Socialist

Labour League I was already a convinced supporter of the African and Arab liberation struggles, and of the Vietnamese. It was only after I joined the SLL, however, that, like every other member, I began serious and continuous reading, study, and discussion. In the study of philosophy and the history of philosophy, considerable attention was given to the study of developments in all the sciences, especially historical science, natural science, and nuclear physics. I came to understand the abyss between the political character of left demagoguery, however sincere, and the deep analytical approach based on consistent training and study.

This is to jump ahead. But on that day my mind was alerted to a perspective and an approach to the analysis and resolution of problems that was a far cry from the superficial impressions and opinions of those engaged in politics whom I had met and worked with so far. I was thirty-six years old on that day when I telephoned Corin, having read *A Marxist Analysis,* and told him that I definitely wanted to join his party. I have been a member of our party and the Committee of the Fourth International for twenty years now. I can truthfully say that I remain absolutely convinced of the necessity of Marxism, and that not for a single day has this conviction been shaken. A Marxist approach to life and its problems and wonders is the opposite of the Stalinist dogma and rhetoric that blasted the brains of several generations, and I sensed this as soon as I read Corin's pamphlet.

The day after he gave me the book and the pamphlet Corin took me to the offices of the Socialist Labour League in Clapham, South London. Gerry Healy's office was on the ground floor, a small room, very simply furnished, with a plain wooden desk and some hard chairs. He greeted me warmly—he had been genuinely surprised when Corin told him I was interested in joining the party. We talked about the Heath government, and the League's plan to hold a conference at the end of the year and adopt a new party name and constitution for the thousands of new members who would join in the coming months. At the end of our talk he said, "So, I hope you'll consider joining too." "Can't I join now?" I asked. "I've made up my mind already." Gerry laughed, and said yes, of course, and, turning to Corin, said, "So now Mary, Queen of Scots, has joined us." We talked about the situation of the Irish, many of whom were held in isolation in British prisons. He knew that I had offered to guarantee bail for

Dolores Price and her sister. "That was courageous of you," he said, "to support those young Irish women."

Gerry Healy was Irish himself, born in Ballybane in Galway in 1913. He went to sea in the merchant navy at the age of fourteen, and a year later joined the British Communist Party. As a seaman and a young communist, he became a courier for the Comintern, carrying messages to leaders of the German Communist Party in the cruel and dangerous days when fascism was coming to power.

In 1936 he discovered by chance, looking at the Lloyd's shipping register, that oil from Batum in Soviet Georgia was being shipped to Barcelona via Genoa for the Spanish Republicans. But at Genoa the Soviet tankers were unloading half their cargo. So the USSR was supplying oil to Mussolini, which would be used to fuel the bombers Mussolini had sent to Spain to bombard the Republican forces. He went to Harry Pollitt, a very senior leader of the British Communist Party, and asked for an explanation. Pollitt sent him to William Joss, who headed the party's control commission. Joss said his question was "Trotskyite," and he would be expelled if he persisted with it. Gerry protested that he knew nothing of Trotsky and had never read a word he had written, but he wasn't prepared to drop his question. He was expelled, and there and then decided he had better make good the omission by reading Trotsky. And so he became a Trotskyist.

The next few weeks were among the most exhilarating of my life. It seemed to me that I learned more in that short space of time than in the whole of my previous existence. I traveled with Gerry to a meeting of automobile factory workers at Cowley in Oxford. Many of the workers in the huge British Leyland car plant, including several shop stewards, had joined the Socialist Labour League. I was struck by the amount of time that Gerry devoted in his political report to international events, and to analyzing every aspect of the world economic crisis, and by the long and thorough replies he gave to the questions that followed his report. It was evident from the discussion that Gerry knew everything about the history of the factory at Cowley, about its trade union agreements, its working practices, and the many disputes that constantly arose there. He could sense the workers' mood as keenly as if he worked there himself. Yet he did not confine himself to questions concerning the car factory. Much of the discussion that day centered on events in Chile, where it was clear that the Allende government was about to be overthrown.

Soon after this Gerry asked if I would speak at a public meeting in London. I felt inadequate, but I knew I must speak on the terrible brutality of the Chilean coup. There had been ample advance warning in the months before September. There had been the dress-rehearsal coup in June, after which the rebellious regiments had been sent back to barracks by the senior general in Allende's cabinet, and not a single leader was brought to trial. Then the transport "strike" had crippled the economy. All the big trucking firms had refused to make deliveries. Factory workers and trade unionists in Santiago had demanded arms from the government to defend themselves against the coup they knew was coming, and Allende had refused them. Allende himself died a courageous death, gunned down in his presidential palace. His body was later exhumed from its anonymous grave in the suburbs of Santiago and reburied with dignity. That is right and fitting, but neither his bravery nor the courage of his followers should ever obscure the fact that it was the policies of his Popular Unity government and their failure to disband and disarm the Chilean armed forces that opened the way to the counterrevolution, which destroyed not only that government, but hundreds of thousands of men and women. That counterrevolution was backed by the U.S. government.

In my speech I drew a parallel between the events in Chile and the situation in Britain. I said that Chile was not some Latin American "banana republic" where the military regularly ruled but was a state with a forty-year history of constitutional, bourgeois democratic government. There were serious lessons for us all in that coup. There were those in Heath's government and in the British army and some sections of big finance who would favor using the army if they felt threatened by a democratically elected socialist government in Britain. The British Communist Party was mourning the coup and the brutal killings in the stadiums and army barracks. However, until the last days, the Chilean Communist Party had been insisting that the Chilean army was the people's democratic army. Did that party not bear a responsibility also therefore for the success of Pinochet?

≡

In August 1973 I was working again with Tony in *Antony and Cleopatra* at the Bankside, an open-air theatre on the South Bank near the site of the ancient Globe Theatre, which Sam Wanamaker hoped to rebuild. Tony set the play in the late 1930s. He said that Cleopatra was like a spoiled movie star who thought the whole world was her oyster. Bob Hoskins was great casting as Enobarbus, and young David Schofield played Octavius. As always, working with Tony was exhilarating and eye-opening. We had run for two and a half weeks when a summer thunderstorm broke, filling the tarpaulins that covered our stage and the audience. The tarpaulins swelled threateningly; audience and actors looked up with alarm as they bulged even lower with the weight of the water. Sam Wanamaker leapt up a ladder with a bucket and started bailing out the water with vehement cries of "The show must go on!" However, the show collapsed, along with the tarpaulins, and the audience sped off never to return.

That autumn, President Sadat of Egypt tried to reconquer the Egyptian lands seized by Israel in 1967. The Egyptian army made a tremendous advance in a surprise attack. But then Brezhnev withdrew Soviet support and put pressure on Sadat to halt the offensive. The result was victory for Israel, and terrible losses for the Egyptian army. The Arab states put up the price of oil, out of sheer necessity, following the example of the Americans, French, British, Germans, and Japanese, who all sought the highest possible price for their commodities. Prior to the price increase, the differential between what the Arabs received, as producers, and what Western consumers paid was 400 percent. Such was the margin of profit for the Western oil corporations.

In Britain, the miners had voted for a ban on overtime. Coal production was down by an estimated 20 percent. Electricity workers were on strike. The cost of oil, following the embargo, had risen fourfold, from three dollars to twelve dollars a barrel. Winston S. Churchill, the Tory MP for Stretford, fulminated against "an unholy alliance of miners and Arab sheikhs" holding the country to ransom.

I was rehearsing Noël Coward's play *Design for Living* when the SLL held a conference, on November 4, at the Odeon Cinema in

Hammersmith, transforming the Socialist Labour League into the Workers' Revolutionary Party. Three thousand members attended the conference. In addition to the daily newspaper, *Workers' Press,* we had a weekly paper for youth, *Keep Left.* The party had its own printing presses and publishing company, and a bookshop in Charlotte Street, off the Tottenham Court Road.

Design for Living is a romantic comedy about a triangular love affair between a woman and two men. Noël Coward wrote it in 1932 and played in it, with Alfred Lunt and Lynn Fontanne, in New York the following year. Strangely, it was not produced in London until 1939. In his introduction to the published version in *Play Parade,* Coward says that audiences found it "unpleasant ... these glib, over-articulate and amoral creatures force their lives into fantastic shapes and problems because they cannot help themselves." *Not* a political play, unless in the sense that the Soviet poet Mayakovsky claimed that every poem is political, "even a lyric about two lovers, hand in hand." And yet I continually sensed, in those three characters twisting and turning as they tried to find relationships they really wanted, the social crisis of the period in which Coward conceived his play, which found its own peculiar expression in the political drama of the abdication of Edward VIII.

Coward's only recorded comment on the Stanislavsky method, as I remember from my father's book *Mask or Face,* is scathing: "Isn't that the little company who went away to the country to rehearse for two years, and found they weren't ready?" But my guess is that such sarcasm was a deflection. He was critical, very demanding, and highly intolerant of anything he considered slipshod or unprofessional. An "infinite capacity for taking pains" was contained in the seeming effortlessness of his performances. His best-known mannerism, a very light, flutelike quick-fire delivery, was really not a mannerism so much as a method of thought and speech ideally suited to the performance of his own work and the comedies of Oscar Wilde. It is easily imitated, and that is the problem with most performances of his work. In the few productions I had seen of his plays the cast imitated what they thought to be the Coward style, whereas what Coward wanted was the truth of human beings in certain circumstances. As I rehearsed *Design for*

Living I tried to remember what Coward had said to me on one of the two occasions he had seen me in the theatre: "Your work is completely truthful. There is not one false moment in it."

The first thing the Stanislavsky method requires is research and study of the historical circumstances, customs, and social life of the play's period and its characters, and there are few directors or actors who would not enthusiastically agree that the cast should do this work. However, a diligent study of the historical context, necessary as it is, and indeed invaluable as a source for the raw materials with which to build a character, cannot of itself bring out the essential life of a play. No amount of careful study can re-create the life of a century, a decade, or even a year ago, because that life has ceased to be. It has passed into our memory. Yet we can find what was essential in that past life, the life of the play, by turning to the present. The more the actor is engaged in trying to change the conditions of his or her life, to grasp the meaning of problems and to analyze them, the more, in the course of rehearsal and performance, impressions will emerge. In further rehearsal and thinking, these will become definite notions, which seem to have their own life. In fact they *do* have their own life. They reflect all that is essential now and all that was essential then in its clearest and most advanced form.

Every actor knows such moments, when it seems that someone else has taken possession of him. It is the union of the conscious with the unconscious. The problem is that everyone knows it when it happens, but artists spend most of their lives trying to understand *how* it happens, especially when they run into difficulties.

The actors will be surprised and look at each other with excitement. Suddenly the atmosphere of rehearsal becomes charged. All will know, even if few or none can understand how or why, that from somewhere a living truth has convinced them and made them convince each other and has taken physical shape in the thought and actions of the characters.

The week after the WRP's founding conference, as I was coming out of the theatre after the first performance, the streetlights went out in a power cut. Next morning, Tuesday, November 13, the home secretary declared a state of emergency, giving the government powers to use troops to take over public utilities, transport, and power supplies. It was the first time a national state of emergency had been declared since the end of the war. Prime Minister Heath announced that from January 1, 1974, industry would be put on a three-day week. It was on the same day that a number of British secondary banks, which had been lending money hand over fist in the credit boom the government had encouraged a year before, went broke and had to be bailed out.

Suddenly a wave of stories appeared in the national press about Arab terrorists at Heathrow Airport armed with Soviet missiles, ready to shoot down civilian airliners. And, lo and behold, one January afternoon, tanks, armored cars, army and police units, occupied the airport perimeter and the area around Heathrow, setting up roadblocks. Neither the Labour Party in Parliament, nor the *Morning Star,* the paper of the British Communist Party, challenged the government story about Arab terrorists with Sam-7 missiles. Not one Arab terrorist was ever subsequently apprehended, nor a single Sam-7. The story was as conveniently forgotten as it had been conveniently invented. We increased the print run of the *Workers' Press* from fifteen thousand to twenty thousand copies a day, warning of the danger of police-military rule as in Chile. We were denounced as scaremongers. But two years later, in 1976, two *Sunday Times* reporters, Stephen Fay and Roger Crozier, revealed—quoting sources that have never been denied or disproved—that several of the most senior army officers, city financiers, and top civil servants were in favor of military intervention. At a meeting at No. 10 Downing Street in early February 1974, Prime Minister Heath had warned Joe Gormley, president of the National Union of Mineworkers, that this might be the consequence if the miners voted for an all-out strike. In February, the miners' executive committee met to discuss the strike, with Gormley arguing heatedly against it. But the vote was 8 to 1 in favor. Then, on February 7, Heath called a general election.

At night I was playing *Design for Living* at the Phoenix, and rehearsing *October,* a play about the October socialist revolution of 1917, at the Oval House in Kennington. There were about forty professional actors and musicians working without a script. Many of us knew only the most elementary facts about the October Revolution, so that much of our time was spent reading and discussing Trotsky's *History of the Russian Revolution,* improvising, then writing down the scenes we had sketched out. We had no funds for the production whatever, and in between our rehearsals, which lasted for about eight weeks, though often for little more than two hours a day, we had to find costumes and props and construct a set, including an armored car and the battleship *Aurora,* whose gunshots signaled the beginning of the uprising.

Some of us were party members; most were not. Some had a certain professional reputation and experience; others were just beginning to make their way. Yet our cast became Lenin, Trotsky, Stalin, Zinoviev, Kamenev, Kerensky, Kornilov, and we peopled the hall with soldiers, sailors, workers, and peasants in a way that was utterly convincing and completely transcended our own egos, inadequacies, and different levels of professional experience and ability. We were united by an urgent political crisis. The miners were on strike, despite the attempts of the Labour Party to make them return to work, and the Tories were fighting the election on the slogan "Who rules Britain?"

My experience with this play was to prove enormously valuable. I found, in the course of the run of *Design for Living,* that I was able to carry out my professional and artistic work and participate fully in the political life of my party. At an emergency Central Committee meeting, we had decided to put forward eight candidates in constituencies where there was a large Labour majority. In the country as a whole we would call for a Labour vote and warn that if the Conservatives were allowed to return, they would come back with a dictatorship, based on the army and the police. We chose eight constituencies, one each in Scotland, the Northeast of England, the Midlands, and Wales, and four in London. The play, *October,* was to be presented as the climax to our party's main election rally in the great hall of the Alexandra Palace, which seated about four thousand people. I was asked to be the party's candidate in Newham Northeast, a large working-class district in the East End of London, between Canning Town, Barking, and Dagenham. It was there that Eleanor Marx, Karl Marx's daughter, had organized the gas workers and thousands of the poorest-paid semiskilled and unskilled workers in the last decade of the nineteenth century. Now the seat was held by Reg Prentice, Labour's shadow minister for education, a right-winger, with a huge majority for Labour. I accepted.

CHAPTER 16

Our party members in Newham found a vacant shop in Green Street and rented it for three weeks for our election headquarters. Their families, friends, and supporters supplied trestle tables and chairs, made cups of tea and sandwiches, and sat for hours cutting out columns of names and addresses on the electoral register and pasting them up into canvassing cards. The party press printed sixty-five thousand election statements, and we folded each one and addressed it for the Post Office to collect each day. Electoral law in Britain gives a political party the right to free postage for its campaign material in a general election.

We had barely three weeks for the election campaign. Heath had dissolved Parliament and set the election date as early as was allowed by law. By the end of the first week it seemed that every other house had a "Vote Prentice, Vote Labour" sticker in its front window, but we soon found that Prentice and his policies were far from popular. Scarcely any householder had a good word to say either for the Labour Party or for their MP. We were on the streets at six-thirty every morning, outside the huge Ford plant in Dagenham, the Tate & Lyle depot in Silvertown, the docks, the railway stations, and the bus stops. We held open-air meetings on the High Street outside the supermarkets, indoor meetings in the colleges and hospitals. In the evenings we canvassed door to door, from six until nine o'clock. Our campaign grew in strength as the number of our canvassers and helpers grew. By the eve of the poll more than eight hundred had applied to join our party. We had canvassed every household in the borough at least once.

Again and again I was told: "You are the only party that has bothered to come and see us." A huge part of Newham consisted of rows of small terraced houses, split into bed-sitting-rooms and rented out privately or from the Council. The average wage was about £20 a week, or £30 if the job was skilled. Wages in industry were held down by law, and prices were rising fast. Economic conditions were deteriorating rapidly, but prices, wages, and unemployment were not the only subjects that workers talked about. In my election address I had warned about the plans for a military dictatorship in Britain. I said that the economic crisis could not possibly be resolved by Parliament or through the ballot box, but only by building the Workers' Revolutionary Party as the means for the working class to take power. I called for Councils of Action, the occupation of factories, and a workers' militia to replace the standing army and the police. When I explained this program at a press conference it evoked a largely hostile coverage. *The Guardian* said that the Workers' Revolutionary Party program was "alarmist," but in the front rooms of the terraced houses where I was invited for a talk and a cup of tea, and at the four public meetings we held in different wards in the constituency, people listened, asked questions, argued, and often agreed.

The Tory election theme was "moderation versus extremism." The miners were "holding the country to ransom." They were blamed for inflation, for the energy crisis, the three-day workweek, and the plight of pensioners and small children. The predominantly Tory newspapers ran stories about orphanages where children huddled in the dark during power cuts, and about old-age pensioners dying of hypothermia. Despite this, it was evident that the Tory campaign was not succeeding. No one believed that the miners were to blame for the three-day workweek. Some dock workers told us of oil tankers deliberately kept at anchor by the port authorities, unable to discharge their cargo.

It rained on election day, as it had done throughout the campaign. Our canvassing returns promised us about one thousand votes, and we pressed every car we could find into service to call on our supporters and transport the pensioners among them to the polling stations. Soon after the polls closed I walked up to a door and was welcomed by a middle-aged worker who had promised to vote for me. "I'm sorry," he said. "When I got there, I voted Labour. I was anxious and I wanted to make sure we kept the Tories out." But he insisted on inviting me into his home. He said he still agreed with our manifesto and had been so impressed with the way our party worked in the area that he wanted to join.

The Labour candidate won the Newham seat with a big majority over the Conservatives. I had just over seven hundred votes. In the country no party had an overall majority. The next day there was no formal announcement that the Palace had summoned Labour leader Harold Wilson, and as we walked down Oxford Street we saw a convoy of armored cars with soldiers in full battle dress crossing Oxford Circus into Regent Street. On Monday, March 4, 1974, Prime Minister Heath resigned, having failed to persuade the Liberals to support his government. Wilson became prime minister, and two days later Michael Foot met the miners' leaders at the Coal Board and settled their claim.

Wilson's government was unstable from the outset, not because it lacked an overall majority in Parliament, but because the state security services and army intelligence were at work to destabilize it. In the North of Ireland, operation "Clockwork Orange" was started. Its purpose was to change the leadership of all three parties at Westminster. A journalist on the *Investors' Chronicle* made a tour of officers' messes and wrote: "The most serious fact is that one top general apparently took three months' leave of absence to write a manual on how and in what circumstances the army would take over."

In July the *Evening News* published on its front page a statement by a retired army officer, General Sir Walter Walker. "Perhaps the country might choose rule by the gun in preference to anarchy," he commented. He had spoken with officers who had fought in the

Burma campaign and who were saying, "What we want is a leader who will put forward fundamental democratic principles like rule by the gun under an army junta that the man in the street can follow." In August, *Peace News,* the pacifist weekly, published a memorandum by the founder of the Special Air Services (SAS), Colonel David Stirling. He had founded a paramilitary strike-breaking organization called Great Britain '75. "The immediate purpose of our project," he wrote, "is to provide on a volunteer basis the minimum manpower necessary to cope with the immediate crisis following a general strike or a near general strike, in the knowledge that the government of the day must welcome our initiative and would assume responsibility for our volunteer force and reinforce it as best it can."

Alex Mitchell, on the editorial board of the *Workers' Press,* wrote an article headlined WHAT IS THE CIA UP TO IN BRITAIN?, revealing that the former assistant deputy director of the CIA's planning department in Washington (the "Department of Dirty Tricks") had been sent to London. With thirty or forty operatives, the CIA was gaining information about the trade unions' left-wing organizations. The year's events brought another general election, on October 10. Our meetings in the October election campaign in Newham were packed. I must have made a score of speeches in public since my first effort a year before, and although I had gained in confidence, I still needed sheaves of notes to make a twenty-minute speech. Gerry, who spoke after me, was the best political orator I have ever heard. He would use three or four cards, with at most two or three lines of notes on each card. He would invariably begin very quietly, as if thinking aloud, his hands thrust deep into the pockets of his jacket. Then, as his speech progressed, he would seem to summon all the force of his intellect and personality, binding himself and his audience together. If it is said that Marxism is the conscious expression of the unconscious historical process, such a union could be observed for sure on those occasions when Gerry spoke to an audience of workers. Without rhetorical tricks or flourishes, he would use the full range of his political vocabulary, expressing complex ideas in a way that everyone understood. I never saw an audience who did not respond.

At the final meeting of the campaign, Gerry concentrated on the issue of the racist MP Enoch Powell and the danger of a military coup. The fascist National Front were campaigning all over the East

End. At first they thought we might be friendly. They assumed that because we supported the PLO we were anti-Semitic. They soon discovered that we believed in the joint struggle of Jews and Palestinians against fascism and racism, and we got several threats. I discovered that quite a few former Communist Party members were as racist as the National Front, which set me thinking.

≡

It was a very busy period. My children suffered from the amount of time I had to spend away from them, Natasha and Joely the most. It was difficult for me but worse for them, and it would not have been possible without first of all Christine, then Linda, and finally Silvana. Thanks to them there was always a caring, loving young woman to take responsibility, listen to the children's problems, and be there for them when I was unavailable. I had made Natasha a new bedroom with a small desk, because she now had so much homework. One night I sat by her bed, my knees on the floor, kissing and hugging her good night, having sung songs to Joely and Carlo in their bunks in the adjoining room. Natasha appealed to me to spend more time with her. I tried to explain that our political struggle was for her future, and that of all the children of her generation. She looked at me with a serious, sweet smile. "But I need you *now*. I won't need you so much then." It was true. She and Joely needed me. The time we spent talking, laughing, or playing together was seldom long and always very precious. They naturally did not understand when I told them that many children could not live a happy life with their parents because of the injustice and cruelty of our society. Or rather, they did understand, but understanding did not lessen the loss they felt.

They understood my grief when Timothy Dalton broke off our relationship because I told him I was going to a big rally for trade unionists in Manchester one Sunday afternoon when he wanted me to stay with him. We had both been very much in love, and so it was all the worse that he could not accept what I was doing. I went to the rally and sang at a concert afterward. I listened to the speeches and knew that I could not and would not give up. Since my early childhood I had been convinced that fascism, war, and the destruction of peoples because of their race, religion, or politics must be fought against. I cried coming back on the train, and again the next morning at breakfast. Tasha and Joely put their arms about me. I told them why I was crying and they comforted me.

I set off for Los Angeles in December 1974 to play Lady Macbeth, with Charlton Heston in the title role, in a production at the giant Ahmanson Theatre. Before my departure I discussed with Gerry our plan to buy a house and convert it into a school, a college of Marxist education. We wanted a house in the country with enough room for fifty students, a lecture room, and a library. We decided that I would give four lectures on Marxism in Los Angeles to raise as much money as possible.

Joely, Tasha, Carlo, and I spent the Christmas holiday in Tony's house above Sunset Boulevard, where he now lived permanently, astonished and delighted with the warmth of the Los Angeles weather, and the luck of having a small swimming pool. With Tony's help I found a school for Joely for the spring term, among the eucalyptus trees in the valley in north Los Angeles. Tasha had to leave us to return to St. Paul's Girls' School in London. Tony had decided she should leave the French Lycée and have an English education, and that Joely would join her at St. Paul's in the autumn term.

I was looking forward to working with Peter Wood again. He had directed me in *The Prime of Miss Jean Brodie*, and would now direct *Macbeth*. When Tasha flew back to London, Joely, Carlo, and I settled down to our California life, which for me meant rehearsing *Macbeth* and preparing my four lectures on Marxism. In this way we saw in the New Year of 1975.

The first rehearsals were lively and interesting. Charlton Heston, John Ireland, and I were excited by Peter Wood's idea of the witches. They were embodied in the corpses of Cawdor's rebel army on the battlefield in Act I, scene i, rising up from the stench and smoke of the battlefield to chant "When shall we three meet again?" The assassins hired by Macbeth to murder Banquo, Fleance, Lady Macduff, and her son were also the witches. It was a brilliant conception, connecting the witches with the violence and cruelty of war and Macbeth's superstitious despotism.

For all that, some fundamental concept was lacking through which to grasp the essence of the play as a whole. What is Macbeth's superstition? A company of actors may readily conclude it was the superstition of the age, and yet, less than half a century after *Macbeth* was written, no one believed in "hobgoblins" or such creatures anymore, according to contemporary observers of Cromwell's republic.

Scholars have debated over the dating of *Macbeth.* From internal evidence it seems likely that it was performed at the court of King James I of England and VI of Scotland, probably in 1606. Shakespeare's company then had a royal charter, and Malcolm, crowned King of Scotland at the play's end, was James's ancestor. In Act IV, scene iii, Malcolm describes the English king, Edward the Confessor, as having miraculous powers of healing:

> and 'tis spoken
> To the succeeding royalty he leaves
> The healing benediction. With this strange virtue,
> He hath a heavenly gift of prophecy . . .

James, though affecting to belittle his own healing and prophetic powers, made sure that his bishops promoted belief in both. He wrote a treatise on witchcraft and possession by evil spirits, *Daemonologie,* published in 1597, which became a rubric for religious and political persecution during his reign and his son's. James also murdered two Scottish nobles, the Ruthnen brothers, chieftains of the Gowrie clan. He arrived at their castle with a company of soldiers on a surprise visit and requested dinner. After supper the two Ruthnen brothers were stabbed to death, and James declared he had been forced to kill them because they had attempted to assassinate him. He made his ministers sign their names to corroborate his story, but none of his contemporaries believed it. On March 28, 1606, Henry Garnet, Provincial of the Jesuit Society in England, was brought to trial, having been indicted for complicity in the Gunpowder Plot. James was present in the court that day, incognito, disguised as a commoner. The more we read of James's rule, the more his features merge with those of Shakespeare's Scottish tyrant, Macbeth. "Stands Scotland where it did?" asks Macduff, and Ross replies,

> Alas! poor country,
> Almost afraid to know itself. It cannot

> Be called our mother, but our grave; where nothing,
> But who knows nothing, is once seen to smile.

Macbeth cannot be understood without a knowledge of this history. And yet that knowledge will not, of itself, bring the play to life. To do that, we must examine our own times. The poet Osip Mandelstam, for instance, called Stalin "the Kremlin Highlander,"* and indeed the play was never performed in the Soviet Union during Stalin's reign of terror. Stalin also liked to be present, unseen, at the trials of his victims. A recent Soviet documentary pointed out a small window high in the wall above the judges' bench in the hall where the Moscow trials were held, from which an invisible Stalin could look down directly into the dock. If we had discussed the simplest, most fundamental everyday facts of political life, facts, so to speak, right under our noses, the essence of *Macbeth* would have emerged more clearly for us and for the audience. Memories of Nixon's downfall were still fresh, and there were many accounts of his last days in office. According to one witness, Nixon, abandoned by his former colleagues, wandered the corridors of the White House, praying to the portraits of his predecessors.

> Now does he feel his title
> Hang loose upon him, like a giant's robe
> Upon a dwarfish thief.

But these are notes for the *Macbeth* that might have been, or for some future *Macbeth*. The *Macbeth* that filled every seat in the Ahmanson Theatre was bloody, bold, and resolute—and essentially rather decent. One day, perhaps, I will get the chance to make another attempt.

I gave the four lectures on Marxism during my stay in Hollywood, and learned something of that town's political history. I met technicians who remembered the ferocious battles with police and strikebreakers in the 1930s, when the bosses tried to stamp out the unions in the studios. Many actors and writers who came to hear my lectures had been members or supporters of the Communist Party in the

---

*A double entendre, "Highlander" also referring to Stalin's Georgian nationality.

forties and fifties and had suffered from the blacklist. A beautiful and talented actress whose career had been blasted by the McCarthy purges said I was brave to speak out. I tried to turn the compliment aside, because I spoke in the way I knew and had learned to speak in my party, and bravery didn't come into it, but I understood what she meant. When the purges began, the Communist Party of America took a "low profile" and told its members to do the same, claiming the Fifth Amendment or the First Amendment; it did not lead any political struggle against McCarthy. And so its members—who were courageous, or wanted to be—were abandoned politically, with no movement to support them and, worse, with no clear theoretical lead to explain why they were being persecuted or what to do about it. I thought again of my father, how he had feared for me, and how cynically the Communist Party leaders had treated his questions when he had been blacklisted and went to them for advice.

The collections at my lectures and the many donations I received from film and theatre people in Hollywood came to more than twenty thousand dollars, at least half the sum we needed to buy a house in the country and convert it into a full-time school of Marxism. One visit—with Groucho Marx—I remember with special pride and pleasure. It gave me a great deal of inward satisfaction at the time because Elliott Gould, who could be very funny and very helpful, would try to irritate me by answering my telephone calls with "Hello, this is Groucho Marx." So it was thrilling to sit with Groucho in his house and listen to this old gentleman, who was *very* funny and very courteous, talk about his battles with the studios. We told him why we wanted a school of Marxism in Britain. "There's one thing I don't like about Britain," he said. "On second thought, there are several things. But the thing I least like is the monarchy." He promised a donation, which never materialized, not because he changed his mind but because his affairs were complicated by a dispute, which broke out soon after his death, between his family and his companion.

At the end of March 1975 we returned to England, where Natasha joined us again. We had missed each other terribly. I went up to Parwich in the Derbyshire Peak District to see White Meadows, a large, empty house, once a youth hostel, that Corin had found. It was half derelict and would need a great deal of work to restore, but the dollars we had raised in America meant that we could buy it and do the work of restoration ourselves. We got planning permission from the Peak Park Planning Board and set about converting White Meadows into a school. One of our members was an architect. He was not young, so we booked a room for him in the nearby Bentley Brook Hotel. But when he saw that our younger members, workers in the building trade, were camping in the house itself so that they could start work at first light, he gallantly said to hell with the hotel and joined them with his sleeping bag. Roy Battersby, who was to be warden of the school, camped there too, and the work proceeded at a terrific pace all summer. The derelict part of the building was gutted, and in its place a canteen for sixty people took shape: a kitchen, a laundry, storerooms, and above, a flat for Battersby and his family. A new wing was added to the main part of the house, with a large dormitory above and a lecture room and library below. Carpets were laid, bathrooms and showers fitted and plumbed, and new wiring was installed throughout. We were all determined to open the school on August 27, and I enrolled for the first course. We had decided that it would be for our comrades in the entertainment unions.

≡

It must have been about this time that the national press, one of whose chief functions is to invent misleading labels, came up with a new term for right-wing trade unionists: they were called "moderates." Their opponents were "extremists." Equity had a right-wing leadership. When you explain to people that in Equity's constitution the annual general meeting has absolutely no powers whatever, that whatever policy the members may decide on at AGMs can be immediately overruled or simply ignored by the Council, they are amazed. In fact, the only body in political life in Britain whose annual conference is as powerless, constitutionally, as Equity's is the Tory party. And that system was what the "moderates" in Equity were seeking to preserve. There was only one area in which the members had some power at an AGM, and that was in the matter of the constitution itself. Union rules could be changed only by a two-thirds majority vote at an annual general meeting. This the new Council immediately set out to change. They announced a special general meeting for October 12. A resolution would be proposed by the

Council for power to change rules by referendum, in a postal ballot.

The postal ballot is not a democratic method for deciding issues. When an answer must be either Yes or No, much depends on how the question is put, what arguments for and against it are printed, and who is selected to put forward each side. It is, in fact, far less democratic than a series of member meetings on the issue, since only in meetings can questions be raised and further implications be discussed. An informed process is the most democratic. A summary paragraph or two on a ballot is clearly the lowest level of information. In this case the leaders of the union would have total control over the presentation of the issue, and many of its aspects could be evaded or neglected.

In the summer of 1975, when I was filming *Murder on the Orient Express* at Elstree Studios with Sidney Lumet and a galaxy of stars playing Agatha Christie's murder suspects, Sidney suggested we should have only a half-hour lunch break, something that was unheard-of at that time. I rang Equity, who sent the film organizer down, and the cast met in the lunch break. Around the table sat Sean Connery, Albert Finney, Rachel Roberts, Ingrid Bergman, Michael York, Jacqueline Bisset, Richard Widmark, and Colin Blakeley. The organizer said it was up to us; we could make our own decision on whether to accept the half-hour lunch break or not. I said it was not only ourselves we were deciding for. I spoke of the economic crisis, the continuous attack on the unions, and the fact that Elstree Studios were soon to be closed. I said that if we, who no doubt had the power to refuse, said that we could manage without a full lunch break, others would soon be forced to accept it, and we should have opened a door for all employers to increase the workload and thereby cut pay throughout the industry.

Our famous cast considered the question seriously, but since the organizer had said that they could accept the half-hour break, and since they had disagreed with my view that there was a danger of our setting a precedent, they voted to accept. Almost immediately stories appeared in the press that Vanessa was causing trouble at Elstree on Sidney Lumet's film. It seemed most unlikely that any member of our cast would have volunteered such misinformation to the press, and I was forced to consider the possibility that someone from the union offices might have telephoned them. Sadly, my suspicions proved correct. There was indeed a regular two-way channel of communication between the press and Equity's offices for stories about me and my party. In any event we all thoroughly enjoyed the filming, and I was especially pleased to get to know Sean Connery, whose fiancée I played in the film.

≡

I spent two weeks up at our college in August and September, and from 1975 to 1985 I went there to study at least two weeks every year. We worked from 9:00 A.M. to 1:00 P.M., and from 3:00 P.M. to 6:30 P.M., and read and discussed questions that had arisen until the ten o'clock news on television. It was difficult but immensely exciting to learn to think about and discuss the process by which the changes in the world of nature and social life are reflected in thought. The students included some who had studied at universities, some who, like myself, had had training in a profession, industrial workers, and young people who had never had the chance to get a real education in anything.

Tasha and Joely were both now at St. Paul's Girls' School in Hammersmith. Carlo was in his first year at primary school. They had a new nanny, Silvana Sammassimo. She and Carlo spoke Italian together, and thanks to her he grew up as fluent in Italian as in English. As time went on she became my secretary, and then my agent and dear friend. Corin had separated from his wife, Deirdre, and for a while he lived in the basement of our house in St. Peter's Square.

My party branch was in Central London, and when I wasn't filming I worked with the branch every day. We sold papers early in the morning outside the post office in Rathbone Place, and at hospitals and colleges. We delivered them to our daily readers before they went to work and at lunchtime. In the evenings we canvassed new readers, had pub sales, and took our paper to sell to printworkers in Fleet Street. Every morning at eight o'clock we analyzed political developments and made day-to-day decisions. At nine the editorial board of the *Workers' Press* met to discuss the main stories and analyze the news. The paper was still produced with "hot type" at this time. Molten metal was used for the letters, which then cooled as they were "set" on boards in a complicated process that required skill and speed. When the type had cooled and been inked, paper was rolled over it and then cut into pages the size of the *New York Post.* It went to press at lunchtime and was then sorted into parcels, which were sent overnight to Scotland, the Northeast, the Midlands, and Wales. Comrades in London came into our center in Clapham around midnight to collect the papers and take them to the main drops throughout London.

Early on Sunday morning, September 26, 1975, I had a telephone call. One of our comrades said, "Get a copy of *The Observer* immediately." I ran upstairs to the front door and found the newspaper lying on the mat. I saw my photograph and the headlines on the front page: POLICE RAID THE RED HOUSE, with a photograph of White Meadows, our college. The report alleged that the WRP ran a military-style organization at the college and that police had raided it the previous night looking for weapons in the grounds. About a hundred police with dogs and pocket flares had burst into the college as the students were having a cup of tea at about ten o'clock. They had no search warrant. They had confined Gerry to his study and searched all the students, including a couple of elderly women. One of the policemen had put his hand into a cupboard where we kept cleaning brushes and detergents and pulled out five bullets. Apparently they were .22 bullets of the kind farmers use for shooting rabbits, but no one in the college had a gun, and the bullets could not have been in the cupboard unless someone had put them there deliberately.

I knew an enormous political frame-up had taken place, in the context of the destabilization of the Wilson government. As Marxists, we were totally opposed to terrorism. We were not terrorists. We did not carry, store, or trade weapons, and if we had ever discovered a member involved with weapons or drugs, such a member would immediately have been expelled from the party.

Clearly Marxist ideas were now considered to be dangerous. This was the first political raid in Britain since World War II, when the homes of Gerry and his comrades had been raided, and some members had been tried and imprisoned, accused of "incitement" because they alone defended the young miners from exploitation during the war.

Tasha and Joely were very frightened, and they spent that day and the next night with Corin's wife, Deirdre, and their two cousins.

They dreaded what might be said at school that day, thinking everyone would be talking about their mother and father and asking questions. Happily school went by normally. When I and my party have been attacked or libeled in the press I certainly feel the pressure and can be very hurt. But my children and Corin's are far more vulnerable, and that has been hard for them and for me.

All the television news programs contacted our newspaper office, and on Monday I agreed to appear on two of them, just after the main news at six o'clock in the evening. I would be interviewed first by Eamonn Andrews for ITV and next by Sue Lawley for the BBC. I met Eamonn Andrews, and we went on the air "live." I took a deep breath and warned the trade unions and Labour Party members that this organized frame-up of the WRP meant that we all faced a new and major struggle for our basic democratic rights. That Monday every single newspaper carried headlines and news stories about the police raid. Featured prominently were quotes from Peter Plouviez, Equity's general secretary. Equity members were warned that they must defeat the Redgraves at the special general meeting, which was to discuss the rule changes on October 12.

On Thursday, October 2, I went up to Blackpool and joined other comrades who were getting signatures for our petition, "Hands off the Workers' Revolutionary Party." Jack Jones, general secretary of the largest trade union in Britain, the Transport and General Workers' Union, signed, and so did Communist Party trade unionists, including Jack Collins, leader of the Kent miners, and many others. Some of them telephoned the *Morning Star* and said that they would cancel their subscriptions unless the paper took a united-front position and defended our basic democratic rights. "An injury to one is an injury to all," the fundamental historical position of the trade unions, was no empty catchphrase. Workers, and many trade union leaders, knew that we had been framed.

In a few weeks about seven million trade unionists had come to our defense. Most Equity members signed our petition. I remember my shock and bitterness when an actor, a close friend, not only refused to sign but even refused to talk to me. In 1975 many middle-class people still had illusions about British democracy, and many tended to believe what they read in the press. "If you call yourselves the Workers' *Revolutionary* Party," said one, "surely you must expect this kind of thing to happen to you."

We worked night and day to collect signatures and to rally Equity members to the Coliseum Theatre on Sunday, October 12. The Coliseum was packed and the overflow had to be accommodated in another theatre. Press reporters and photographers were everywhere. Lord Olivier, then Sir Laurence, had appealed for the defeat of the "extremists" in a letter to *The Times*. I remembered that he had been a guard on the Underground to help break the General Strike of 1926. In 1975, the acting élite—who had regular employment and close ties with judges, lawyers, newspaper proprietors, and the armed services—lined up, with honorable exceptions, against "The Redgraves." The actors and actresses who suffered all the slings and arrows of our profession, including unemployment, low wages, and constant humiliation, were on the whole distrustful of the Equity Council, which had never lifted a finger to change the terrible conditions in which most performers work. Today leading actors and directors and most professional people are extremely alarmed and angry about the drastic deterioration in living conditions, in the arts, education, and health, and are deeply offended by the government's contempt for truth and for basic democratic rights.

In spite of the police raid, the press witch-hunt, and an appeal by Sir Laurence Olivier, the Equity Council failed to get the two-thirds majority needed to institute the referendum. Immediately after their defeat, they took Equity's constitution to court, where it was judged that Equity's rules *could* be changed by referendum. We engaged a solicitor and a barrister and got the High Court decision overturned on appeal. Then they went to the House of Lords, which overruled the Appeals Court.

In December 1975, six thousand trade unionists marched with us to Trafalgar Square. Robert Bolt, the playwright, who was at this time president of the Association of Cinema and Television Technicians union, spoke on our platform, along with other trade unionists. Some Labour MPs stood up in Parliament and challenged Home Secretary James Callaghan (responsible for the police and the secret services) to declare whether or not there were grounds for the raid and for prosecutions of members of the Workers' Revolutionary Party. What happened, and how this provocation was organized, could be exposed only if we sued *The Observer* for libel. It was in the course of this libel case, which came into the High Court in October 1978, that we officially cleared our names and put on record the truth of our party's position on terrorism, and the truth of the role of the state and the Labour government in the police raid.

The support we received indicated that a great many people, and many of them in the theatre profession, were very uneasy about the role of the press. This was particularly true for older people in the profession, like Rachel and Michael. As often happens, my marriage, family, and career had taken me away from my parents, and then my intense involvement in political work in the seventies distanced me from them. I found it difficult to explain this work to Michael and Rachel initially, but with the *Observer* case, they, like many others, supported our demand for basic democratic rights and were not deceived by the avalanche of articles in the press. In the late seventies and early eighties, when Corin and Michael worked together on his autobiography, the distance between us all closed again, and Michael became involved in both film and theatre projects organized by the party, which meant that I had the tremendous pleasure of acting with him again in 1982.

CHAPTER 17

Circle in the Square is a protected island in the middle of Manhattan's tempestuous theatrical seascape. At Circle in the Square the plays, some new, some revivals, run for two or three months, and the theatre has an audience that likes and understands what it is trying to do. It takes much dedication, imagination, and knowledge of plays and audiences to build up a theatre like that in New York, and its artistic director, Theodore Mann, has all those qualities and more. I first came to know him in 1975, when Tony and I asked if we could do Ibsen's *Lady from the Sea* there. Both of us were excited to try theatre-in-the-round, and fortunately Ted was excited by us, so he made some space in his program and we got down to business.

Since that time I have got to know Ted and his gentle, brilliant wife, Pat, really well, and they let me stay at their apartment on Seventh Avenue when I come to New York. It is old and spacious, with high ceilings and lovely old brown furniture, and hot-water pipes that hiss, gurgle, and spit during the night. It's very peaceful for Manhattan—which means it is shatteringly noisy between one and four in the morning, when the garbage trucks load up all the refuse from the Carnegie Deli and the apartment blocks along Seventh. We celebrated my son's twentieth birthday there, and the opening of *Orpheus Descending* in September 1989, and the apartment almost split its capacious seams when all the artists from America and Russia celebrated after our "Wall Breaks" concert that December. We chatted into the early hours with Ted's son and daughter-in-law, John and Claudia, eating pints of Häagen-Dazs ice cream. We gathered with Russian and American historians, prepared poetry recitals, and listened to Pat's mother play piano rags in celebration of Thanksgiving. I've received coaching from Ted and shared many loving and important moments with Pat and Ted.

But back in 1976, Carlo was six and a half years old, and I'd rented a painter's apartment on Third Avenue. For my thirty-ninth birthday I sat at a small wooden table with Carlo and Silvana, celebrating with a bowl of Rice Krispies. This time both Tasha and Joely stayed behind in London—Tasha with her schoolfriend Elisa, and Joely with her cousins, Jemma and Luke. Even though Deirdre was now divorced from Corin, she was really kind and agreed to look after Joely while I was away.

The Lady from the Sea was my first appearance in New York, and as things turned out, my only appearance until, fourteen years later, I played another Lady in *Orpheus Descending.* There were plenty of offers in the 1960s to appear on Broadway, including the chance to work with Mike Nichols in *The Little Foxes,* but I turned them all down. I did not feel that playing on Broadway was a goal in my life, and what is more, I felt certain I could do no good work under the kind of excessive pressure and hype I had seen at close quarters when Tony worked there soon after we were married. But to work at Circle in the Square, a theatre that depended on subsidy and could measure its success or failure in terms other than the weekly gross at the box office, was closer, in my experience, to working at theatres like Stratford, Manchester Royal Exchange, or the Royal Court in London. I greatly admire the people who make theatre in America. The work of many American actors, directors, designers, and companies—Steppenwolf, for example—has been inspirational. But the Broadway system can be very damaging. The West End today is becoming increasingly like Broadway; both places make it practically impossible for new plays to be performed unless there are several leading names in the cast. But Theodore Mann and his partner, Paul Libin, were from the generation whose creativity I had glimpsed back in 1955, and twenty years later I was delighted to be working with Tony again.

Rehearsing with Tony was one of the greatest pleasures I ever had. He was very sharp and intelligent, and because he knew his own mind and had a firm conception of what he wanted, he really listened to others and was never afraid of asking or taking advice. He had an absolute scorn of playing things safe and could be very provocative. One day in rehearsals, Pat Hingle, our leading man, became exasperated with Ibsen's portrayal of Ellida. He simply couldn't tolerate her and became more and more impatient with her suffering. Tony urged him to think of his own wife, whereupon Pat burst out: "If she was my wife I'd hit her." Tony was thoroughly delighted. He laughed and clapped his hands, as if this was the funniest joke he'd heard that year, and urged Pat to drop all restraint and do just that. "Go on, hit Vanessa! Hit her hard! It'll do her good!" I have been hit a few times in my life, but no one had ever suggested this should happen, apart from Edith Evans when I was very small, and I waited anxiously for a box on my ears. But despite Tony's prompting, it never came.

Ellida is Ibsen's most sensitive and profound exploration of a woman's longing to discover and share fully in the life of her times. The play deals with the awful harm inflicted on women, especially married women, by the hypocritical morality and laws of bourgeois society. I identified very much with her yearning for the unknown, and for the freedom she had before marriage, when she was a lighthouse keeper's daughter on the seashore. Nonetheless I found many areas of the play very difficult to grasp, and as often happens when we don't fully understand something, I resorted to demonstrating what I thought the scene was about.

Tim Dalton and I had got back together again, and he came to New York from filming in Los Angeles with Mae West. He saw the play, and his criticism drove me to reexamine what I was doing. I realized that in demonstrating what was happening to Ellida I was avoiding the contradictions in her moments of development. I was acting what she knew, and avoiding all the things she did not know or understand. "Science," Engels says in *Dialectics of Nature*, "has to investigate what we do not know." And so, though it is not a science, does acting.

After the first night Tony and I went to a café, and his assistant went off to get the reviews. When Clive Barnes, the drama critic of *The New York Times,* said I was "a child of nature" and praised Tony's production, we all heaved a sigh of relief and knew we had a success. I was contracted to play for twelve weeks, at one thousand dollars a week, less than half what I had earned the last time I had worked with Tony, in 1972, in *The Threepenny Opera* at the Prince of Wales Theatre in London. I mention this remembering my father's advice to his mother, when she was old and in a nursing home in Stanmore. He sent her some school copybooks, suggesting that since she remembered so much about the theatre of her days, it should be recorded. "Don't write what you thought of this or that actor or actress," he said, "so much as what you were paid, working conditions, landladies, Sunday 'train-calls,' and the rest of it." His father, Roy, died penniless, with only just enough to pay for a plain tombstone. Michael died with no savings in the bank, and my mother, in her eighties, still has to work as often as she can to pay the bills.

In the sixties and early seventies I had earned some large salaries for films, *Mary, Queen of Scots* and *The Devils,* which I had put into the Vanessa Redgrave Nursery School. I don't remember ever reading an article in the press that complained that I gave my money to a school. But from the time I joined the WRP in 1973 the press continually wrote: "She gives all her money to the party," as if to warn employers not to hire me because they would be subsidizing the WRP, and, in fact, my earnings fell very considerably. For *Agatha*, costarring with Dustin Hoffman, I was paid £25,000. From that I paid a 10 percent agent's commission, a 60 percent corporation tax, national insurance, and employee taxes for Silvana and Sandra Marsh, my secretary, which left about £7000 for the year to pay the bills. I paid my weekly subscription to the party, like every other member, and if I could lend a sum to the party for some special need, I did; it was always paid back. Franco has been a truly kind and generous friend, helping me to find work when I have been in difficulties. After we separated, Tony gave me about £200 a month to bring up the girls. I am proud of the men I loved, the fathers of my children. All of us despise professional women who drain their former husbands of money when they divorce, so we shared everything, which is how it should be.

One night as I came into the Circle in the Square to get ready for the performance, Pam, one of the usherettes, who used to baby-sit for Carlo on her night off, gave me a book. "You must read this—it should be made into a film and you should play Julia." That night when I got home I read Lillian Hellman's *Pentimento* from start to finish. It is a memoir, and in it she tells the story of a remarkable woman who had been her friend from childhood, and whom she had last seen in Germany just before the war, when Julia asked her to participate in a risky couriering exercise between Paris and Berlin. Julia was killed by the Nazis for her resistance work. Next day at the theatre I found a message from Fred Zinnemann. I telephoned his office the following morning and heard that he was casting for the film *Julia*, with Jane Fonda, and wanted to meet me.

Zinnemann was kind, but he was also extremely cautious. I decided to take the bull by the horns and told him I wanted to play the part of Julia. He gave me the script to take away and read. Julia's role was very small, but that did nothing to affect my desire to play her. I rang my agent and told him that he should accept their first offer without argument.

Julia, as described by Lillian Hellman, was a communist in outlook. Also, like Lillian, she was Jewish. She was one of millions of ordinary/extraordinary people who sacrificed everything to defeat German fascism. I knew that *Julia* was a true story before Lillian Hellman confirmed it. Every line in her book told me that. Not long before she died, Lillian also told me that her own part in the story was true, and I believed her. I did not meet her until 1984, but after I had done the film she revealed that she had insisted on my being cast as Julia. "You're so like the lady in question, it's uncanny." A controversy arose because Mary McCarthy and others accused Lillian Hellman of lying. It was said that *Julia* was based on the story of an American woman, Muriel Gardiner, whom Lillian had not known. "Every word she writes," said Mary McCarthy, "is a lie, including *and* and *the*." Lillian began a libel action but died before it came to court. No one can say what the outcome would have been, but one thing is sure: her story has survived, and will survive, as a compellingly truthful account of a woman's struggle against fascism, long after the attacks by Lillian's opponents have been buried and forgotten.

The part of Julia became even smaller in the second and third versions of Alvin Sargent's script, and many of the political references in the first draft were cut out. Fred asked me to discuss each new version with him. I told him I was sorry at what had been cut, not because it affected the size of my part, but because the political references were true, and were taken directly from Lillian's book. Fred looked at me with his serious eyes. "But I *told* you it was not going to be a political film. Are you not happy with the script?" I assured him that I was very happy, and realized almost at once another reason for Fred's caution. Some of his greatest films had been made when the House Un-American Activities Committee was at work: *High Noon* with Gary Cooper, which no studio had wanted to finance, and which had a script by a blacklisted Hollywood screenwriter, had been considered possibly subversive by the committee.

I learned a great deal from Zinnemann, whose work I had admired ever since I saw *The Search* as a young girl, and later *From Here to Eternity*. Fred is a master storyteller with an expert control of his narrative. Two nights before Jane and I filmed the café scene where Julia and Lillian meet in Nazi-controlled Berlin, he asked us both to look at the scene for cuts. "It's too long," he said. "Please give me your suggestions tomorrow." That's the main scene of the film, I thought to myself, and I approached the task with some reluctance. But when I looked at the script, trying to see the scene in the context of the whole film, I found that he was right: a lot could be cut, especially from Julia's lines. Fred was very pleased with my ideas, and I was excited that he trusted me enough to make my own cuts.

Jane and I had traveled along very different roads since the time we worked together with GIs against the Vietnam War. But we worked on *Julia* in perfect harmony. Four years later, in 1980, *Time* magazine wrote a feature article about me, to coincide with the screening of *Playing for Time*. As usual with such articles, they approached a number of artists who had worked with me, including Jane. I knew her to be a generous friend, generous to other artists in a way that only actors who are confident in themselves and take pride in their work can be. I knew her to be very intelligent and perceptive. But her interview moved me to tears. I was astonished by what she had observed in me. I made a silent wish that I would one day have the chance to talk about her with the same generosity and breadth of mind that she had shown to me.

In Paris, where most of *Julia* was filmed, I lived for some weeks with a Palestinian couple near Billancourt. They were students with very little money and their flat was tiny, one small living room with a gas stove, and an even smaller bedroom. One night they invited a friend to dinner, a Palestinian engineer living in Kuwait, who told me, in a voice choking with emotion and fatigue, of the treatment of Palestinians there. He spoke of the astonishing riches of the Kuwaiti sheikhs, with their palaces and Rolls-Royces.

We spoke of the siege of the Palestinian camp at Tal al-Zaatar, in Lebanon, and how the young men, women, and children had to run a gauntlet of sniper fire when they crossed open ground to fill their cans with water from the only pipe within reach of the camp, all other water having been cut off; and of the horror of the continual bombardment, day after day, month after month. The siege had begun in January 1976, and after many months its sheer savagery had begun to penetrate the indifference of the European press. When the civil war in Lebanon started, it was portrayed in the British press as a fratricidal war between Christians and Muslims, and their many sects. In fact, it was a war, first and foremost, of the rich against the poor, fascist feudal landowners against Lebanese poor peasants and workers organized in their trade unions. And side by side with the Lebanese poor were the Palestinians who had been driven to take refuge in the camps by the Israeli massacres in 1948, 1967, and 1973. The camp of Tal al-Zaatar, the "Hill of Thyme," was next to some of the largest factories in Beirut, which used the camp dwellers for cheap labor. The civil war began with a demonstration by Lebanese fishermen and trade unionists led by Ma'arouf Saad against Camille Chamoun, the feudal boss of the city port of Sidon and its fish-processing factories. The Sidon Lebanese battalion was ordered to fire on the demonstration, and a soldier's or a sniper's bullet killed Ma'arouf Saad. That was the flashpoint for the war.

In the Lebanese civil war the Palestinians—who had organized clinics and hospitals, schools and sanitation, factories and workshops, where before there had been none—joined forces with the Lebanese poor and Kamal Jumblatt's Druze mountain farmers. Some of the rich merchant families, whether Muslim or Christian Druze, supported the Palestinians because their communities had suffered under the old French colonial regime. Opposing them were the Phalangists, feudal absentee landlords and industrialists, Pierre Gemayel's fascist party, and other feudal clans with their militias, all of whom had had acknowledged ties with Hitler, Mussolini, and Franco. They laid siege to the Palestinians in Tal al-Zaatar and vowed to exterminate every man, woman, and child.

What had happened at Tal al-Zaatar was so hideous that I immediately wanted to do something to assist the situation, so I suggested to Gerry Healy that I should go to Lebanon, as Jane Fonda had gone to Vietnam, with a camera team and make a documentary about the Palestinians. He was enthusiastic, and our proposal was endorsed by the Political Committee.

As the tide of the war turned against the Phalangists, the Syrian army, which had been sent into Lebanon by the Arab League as a peacekeeping force, was ordered to turn its guns on the Palestinians and destroy Tal al-Zaatar. What the Phalangists could never do on their own they now did with the assistance of Syrian army detachments. The Palestinians kept silent, at least in public, about this treachery. They knew the Syrian masses still supported them. They knew too that Hafez Assad's regime twisted and turned, now stabbing them in the back, and the next moment offering support. Thousands of Palestinians were refugees in Syria, and many of their fighters were based there. Syrians, as Arabs, were their brothers and sisters, and they too had suffered bombardments, massacres, and the seizure of their villages and pastures in the Golan Heights. I started to plan for the documentary in Paris in 1976, asking French artists if they would take part. I made contacts with film producers and technicians in Italy. Roy Battersby, who had directed many excellent television feature films and documentaries, agreed to direct and brought a first-class cameraman, Ivan Strasberg, into the project.

Back home I sat down with a sheet of paper and made some calculations. Our home at No. 18 St. Peter's Square was a freehold and I had another house around the corner, which I had bought for Jann Stevens and her family when I built the nursery school. She had returned to California, having trained an English swimming instructor to take over her work. I could hope to get £40,000 for my home, and perhaps £25,000 for the other house. I found a small house near Ravenscourt Park, almost opposite Carlo's primary school, for £23,000. I managed to get a mortgage of £18,000 and we moved into 1 Ravenscourt Road. Now I had the money for *The Palestinian.*

In the spring of 1977, Roy flew out to Lebanon about four weeks ahead of me. We had budgeted for a six- to seven-week shooting schedule. Silvana would stay in the house with Carlo, Joely, and Tasha, who was now fourteen. Tasha and Joely discussed plans for a new kitchen with me before I left. Our new house had a tiny old kitchen and an outside lavatory. We needed a new kitchen/dining area and an indoor lavatory, so we agreed that the girls would organize this while I was away. I told them it was unlikely that I would be able to telephone from Lebanon, because we would be constantly on the move. They were both frightened for me. Joely had great difficulty sleeping, sometimes lying awake for hours in the dark. I remembered how Rachel would sing me to sleep, so I sang her a lullaby Jock Addison had composed for Tony's *Midsummer Night's Dream* back when we'd fallen in love.

> You spotted snakes with double tongue,
> Thorny hedgehogs be not seen;
> Newts and blind-worms, do no wrong;
> Come not near our fairy queen.
> Philomel, with melody
> Sing in our sweet lullaby;
> Lulla, lulla, lullaby; lulla, lulla, lullaby.
> Never harm nor spell nor charm
> Come our lovely lady nigh.

CHAPTER 18

The sunshine was hot and dazzling as I came out of the airport at Beirut in May 1977. A group of women came to meet me, kissed me, and gave me some red carnations. They were from the General Union of Palestinian Women. One was the widow of Hani Jawharieh, the Palestinian cameraman who had been killed in the mountains while filming during the war. She took me home and I met her two small children. She told me how she and Hani had first met, arranging the first exhibition of photographs organized by the PLO to show the life of their people. She showed me the handful of Palestinian earth she kept and took me to the cemetery to see Hani's grave. The pine trees stood warm and silent above row upon row of graves, each covered with wreaths and palm leaves and a large photograph of the martyr.

Roy Battersby, Ivan Strasberg, our cameraman, and I were lent a flat to stay in, and we sat down to discuss our schedule. There was a Phalangist conference in a few days' time, and we agreed the crew would go without me and try for an interview with Pierre Gemayel, the Phalangist strongman. Roy Battersby succeeded in persuading him to do an interview for our film and this is what he said:

Everything that happened in Lebanon was due to an intervention by international communism. We were one of the happiest countries in the world. Our people, the workers, the social laws.... Only Lebanon had such liberty and democracy, no other Arab country. Naturally, that challenged international communism to get rid of the government. So we had to fight international communism. I think we overcame it, despite its great strength.

Gemayel spoke in French, sitting in front of the Lebanese flag. He continued:

I began life as a sportsman. I was captain of the football team, president of the Lebanese Football Federation. We attended the 1936 Olympic Games in Berlin. I was impressed by the discipline there, by the bearing and sense of nation.

One of Gemayel's sons, Bashir, was head of the Phalangist militia that had spearheaded the assault on the Palestinian camp at Tal al-Zaatar in 1976, butchering women and children with disgusting savagery. But the Phalangists could never have overcome Tal al-Zaatar without the backing of the CIA, the Israelis, and the Syrian army. The CIA funded Bashir Gemayel and Israeli "advisers," trained the Phalangists, and coordinated the whole operation.

Kamal Jumblatt, leader of the Druze and Progressive Socialist Party, had been assassinated a few months before because he and the Druze supported the Palestinians. No one knew who the assassin was, but everyone knew the CIA was behind the murder, because Jumblatt's people and his party were the strongest Lebanese opposition to the Phalangists and their allies. The director of the CIA from January 1976 to January 1977 was George Bush. Our team got interviews with Bashir Gemayel and Danny Chamoun, and the archbishop who headed the Christian Maronites. One of the Phalangist leaders stated on film that they would kill every Palestinian child they could get their hands on and would welcome the destruction of every city in Lebanon.

I drove with our crew into the eastern zone of Beirut, now controlled by the Phalangists. We had to keep a constant lookout for their militia. A month earlier a young nun had been kidnapped and murdered during a visit to her family in the eastern sector. We parked the car on a sandy road beside some deserted factories. Below us, mounds of rubble stretched to the perimeter of the city. Thirty-five hundred men, women, and children had been slaughtered there during the six-month siege of Tal al-Zaatar. One thousand had been killed on a single day, the final day of the evacuation, as the Red Cross trucks waited at the checkpoints, which were controlled by Syrian armed forces. We filmed there for about an hour, slowly panning the camera across the shattered cinderblocks, the remains of a mosque, twisted corrugated iron, and broken water pipes.

A few days later we met Abu Jaffar, one of the defenders of Tal al-Zaatar. He sat on the floor of a small room with some eighteen-year-old boys in battle fatigues and about fifteen women, some Lebanese, some Palestinian, all of them in black. After a long discussion together, Abu Jaffar said: "Now I am going to sing you Abu Jaffar's song of Tal al-Zaatar."

> O Tal al-Zaatar, you held out against an enemy
> that came like a swarm of locusts.
>
> I sing in honor of your brave heroes,
> who fought and faced rockets and bombs.
>
> I will tell what happened, the truth,
> and I need no witness.
>
> For from the first bullet to the last bomb
> I was there.
>
> The first day twenty thousand bombs fell
> on civilians and soldiers alike.
>
> On the second day there were fifteen thousand
> bombs, and you could see the flames and smoke rising.
>
> On the third day there was a lull while they
> stopped for a rest, only to start again.
>
> And the worse it got, the more like tigers
> our heroes fought.
>
> For two long months we lived through that
> battle, and our hearts turned hard like stone.

We had no water and the food ran out.

And the children were thirsty and cried to
their mothers, "I want my dad," until their
mouths were dry.

And mother says, "He'll be back in the morning,
I promise."

And in the morning the boy asks again,
"Where's my dad?"

And they tell him, "Your father is missing."

And the girl asks her mother, "Where is my brother?"

She says to her, "He is in the trenches."

"Oh my son, he is fighting for honor and dignity,
in a few short hours he is learning the struggle
of a lifetime."

So many young people were victims, so many
martyrs for heaven.

Every mother has to say, "Oh my son,"
and the tears run down her cheeks.

And the girls say, "Oh my brother,"
and visit his house in mourning.

Who can have guests anymore when you've
seen your son lying on the ground?

I had two sons, dearer to me than my sight.
They were so good, it's hard to believe.

Whenever I saw them it was like sunshine,
their cheeks were so rosy.

Yar Yar joined Fateh, and Fawzi the Democratic
Front. You'd say they were like a couple of tigers.

And they went to the mountains and they didn't
come back.

And that day my heart broke.

O God, dear God, bring them back to me.
Bring back all our lost relatives. O God,
whom we worshiped.

It is God's will—the vine is growing but
we pick no grapes.

O God, O merciful God, hear our prayers
and bring them back to us, these miserable
nights.

O Zaatar, the Arab leaders who betrayed you,
now praise you for the way you fought.

They offered you a helping hand to stab you
in the back.

And I know for a fact they are conspiring
again, and those who were martyred live on.

His rough voice rose from his soul. The coal miners of Kentucky and
the old miners from the copper mines of Sicily sing their stories in
the same way. Harsh and deep from the throat, they sing of their
tragedies, the fights, the low wages, the strikes, the deaths of their
sons on the picket lines.

There were about five hundred thousand Palestinians in Lebanon,
living mostly in camps together with the poor Lebanese families.
Before the war in 1976 there had been seven camps in Beirut. Now
there were five. They were similar to the black townships, like
Soweto, in South Africa.

We searched for Dr. Youssef. He and his one colleague, Dr.
Labadi, had run the hospital in Tal al-Zaatar throughout the six-
month siege, and had trained a team of nurses to tend the six thousand casualties. We found him in a small clinic. On his desk beneath
a glass top were photographs of fifteen boys and girls who had been
lined up and shot in front of his eyes. He, too, would have been shot,
but for one of the Syrian soldiers, a captain, who recognized Dr.
Labadi and remembered that he had saved his life about a year before

the siege. Dr. Youssef had seen the Phalangists shoot his nurses while the Syrian forces stood by and watched. "I'll not forget that moment. What is civilization? These people consider themselves the representatives of European civilization in the Middle East. I don't know if European opinion agrees with that. Maybe there is a new definition for civilization? I don't know."

In the Bourj al-Barajneh, Sabra, and Shatilla camps, we visited wounded fighters and children. The Palestine Red Crescent Society, the equivalent of the Red Cross, had built hospitals and clinics where they could receive therapy and be fitted with artificial limbs. We saw a tiny baby with pneumonia struggling for breath with an improvised humidifier made out of a cardboard box over her head. A six-year-old boy lay writhing on his back in a cot, his limbs shaking with uncontrollable spasms, his mouth twisted into a terrible smile. His entire family had been killed in the siege. The doctor introduced me to him, speaking with deep affection. "We love Mohammed: we are his family and he is our brother."

We walked down the narrow alleys between the houses and shacks in Sabra and Shatilla, our guide introducing us to the families. When we said we were from Britain, a sixty-year-old woman invited us for a glass of tea. In the back of her home her daughter was stirring a pot, making sweets for their family business. She told us about life in Palestine under the British mandate. "They took our fields, our flour, and our food. They killed our men and our sons, and they took our land and gave it to the foreigners, the Jews."

We went south to Sidon, the seaport where Queen Cleopatra of ancient Egypt built her fleet from the cedar trees of Lebanon. Here we met the commander of the joint Palestinian and Lebanese armed forces of the south, with his wife, Princess Dina. In the ancient port of Tyre, a few miles farther south, we met leaders of the Lebanese fishermen's union, all close comrades of the Palestinians. We gathered in a small group on the jetty, introduced ourselves, and began filming. "This region of Lebanon was an absolute dictatorship before the war," they told us. "The Lebanese Deuxième Bureau was everywhere—if they caught you listening to a radio broadcast from a revolutionary country, they would take you away to prison. To organize a trade union that would fight for us was illegal; you would be arrested for that." They told us that fishing had become almost impossible because the Israelis patrolled the waters a few miles out and sank their best boats.

The PLO helped the Lebanese peasants form cooperatives, and provided funds and assistance for hospitals, welfare clinics, and schools. They built small factories where young people could get skilled training and a weekly wage. The United Nations Relief and Rehabilitation Administration provided some schools that opened the door to a college education in the United States, and the PLO tried to provide the fees, since the majority of families could not afford such an education. Not many, even with the PLO's help, could send their children abroad. However, the UNRRA schools taught English language and literature, and we met very few Palestinian children in the camps who did not speak some English. I met a girl of fourteen in Bourj al-Barajneh and asked her what her favorite subject was. "English," she replied. "And your favorite writer?" "Shakespeare." "Will you read me something?" I asked. She sat there on the sofa, her hands folded on her lap, and began to recite:

> Shall I compare thee to a summer's day?
> Thou art more lovely and more temperate.
> Rough winds do shake the darling buds of May
> And summer's lease hath all too short a date . . .

The children in the camps all belonged to the Cubs and the Flowers, Palestinian youth organizations. On weekends they studied Palestinian history, sang Palestinian songs, and learned the old dances or performed their own sketches. They learned the embroidery of their Palestinian villages and how to shoot. They had to know how to defend their camps from attack, and they all hoped to take part in the struggle of their armed forces to liberate their country, and return to their parents' and their grandparents' homes in Palestine.

These young people of eleven or twelve were all politically conscious and could distinguish quite clearly between the political ideology of Zionism and the Jews as an oppressed people. This could only be the result of an honest and advanced political outlook on the part of their teachers and parents.

When I first met Salah al-Tammari he was playing football with some teenage boys in the early evening in the Ain al-Helwe refugee camp. After the game we sat on the grass and he spoke fast and passionately: "Zionism is a racist movement. It's the same as Nazism. Nazism was not a threat against the Jews only, it was a threat against the whole world, against humanity. It was a *bad event* in the history of man." He said "bad event" with great emphasis. "This event is being repeated. That's why Zionism is not a threat to Arabs only— it's a threat to the Jews themselves. Zionism is dangerous to Judaism itself. It's a racist movement. It seeks what differentiates the peoples of the world, although we are in the epoch where we should seek what unites the peoples of the world." Salah's outlook, like that of all the Fateh political and military men we met in Lebanon, was reflected in the answer of a young girl of thirteen to my question "What would you do if you met a wounded Israeli soldier?" "I would look after him and make his wounds better and I would explain to him that we are not against Jews, only against Zionism. I would explain that we need our homeland back and we would share it with the Jews. We could live together in a democratic state of Palestine."

We slept at night on floors or cots and drove on each morning. At breakfast in Sidon we met Elias Shoufani and one of the Lebanese trade union leaders. Elias gave us an interview in a tiny villa as we waited for transport to go down the narrow road leading to the Crusader castle Beaufort. "The so-called South Lebanon," he told me, "is nothing more than an extension of the Upper Galilee of Palestine. Geographically, ethnically, historically it has always been so. The Upper Galilee extends in Palestine from the road linking Acre to Safad all the way to the Litani River. This is one block of mountains and it is the same all the way."

He smiled at me. "As my name, Shoufani, indicates, I am from this area near Sidon." He was speaking of the Shouf Mountains. "My family lives south of the border, half of which is Lebanese and the other half Palestinian. So how could I recognize a border, a line that was drawn in 1926, I think, by two imperialist powers, the French and the British? To split one clan into two halves—that is totally unacceptable to me."

We stopped in Taib and Nabatiya. The few remaining Lebanese families welcomed us and showed us their houses, wrecked by shells. Some shell cases had Hebrew writing and some were made in the

United States. The CIA funded a small Lebanese army of fascists down south, commanded by Major Sammi Haddad. They seized control of some of the small villages. A schoolteacher told me how his village had been occupied in 1976. Everyone was ordered into the main square. Then twelve young men were pulled out of the crowd, lined up against a wall, and shot, as an example of what would happen if the village refused to collaborate with the Lebanese fascists. He trembled as he spoke, reliving those days.

Here, two miles from the border between Lebanon and Israel, the night sky was full of heavy red rain as rockets poured into the Lebanese villages. Every night the shelling began. Dozens of 155mm and 175mm shells came over the border from Israel. At night, as we moved from village to village or sheltered in a dugout or cellar, the earth shook and thudded.

I visited the UN post on the border. The United Nations officer was pleasant, courteous, and suntanned. "Do you report to the United Nations how many rockets and shells are fired from Israel into Lebanon every night?" I asked him. The officer shook his head. "What do you do, then?" I asked. "I'm trying to find some garlic I need for the dish I'm cooking this weekend," he replied.

Refugees poured out of their houses, packing bundles and suitcases into cars and trucks, preparing to leave their homes. Seeing our camera they spoke angrily, some of the women crying, "Israel! Israel! Look what they are doing!" The Israeli Defense Forces were using terror-bombing and a scorched-earth policy. The aim was to force Lebanese civilians to leave their homes and land, and then invade. Everyone knew an invasion was coming. The families were frightened, but they spoke up with pride for the Palestinians, and they held on as long as they could, until their homes were completely wrecked. I noticed that the nearer to the front lines people were, the more courage and strength was shown by Palestinians and Lebanese alike.

We met Abu Jihad, and he gave an interview for our camera, and last of all we met PLO chairman Yasser Arafat. He asked about our work and where we had been, then gave me an interview. He was extremely tired, but he spoke effortlessly and spontaneously, and his smile was warm and direct.

"We are not against Jews. We are against Zionism. And you remember that in the first slogan we gave, we said that our aim is to establish our democratic Palestinian state where Muslims, Christians, and Jews can live together—together. And I'm saying now, they are speaking of settlement. Okay, I am saying why speak about settlements? Why not speak about living together, all of us in this homeland? I am offering this in the name of my people.

"Without a civilized, ideological theory you can't have victory. And I think that in the future, all the Jews will understand that we are fighting for them too."

Arafat has been slandered and attacked more than any other leader of our time. His life is in constant danger from assailants, yet I doubt if he has any personal enemies. In conversation—and that was all my interview was, a filmed conversation—he is absolutely unselfconscious and transparent, with a warmth that lights up his audience. Small wonder that when *The Palestinian* was shown in America and Britain, Zionist organizations did their utmost to prevent it from being screened.

returned to London on a sunny June morning, and the children met me at the front door with a big Welcome Home sign. Tasha had permed her hair, and was directing scenes from *West Side Story* at her girls' school, with all the boys' parts cut out. The fourteen-year-old girls danced and sang "America" and "I Feel Pretty" with such gaiety and excitement that all the mothers, including me, got to their feet shouting "Bravo!"

The editing of *The Palestinian* proceeded apace. We hired a Steenbeck editing table and Battersby and the two editors worked into the night for weeks. In November the film was premiered at the London Film Festival on the South Bank, and the Workers' Revolutionary Party held public meetings all over the country for trade unionists, students, and young people to see the film.

Later in June I was invited to Los Angeles, Chicago, and New York to do a publicity tour for *Julia*. I took cassettes of *The Palestinian* with me and invited a number of filmmakers to private screenings. I also showed the film to various Public Broadcasting Service producers, who said they would lose their oil sponsors if they screened it. I took the film to CBS, who said it was their policy never to buy a film by an independent producer whom they had not commissioned. I pressed on higher up and was told that the film was "not objective." This was at a time when not one American or European network had shown a film about the Palestinians. I did the Mike Douglas TV show in Las Vegas.

From there I flew to San Francisco, where Timothy Dalton and I sat spellbound in the Old Theatre watching my father in *Shakespeare's People*. Parkinson's disease had robbed him of his ability to learn new parts, and his walk had become a shuffle. But he could still remember all his Shakespearean roles, and when he set foot on stage, his muscles loosened and he stood upright. He played some scenes from *Hamlet*, *As You Like it*, *Macbeth*, and *King Lear*, and then he came forward to the podium and looked out:

> Shall I compare thee to a summer's day?
> Thou art more lovely and more temperate . . .

He could recite Shakespeare's best-known sonnet as if he had written it himself that afternoon, and he made you forget you had ever heard the poem before. He was touring North America with the show that summer of 1977. There were five of them in it—Dad, David Dodimead, Philip Bowen, Rosalind Shanks, and Rod Willmott. They spent a week in San Francisco, but in some places they did only three performances and then would get back into their tour bus and travel to the next city.

An article about *The Palestinian* appeared in the *New York Post*. One of the actors I had invited to a private video screening had given the story to Liz Smith, the *Post* columnist. In February I had won the Golden Globe Award for *Julia* and was nominated for an Academy Award as best supporting actress, and now the press all over the United States were running stories about my support for the PLO. Rabbi Meir Kahane's Jewish Defense League went to 20th Century–Fox and said they would cause every kind of problem unless Fox issued a statement that they would never employ me again.

In Los Angeles, my friends said that I was unlikely to win the Oscar because of the press campaign against me. Sandra Marsh, my secretary, told me that a British producer was putting it about in the film community that I was a terrorist. She had saved me some news cuttings, including a long report of a meeting of the Jewish Defense League in Los Angeles where one speaker had waved a fistful of dollars and asked: "Who is willing to rid the world of a Jew-baiter?"

The day before the ceremony, Howard Koch, chairman of the Academy Awards Committee, urged me not to say anything more than "Thank you" if I won the Oscar. Then he explained the security arrangements. There would be armed plainclothes security backstage and in the auditorium, and police sharpshooters on the roof. I told Howard that I must reserve the right to say whatever I thought was right and necessary, and I thanked him for all the care he had taken with security. That evening I stayed in a hotel owned by an Arab-American businessman. A large reception room was packed with members of the Arab-American community in Los Angeles, who were there for a showing of *The Palestinian*. Waiters and kitchen staff stood in the aisles and doorways to watch. There had never been a film in the United States that showed the Palestinian-Arab cause, or a news report that allowed ordinary Palestinians to speak out. In our film many ordinary men, women, and children spoke, truthfully and directly.

As we drove up to the Dorothy Chandler Pavilion for the fiftieth Academy Awards ceremony, there were dense crowds behind police barriers. Opposite the theatre several hundred Arab-Americans stood waving the red, green, white, and black Palestinian flag. On another sidewalk about twenty members of the Jewish Defense League were burning an effigy of me. "Arafat's whore," they called it, dancing and shouting around the smoldering heap.

Inside the artists' entrance a beautiful actress I recognized but had never met turned to me and came up and put her arms around me. The embrace was honest and warm, and she could have pretended not to see me. When we finally met properly, a year later, she told me of the poverty and suffering she had seen while on a publicity tour of Latin America. "I wish I had the same courage as you," she said. "I wanted so much to speak out about what I saw, but I knew that my career would be destroyed if I did."

I came into the auditorium and sat down. I had been given a seat next to the aisle, so I thought that I would probably get the Oscar that night. I thought of the Palestinians in the camps and the hospitals, and the socialist and communist Jews who were the first to be sent to the concentration camps. I thought of Lillian Hellman, categorized as a "premature anti-fascist" by the FBI and blacklisted in the 1950s. I thought of all the American artists and workers in the film, TV, and theatre industries who were persecuted because they were trade unionists, or communists, or Jews, or all three. John Travolta came into the center of the stage, opened an envelope, and read out my name. I got up from my seat, he gave me the Oscar, and this—verbatim—is what I said:

> My dear colleagues, I thank you very, very much for this tribute to my work. I think that Jane Fonda and I have done the best work of our lives; and I think this was in part due to our director, Fred Zinnemann, and I also think it's in part because we believed in what we were expressing—two women, out of the millions who gave their lives and were prepared to sacrifice everything in the fight against fascist and racist Nazi Germany. And I salute you and I pay tribute to you and I think you should be very proud that in the last few weeks you have stood firm and refused to be intimidated by the threats of a small bunch of Zionist hoodlums whose behavior is an insult to the stature of Jews all over the world, and to their great and heroic record of struggle against fascism and oppression.
>
> And I salute that record, and I salute, salute all of you for having stood firm and dealt a final blow against that period when Nixon and McCarthy launched a worldwide witch-hunt against those who tried to express in their lives and their work a truth that they believed. I salute you and I thank you and I pledge to you that I will continue to fight against anti-Semitism and fascism. Thank you.

When I referred to the "Zionist hoodlums," I meant, of course, the Jewish Defense League and their death threats. There was a round of booing from upstairs. And then enormous applause when I finished.

I received many letters of goodwill and support. Many of those who wrote were American and some were Jews. This letter, written in English, came from a Palestinian in Kuwait:

Struggler Vanessa Redgrave,

You'll stay as a candle in our hearts that lights our way and leads us to all what we want and we'll stay grateful to you for what you are doing for our cause which you believe in its justice.

I wish I could help you, but anyhow you realise that my conditions as a student decrease the possibility of offering the necessary help you deserve. Very, very much, at last, with my compliments to her who offers herself for the Palestinian problem and for the freedom problems in the world.

Dawood K. Almani, April 4, 1978.

I returned to London, kissed and hugged my children, and then left immediately for the Palestinian Film Festival in Baghdad. In March, Israel had invaded Lebanon. I met a number of our friends from the Palestinian Film Institute at the festival, and they asked me to return to Lebanon and do interviews for a film of the invasion. So I flew to Beirut again and drove down south. Sidon was devastated and Tyre was very badly damaged. Whole apartment blocks and districts were mounds of rubble. Rescue teams were still pulling bodies out of the wreckage. The pools of water in the streets from shattered water-mains were red with blood. The camp of Rashidiye had been evacuated, street upon street of ruins.

I interviewed a group of fighters, including a seventeen-year-old girl, who were defending a hill position very close to a group of Israeli tanks. I spoke to youngsters who had ambushed tanks and held them back for several hours before they were forced to retreat. I met the widows of two of my friends, both Palestinian cameramen. They had been surrounded by tanks where they stood in the middle of the road and shot on the spot, although they had no weapons and were holding a piece of white cloth to show they had surrendered.

The Israelis had now acquired a new five-mile-deep strip of territory across the south of Lebanon. Thousands of civilians were dead and wounded, their homes, farms, and workshops destroyed. No medicine, food supplies, or aid were sent from America or Europe. There was no vote from the U.S. Senate or House for economic sanctions against Israel. In the Security Council and in the UN Assembly, the United States and Britain blocked and vetoed all resolutions of condemnation. Cluster bombs and other weapons made in the United States and sold to the Israelis by authority of the U.S. government were used in the invasion. In his memoirs, President Jimmy Carter complained about this: "I was particularly disturbed because American weapons, including lethal cluster bombs, had been used in the operation, contrary to our agreement when they were sold." Here was the former president of the United States actually admitting that the United States sells "lethal" weapons, which are specifically *anti-civilian* weapons (they were dropped on villages in the Vietnam War), claiming that a written agreement was made that they would not be used, and then complaining that they had been.

The news stories of the Israeli brutality, which left more than one hundred thousand civilians injured and homeless, forced the State Department to agree to a UN resolution calling for a United Nations peacekeeping force and the Israeli withdrawal from Lebanon. The Israeli Defense Forces did not withdraw. The Likud government got the agreement of a small army of Lebanese fascists commanded by Major Haddad to provide a political cover for complete Israeli control of the five-mile-deep border area. The United Nations Intermediary Forces in Lebanon (UNIFIL), when they arrived, never entered the area: "No can see, no can hear, no can do."

The Israelis claimed the invasion was provoked by a Fateh military operation in March against an Israeli army position near a beach outside Tel Aviv. Our party published a two-page statement that told the truth about that operation and paid tribute to the bravery of the Fateh fighters who led the assault. In our view the Palestinians had every right to pursue their armed struggle in their own country against the Israeli state. They had the same right as did Mandela's African National Congress, whose armed wing, Umkonto We Sizwe, fought the apartheid state of South Africa. Mugabe and Nkomo's armies had the same right when they fought the colonial state of Rhodesia. The people of Nicaragua and the Sandinistas had the same right to fight for their liberation.

In June 1978 came the annual general meeting of British Actors' Equity. Our "Defend Equity, Defend the Union" faction presented a number of motions: to raise the minimum wage, which won the vote; for Equity to unionize and give protection to hostesses in nightclubs and performers in porno bars and porno films—this also won a majority vote. We also put a resolution confirming Equity's ban on members' working in South Africa while apartheid was in place. Because of the Israeli invasion of Lebanon, we prepared a motion, which I was to propose, with seventy-three signatures, asking the Council "to instruct all members working in Israel to terminate their contracts and refuse offers of work in Israel." This was exactly the same as Equity's official policy on South Africa. Due to the schedule and time allotted, the motion was never debated and voted on, but someone in Equity sent a copy of the motion to the *Jewish Chronicle*. Three weeks before the AGM meeting the *Jewish Chronicle* ran a story that was immediately taken up by *Variety* and *The Hollywood Reporter:* "Vanessa calls for boycott of Israel." On June 27 *The Hollywood Reporter* ran a full-page advertisement from the Association of Motion Picture and Television Producers, the Producers Guild of America and the Writers Guild of America West:

> To our colleagues,
>   We emphatically reaffirm our position against any blacklist, censorship, or boycott of artistes and their work. Just as 20th Century–Fox was commended for its refusal to blacklist or boycott Vanessa Redgrave as an artiste because of her political position, so we unreservedly condemn her recent attempt to institute a blacklist boycott of the film industry and artistes of Israel. We consider this a threat to all of us. Therefore we call upon the entire entertainment industry to join in public support of this stated position.

I categorically had not called for a boycott of Israeli artists or their films or theatre companies. Our resolution was a cultural ban on English artists' working in Israel and English films' being sold to Israel; it was similar to the cultural ban against English artists' working in South Africa.

For all the reasons we supported a ban on British actors' working in South Africa, we believed such a ban should apply to Israel. Palestinian trade unions were *illegal* in Israel. Palestinian writers, poets, and musicians were censored and imprisoned on mere suspicion of being members of an illegal Palestinian organization. Indeed *all* Palestinian organizations created by Palestinians were illegal: the General Union of Palestinian Workers, the General Union of Palestinian Women, and the General Union of Palestinian Students. For us to take money in the state of Israel as English actors, dancers, directors, or designers was to take blood money when our Palestinian brothers and sisters were being killed, imprisoned, censored, and denied their cultural freedom of expression. But we categorically did *not* call for the banning of Israeli artists, or seek to prevent them from working in England, the United States, or anywhere else, or to prevent their work from being seen or sold. We sought, as trade unionists, to establish a unity of all artists to defend the basic democratic rights of all workers in the entertainment industries. Whether Jew or Arab, black or Hispanic or white, we have a common identity; we are all exploited. But "white" artists especially have the duty to defend the basic democratic rights of African, Asian, Hispanic, Jewish, or Arab artists and workers against discrimination of any kind, whether racial, political, or religious.

On June 6, *Variety* reported that *The Palestinian* would be screened on June 16 at the Academy of Motion Picture Arts and Sciences in Los Angeles. The Academy canceled the booking. The Workers' League sponsored two screenings of the film on June 17 and 28 at the Marc Ballroom on Union Square, New York. In May they had sponsored a screening at UCLA that drew four thousand students. Theodore Bikel, president of American Actors' Equity, was quoted as saying that he had read a transcript of *The Palestinian,* that Arafat had called for the liquidation of Israel, and that I had agreed. That was a lie. I wrote to Donald Grody, American Equity's secretary, pointing out that nowhere in the film was such a statement made, nor could Chairman Arafat have said such a thing, which was directly contrary to the policy of the PLO. Perhaps, I said, Theodore Bikel had been misquoted. If so, would he correct the reports?

At the screenings in New York, the auditorium was filled to capacity. The Jewish Defense League threw a bomb at the box office of a small independent cinema in Los Angeles that had booked the film for two weeks. The owner, to his credit, did not cancel and ran the film as advertised.

I have certainly lost much of my film career because of this kind of misreporting. Did any one of those film and television producers actually read the motion I proposed? Or did they read a newspaper report on the motion that presented only part of what I said, with a headline calculated to mislead the reader? Did that reporter read the motion and falsify my words intentionally? Or was it an editor who added the headline REDGRAVE CALLS FOR A BOYCOTT OF ISRAEL, knowing this would imply an identity with the boycott of Israeli products by some Arab states?

In the case of the press, I have to say that I have learned the hard way. Some newspaper owners and their editors appear to have lost the faculty of distinguishing between truth and falsehood. Since I discovered this was the case in regard to myself, I have also learned always to read source material before jumping to a conclusion about someone else. In the case of Theodore Bikel, I sent a transcript of the interview I filmed with Chairman Arafat to prove the allegation was false. I never received a reply or an apology. In the case of the alleged call to boycott/blacklist Israeli artists, that lie lived on, deliberately perpetuated, no matter how often I sent the true text. Trotsky, more falsified and libeled than any other man in our century, often quoted a proverb that says a lie travels all round the world while truth is still struggling to pull its boots on. In a descriptive sense the proverb is attractive and apt. However, intelligence services have "disinformation" departments and ready media channels for lies. For this reason, while nothing can negate the value of an honest documentary film, I often feel that only drama, or fiction, can be deeply trusted. A skillful editor can make any fact appear in a false light, to fit the story he or she has already predetermined. In drama, which we know as "fiction," you hear the ring of the soul. Be it ever so slightly cracked or faulty, we all hear the pitch.

CHAPTER 20

In October 1978, three years and eleven days after we had issued a writ for libel against *The Observer*, the trial began. English law requires two sets of lawyers. The first, the solicitors, gather all documents for a case and advise their clients on choosing the second set of lawyers—a senior counsel to plead the case in the court, called a Queen's Counsel, and a junior to advise him. When we met John Wilmers, Q.C., in his chambers in Pump Court, he warned us that our case would be difficult to win. Nevertheless we felt bound to go ahead. We had been libeled as terrorists, and a police raid was the immediate result. Despite all the petitions and protestations on our behalf, we had to prove our case in a court of law; if we did not, any other newspaper, informer, or police force could libel us and raid us again. Moreover, only by going to court could we find out all the facts of our case.

The WRP was a legal party; socialist parties had a long history of struggle, both for legality and for the right to put forward their policies like all other political parties. We had to defend our party's right to exist politically.

There were six of us in court: Corin and I, Gerry, and three others, all named in the *Observer* article. From the moment John Wilmers completed his examination of Corin, and Colin Ross-Munro, Q.C. for *The Observer,* took over, we realized that the case had been turned around. It was we who were on trial. Corin was examined for two and a half days. Ross-Munro produced one article after another from back issues of the *Workers' Press,* quoting sentences out of context for Corin to explain.

"The working class should take power?"

"Yes."

"And here, do you see, you advocate a struggle for power?"

"Yes."

"By an armed uprising?"

"No," Corin said, "by peaceful and constitutional means." There came a flurry of papers and whispers, as if a mouse or a ferret had been let loose. Again and again Ross-Munro returned to the fray with the phrase "peaceful, legal and constitutional," which he uttered in tones of rising incredulity to press his disbelief home to the jury. He pulled out pamphlets and news articles against continued objections from our Q.C., which were overruled by the judge, Mister Justice O'Connor. When it was my turn to get into the witness box I was questioned about a *Daily Mail* article, "The Grandmother of Hate." This referred to Maire Drumm, the Irish Republican leader who had been murdered in her hospital bed by the Ulster Volunteer Force or the British army. I had attended her funeral. I told the court I opposed terrorism but I defended the right of the Irish Republican Army to undertake military actions against the British army and the UVF. I was in the witness box for a day and a half. Chiefly I had to explain and defend our party's position in support of the Palestinians' right to self-determination and to their elected leadership in exile, the Palestine Liberation Organization. I had to explain many times that terrorist acts are acts of violence against civilians, and that the PLO's military actions were similar to the actions of partisans in Nazi-occupied France, for instance, designed to fulfill military objectives.

I supported the PLO's right to conduct military operations inside Israel, since their land had been illegally occupied by military force. The United Nations had no legal right to partition Palestine, nor to recognize a State of Israel created in 1948 through terror and mass expulsion of the Palestinians. When the West Bank and Gaza Strip were occupied in 1967, the UN issued Resolution 242, which called on Israel to withdraw from these territories.

At four every afternoon after the court session, I ran into a waiting taxi to Euston Station, caught the train to Manchester, jumped into another taxi, and with twenty-five minutes to spare arrived at the Royal Exchange Theatre just in time to step into a robe, wet my hair, and go on stage as Ellida in Ibsen's *The Lady from the Sea,* directed by my dear friend and mentor Michael Elliott. Immediately after the performance I had to get back to the station and return to London on the overnight sleeper, in time for court in the morning.

At the beginning of the second week it was the turn of the police to be questioned. The first officer into the witness box was Deputy Assistant Commissioner Victor Gilbert, who had headed the Special Branch in 1975. He submitted to the court a confidential report from the Metropolitan Police, dated September 25, 1975.

Walter Stansfield, chief constable of Derbyshire, and then Colin Smith, the *Observer* journalist, took the stand, and the contents of the report were revealed. Gradually, the following chain of events culminating in the raid at 10 P.M. on September 25 and the front-page headline POLICE RAID THE RED HOUSE on September 26 became clear.

On Friday, September 24, Scotland Yard had received a call from David Astor, the editor of *The Observer,* to say that the paper would be running an article on the activities of the WRP. He mentioned that "reference had been made by their *informant* to Special Branch." A meeting was held at the *Observer* offices between Deputy Assistant Commissioner Gilbert, David Astor, and Colin Smith. Gilbert stated that he was instructed to have the meeting by Sir Robert Mark, the chief commissioner. *The Observer* did not name their "informant" to the police, but stated that the name would be published in their article that Sunday. Gilbert did not appear to have been concerned that the informant's name was withheld. A woman, referred to as a "former girlfriend of WRP activist Corin Redgrave," had alleged, according to *The Observer,* that Corin had made a remark "to the effect that the WRP had a quantity of arms buried (or secreted) in the grounds of their Derbyshire establishment." Gilbert's report to Sir Robert stated that Special Branch had no "collateral" to support this allegation. However, they would investigate, on the understanding that "no overt action would be taken by any agency to destroy the impact of the story without prior reference to the editor of *The Observer*."

Gilbert reported that relevant government departments had been notified about the article, including the Security Service (MI5) and the Derbyshire police. It would seem that the biggest police raid on a political party since the war had been authorized on the basis of an *alleged* remark reported by an *unnamed* person, for which Special Branch had no supporting evidence. Our counsel, John Wilmers, established that the first edition of *The Observer* was on the streets for sale on Saturday night around nine-thirty to ten in the evening. The raid took place at ten P.M.

Colin Smith told the court that the general secretary of British Actors' Equity, Peter Plouviez, had telephoned *The Observer* and arranged a meeting with a journalist, Robert Chesshyre, outside the Coliseum Theatre. Plouviez told Chesshyre that an Equity member, Irene Gorst, had given him the story about Corin. Smith told the court he had not telephoned either myself or Corin to check the story, because Irene Gorst was frightened. Peter Plouviez had not contacted us either.

The *Observer* lawyers concentrated their case on the fact that we supported the Palestinians' right to self-determination, and their right to take up arms in their country against the military force that was occupying their land. For the *Observer* lawyers this was terrorism. On the eleventh day of the case, John Wilmers made his concluding speech, and addressed this question. He reminded the jury that the *Observer* article had been published at the height of an IRA bombing campaign in Britain. Then he came to our policies, which had received so much attention from the *Observer* lawyers, especially our support for the Palestinians. Mr. Wilmers had fought behind enemy lines with the partisans in Italy, and he spoke from his own experiences, very movingly. He spoke quietly and modestly, as if the jury were sitting with him in his living room, asking them to see things from another point of view. "It isn't popular to say that the Palestinians fight for their own land. Many of us would not think it right to support them when they carry the fight into Israel by measures which undoubtedly injure civilians. But ask yourselves this: Is there just possibly another side to it?"

At the lunch break, Corin and I walked with our friends into the public gardens at the back of the courts, where we could get a sandwich and a cup of tea. It was there, one day early in the trial, that Corin had showed me the opening chapters of Dickens's *Hard Times*, where the teacher browbeats a girl called Sissy Jupe to give him the definition of a horse. I read it on the train going up to Manchester that afternoon, laughing out loud. Lawyers browbeat witnesses using the same formal logic: yes or no, nothing else permitted.

On Wednesday, November 8, the jury gave their verdict. The headline in the *Express* read: BLOW FOR VANESSA—ACTRESS PROVES SHE WAS LIBELLED. JUDGE ORDERS HER TO PAY MASSIVE COSTS. On November 10 a lengthy editorial in *The Times* noted that "the unfairness to the plaintiffs is that, though having shown to the satisfaction of the jury that the *Observer* article had been defamatory and wrong, they are now saddled with a bill for tens of thousands in costs. The Redgraves' action has demonstrated, not for the first time, the inequity of, in many respects, Britain's libel laws."

Corin and I spoke at a press conference on Friday, November 11, to announce the launching of a £70,000 appeal fund. Corin said that the results of our case set a dangerous precedent because it suggested that a newspaper could act on the information an "informant" had brought it, which could be proved to be untrue, and yet the victim had to pay the costs of a libel action.

I learned a lot from the trial. We had proved our case and cleared the name of the Workers' Revolutionary Party. The jury was asked: "Are all the words complained of substantially true?" They answered no. They were asked this question in respect of each of the six plaintiffs, one of whom, Gerry Healy, was connected only with the allegation about arms caches, and another who was connected only with the *Observer* allegations about Irene Gorst. Since the jury answered no in respect of all six plaintiffs, it followed that the jury believed neither the "arms caches" allegations nor the allegations about Miss Gorst.

We had proven the libel, but we lost the case because the jury said our reputations had not been materially damaged, a point of view the judge emphatically agreed with. Under a Labour government, a socialist party had been libeled and victimized in a provocation in which Special Branch had coordinated their activities with the Home

Office, the Security Services, and *The Observer,* on the basis of an allegation that the police had not checked, allegedly made by a person whose name they did not even know. In December 1975, the attorney general was obliged to state he had no grounds for any prosecution. The Derbyshire police, whom we had sued for wrongful entry, later agreed to settle the case by issuing a statement that they acknowledged we were nonviolent and had the same right to police protection as anyone else.

To help raise the £70,000, we organized a concert at the Lyceum Theatre. Our mother agreed to take part. What a relief, and what strength it gives you when you know that so many workers, youths, and intellectuals from different generations will come forward to defend basic democratic rights.

≡

Gerry Healy and I went to Kuwait in April 1979 at the invitation of the Kuwait Cine Club to present a special screening of *The Palestinian.* We had a meeting with the Crown Prince, Sheikh Sabah al Sabah, and discussed our proposal to make a second documentary on the Palestinians living under Israeli military occupation in the West Bank and Gaza. He donated £25,000 toward the budget. We were driven out to Ahmadi to have lunch with the governor, Sheikh Jaber. His colleagues took us on a tour around the gigantic petrol refinery that produced gas in icy temperatures in the middle of the blazing desert. We were welcomed by Kuwaitis and Palestinians and spoke at a special showing of our film in the PLO offices. Here we met for the first time Abu Jihad's brother and some of the women teachers in the General Union of Palestinian Women. From Kuwait, we went to the United Arab Emirates at the invitation of the minister of culture. We met many young Palestinian girls who helped us to collect money for the new film, and I was introduced to Benazir Bhutto, whose father had recently been hanged in Pakistan. On the last night of our visit we watched TV, extremely excited to see our film, knowing that the story of the Palestinians was being watched all over the Gulf.

We returned to London to take part in the general election campaign. I was a candidate again, this time in Moss Side, Manchester. Corin was standing as WRP candidate in Lambeth, an equally poverty-stricken area in South London. Workers were convinced that Labour would win, and I remember one building-site worker opening his eyes wide with disbelief when I told him that the record of the Labour government had ensured Mrs. Thatcher's victory at the polls. He told me he would bet me a pound that she wouldn't win. But she did. She had become the patron saint of the frustrated reactionary sections of the middle class, whose former Liberal and Labour votes now went to the Tories in support of Mrs. Thatcher's policies of anti–trade unionism and anti-immigration. Thousands of workers did not vote at all or voted against Labour as a protest.

In June that year Michael Elliott brought his Manchester production of *The Lady from the Sea* to London. We performed at the Round House Theatre, whose artistic director was Thelma Holt. Since the time when we had shared digs while we both worked in *A Touch of the Sun,* Thelma had done a lot of exciting work as an actress with Charles Marowitz at the Open Space. Thelma is practically unique in the British theatre; apart from Peter Daubeny I cannot think of anyone who has been so involved in bringing theatre work from other countries to England. When she was at the Round House she opened its doors to every kind of event, including performances by unknown and established poets and musicians, and various benefits that we organized to finance our youth training centers. She is engaged wholeheartedly and thoughtfully in her work and I admire her tremendously.

I was very glad to have the chance of working with Michael Elliott again, especially at the Round House Theatre, where seats were cheap compared with the West End and the arena stage established an immediate contact between audience and players. One night a woman came up to me after the performance and said: "You know, your production made me feel so alive! I have never felt like this in the theatre before."

That same month I received an invitation to the Moscow Film Festival. I thanked the organizers and accepted, on condition that they acknowledged my belief that Soviet Jewish citizens had the right to emigrate to any country of their choice, including Israel. They never replied, and I did not go.

As a result of visiting Kuwait with Gerry for the special screening of *The Palestinian* at the Kuwait Cine Club we made a documentary called *Vanessa Talks to Farouk Abdul Azziz*. Farouk Abdul Azziz was the secretary of the Kuwait Cine Club, and he wanted to interview me about my life. I discussed the idea with Corin and Gerry and we agreed that he could come to England and I would spend time with him doing the interview. We decided to include a scene that Dad and I could act in together. In the early spring of 1980 we went to Wilks Water and Michael and I did the scene from *King Lear* where he awakens from his madness and is reconciled with Cordelia. We filmed it by the little lake, and it was a marvelous experience. Michael played the scene extraordinarily—he had never played any leading Shakespearean role on film—and it was terribly moving to watch. I would act that very same scene with him the last time that we performed onstage together, which was at the Round House in October 1982 in a benefit for the Young Socialists' youth training centers.

I will always remember him coming to see the finished documentary. He was stricken with Parkinson's but he walked out of the viewing room singing, and sang all the way home in the car. He was obviously extremely happy, and said that now for the first time he could really understand the relationship between my political life and acting.

CHAPTER 21

P *laying for Time,* the story of the women's orchestra in the Nazi concentration camp at Auschwitz in Poland, was written for television by Arthur Miller. All Miller's writing is superb, but historical subjects, the main events of our times, have inspired his best writing, and this story, in my view, is his masterpiece.

We were to rehearse in New York and film in Pennsylvania. I had given the script to Gerry, and before I left for New York he gave me three pages of notes. He said it was the best description of fascism and fascist ideology he had ever read and advised me to pay close attention to all the physical details in Miller's script. Very good advice. From his knowledge of our history, and of the many men and women who had spent years in prisons and prison camps, Gerry knew how these physical details shaped their lives, expressing not only their suffering but their will to resist. He also reminded me that it is the present, the times we live in, that gives life to the past, stirs and activates the historical truth of a script.

Both of us knew that rehearsals would be a battle. Linda Yellen, our courageous producer, had stuck out her neck to cast me as Fania Fenelon, on whose autobiography the script was based, and now her decision was coming under fire. I arrived in New York to find a security guard posted outside the rehearsal rooms. Linda's office in downtown New York had been broken into by a gang who rushed a guard and sprayed red paint on the walls. She herself was virtually in hiding in a friend's apartment, and Bill Paley, the head of CBS television, had pickets outside his house demanding my removal from the cast. Worst of all, Fania Fenelon herself was in the States on a speaking tour, denouncing my being cast to play her.

Two months previously I had met Fania in the CBS studios in London, where we were interviewed by Mike Wallace for *60 Minutes*. She said I was too old for the part and Jane Fonda would have been more suitable. Jane certainly looked remarkably young, but as we are the same age I didn't take that objection seriously. Then Fania declared that Yasser Arafat wanted to wipe out all Jews in Israel and sweep them into the sea. This was as big a lie as the infamous "Protocols of the Elders of Zion," and I said so. Then she compared casting me to play herself to hiring a member of the Ku Klux Klan to play Sammy Davis, Jr., and I put the record straight on that. After the interview, we found ourselves sitting together in a small room, drinking cups of coffee and waiting for our transport home.

"Well," she said, "since you are playing me, you had better know something about me." She told me her father had been a member of the French Communist Party, which was the main organizer of the resistance, and that she herself had joined when she was twenty. Her job, as a cabaret singer, was to spy for the resistance. She sang in the cafés, entertaining and chatting with Nazi officers, gleaning every piece of information she could and passing it on.

I discovered that no car had been arranged for Fania, so I offered her a lift. We stopped first at my home in Ravenscourt Road, and I ran inside to get her a copy of the script, which she said she had never received. I found my copy of her book, brought it out to the car, and asked her to sign it for me. She wrote: "For Vanessa, with friendship, Fania Fenelon." I promised I would do everything in my power to persuade CBS and Linda Yellen to engage her as adviser for the film, and I kept my word. Linda said they telephoned her but she never answered their calls. I feel a deep sadness to this day that in spite of all my efforts, Fania did not get to join us on the film.

This was 1979. In the summer of 1993, through the violinist Chris

Warren-Greene, I made contact at last with another survivor of the Auschwitz women's orchestra, Anita Lasker. I say "at last" because when I telephoned her, asking her to speak at a meeting and concert, *Wake Up, World,* of International Artists Against Racism, she told me she had sent me and Arthur Miller many letters while we were filming *Playing for Time.* I had never received one of them, so I am sure Arthur Miller had not either. Anita told me she had totally disagreed with Fania's publicity tour and her denunciations of me. "But you have to remember this—Fania was quite different when she was in the orchestra." I do remember that. I remember there was a brave young girl who was a communist and fought fascism, who risked her life and suffered the horrors of Auschwitz. That is what should be remembered about Fania Fenelon.

In Harrisburg, Pennsylvania, where we were to film, there was a tight security guard around the compound, part of the Indiana Gap air force base used in World War II to intern civilians. The barracks consisted of row upon row of wooden buildings—a chilling sight. They seemed almost identical to the wooden huts in Auschwitz. The citizens of Harrisburg, many of whom had been cast as extras in our film, had plenty to talk about, and plenty to worry about. Life had overshadowed the drama of our arrival. On March 28, 1979, a major accident had occurred at the nuclear power plant at nearby Three Mile Island. It was the worst disaster in nuclear power until Chernobyl seven years later. A meltdown had almost occurred. Radioactive gas had escaped from the plant, contaminating a ten-mile radius around the power station. The accident radicalized the local population. Talking to them, I realized how swiftly ordinary people's views can change in response to such a shock. I doubt whether many of them were political before it happened, but it had made them realize that the government was not in the least concerned with their health or safety. Some of them told me that this event, combined with their desire to learn more about German fascism, was why they were keen to take part in our film.

Jane Alexander, Robin Bartlett, Marcell Rosenblatt, Mady Kaplan, Melanie Mayron, Marisa Berenson, Lenore Harris, and I played the women in the orchestra. Shirley Knight was the commandant, and Viveca Lindfors one of the guards. The day came when we were to have our heads shaved. When it was done, we looked at the piles of hair on the floor; we looked at each other, and saw how we had been dehumanized, shorn of our identity. I have sometimes been complimented for cutting off my hair for *Playing for Time,* but in fact all of us did. The cast of the *Holocaust* television series, on the other hand, wore special rubber skullcaps. As far as I was concerned, shaving our heads was one of those details that Gerry had asked me to pay close attention to: a tribute, albeit a very small one, to the millions of Jews who had been made to undergo this humiliation before they were killed. It made us understand Nazism more sharply.

For the first three weeks of the six-week shooting schedule we had a well-known and successful television director. During a rehearsal, before shooting had started, he said, "This scene is rather melodramatic." I was alarmed and could not understand how he could say this unless he was nervous or hostile to the entire story, because what was true of that scene was true of the whole script. In any event, our producers decided he must be replaced. Arthur Miller discovered that Daniel Mann was free. He was a great director, and a very generous man. With half the footage already in the can, and no budget to reshoot, he agreed to shoot the second half of the film. Each day's work was terrifying. We were frightened we should not do justice to Fania's story and to the memory of those who had died, and now we were frightened by the technical problem of having to complete so much footage each day, to finish the film on schedule. We, too, found we were playing for time, and this became a factor sharpening our consciousness of what each moment meant. We had to work well together, and we did. All the actresses told me they had received telephone calls and letters requesting that they make a statement against my casting, but none of them had. Instead they signed a press release saying that there should be no blacklisting, and that they had been looking forward to working with me. Many had relatives who had been killed in the Holocaust, and some had family who had been blacklisted in the fifties.

Later that year I went to Bahrain, and for the second time to Iraq. In Baghdad I met the film director Mohammed Shukri Jamil, who asked me to play the role of Gertrude Bell. She was one of those who were involved in setting up the British Mandate after 1918, putting King Faisal on the throne to serve British interests and crushing the Iraqi revolution of 1920. The Iraqis were brutally defeated. The

British used airplanes in a campaign of bombing and strafing villages and camps. They also used gas, from large quantities stockpiled after the war against Germany.

I spent some wonderful hours with Mounir Bashir, the director of the Baghdad Music Conservatory, who was gathering on cassette an archive of ancient music, going back to Nineveh and Babylon in 3000 B.C. I had heard Mounir himself play for the first time at a concert in Bahrain. His mastery of the twelve-stringed oud was extraordinary. It seemed to me I could hear a spider spinning her web, or frozen twigs thawing in spring, so delicate were the vibrations. Mounir's passion was to train his students in the knowledge of their own musical history. He traveled all over the country making recordings, always anxious to preserve what was there in case it should be lost forever. In the oral music of the tribes, he said, he could trace connections with the music of the ancient civilizations of Assyria and Babylonia, later called Mesopotamia, and later still, Iraq.

I went to Iraq as I went to every Arab country, to give my support to the Palestinian struggle for the right to self-determination. I came to understand, as I had not understood before, how much this struggle meant to the Arab peoples. Iraqis had always supported the Palestinians. In Kuwait, Saudi Arabia, Iraq, Libya, and Syria I made many friends, and I will never forget their kindness and hospitality. Without their help *The Palestinian* and then *Occupied Palestine* would not have been financed or shown. I learned an important lesson—to have respect for the Arab peoples, be ready to learn, and never be hasty to judge on the basis of fixed categories such as "right-wing" or "left-wing."

In March 1980 I was a guest at the General Popular Assembly at the Libyan Arab Socialist People's Jamahiriya, where I was introduced to a delegation of slender, beautiful women from the Polisario Front, the national liberation movement in Morocco. Every one of them looked too fragile for any physical work. Then they showed me a documentary of their struggle in the Sahara Desert, and I saw these same women pitching tents, cooking, hauling metal water wagons, feeding the children and the soldiers, always on the move. I met with young Libyan women, students, some of them dressed like nuns, in cool, plain linen veils and tunics. They reminded me of young women in the Middle Ages and Renaissance who became abbesses, renowned poets and intellectuals. Selwa, a woman of my age who told me her story, was quite typical of her generation. She had been a medical student in the sixties, during the last years of the rule of King Idris of Libya. As the daughter of a privileged family, her education was exceptional. For most young people, and especially girls, education was minimal. Selwa was a supporter of President Gamal Abdel Nasser, and she agitated against U.S. military bases in Libya. When the authorities discovered this, her scholarship was canceled. Her father was furious; he ordered her to stop busying herself in politics and concentrate on her studies. Somehow she managed to get a scholarship from President Nasser, worth £9 a week, to go and study for four years in Cairo to learn to be a journalist. In 1964 Nasser told her there would be a revolution in Libya. She said, "You're dreaming; all the men in Libya are cowards." She was in Cairo in 1969, when the September 1 Libyan revolution took place. All Libyan airports were closed, so she drove for five days to Benghazi, found some soldiers, and asked them, "Where are the leaders? I want to see them." They took her to Colonel Muammar Qaddafi and the young men of the Revolutionary Command Council.

We traveled by bus for miles into the desert to a celebration in Taghrit, stopping only to wash our hands and drink coffee, and singing songs all the way. We arrived on a plain with ridges so oxidized by the sun that the wind blew fine layers of rock off them. This was the scene of the famous battle when the Libyans, led by the legendary Omar al-Mukhtar, the Lion of the Desert, armed only with rifles, had defeated Mussolini's armored columns. We sat under an awning and watched the commemoration of this great victory, which was celebrated every year. Tanks rolled by, followed by armored cars, and then a group of horsemen in white Libyan togas and flat hats. The loudest applause was for a group of veterans from the war with fascist Italy. Only five could take part in the ceremony that day. Mussolini's forces had massacred half the population of Libya, and it was rare now to see men and women of my father's generation, or even of mine.

That summer the European Parliament passed a resolution recognizing the right of the Palestinians to self-determination. It also condemned as illegal Israeli settlements in the occupied territories and all "modifications" in population and property in the West Bank, Gaza, and the Golan Heights. In the autumn, on September 17, Iraq invaded Iran. Our party Central Committee condemned the invasion and called on Iraq to withdraw. No matter what the rights or wrongs of the dispute over the Shat-al-Arab waterway, Iran, through revolution, had defeated the brutal tyranny of the shah. The invasion would weaken Iran's economy, as it would Iraq's, and undermine the cause of the Palestinians. The Americans, British, and French publicly lamented the war and privately got on with the lucrative trade in arms, hoping Iraq would deal a mortal blow to the Iranian revolution.

I was working night and day for the party, finding premises for youth training centers in London, Liverpool, and Manchester. Our idea was to set up such centers in all the main towns in Britain, where high school graduates without jobs could find skilled training and also enjoy themselves socially. We opened our first two centers in January 1981, and very soon the press started a witch-hunt. *The Times,* the *Daily Express,* the *Daily Mail,* and the *News of the World* ran stories about the centers, referring to "bomb factories" and "brainwashing." In spring and summer, when there were riots in Brixton and Liverpool, some of the reports tried to make out that these were instigated by our youth centers. I was kept busy for several weeks answering these reports, and in almost every case I received an apology or the right to reply. By the time our center in Glasgow opened we had got support from the assistant secretary of the Scottish Trades Union Congress, trades councils and branches, and prominent sports people.

That spring, 1981, I was in Nashville, Tennessee, shooting a television film for ABC called *My Body, My Child.* On the night of May 4 I was standing with a group of truck drivers, watching a scene I wasn't in and listening through the cab door to a driver's radio. Bobby Sands, on hunger strike in Northern Ireland's Maze prison, had died. It was the first item on the news. Those who were brought up, as I was, in Britain, reading the *Daily Mail* and listening to or watching the *Six O'Clock News,* might find it hard to imagine or believe that a bunch of Tennessee truck drivers would bow their heads in respect and sorrow at this news, and that one of them would wipe a tear from his eye. But that was how it was. Next morning the *New York Post,* a newspaper owned by Rupert Murdoch, whose papers in Britain vilified Bobby Sands and the hunger strikers, had a banner headline

with a black border: BOBBY SANDS, IRA MAN AND MEMBER OF PARLIA-
MENT, DIES IN MAZE PRISON, BELFAST. IRELAND MOURNS.

When the editor rang Murdoch for approval of his headline he
must have reminded him that the *Post* has a large Irish-American
readership. I cut the headline out, and when I got home I taped it to
the wall above my desk. It is there now. Bobby Sands was a true hero
of our time. He was not a terrorist but fought as best he could,
politically. Every British government, Tory or Labour, has denied
the Irish their right to self-determination. We in Britain have a
special responsibility to right that wrong, which has been the cause
of so much tragedy and suffering.

Much more precious than the *Post* headline is the letter I have kept
from Bobby Sands. It was written on toilet paper and smuggled out
of the H-Block. Sands was a member of Parliament, elected by the
people of Derry while he was a prisoner. All his rights as a prisoner
of war had been denied by the Thatcher government, which had
refused him political status. As a member of Parliament elected by a
large majority he had no rights, and his constituents could neither
hear from him—except for the occasional message smuggled out—
nor communicate with him. His letter is full of humor, courage, and
defiance.

Hiya! Vanessa,

How are ya? I'm sure you're a bit surprised to receive this little
letter, but I'm sure that you recognise the good old H-Block
writing paper. Well, anyway, I'm Bobby Sands, blanket man,
H-Block 6. I'm not really writing to tell you about H-Block,
Vanessa, as I'm more than sure you know as much about it as any
one else, but all the same, things remain more or less the same here.
We continue to resist here and they continue to torture us. Sometimes we make the mistake of saying 'this is total boredom.' That
is very true most of the time, but there are times here when there
is never a dull moment, so to speak, for if the screws aren't beating
someone up, they're hosing someone down, searching remains
nightmarish. Bedding as ever is damp, food cold and most times
inedible. They've blocked up the windows and the flow of air is
minimal, our view of the outside an eyesore of a few inches of
barbed-wire. Bad and degrading searches remain the in-thing, you

know the way it feels going into a dentist's surgery, well it feels about ten times worse when you walk naked into a group of screws armed with mirrors, torches and metal detectors, the tools of the searching trade and as they say 'they're only doing their job' God help us! Anyway, Vanessa, we don't know very much of how things are in England (or anywhere else for that matter), but we did hear that there were ten-thousand at the London march and after the reports of the Belfast march we were very pleased and morale is quite high. I'm putting a few wee odds and ends in along with this letter to you: perhaps you can use them for some of the papers or for leaflets. 'Sort of a direct from H-Block thing', anyway I'm also putting in five letters to other people, who we think may be interested in H-Block. We would appreciate it if perhaps you could pass them on to them, as they're in the film world, we can hardly get a letter to the Falls Road, let alone these people, so hope you could manage it. We're sort of pushing on the propaganda front and trying to get as many people as we can to tell them and explain to them about H-Block and Ireland. From in here all we can do is write some articles and letters, etc., when the situation permits, but we try. Well, no matter, if you wish or get the chance, you could drop us a note letting us know how things are with you. You could send it to the incident centre, 170 Falls Road, Belfast. Also (before I forget) if you can, could you send us the names and addresses of anyone you think would like to hear from us, or whom you think we could tell of H-Block, be they individuals or organisations, come to think of it, you can add anyone at all approachable or unapproachable. Perhaps I'll be able to get you another letter again shortly to let you know how things are here. But anyway it's been nice writing to you and thanks to you from us all here for the great work yourself and your comrades have done for us and our people. Regards to everyone.

Sealadaigh Abu   See ya!

Bobby Sands

O*ccupied Palestine* was completed in the summer of 1981. From September until spring the following year I did nothing but travel from one city to the next, showing the film or arranging for it to be seen, and speaking for the Palestinian cause. I was proud of *Occupied Palestine,* and I think even now, years later, when many remarkable films have been made about Palestine—for example Mei Masri's *Children of Fire*—that it stands among the best. It shows how the settlements in the occupied territories functioned, what a "settler" was, what his or her mentality was. In one scene in *Occupied Palestine* we see a "park" where there was once a Palestinian village. A guide welcomes Americans and Canadians to look it over. They will receive cash and a house, together, of course, with Israeli citizenship, if they settle there. Water will be pumped from artesian wells, which once supplied the village, so that the "park" will be well irrigated. Barbed wire and watchtowers will protect the "park" from those who once grazed their flocks, drew their water, and tended their orchards on its slopes.

"Settlers," whether British, German, French, Dutch, Belgian, or Romanian—many came from Romania during the Ceauşescu regime—are reactionary individuals. I do not mean refugees, those who fled persecution, but those who after 1967 left Manchester or Johannesburg or somewhere in the States to "settle," as colonists, in the West Bank. It is not a case of nationality or religion; it is a question of racist mentality. They too, with guns and guard dogs, lived behind barbed wire. But they had all the rights. The Palestinians whose land they took had no rights at all.

In Jordan I was taken to the ancient Roman city of Jerash. My host, a deputy minister, showed me the theatre, and as we walked in the winter sunshine down Roman streets, long deserted, I thought of the Roman colonists and of their civilization. I thought of Shelley's fable of an ancient empire buried beneath the desert sands, and despite the beauty of the place and the warmth of the winter sun on pink stones, I was shivering.

Crown Prince Hassan met me in the palace and showed me a series of photographs demonstrating how Israeli policy on the West Bank had reduced the Palestinian areas to tiny enclaves, dominated and engulfed by the settlements of "Greater Israel." It was a very clear and objective presentation. I suggested that the Ministry of Culture should buy the rights to *Playing for Time* and screen it on Jordanian television. It had been banned in Israel, but if it were broadcast in Jordan, Israelis could see it on their screens. One of the greatest tragedies of the whole conflict is that so much injury has been done to the Arab peoples, and there has been so much racism that they do not feel they can show something like Fania Fenelon's story, which proves again not only the crime against the Jewish people but the common experience of both peoples, suffering from the crimes of racism and imperialism.

In the new year, 1982, I flew to Australia to speak at the premieres of *Occupied Palestine* in Sydney, Melbourne, Canberra, Brisbane, and Perth, and at public meetings sponsored by the Socialist Labour League, which at that time was affiliated with the International Committee of the Fourth International. I was guest speaker at the Australian Press Club, and the film drew large audiences everywhere. In Sydney, where it was shown first, someone rang the caretaker of the town hall to say that a bomb had been planted. The police searched the place, and the mayor provided extra security. I rang a number of trade union leaders and asked if they would join me on the platform and help protect people's democratic right to see the film if they wished. They came, and the hall was packed. The Australian Congress of Trade Unions had a despicable record for abusing the rights of the Palestinians and other Arab peoples, but that was by no means true of all the unions that made up the Congress, nor of their leaders. And Australian trade unions have a record second to none for defending democratic rights, including the right to free speech. So they came, and we spoke, and of course there was no bomb.

In all I spent six months on the road with *Occupied Palestine*, and during that time I spent seventeen nights at home. Tasha and Joely were nineteen and seventeen, almost grown-up. Carlo was only twelve; I missed him terribly and longed to hear him speak and hold him in my arms. Nothing can make up for the time you lose with your children, but the time you have becomes more precious. Our children see what we are doing and understand it, but sometimes they despair when things change slowly, or not at all.

I was really tired every night when I got home. Tasha and Silvana did most of the cooking, or we'd get a Big Mac, or I'd make what Carlo called my dinosaur soup—lamb with lots of gravy, potatoes, carrots, and bones. Carlo came and sat with me one night at the kitchen table with a tape recorder in his hand. We started talking and suddenly he burst out laughing. I woke up with a start and looked at him. He played back a tape of our talk—I'd gone to sleep while we were talking, and I'd gone on talking in my sleep.

I had a good new piece of work: the small but fascinating role of Cosima Wagner in a six-part television series about Richard Wagner, to be played by Richard Burton. We had a week's filming in Venice in March, which was a wonderful opportunity to see that fabled city when almost no one else was there. Franco had a part in the film, and so did Corin. I stayed in a small hotel near St. Mark's Square, and one morning I got a call from Silvana to tell me I'd been offered six concerts with the Boston Symphony Orchestra in honor of Stravinsky's centenary.

When I got back to London I told my agent to accept the offer. Seiji Ozawa would stage Stravinsky's *Oedipus Rex*. Jessye Norman would sing Jocasta, and I would take the role of the Narrator, written and created by Jean Cocteau. I had discussions with Bill Bewell, the music director, who said he would send tapes right over. Rehearsals would start very soon, and he said he'd put me in a hotel by Symphony Hall in Boston.

≡

The telephone at my bedside rang at one in the morning on March 31. I was very annoyed to be woken up, but when I heard the voice of Bill Bewell I got out of bed and went to the kitchen, where the cold and a cup of tea would pull me together. Bill sounded very excited. "Vanessa! I had expected some protests but nothing like this!"

There was a pause. "Like what?" I said, pushing the switch to set the water boiling for my cup of tea.

"The symphony switchboard has been inundated with phone calls!"

Another pause. "Yes?" I said.

"We've had dozens of letters protesting your engagement!"

Another pause. "Have you?" I said, quite surprised, but still concentrating on my cup of tea. Bill talked and talked, saying the same thing so often that I began to think there was something else he had to say but didn't want to say, or didn't know how to say.

"Supposing there's violence!"

"Why should there be any violence?" I asked, again somewhat surprised by this agitated exclamation.

"We've had phone threats!"

I explained that people who make phone threats never do anything. He continued to talk and talk; it seemed to me he was expecting me to say something. I told him that way back in 1969, when I was working at a theatre in Manchester with Michael Elliott, someone had phoned—we presumed from the fascist National Front because our play, *Daniel Deronda*, had a Jewish theme and a number of Jewish actors—saying there was a bomb in the theatre. Michael Elliott had called the police. It was the first night, and they checked through the theatre and found nothing, and we had a very good performance.

I thought this story might put things into perspective for him, but my sangfroid seemed to worry him. "What will you do if they shoot you?" I really was amazed by this. I couldn't imagine what he was talking about. *Oedipus Rex* is a great musical work, and it did not seem likely that the ancient story of the King of Thebes was controversial anymore.

I explained to Bill that if this was a political protest, whoever was making it would know that a great orchestra like the Boston Symphony would not change its plans, and there would be a lot of people who would want to hear Jessye Norman and myself in *Oedipus Rex,* this extraordinary piece by Stravinsky. There would be no bombs, no shooting, perhaps one picket, and the concerts would be a big success.

The next evening, April 1, my agent rang me from Los Angeles. The BSO had canceled all the *Oedipus Rex* concerts. They had prepared a press statement without mentioning my name: "The Boston Symphony Orchestra regrets to announce that due to circumstances beyond their reasonable control the concerts of Stravinsky's *Oedipus Rex* are canceled." That was how my case against the BSO began.

A contract properly made is legally binding, but a *force majeure* clause in every contract permits an employer to cancel in case of flood, earthquake, fire, or war, events that are presumed to be beyond his control. I rang lawyers in New York. I said I thought the BSO's reasons for canceling my contract were political, so would they demand that the BSO reinstate my contract and resume their planned program. I rang Mike Wallace at CBS. Then I had a call from a radio station in Boston inviting me to fly there and talk to callers. ABC had invited me to do some publicity for *My Body, My Child,* so fortunately I had a visa; otherwise I could not have gone. I flew to New York and spoke on the *Good Morning America* program, saying I hoped the concerts would be rescheduled and that I had instructed lawyers to make this request for me. If they were not, it meant that blacklisting and political censorship of artists had come back to America. Then I flew to Boston and spoke with telephone callers on the *Jerry Williams Show* for three hours. One of these, a violinist from the Boston Symphony named Jerome Rosen, said that a few members of the orchestra had signed a petition objecting to my appearance in the concert, but that they were shocked and upset to learn that it had been canceled. He had been told by a member of the orchestra's management that their petition had nothing to do with the decision to cancel.

JERRY WILLIAMS: How many members of the orchestra were upset?

JEROME ROSEN: Well, you see, half the orchestra were on vacation at the time . . .

JERRY WILLIAMS: So, there couldn't have been very many, obviously?

JEROME ROSEN: Do you mean upset at the cancellation, or . . .

JERRY WILLIAMS: No, upset at the fact that Miss Redgrave was going to appear.

JEROME ROSEN: I think many of us were disturbed, but with little thought about what was really at stake, which is freedom of expression. I think most of us realized that many of us are Jews, who know our own history. Many of us are old enough to remember McCarthy in a more personal way, and the parallel was obvious and immediate. And as many people have said, the First Amendment in this country was not designed to protect popular opinions because popular opinions don't need protecting. It's the hard cases where you have to hold to the principle.

After the broadcast I went to my hotel to meet Peter Sellars, who was to have directed *Oedipus Rex*. I was surprised to find a very young man of twenty-four who was thoughtful and articulate. He, of course, had been at the meetings in Symphony Hall with the general manager, Tom Morris, Bill Bewell, and two press officers, Caroline Sandrig and Judith Gordon. I will always be grateful to Peter Sellars. He is one of those who, as Jerome Rosen said, knows that there are "cases where you have to hold to the principle." He told me the sequence of events as he knew them.

On March 29 Tom Morris had told Peter that they wanted to replace me, and that evening Peter told Morris that if they did fire me he would not direct *Oedipus Rex*. When he asked Morris for his reasons, he was told that although no threats had been made, the BSO was afraid there would be. Morris told him the B'nai B'rith was *considering* issuing a statement condemning my engagement. From the moment Peter refused to accept my being fired, the BSO had a problem. If they went ahead and fired me, they knew he would resign and would speak out publicly. Nonetheless, on the morning of March 30 Morris had my name removed from the artwork of a display advertisement that the press office was placing in *The New York Times* on April 4. That same Tuesday, Peter was told that the B'nai B'rith had decided *not* to issue a statement. By late afternoon the BSO had still not received any threats, or any call from the Jewish Defense League. Peter's rehearsal in New York that Tuesday night was postponed. On Wednesday evening, March 31, he was due to rehearse the chorus. Tom Morris called him and asked him once more for the record if he still refused to direct the concert without Vanessa Redgrave. Peter said he hadn't changed his mind, and that he was going to call Seiji Ozawa in Paris and wanted to speak with the BSO trustees.

So by the time of my midnight telephone call from Bill Bewell on Wednesday, March 31, there had been no threats of violence or bloodshed. Why then had Bewell spoken to me about violence? Why had he asked me, "What will you do if they shoot you?" Why had he not told me that the BSO general manager had already decided to replace me, going so far as to remove my name from the artwork for the display ad on March 30? I realized that if I had withdrawn from the concerts during this telephone call, then the BSO people could have told Peter Sellars, "Vanessa has withdrawn, so you don't have to resign; you can go ahead and direct *Oedipus Rex*." But I had not withdrawn.

On Thursday, April 1, Peter Sellars was told that someone from the Jewish Defense League had telephoned. Tom Morris told Peter this call had clinched the cancellation of my performances with the BSO. Peter asked for a conference call with Seiji Ozawa. He urged Ozawa to go ahead with me, speaking of the Rights of Man, of Beethoven's beliefs, of the perils of allowing blacklisting. Ozawa did not agree, so Peter told him he would resign rather than allow me to be removed from the concerts. Following that conference call, the BSO press office and lawyers started drafting their press release, which was published the next day, April 2.

Alan Eisenberg, for American Actors' Equity, wrote to Tom Morris: "An orchestra of renown and standing such as the Boston Symphony should be a major champion of the artist's right to work and to espouse whatever political views he or she chooses. Your denial of Ms. Redgrave's right to do both poses a threat to the basic democratic principles we cherish and upon which art depends." The Screen Actors Guild also made a statement on my behalf. Then, on April 6, Ed Asner, the star of the CBS *Lou Grant* series, had his show canceled, because of "falling ratings," CBS said. But everyone knew that Ed was being victimized because he had led a fund-raising campaign for medical aid for Nicaragua and El Salvador and had supported PATCO, the air traffic controllers' union, which was in dispute with the federal government.

The BSO refused to reinstate the concerts. The Arab American Association in Washington said they would sponsor me to appear in a performance in Boston to help prove I could perform there without any public disorder. They booked the Orpheum Theatre for April 29 and I prepared a program of songs and scenes from *As You Like It*, *The Seagull*, and *Isadora*, with Philip Casnoff, a brilliant young actor who was then not well known. I rang Tennessee Williams and asked if he would join me, and read something from his own work. He said fine, he would read an essay called "Misunderstanding of the Artist in Revolt." We arranged to meet in the Ritz-Carlton Hotel in Boston on April 8.

I flew in from London that day and checked with the desk to see if Tennessee had arrived. They said, no, Mr. Williams had not made a reservation. My heart sank. I knew there must have been great pressure on Tennessee not to come and read with me that day, and I supposed he must have bowed to it. My body felt heavy and exhausted. I sat down on the hotel bed, took a deep breath, drank a glass of water, and then the phone rang. I picked it up and heard a warm, cheerful, deep Southern voice. "Vanessa? It's Tennessee." "Oh, Tennessee, where *are* you?" Distress does strange things to the voice, and I must have sounded like an anxious mother or a harassed schoolteacher, because Tennessee laughed and laughed until he had a coughing fit. "I'm downstairs in the lobby of course. Won't you come down?" "Of *course* I'll come down," I cried, and I really did cry, all the way down in the elevator. Tennessee was sitting in a huge green chair in the quiet old lounge, and we hugged each other and ordered tea and muffins. He said, "You were right, they *all* phoned me and told me not to come, but damn it, here I am." We gave two performances next day. A very small, orderly picket line appeared for one hour, then shuffled off. A dozen policemen shifted from foot to foot in the foyer and on the pavement outside, with nothing to do but look at their watches. The press said practically nothing. Not one paper even mentioned that Tennessee Williams had come.

When he died the following year, Tennessee's friends and fellow artists paid him a tribute at Circle in the Square. They recalled his definition of happiness: "Insensitivity, I guess." That is the key to Tennessee as a human being and as a writer. When he drank or took pills, he did so, like Brick in *Cat on a Hot Tin Roof,* to hear "a click in my head," to have a few hours' oblivion, because he could not bear the cruelty he saw in the world. His agent, Milton Goldman, was a very kind and noble man. When Tennessee died he wrote to tell me he had done his very utmost to stop him from coming to Boston. He sent me a copy of the letter Tennessee sent him after the Boston performance. He wrote about the agony of the artist who feels that he's alone, that no one is listening to him or seeing what he sees. That was why he had joined me in Boston, he said. Not because of my politics, but because I felt the suffering of human beings as an artist, and he did not want me to be alone in that.

It took two and a half years to get my case against the BSO into the Massachusetts courts. It made some legal history and is a landmark in the struggle for civil rights because, in the final judgment, it set a precedent for legalizing blacklisting. To tell it in proper detail would require a whole book.

Many things were revealed in the legal process of "discovery." There had been exactly four letters protesting my engagement by April 1, the day the BSO press release was prepared. Also, the Jewish Defense League member had obligingly left his telephone number and name when he telephoned Symphony Hall. Two years later, in November 1984, Arthur Burnstein appeared in court, summoned by my lawyers. He testified that he had told the press office he would organize a picket line outside Symphony Hall. The fact that he had left his name and telephone number corroborated his sworn evidence that he had made no threats; he had merely said he would exercise his democratic right to organize a picket line. He also confirmed that he was the only Jewish Defense League member left in Boston. The rest had left the United States and gone to Israel with Rabbi Meir Kahane to found the Kach party (which was made illegal by the state of Israel in 1988).

Money was a problem. I borrowed heavily, and my lawyers allowed me to get deeply in debt with them so long as I paid them small sums fairly frequently. But even those small sums were hard to find. I discovered that my previous accountants had completely neglected my taxes; the Inland Revenue was now demanding large amounts that had been left unpaid, and for over a year I could get no work, owing to the publicity surrounding my case against the BSO. Things began to change in my favor when the BSO failed to get a summary judgment to dismiss my case in 1983. Ismail Merchant rang asking me to play Olive Chancellor in a film of *The Bostonians,* with Christopher Reeve. He told me the Bank of Boston was putting money in the film and was pleased to hear I would be starring in it. But when Anthony Page wanted me to play in *Heartbreak House* at Circle in the Square, Ted Mann and Paul Libin said they couldn't engage me because of the BSO cancellation. They, too, depended on subscriptions, and if the BSO was unable to withstand political pressure and blackmail, they, a much smaller organization, could not risk employing me.

The weekend before the case began, in October 1984, I needed $150,000 to carry on and I had $20,000 in the bank. I telephoned the Washington embassy of the Royal Kingdom of Saudi Arabia and asked for Prince Bandar Bin Sultan's secretary. The ambassador came on the phone and invited me to see him and his family in Virginia. I flew down from Boston and we sat and talked, and I explained that without his help I would be forced to withdraw my case from the court for lack of money. I flew back to Boston with a check for $150,000 in my shoulder bag.

For three weeks I was in the district court every day. Among my witnesses were Peter Sellars, Sidney Lumet, Ismail Merchant, Ted Mann, and my agent, Bruce Savan. Lillian Hellman had promised to appear for me as an expert witness on blacklisting. I had met her, at last, in the summer of 1983 on Martha's Vineyard—a fragile, indomitable woman who could hardly see and barely walk. She welcomed me, and we talked like sisters about the Rosenbergs, *Julia,* and the BSO. She had prepared an affidavit outlining the economic consequences of her own blacklisting. She died before the trial began, but her affidavit was read to the court. My dear friend Thelma Holt flew to Boston and told the court that during the visit to London of the Rustaveli Company from Tbilisi, Georgia, soon after the Soviet invasion of Afghanistan, there had been bomb threats every night for ten days. Two busloads of police had arrived every evening at her theatre. "I would announce to the audience each night that we had received a threat. The people making the threats always told us when the bombs were to go off, shortly after the intermission began. So while people were filing out of the theatre for the interval the police went in and made their sweep. It was a bore for all of us and very expensive for the British police, but if we had canceled, if we had given in to every nut who wanted his name in the papers, nothing could go on."

On November 9, 1984, the jury found that there were no causes beyond the reasonable control of the BSO to justify cancellation and awarded me $100,000 of consequential damages, saying that the BSO caused "foreseeable harm" to my career when it canceled the concerts. They did not find for me on the separate issue of the abrogation of my civil rights, but a few days later they made legal history. They wrote a letter to the district court judge, Robert E. Keaton, saying that they were indeed convinced that my civil rights had been abrogated by the BSO, but could find no way "to express [this view] within the confines of the [questions put to us] and your explanation to us as to the parameters within which the law required we must decide."

The judge overturned the jury's findings and the award of $100,000 consequential damages. He ruled: "It is not illegal for a private entity to make a choice not to contract with an artist for a performance if its agents believe that the artist's appearance under their sponsorship would be interpreted by others as in some degree a political statement. Thus the BSO was entirely free not to make a contract with Redgrave for such reasons even though its agents considered her a superb actress and exceptionally qualified to perform as narrator in *Oedipus Rex.*" Therefore, Judge Keaton ruled in January 1985, the cancellation amounted to no more than standard breach of contract, and an award of $100,000 damages would signify an attack on the constitutionally protected rights of the BSO.

The judge's ruling was staggering. It meant that all laws and provisions against discrimination were undermined. No employer would be obliged to employ someone, however qualified for the job in hand, or keep a person in employment, if in the opinion of the employer or his agent to do so could be construed as "a political statement." Nor could it be illegal, beyond a "standard breach of contract," for an employer to make a political statement by firing someone.

I had no choice but to appeal. The Lawyers' Committee for Civil Rights of the Boston Bar Association, the Civil Liberties Union of Massachusetts, and finally the attorney general of Massachusetts himself entered amicus curiae briefs in my behalf.

I announced my appeal at the Los Angeles Press Club on March 21, 1985. Peter Feibleman, one of Lillian Hellman's executors, had joined me. Half an hour before the conference I had a call from Corin from a nursing home in Denham, in Buckinghamshire, to tell me that Michael had died. I wanted to cry and cancel the press conference, but I couldn't, and I knew that if I spoke, I must speak strongly and well.

Michael had followed his political convictions in the thirties. So had Lillian. She had kept hers until her death. He had lost all conviction until, already shaking with Parkinson's disease, he had made his way to a rally in Hyde Park where I was speaking and, standing well away at the back of the crowd, unnoticed by anyone, had found, he told Corin, that he liked the "revolutionary flavor" of what he had heard. The night before he died, struggling for breath and shaking with fever, he took Corin's hand and whispered, "You put the wind in my sails."

I thought of Michael and felt him with me, knowing he would want me to take a deep breath and speak as well as I could. So I did.

CHAPTER 23

The Bostonians in 1983 was my first film with Merchant-Ivory Productions. Since then I have done *The Ballad of the Sad Cafe* and
Howards End. I was immensely grateful for the work, in the midst of
the BSO case, but I approached the job with some fear. Corin had
read most of Henry James, as had the majority of his generation who
studied English at Cambridge and attended Dr. Leavis's lectures. My
father was a devotee. He had faithfully and very creatively adapted
James's novella *The Aspern Papers* for the stage, and his bookshelves
were lined with Leon Edel's editions of James's letters and novels and
countless studies of James. But I was far from devoted. Every time I
picked up a novel, James's spiteful verdict on Ibsen—"Yet I feel, to
the pitch of almost intolerable boredom, the presence and stirring of
life"—rang in my ears, coming back, like a boomerang, to James
himself, or rather to my response to his writing. Life there undeni-
ably was in his portrait of Olive Chancellor, the sensitive and highly
prejudiced view of a brother toward his sister, Alice James. He writes
cynically, and often maliciously, yet he was touched in spite of
himself by the fate of those middle-class women, treated like pariahs
by their contemporaries, who set their faces against the mores of their

society and campaigned for women's right to education and the vote, and often for women's rights in the factories. Reading James's novel, and Ruth Prawer Jhabvala's very good script, I felt his prejudice all the time in conflict with his artistry as a writer, and the fact that despite himself he was drawn toward the woman he portrayed.

"Forget the novel," James Ivory told his cast two or three times a day during our first days of shooting. "We're not filming the novel, but a story by Ruth Jhabvala." We had some friendly arguments about that. I could see why he said it, and I could imagine how it would try a director's patience to be told that such and such a scene "worked" better in the novel, often because an actor would be disappointed to discover how much shorter his role was in the script than in the original. Nevertheless I could not forget the novel, simply because it seemed to me that I must understand James's very contradictory view of Olive Chancellor. Some arguments in filming can be debilitating. Ours were invigorating, and I would spring out of bed, looking forward to each day's work. I loved Madeleine Potter, who played Verena. And Christopher Reeve was a joy to work with, dedicated and full of ideas. He's a wonderful actor, very inventive and immediate. He became a good friend, and in 1984 we played together again in my father's adaptation of *The Aspern Papers* with Wendy Hiller.

The Aspern Papers was a wonderful experience. It is an extremely well written play because Michael had a real feeling for the story. James does not explain very much, and in writing the play Michael strengthened all kinds of human touches that you might easily miss on a first reading of the novella itself. I was delighted when I finally convinced Christopher to play Henry Jarvis. I felt that casting an American in the part was important. Michael was very quiet when he met Chris and looked at him intently, wondering how this very tall and muscular man would appear as Henry Jarvis. Before we brought the play into London, Michael spent a lot of time with us, and I valued being able to share the production with him professionally. When he came to the first performance he sat in a box, and Rachel said that at the end he waved his arms and clapped his hands above his head in admiration. He thought Christopher was a truly fine actor, which meant a lot to us both, particularly before the play opened, when the British press tried to put Christopher down. Christopher has worked in the theatre since he was fifteen, long before he became known to British journalists as Superman, and he continues to work in the theatre today. He is a fine stage actor, and when we opened he rightly received unanimously good reviews. The critics agreed with Michael.

Shortly before he died, Michael had seen Natasha as Ophelia in *Hamlet* at the Young Vic Theatre in Waterloo. The Young Vic's policy at that time was to present classic plays for school and college students, so the Saturday matinees were boisterous affairs, with a good deal of whistling and giggling from sixteen-year-old kids who probably thought they had better things to do on a Saturday afternoon than watch Shakespeare and be bored. Michael's wheelchair was parked in an aisle, and he was surrounded on all sides by teenage schoolchildren. Tasha's was the sweetest, dearest, most affectionate Ophelia I had ever seen. Her "mad scene" was not mad, but she was so grief-stricken at the horrors she had seen that her nerves gave way, and to the adults around her she appeared mad. It struck a chord with the Young Vic audience, who watched and listened in silence, totally concentrated, and applauded and cheered at the end. Michael said almost nothing as we drove back to the nursing home, but I knew from long experience that that was a good sign. When he was most absorbed he lapsed into long, impenetrable silences, and a look of deep melancholy, even boredom, settled on his face. It was exasperating for those who didn't know him well, but we knew that it meant he was turning something over and over in his mind. His grandchildren saw him very little, yet they loved him for his gentleness, and the way his eyes would follow them round the room. As we reached Denham he said, after a pause which lasted almost the length of the journey, "She's a true actress."

Michael had been moved into a clinic run by the Licensed Victuallers' Association—a jolly place for retired publicans where all the patients could get cut-price drinks. No hospital could afford to have him because his disease was incurable and to keep him in a bed would mean depriving another patient. The acute shortage of hospital beds caused by the Tory government's cuts in funding meant that there was a crisis in the National Health Service. The nurses welcomed him back and wheeled him to his room, teasing him about his "outing" and helping him to undress. He shared a room with an elderly retired publican who had kept a pub in Whitechapel in wartime and remembered all Michael's films, like *The Way to the Stars* and *The Dam Busters*. I tucked him up in bed, kissed him good night, and wished him Happy Birthday for the following Tuesday, his seventy-seventh birthday, when I should be back in America.

Parkinson's disease had muffled Michael's voice almost to a whisper, and at times he could not speak at all. His greatest tragedy was that people would talk to him as if his mind were disabled. Because he often could not reply quickly, or stopped in mid-sentence, they spoke to him as if he were a retarded child. I have seen many retarded children with disabilities that have their origin in a chemical breakdown in the system. Even in the most severe cases, given proper medical and above all human treatment, such children can develop their mental abilities to a degree not commonly imagined. If, however, they are shut away in institutions and tied to their beds, for lack of staff, or out of sheer bureaucratic ignorance, they become hopelessly handicapped. Professor David Watkins, the leading neurological surgeon at the London Hospital, who had taken a close interest in Michael, explained that "the more input the better. People hallucinate when they don't have enough input or stimulus from outside. Human beings are social beings. Without discussion, walks, activities, videos, they lose their human faculties."

≡

March went out like a lion and the daffodils in Mortlake crematorium tossed to and fro in the wind. But Michael's funeral was a celebration. Cecil Beaton's wonderful photograph of his Antony, the best theatre portrait I ever saw, lay propped against his coffin in the chapel. His friends and colleagues sang or spoke poems in eulogy. Natasha read Perdita's speech from *The Winter's Tale*—"My fairest friend, I would I had some flowers now o' the spring . . ." Ian McKellen spoke Milton's "Lycidas," and the final, famous couplet— "At last he rose and twitched his mantle blue:/Tomorrow to fresh woods, and pastures new"—never sounded so fresh and hopeful. Ian Charleson, a beautiful, sensitive actor, who died in 1990 after a heroic struggle with AIDS, and who had a special place in the affections of his colleagues, sang Sky Masterson's solo from *Guys and Dolls*—"My time of day is the dark time,/A couple of deals before dawn . . ." It was Michael's favorite song. Walking the streets at night in a black overcoat and black felt hat, calling on his friends at two in the morning, and coming home just before dawn was his favorite occupation. Yehudi Menuhin and his wife, Diana, came, and afterward Diana told me a story. "I always loved your father and I told him everything. People said he was aloof and difficult to know, but not me. I could say anything to him. So when I met Yehudi, Michael was the first person I wanted to tell. I went to his dressing room at the theatre and said, 'I'm in love with Menuhin and I want to bring him round to meet you. Can I?' 'Oh no, no, no,' Michael said, 'you can't. Please don't.' 'Why ever not?' I asked. 'Because he's a genius,' Michael said, 'and I won't be able to talk to him.' 'Don't be silly,' I told him, 'you're quite a genius yourself, and I can still talk to you.'"

In April 1985 I was on the road again. The miners had returned to work after their year-long strike, betrayed by the Labour leaders and the Trades Union Congress but not defeated. But now a terrible toll of reprisals began, in which the government, the courts, and the Coal Board did their utmost to take their revenge on the miners and smash their union. Thirty miners were in jail, and more than seven hundred had been sacked. Their offenses ranged from manslaughter, in the case of Russell Jones and Dean Shankland, who were jailed for life, to the most trivial charge of trespassing on Coal Board property. But whatever their charges or their sentences, their real offense, in the eyes of their accusers, was that of fighting for their jobs, their families, and their communities, and loyalty to their union, the National Union of Mineworkers, and to the trade union movement and the working class as a whole. They were victims of class warfare, and those who were in jail were political prisoners. If you said that to a member of the front bench of the shadow cabinet or to a leader of the TUC, he would roll his eyes heavenward or turn on his heels and walk away. The very concept of classes and class warfare had become anathema to the bosses of the labor and trade union movement, who preached a vision of classless harmony called "new realism." But it was true, and if you wanted confirmation of that from the horse's mouth, you need only have listened to the seventy-year-old American Scot Ian MacGregor, brought over to Britain for a huge fee to run the Coal Board. On the day after the miners were forced back to work in March 1985 MacGregor said, "People are now discovering the price of insubordination and insurrection, and boy! are we going to give it them."

I set out with a camera crew and a reporter to visit all the mining communities in Britain and talk to the miners' wives. Our Central Committee had asked me to make a film about the women, because their movement, the miners' wives' support groups, was one of the most remarkable political developments of the strike. They had sustained the strike for twelve months. They had traveled up and down the country for demonstrations and meetings. They had spoken on public platforms. They had traveled abroad, to speak and to raise funds. They had seen how other workers lived and struggled. And they had learned that Britain, under Margaret Thatcher, had become a police state.

Liz French, whose husband, Terry, from Betteshanger Colliery in Kent, had been jailed for five years, told me how it had begun. "He'd been picketing in Warwickshire and when he came home, he said, 'You wouldn't believe the kickings we're getting.' Now me, personally, I was saying to Terry, 'Come on, six of one, half a dozen of the other,' but he said, 'What you've been seeing on television isn't half and half. Television hasn't shown you what they're doing. It's too busy making us out to be criminals and thugs.' " And then, Liz said, the police moved into their communities in Deal and Aylesham and the women were shocked. "You couldn't walk down this street. The police stopped you on every corner, where were you going, what were you doing, who were you married to? And then they came bursting into your home, trampling down your fence, knocking down your door, accusing your men of crimes they'd never committed. We experienced the police state, and it was frightening."

In Barnsley I interviewed Anne Scargill, the wife of the leader of the miners' union, and then went back to her home to meet her husband and daughter. Their home was modest, warm, and welcoming. Arthur Scargill told me there had been three attempts on his life during the strike. In no instance were arrests made or charges brought by the police. Arthur himself had been arrested for picketing at Orgreave in Yorkshire. He led the miners from the front, picketing with them, being arrested with them, and for that, as well as his other very great qualities of leadership, he had retained their support and loyalty against the most sustained onslaught that had been waged against a trade union and its leader in our times.

I visited James Waddell, a young married miner from Kent, in prison on the Isle of Sheppey. Outside the prison an enormous site was being scraped and bulldozed for another high-security wing. We met in the canteen, which was unusual, and had a cup of tea at a plastic-topped table in a room full of other men and their relatives. He told me it was impossible to get *Newsline*, our party's daily paper, although we were mailing it to him. He was allowed only the *Sun* or the *Daily Express*. I looked at James, who was young enough to be my son, knowing that when he came out he would be unable to get a job in the pit, which had been his life ever since he left the Royal Marines. He would be blacklisted by every employer in the country. In a short while every colliery in Kent would be closed, and Betteshanger Colliery would be turned into a yacht marina or a leisure center, and families like James Waddell's, who had come down from Scotland in the 1930s in search of work, would be at a dead end. James knew this and explained it very well. He had fought for jobs, for his family, and now he was in a high-security prison on the Isle of Sheppey.

I learned a lot during the making of this film. The more I listened to the miners' wives, mothers, and daughters, the more it became clear that their main concern was for the men, like James and Terry, who were in jail, and the hundreds of miners who had been sacked. The party was preparing a march, from Edinburgh, Liverpool, and Swansea to a rally at Alexandra Pavilion, against unemployment and the cheap labor schemes for youth, and as soon as I returned to London I wrote a letter to the Political Committee suggesting that the main demands of the march should be that the jailed miners be released and that the sacked miners get their jobs back. Gerry agreed and formulated a new proposal for the Central Committee, a concept in which the particular case of the jailed miner would be connected to the universal threat of mass unemployment, the destruction of industries, and the exploitation of young people, denied the right to join a trade union.

Political parties are tested and prove themselves in a very concrete way at times of great social and political conflict. Elections and opinion polls provide one kind of test, but a very imperfect one. This is chiefly because opinion polls are now governed exclusively by the needs of the party in power. But it is also because every poll, no matter how "objectively" the pollster approaches the task, addresses its sample of opinions as a passive object. It is incapable of analyzing the changes in large masses of people, connected to one another in a struggle, or of listening to *their* questions. It is certain that no opinion poll could have detected the changes in the influence of the Workers' Revolutionary Party among decisive groups of workers and working-class communities in 1985.

But the miners' strike provided a test of another kind. Many workers joined the Labour Party in 1984 and 1985, realizing that their struggle was political, and wanting to become politically active. But far more significant was the number of miners and politically conscious workers who left the Labour Party, tearing up their cards in protest at Labour's refusal to back the strike. These workers and their wives, the vanguard, not in the sense of an elite but in terms of their political development, were searching for an alternative. And they now turned to the Workers' Revolutionary Party. Not to the Communist Party—which was conducting a half-open, half-clandestine campaign against Arthur Scargill—but to the WRP.

This was the situation for which Gerry had spent his life working, teaching, and preparing. The party had a full-time college of Marxist education. We possessed a printing factory in Runcorn with £750,000 worth of plant and equipment. Astmoor Litho, our printing works, could produce a quarter of a million copies of *Newsline* each day, with full-color printing superior to that of any Fleet Street newspaper. We produced a steady stream of books and pamphlets, with six bookshops in the largest cities. Youth Training, the movement sponsored by the Young Socialists, had eight youth centers. In Britain we had a political alliance, a united front with the most progressive elements in the Labour Party. Internationally we supported every revolutionary movement and national liberation struggle and had firm political alliances with all the most important trends and tendencies in such movements.

Then, on July 1, the day after our rally at Alexandra Pavilion, an attack was launched that had been prepared for a long time. Gerry's secretary, a young married woman who had been in the party for over twenty years and had been his personal secretary since before I became a member in 1973, disappeared. She left a letter accusing Gerry of sexually assaulting women in the party. The Political Committee voted by a large majority for my resolution that this letter was a provocation. (I never saw or heard of the woman again.) The next morning, however, Mrs. Gibson, who had been in charge of the finance office for many years, announced that two large bills had arrived, for a total of £49,000, and that the party had no funds to pay them. This was indeed alarming, for Mrs. Gibson and her colleagues had checked the weekly accounts in the finance office and submitted them to the Political Committee. These accounts had shown the WRP, and our printing and publishing companies, to be in the black, with no large outstanding debts.

Corin was elected to take charge of the finance department. He found £250,000 of unpaid bills and every bank account in deficit. He also found forged copies of deeds to party property in the finance office. The forger had blanked out entries on the charge sheets showing that the properties, unknown to the party, had been mortgaged to the hilt. The true copies of the deeds were now, of course, in the vaults of the bank that had mortgaged them.

We raised, almost immediately, £100,000 in donations from party members and supporters to pay off the most pressing debts. Corin, together with a subcommittee of members, including Gerry, put the financial affairs of the party companies on a sounder footing. Credit, which had been refused by almost every company we traded with, was restored. The worst of our financial crisis, in the short term, was overcome. Gerry still commanded great support in the party ranks. The members knew that he, more than anyone, had built the party and that his opponents, university lecturers who only yesterday had voted with him for every decision, had built nothing at all. Moreover his work was still intact: no premises had been sold; the party held on to all its assets.

In September and October, our general secretary, Mike Banda, suddenly joined those Central Committee members who were declaring that they had *never* agreed with the political perspectives and manifestos they had discussed and voted for; had never agreed with anything they had voted for since I had joined the party in 1973. They had *never* agreed with the the studies we had made with Gerry in dialectical materialist philosophy. Britain was not a Bonapartist state. We should not be supporting the liberation movements of Chairman Arafat and Nelson Mandela, or SWAPO in Namibia.

Political differences are one thing, but the atmosphere now was abusive, hysterical, and violent. Corin and I became extremely alarmed for Gerry's safety. We and some of our comrades set about finding a new place for him to stay. We arranged to move his library and few personal belongings to a house I bought, where he and I could live and he could study. I was in his small rented apartment packing his books when a gang of men rushed upstairs. Luckily, I had arranged for the police to be called if this should happen. For the next three months, until the house was ready, we found several different accommodations for him. He had been the target of assassination attempts in 1982 and 1983, and we resolved to ensure that neither the enormous stress of the moment nor any physical attack should end his life prematurely.

Corin prepared a financial report for the Central Committee on October 12. His careful research proved that since 1982 five Central Committee members had been forging signatures on documents, mortgaging premises, and running up large debts without the knowledge of any of our other committees. Corin demanded that this report be given to all party members, but Mike Banda and a majority of the Central Committee refused to circulate it, and would not consider it themselves. (The following year we published this report in full in *The Marxist Review* and submitted it in evidence in the Companies Court.)

Two hundred members were summoned to our center in Clapham. Many of them had not been seen at any branch or aggregate meeting for years. They demanded Gerry's expulsion and the resignation of the Political Committee members who supported him. Someone had set up loudspeakers to relay the Central Committee proceedings. A group of men were selected to go to Gerry's apartment and bring him back to the center for some kind of trial. This was when they discovered me packing his books.

Two weeks later, the WRP and the International Committee were split. We called an emergency conference and asked all members to attend who supported the policies of our last congresses and opposed the witch-hunt and slanders against Gerry. The Greek and Spanish sections sent messages of support; our former fraternal colleagues in Germany and the United States had joined the witch-hunt. We retained the name Workers' Revolutionary Party, confident that our opponents would soon reject the name of a party whose philosophy, policies, and perspectives they had repudiated. This proved to be the case. The majority of the Central Committee held a conference, expelled us, and proceeded to invite the British press to the party center, offering stories of sex and violence, for which they found a ready market.

In 1987 I was watching the television news with Gerry at the house where he lived and worked for the last years of his life. The government was fighting a battle in the Australian courts to ban the publication of *Spycatcher* by Peter Wright, a former MI5 agent. I sent off to a friend in America for copies of the book, and found a description of a crucial meeting in the early seventies, when Michael Hanley, the director-general of MI5, had ordered a major shift in the agency's resources and manpower from K Branch, which dealt with counterespionage against the Soviet Union, to F Branch, which was responsible for "domestic subversion," meaning political parties in Britain, including the Workers' Revolutionary Party. An argument had developed between Wright and a senior officer, John Jones, concerning the best method of spying on the WRP. Jones favored electronic surveillance; Wright preferred to use agents. In point of fact, both methods were employed. Every office in our party headquarters in Clapham was bugged, and agents were sent into the party and recruited from among the membership.

The technique of the frame-up is by now all too familiar. The FBI, for instance, bugged Martin Luther King, Jr., in their efforts to build up a dossier of scandal and "immorality" against him. Reports of bugging by state intelligence services and their friends appear almost daily on the front pages of the international press. In our case the state security services had a dual purpose: their stories were intended to discredit Gerry and the party he had built, and to create a climate in which any attempt on his life could be attributed to the blind, incomprehensible vendetta of "Trotskyists." The stories also served as a cover for the liquidation of all the resources that he had built. In a short while the printing presses were sold, as were the party headquarters and the youth training centers. It was a lucrative pro-

As Susan Thistlewood in Robert Shaw's superb play *Cato Street* at the Young Vic, 1971 (*above*); and (*right*) as Polly Peachum in Tony Richardson's production of Brecht's *The Threepenny Opera* at the Prince of Wales Theatre, 1972.

Bertrand Russell's ninetieth-birthday tribute at the Royal Festival Hall, November 23, 1961.

Outside the Ministry of Defence, Whitehall, during the Committee of 100 civil disobedience campaign for unilateral nuclear disarmament, 1962 (*left*); and (*below*) with Tariq Ali, leading the march to the U.S. Embassy against the war in Vietnam, March 1968.

Gerry Healy (*above*) of the Workers' Revolutionary Party in 1974. He led the International Committee of the Fourth International from 1953 until his death in 1989. In October 1974, I was the WRP parliamentary candidate for Newham North-East, London (*right*); speaking to trade unionists in Britain, spring 1978, during the Israeli invasion of Lebanon (*below*).

The Lady from the Sea, directed by Michael Elliott, at the Round House, London, 1979. This was the last time I worked with Michael, a dear friend and a great director (*left*); *Design for Living*, 1973, produced by Bob Regester and directed by Michael Blakemore (*opposite page*).

The marriage of Guinevere and King Arthur in *Camelot*. John Truscott, the designer, used candles and black velvet to create the illusion of a great dark cathedral (*left*). As Anne Boleyn in Fred Zinnemann's *A Man for All Seasons* with Robert Shaw (*bottom left*). Corin played Roper, Thomas More's son-in-law. *Below*: With Glenda Jackson as Queen Elizabeth in *Mary, Queen of Scots*, 1971.

Tony directed the 1973 production of *Antony and Cleopatra* in Sam Wanamaker's tent on the site of the sixteenth-century Globe Theatre (*above*).

As Fania Fenelon in *Playing for Time,* Arthur Miller's television film about the women's orchestra in Auschwitz (*above*); and (*right*) as Sarah, with Ron Hunter, in the *American Playhouse* television film about the Salem witch trials, *Three Sovereigns for Sarah.*

Me as Julia and Jane Fonda
as Lillian Hellman at
Oxford University, filming
Julia (*above*); and (*right*)
accepting the award for
Best Supporting Actress for
Julia at the 1977 Academy
Awards.

With Dustin Hoffman in
Agatha, 1977, the film about
Agatha Christie's
disappearance.

At the Rieka Opera House in Yugoslavia, with Litz Pisk and Karel Reisz, waiting for another take on Isadora's dance to Beethoven's Seventh Symphony (*right*). Working with John Schlesinger in *Yanks*, 1979 (*bottom left*). At the Hollywood tribute to the great director Fred Zinnemann, 1986 (*bottom right*). I was filming *Second Serve*, the story of Renée Richards.

With Michael and Christopher Reeve at the opening of *The Aspern Papers*, March 1984; and (*right*) as Cordelia at a benefit performance of *King Lear* in 1982 for the Young Socialists Youth Training Center. This was the last time Michael and I acted together.

With Lynn, Natasha, Rachel, Jemma, Carlo, and Joely at Michael's funeral, March 1985. Joan Hirst, family friend and Michael's secretary, is standing next to me. Corin is on my left.

cess and large sums of money changed hands. Our center at Clapham was sold in 1987 for £166,000. The following day it changed hands again, for £488,000. In the era of Thatcher and Reagan, when billions of dollars of fictitious value could be accumulated through junk bonds, mortgage bonds, and interest-rate swaps, such transactions hardly raised an eyebrow.

Social being determines social consciousness. The morality of Thatcherism, a gospel according to which "there is no such thing as society, there is only the individual," had percolated into our party, borne in on the flood tide of easy money that had swamped the middle classes. A revolutionary party is built on the devotion and self-sacrifice of its members, who work long hours, forgoing their own comfort and their families', often risking all chance of promotion in their work, and sometimes risking their jobs as well. Only a high level of theoretical understanding will sustain them, enabling them to see their goal clearly when the conditions for achieving it are most difficult and contradictory. That was why Gerry had placed such emphasis on theoretical training and the study of materialist dialectics. From that vantage point he had predicted a split in the party in 1981, four years before it happened. When it began to unfold, he recognized it before any of us and realized, before we did, that it was the work of the state.

≡

All through the autumn and early winter of 1985 and during the most hectic days of the split in our party I was working at the Queen's Theatre playing Madame Arkadina in Chekhov's *The Seagull*. The production had begun at the Lyric Theatre in Hammersmith, with Samantha Eggar and John Hurt as Arkadina and Trigorin, but since they could not move the production to the West End, Jonathan Pryce and I took over. Natasha played Nina in both productions. We had only about two weeks' rehearsal with the new cast, and I will always remember our first read-through. Natasha's eyes were lit up with excitement throughout, and afterward she said, "Oh, what a wonderful read-through that was." I was so happy to see her proud of me. Sadly, we had very little dialogue together onstage. "What is it like to be acting with your daughter?" I was asked. I had to restrain myself from raving on and on about her performance, which might have seemed somewhat too partial. But in truth I did not see how it could be bettered. I had read and thought a good deal about Olga Knipper, Chekhov's wife, who created the part. She had a trace of a Friesian accent, which hinted at her German origins, and she was fiercely independent, and sometimes disrespectful, even of Stanislavsky. Natasha's voice compels you to listen, which is a great gift. But more than that, she made you believe in what she saw in Trigorin, which was of course more than he saw in himself. And what does she see in herself? Nina's extraordinary soliloquy in the fourth act—"I am a seagull"—is impossible if the actress sees only Nina's own estimation of herself, as an untrained ingenue in provincial theatre, finding herself out of her depth in parts that are beyond her powers. What wrecks the lives of Nina and Konstantin is not the cruel limitation of their own talent or their capacity to mistakenly love the best in others, but the restrictions their society set upon all creativity, which meant that *The Seagull* was booed off the stage at its first performance. Our production, however, was praised to the skies, and in the spring of the following year I was awarded the Olivier/ *Observer* Prize for my performance as Arkadina.

≡

Homo sum; humani nil a me alienum puto. Terence's epigram should be a compulsory text, engraved on every magistrate's bench. I thought of it as I read Renée Richards's extraordinary, courageous autobiography. Linda Yellen, our producer on *Playing for Time,* had sent me the book, and a script based upon it, for a CBS film to be shot in January 1986. Linda's note said that there would be a twenty-day shooting period, and though I had had to refuse the chance to play *The Seagull* in New York, which was a great disappointment, since I would have loved Natasha's performance to be seen on Broadway, I knew that Renée's story was something I wanted to do very much. Renée, when she was a man, ranked among the hundred top tennis players in the world. But as she grew up she realized she had a problem that was not psychological but physiological: she was a woman, trapped inside the body of a man, and if she was to become herself, she had to change, not her mind, as many in the medical profession attempted to persuade her, but her body. Reading her story, I realized how many of my notions of what is normal or healthy were based on ignorance and fear, and I was alarmed. If I, who thought myself an unprejudiced person, could have been guilty of such stereotyped thinking, how much more so someone whose ignorance was regularly played upon by politicians, judges, and the press?

I spent a happy and fascinating evening with Renée after we had completed shooting *Second Serve*. It wasn't that I had planned not to meet her before; it simply happened that way. I was glad of that because it made me reread her book and concentrate upon what she was writing about. If I had met her before shooting, I might have been tempted to copy what I saw, or thought I saw, in her. Linda and Tony Page, our director, arranged a meeting, before we started filming, with a group of transsexuals in Los Angeles. They told me that they were often treated as outcasts or untouchables, and that many of them had lost their jobs after they had had their operations. It was amazing, they said, how many spurious reasons and excuses for firing them were forthcoming to explain why they, as women, could not perform the jobs they had been doing as men, jobs that they remained every bit as capable of after their operations as before.

Forrest Stewart, one of the best tennis teachers in Los Angeles, was my coach for the tennis scenes though no one, not even he, could make me into a shadow of the tennis player Joely had become. All the while I was learning from him I was conscious of her critical eye. But my height and my build helped a lot, and Forrest, like every great teacher, including my beloved Litz Pisk, taught me what was essential—how I should move, and how I should think.

I'd asked my friend Peter Owen, an expert wigmaker, to make my wigs, and he, I, and Del Ecevedo, George C. Scott's makeup artist, talked late into the night experimenting to find out how my appearance as Dick—Renée as a man—could carry conviction in close-ups. The consensus was that I should wear a wig as Dick, and my own hair as Renée, so Peter made a number of different men's wigs and we camera-tested them.

And then, when we'd broken for lunch, and Linda, Tony, and the crew had gone for a meal, I sat with Peter, staring at my unconvincing silhouette, profile and rearview, in the three-sided mirror, and said, "Let's go for it. Cut off my hair!" Neither of us had agreed with the consensus, and now I felt sure we were right. Peter explained that almost every man who has a head of hair has, more or less, a widow's peak, so he shaved my forehead at the temples to give me one. Two other things, he said, distinguish a man's head and neck from a woman's: the Adam's apple, and two prominent occipital bones at the base of the skull. Unusually, I have a slight Adam's apple, so that distinction was no problem. And with my shirt collar turned up I could disguise the back of my neck. Linda Yellen had suggested I should have brown eyes, and I remembered how Laurence Naismith, when we were shooting *Camelot*, had wanted green eyes for Merlin and had come back from an optometrist in the San Fernando Valley with a pair of perfect emerald-green contact lenses. Luckily he was still there, and soon I had brown lenses.

Dick, it seemed to me, would have been slow to speak his thoughts, not "chatty" or talkative, precisely because he thought such a lot. Conversely, when I played a scene with Alice Krige in the first serious love affair that Dick had, I thought of the enormous physical and spiritual exuberance some very young men have when in love, especially those who are most silent and uncommunicative.

Twenty days of hard work. *Second Serve* was shown in America soon after we'd completed filming, and it was very well received. I was nominated for an Emmy. But to my great disappointment the film was never shown in Britain. Neither the BBC or ITV companies would buy it, and I can only suppose that some prejudice against the subject must have influenced their decision. A pity, if it was so, because the film served, in a small way, to overcome the fear and ignorance that surrounds transsexuality.

CHAPTER 24

There are certain roles that haunt you, teasing your imagination, daring you to play them again. Cleopatra is one. My first attempt had been interrupted by what insurers describe as *force majeure,* the cloudburst that swamped Sam Wanamaker's tent theatre on Bankside. I waited twelve years before my next attempt. It began well enough. Tim Dalton and I sat down with Duncan Weldon and planned a season at the Haymarket in which we would play *Antony and Cleopatra* and *The Taming of the Shrew* in repertory. In 1986 it was almost impossible to find an impresario who would risk producing a straight play in the West End with a company of twenty-two actors. But Duncan agreed. Having crossed that bridge, we decided that anything was possible and embarked on rehearsals at the Chiswick Social Club in high spirits. I had moved from the house in Ravenscourt Road to a flat in a mansion block on Chiswick High Road. I loved my new flat, which had nice rooms for Carlo and Joely, and relished the thought of walking a mere fifty yards down the road to rehearsals. It had been a cold winter, and the first morning of rehearsal in February was also the first whiff of spring.

By the time we were about to open, in April, for a six-week

pre-London season at Theatr Clwyd in North Wales, I was in despair. I had chosen a long blond wig, which in everyone's opinion except mine was a disaster, and I was using it to hide from the audience. Kika Markham, Corin's second wife, played Octavia. She remembers coming into my dressing room and seeing me covering my face with plague spots. Apparently I said they were freckles. Tim and I had reached a natural pause in our relationship, but I could not recognize it at the time, and there was sadness and tension between us. The local papers were absolutely scathing about our first performance. Actors usually dismiss their notices in provincial papers in the belief that their praise is too easily won and their criticism too uninformed to matter, but in this case we had an uncomfortable feeling that the *North Wales Echo* was right.

I sent an SOS to Corin, who came up the next night with Gerry. We had a discussion over breakfast. Corin talked about Fulvia, Antony's first wife, whose death is reported in the second scene of the play. He rolled the name around his tongue, and conjured up such a caricature of Fulvia that I began to laugh, imagining all the reasons why Cleopatra loathed this Roman matriarch. We talked about why Cleopatra insists on a naval battle with Octavius, and why she is called a gypsy. He said I should read Prosper Mérimée's "Carmen," the short story that inspired the opera. I felt better. I sent my long wig back to London and asked for Arkadina's wig from *The Seagull* to be sent up. It was only a stopgap, but it had tight red curls on top, a step in the right direction.

We were in Clwyd when the news of the Chernobyl meltdown came through. All that week figures in Roman armor and Eastern gauzes, Jacobean ruffs, ribbons, and garters, gathered round the television in the green room as the stories came through of gallant efforts by Soviet helicopter pilots and firemen to prevent the catastrophe from spreading farther. Outside, the sun shone, and great gray rainclouds sent their shadows racing across the hills. Spring had come late, with a burst of bluebells.

It was hard to believe, in all the din of rushing water from the melted snow, and the lambs bleating on the hillsides, that such beautiful country was being poisoned every minute by the Chernobyl disaster. The Ministry of Defence in Whitehall put out a statement and statistics designed to show that whatever increases in radiation had taken place were below the danger level. A rumor that the alarm outside the North Wales reactor had been activated was hushed up. But the townspeople in Clwyd knew better. They lived in the shadow of nuclear power. They had relatives or friends in Cumbria, near the nuclear plant at Sellafield, where stories persisted of uncommonly high levels of leukemia among children, and where fish-and-chip shops have notices in the window saying "No *local* fish sold here." Many had friends or family who were hill farmers, and who knew that their sheep and cattle would be storing radiation in their bones and milk because with every fall of rain it would be building up in the soil and the grass.

There was something else to note in the television film from Chernobyl. Gorbachev had demanded a full inquiry and was said to be furious at the attempts that had been made, in the first days after the meltdown, to prevent the news from breaking out. I wasn't present at our Political Committee's meetings at this time, but I followed the way *Newsline* reported the Chernobyl accident. I couldn't understand why, after the first few days, the reports tapered off. Then came an editorial defending the right of the Soviet Union to have nuclear weapons. I thought yes, of course, our party has always supported that right, but why is this being asserted now—why now? Corin told me that Sheila Torrance, our general secretary after the split in 1985, had criticized the paper's first attempts at reporting the accident, saying they simply followed the line of the Fleet Street press, which was magnifying the disaster because it opposed the Soviet Union's right to develop nuclear power and nuclear weapons. I couldn't understand this line of reasoning. It seemed self-evident that the only people with an interest in minimizing the Chernobyl disaster were those Stalinist bureaucrats in the government and the state industrial planning departments, whether in Moscow or the Ukraine, whose negligence had helped to create it. But for the moment I simply filed these questions at the back of my mind, to return to them later.

Something had changed, though. In May the Soviet Film Workers' Union elected Elem Klimov as their new general secretary. Many of his films had been banned under the previous regime. And then in June the Soviet Writers' Union held a conference and removed more than a third of the old leadership. Georgi Markov, the union's first secretary since 1971, was replaced by Vladimir Karpov, the sixty-four-year-old editor of *Novy Mir*, who had been a prisoner in Stalin's gulags. Yevtushenko, Bulat Okhudzhava, and Bella Akhmadulina were on the new sixty-three-member secretariat.

In August we were playing *Antony* and *The Taming of the Shrew* at the Haymarket. Somehow we had survived, with good reviews and excellent audiences, and Tim's Petruchio was brilliant. The director David Thacker, whose work at the Young Vic with Natasha in *Hamlet* and then with Corin in *The Crucible* I had seen and liked, came to see our productions. Margot Leicester, his wife, was playing Charmian, and was pregnant. The question had arisen whether we should tour with *Antony*. It was impossible to continue at the Haymarket, although we were playing to capacity, because Jack Lemmon was following us in *Long Day's Journey into Night*. I badly wanted to go on and play on tour, even though we had had a hard time making something good of our productions. I felt sure there was still much room for improvement in my own performance as Cleopatra. But I couldn't bear to re-rehearse with a new Charmian, because I couldn't see how Margot could be bettered, especially in Charmian's immensely difficult scene after Cleopatra's death.

It was then that David Thacker suggested we do a play at the Young Vic, and I proposed Ibsen's *Ghosts*. I knew very little about the play. *Ghosts* had been neglected in my lifetime, and one of the stupidest assumptions behind its neglect was that Ibsen's knowledge of the effects of venereal disease was inaccurate, and therefore the play was "irrelevant" to modern audiences. I remembered that Michael was going to play Oswald at the Old Vic in a season he would have shared with Robert Donat, which was canceled when the war broke out in 1939. But two events had made me think about Ibsen. The first was Chernobyl and Gorbachev's insistence that the truth of the disaster be made known. "When you go out to fight for the truth you should put on a new coat," says Stockman in *An Enemy of the People*. Stanislavsky describes in his memoirs how this line brought the audience to its feet one night when the 1905 revolution against the tsar was at its height. And in Stalin's time every political opponent was labeled an "enemy of the people."

The second thing that made me think about Ibsen, and particularly about *Ghosts*, was my dear friend Bob Regester's death from AIDS.

Bob had many friends who loved him. Natasha was with him when he died. But it was terrible to know that thousands of people would have to battle not only against the disease but against the ignorance and fear that were being deliberately stoked up against homosexuals and bisexuals.

In August, I read reports of Gorbachev's visit to Khabarovsk, in the east of the USSR. "Those who are unwilling to change must go," he said, and demanded that Communist Party officials should be "more open in their dealings, more self-critical, and more democratic." Gerry was convinced that perestroika and glasnost, the twin policies proclaimed at the Twenty-seventh Congress of the CPSU in April 1986, were the forms within which a political revolution against the Stalinist bureaucracy was unfolding. It would not be long, he thought, before we saw the rehabilitation of Leon Trotsky in the Soviet Union.

But the more he argued on our Political Committee that a political revolution was under way, breaking up Stalinism and Stalinist dogma, the more we encountered a wall of opposition. For Gerry, Corin, and I it was axiomatic that we must intervene to the utmost of our ability in these great changes in the Soviet Union, supporting them in every way we could. For our opponents, perestroika amounted to nothing more than a counterrevolution, carried out by the political descendants of Stalin. For supporting perestroika, Gerry and I were accused of "capitulating to Stalinism." We realized that the split that had occurred within the WRP a year earlier was still not complete.

Ghosts transferred from the Young Vic, where it played for six weeks "in the round," to Wyndham's Theatre in the Charing Cross Road, for a limited run of twelve weeks, and then a week at the National Theatre in Oslo. I had spent several weeks, before and during the rehearsal period, studying Ibsen and the conditions in which *Ghosts* was first performed: before an invited audience, in a drawing room in Bloomsbury. Ibsen was a socialist, and his first champion in England was Marx's daughter, Eleanor Marx Aveling. It was for this reason, I felt sure, that the first official reaction to his play was fear and loathing. And the other reason was imperial arrogance. If there was one thing the English of the 1880s and 1890s hated even more than being preached to, it was being preached to by a representative of a very small nation on the outer fringe of European civilization.

I began to learn Norwegian, by no means well enough to translate Ibsen's play, but enough to realize that we could not use any of the existing translations without falling into assumptions about Ibsen's meaning that might not be correct. I persuaded the Young Vic to commission a literal translation and to have a Norwegian scholar present throughout the rehearsal so that the whole cast could work collectively on the translation and could check every phrase and nuance against the original. We were taken to task for this by the critic of *The Financial Times,* who, besides finding our production "soporific" (I suppose that meant he fell asleep after an early supper), thought our collective approach to the text too egalitarian by half. In point of fact, it had nothing to do with egalitarianism. But it concentrated our attention on Ibsen's text, and that was a good starting point for work each day.

I am certain that this approach contributed to the success of the production, the most successful run of any play by Ibsen in the West End. But above all it was the spirit of the times, in which the "new thinking" proclaimed by Gorbachev stirred our audiences and made them consider aspects of our own society in a new light. Oswald's "Give me the sun!" had a new urgency and conviction. Mrs. Alving's horror at lies "creeping like ghosts behind the words in newspapers" had an immediacy for the audience as well as for me.

In March 1987 Thelma Holt invited me to accompany her to the Soviet Union. She had been asked to produce an international festival at the National Theatre on the South Bank. Peter Stein's Schaubühne was coming in May with Eugene O'Neill's *The Hairy Ape,* Ingmar Bergman's Royal Dramatic Theatre from Stockholm would arrive in June, the Ninagawa Company would appear in September, and Thelma wanted a Soviet production for October. The new minister of culture had invited her to Moscow, Riga, and Armenia to see for herself and choose a production.

Riga was buzzing with vitality. There was a new exhibition of posters, extremely sharp and satirical, against the bureaucracy, and a brilliant documentary film directed by Yuri Podniecks, *It Isn't Easy to Be Young.* Thelma and I scuttled along icy pavements, seeing every production we could, five in three days. The most exceptional was at the Rains Theatre, *A Day Is Longer than a Century,* based on the novel by Chingis Aytmatov. It was brilliantly staged, adapting cinematic techniques of cross-fading and mixing, from the desert sands on the edge of a military space complex in Tajikistan today, to a space module hurtling through the galaxy in search of life on another planet, to one of Stalin's gulags where prisoners were building the railroad. It was playing in repertoire with a stock production of Schiller's *Maria Stuart,* quite typical of the work that found favor in the pre-perestroika period.

On the road from the airport to Yerevan, the capital of Armenia, we asked our driver to stop for a moment so we could get out and look across at Mount Ararat. It was a gray, cloudy day. Everything was normal, said our driver. And there was Ararat, the ancient mountain of Armenia, except that it wasn't Armenian, and no Armenian could climb about its crags without a visa. The frontier of Turkey had advanced in the 1915–1919 war, devouring a large chunk of Armenia and the Armenian people. It seemed to me I could see eagles high in the clouds around the peaks where Noah's ark had settled and where Noah had planted the first vine, from which sprang Armenian grapes.

The streets of Yerevan were gray and desperately neglected. The Stalinists on the Central Committee of the Armenian CP still controlled everything. They held all the top and middle-rung posts in industry, culture, sport, and tourism, and they used their control to feather their own nests. They toasted Gorbachev, hung his portrait above their desks, voted with both hands for all his resolutions, and carried out none of them, except those laws that enabled them to make their own deals abroad.

Our young interpreter, who spoke excellent English, took us to see his father, and that was how we came to meet Gevorg Emin, the greatest living poet of Armenia and the latest in a centuries-old tradition. This short, rock-sturdy man, nearly seventy years old, was trained as a hydraulic engineer and began to write poetry in 1940. In the preface to the American edition of his work he wrote, "These poems are my true autobiography." I began to read "Ararat," "Thaw," and "Small," and I could not stop, horrified by my ignorance and thrilled by the sense of discovery that comes when another human being opens your eyes and ears, telling you what you did not know and revealing that what you thought you knew amounted to very little. What exhilaration, what excitement, when you read a poem and think "I am not alone." Gevorg Emin wrote "Small" to describe his people, and himself, too.

> Small, yes,
> you have compressed us,
> world, into a diamond.
>
> Small,
> you have dispersed us,
> scattered us like stars.
> We are everywhere
> in your vision.
>
> Small,
> but our borders stretch
> from Pyrragan telescopes
> to the moon,
> from Houssaran backwards
> to Urartu.
>
> Small as the growth
> of marvelous uranium,
> which cannot be broken down,
> put out, or consumed.

Artashes, Gevorg's son, was a wonderful host, discussing and explaining everything, showing us how modern artists work in Yerevan. Making our way through a half-completed building we found a group of young people silk-screening posters and recording music. Their mood was in sharp contrast to the subdued and demoralized atmosphere in the theatre. There we were shown a film, made two years before, of Shakespeare's *Coriolanus*, with a superb performance of the leading role. We could not understand why the director and producer never referred to this fine actor by name and had great difficulty remembering it when asked. Later we learned from one of the cast that he had been banished to a small town.

The theatre director invited us for a special performance. "Will

Gevorg be there?" I asked Artashes; time was racing by and we badly wanted to meet him again. He would not be invited, Artashes told us, unless we asked for an invitation for him. So we asked and he came and sat with us in our box, together with Ramaz Tchikvadze's wife, Natasha, who had come by train from Tbilisi to meet us. We noticed how the directorate treated Gevorg and his wife as nonpersons, as if they simply were not there. There and then Thelma proposed that we invite Gevorg to a poets' platform at the National Theatre in October, as part of the International Festival, and I promised to read his poems in English.

With one exception—*Autobus,* by a Bulgarian author—the productions in Yerevan were poor, and the actors themselves were the first to acknowledge it. The choice of a production to go to London was narrowed down to the brilliantly staged and acted production in Riga of *A Day Is Longer than a Century* and a far more modest production by the Mayakovsky Theatre Company in Moscow of a story by Boris Vasiliev, *Tomorrow Was War.* It showed a group of boys and girls in their final year at high school in 1940–1941. Stalinist persecution was at its height and reached right into the lives of these schoolchildren and their parents, bringing tragedy and a new consciousness of what, in spite of Stalin's crimes, they would fight to defend against the Nazis. The audience wept for these children and their parents, most of them about to be killed in the "tomorrow," which was war. Despite the brilliance of the Riga production, we felt we must choose Vasiliev's play. Thelma announced our choice to Mikhail Ulyanov at the Actors' Club in Gorky Street, and I suggested that when the production arrived at the National Theatre in October, I would read the simultaneous translation.

And so it came about that my first job at the National Theatre was working in their sound booth. My father was one of the very few actors in Britain who had consistently championed the idea of a national theatre during the forties and fifties, at a time when most actors and directors dismissed the need for such a thing. He led the company, with Olivier, in their first season at the Old Vic and gave his last performances in London at the Lyttelton Theatre, directed by Harold Pinter, in 1979. I, on the other hand, was never offered a season at the National Theatre, and as I settled down to work in the sound booth it crossed my mind, as Rosa Dartle might have said, to wonder why. But not for long. I would not have exchanged this job for anything. In fact, a month earlier I had been offered a job that I would have preferred to anything but this, in a film with Woody Allen. I longed to work with him, and still do, but I had promised the Mayakovsky company that I would speak the live translation, and I knew I must keep my promise.

The Schaubühne company was preceded by an immense reputation. So were Bergman's company and the Ninagawa. But London theatregoers knew nothing of the Mayakovsky company or Boris Vasiliev, and only a very few seats were sold in advance. The National Theatre management were skeptical about this new work by a company that had never traveled outside the Soviet Union, and they did not seem inclined to rouse themselves into publicizing it. I remembered how, years ago, we had all turned out to meet the Moscow Art Theatre at Stansted Airport, so I sat down by the telephone and rang everyone I could find. Peggy Ashcroft, Anthony Quayle, Tim Dalton, Kenneth Branagh, and I met the company at Liverpool Street station off the boat train from Harwich, and that earned a picture in the London *Standard*. Michael Billington chaired an excellent, lively conversation-cum-interview with Vasiliev and the Mayakovsky's director, Nikolai Goncharov. It all helped to sell tickets, as did my name on the poster. But in the end the company made its own success. The audience at their first performance warmed to them slowly, slowly, these very accomplished but modest young actors. An audience will cheer and stamp a virtuoso, a showman who astounds them with his skills, and sometimes they will take him to their hearts. These actors were neither virtuosi nor showmen, but they had something more rare, a total trust in the truth of what they were performing. At the end the applause was slow to begin and grew slowly, wave upon wave, until the whole audience was standing. The last three performances were sold out, and to everyone's delight and astonishment, including mine, the Mayakovsky company was second only to the Ninagawa in popularity that season.

I visited the Soviet Union three times in 1987. Each time I had prepared a list of people whom I wanted to meet—historians, writers, artists—and every assistance was given me to meet them. I took books by Trotsky, none of which were published or available in the USSR, and no one ever opened my baggage or suggested I should not give them to Soviet friends to read. The Lubyanka still housed the KGB, and within the KGB were many who were working for a return to the time of Stalin and Brezhnev. Undoubtedly they followed my activities in Moscow and reported on them. But much more evident was the surveillance of the CIA. "Hi," said my new friend, in the lift of the National Hotel near Red Square. "I used to work for *Ramparts*. Remember *Ramparts?*" I did indeed, and remembered how infested that magazine was with agents from Langley, Virginia, so "Yes, I do remember *Ramparts*," I replied with a big grin, and my newfound friend grinned from ear to ear and attached himself like a leech. I remembered an old gentleman in the army telling me that the way to deal with leeches was to burn them with the end of your cigar, but I didn't think Langley, Virginia, would take kindly to such treatment, so I used politeness instead and said "no, thank you" with deadly courtesy to all his invitations.

My second visit, in June, was to the Moscow International Film Festival, as a guest of the Film Workers' Union. They had prepared a center at Dom Kino, their club, for all their foreign guests. In the hall a seminar was about to begin. Vladimir Pozner sat in one of the simultaneous-translation booths with Alla Pugacheva, the rock star. Stanley Kramer, Robert De Niro, and Gregory Peck sat in the audience. Professor Yuri Afanasiev was on the platform, as was the playwright Mikhail Shatrov. When the discussion began I approached the microphone and was about to speak when someone tugged my sleeve from behind. "Please let me speak first," he asked. *"Please."* Since it was clear that he was burning with impatience to say something, I said, "Please, go ahead." It was Sasha Oskaldov. His film *The Commissar* had been shot in the 1960s, with Rolan Bykov as a Jewish carpenter whose family shelters a young pregnant commissar in the civil war. Soon after his film was completed he was fired from MosFilm, and he had been banned from directing ever since. One of the highlights of this festival was a special screening of banned films, and Oskaldov demanded that his film should be included. When my turn came to speak I backed him up. Within a few moments Elem Klimov announced from the platform that the timetable would be altered so that Oskaldov's film could be shown that afternoon. It was an exhilarating taste of the new Soviet democracy in action.

Before I left London, Gerry had urged me to see Mikhail Filippovich Shatrov. We had read excerpts from his plays in translation and we knew that his was one of the most powerful voices in the political revolution. Gerry had selected two books to give him: Trotsky's *The Stalin School of Falsification* and a book by the great Soviet philosopher Evald Ilyenkov, *Leninist Dialectics and the Metaphysics of Neo-Positivism,* which we ourselves had translated and published in English.

With my young friend Julia, who taught English, I drove through the leafy lanes to a small wooden bungalow, Shatrov's dacha at Peredelkino. Born in 1932, he was fifty-five that year, short, gray-haired, and hardly ever smiling. He welcomed me with great warmth, and immediately, without so much as two sentences of small-talk politenesses, began to speak about the reasons for my visit. Shatrov's life was a paradigm of the entire era encompassing the struggle, with all its tragedies, against Stalinism. His parents were leading revolutionaries; his uncle was Alexei Rykov, one of the leading Bolsheviks in Lenin and Trotsky's time. Shatrov's father was shot in 1937. His mother was arrested in 1949. Not long ago she found herself standing in a line at a supermarket behind a very tall man. When he turned round, she was face to face with her former torturer, who had fractured her skull in the Lubyanka prison.

We visited Pasternak's grave. The cemetery was full of trees, a jungle of tangled briars and weeds. One well-worn narrow footpath led through the mass of undergrowth to a small square plot with a stone and railings. "We have weeded it, you see," said Mikhail Filippovich. Pasternak had been officially rehabilitated that year. Gesturing around him at the graveyard, and then at Pasternak's tomb, he said: "It's like this, perestroika. A continual struggle against the weeds."

As we parted he promised to do everything necessary for Gerry and me to obtain visas for a visit in November at the time of the seventieth anniversary of the revolution. His eyes shone when I presented him with Trotsky's book. It was published in the Soviet Union, with an introduction by Professor Vitali Startsev, two years later, but at this time it was still banned and unobtainable. Shatrov knew of it, and knew that it contained the definitive answer to all the Stalinist falsifications and distortions against Trotsky. Of Ilyenkov he said, "He influenced me and my friends more than any other philosopher."

In August, Corin, Gerry, and I founded the Marxist Party. The disagreement within the WRP over perestroika and glasnost had worsened. The majority group said that these were the same old Stalinist leaders up to the same old game. We, the minority, said no, this is new; it is a political revolution against the Stalinist bureaucratic dictatorship. Then a series of articles had appeared in our daily paper, praising Gerry but distorting our party's history. We appealed to have our position discussed before the whole membership. The appeal was rejected, and we discovered that the constitution had been altered—without discussion with us or the rest of the membership—so that we no longer had such a right of appeal. In February we had gone to the International Committee of the Fourth International (the elected delegates from all the national sections), and after protracted discussion the majority of the WRP had rejected the constitutional authority of the International Committee and they were expelled. Those of us who remained, although we were few in number, formed a new party—the Marxist Party. We were clear in our belief that we should support the political revolution against the Stalinists, who we knew could and would do everything in their power to reverse the democratic reforms that were well on their way.

In November, Gerry at last made the trip to the Soviet Union. It was bitterly cold, but he flatly refused to wear the fur hat I had made him. He had prepared himself for weeks for this visit. The foremost Trotskyist of his time, he was coming to the Soviet Union, where for sixty years Trotsky had been anathematized, his family and secretaries murdered. Millions had perished in the mass killings of "Trotskyite-Zinovievite agents of fascism," "saboteurs," "wreckers," "terrorists," and "mad dogs." Gerry was watchful and alert, both tense and relaxed, every second of our visit. At the anniversary parade, where only portraits of Lenin appeared, he was very critical, saying "There are still some blank spots here." I was feeling fairly euphoric and could not understand why he said it or why he returned to it that evening after a performance of Shatrov's *The Dictatorship of Conscience*. I thought at first he was disappointed that there were no portraits of Trotsky, but he brushed that aside, as if to say that of course he hadn't expected that. But Lenin on his own? Without Marx, Engels, Trotsky, or Stalin, what could that mean?

He spoke before an audience of historians, professors, and lecturers at the Moscow Institute of State Archives. But he didn't choose to talk about Trotsky. He invariably approached every task and every problem from the standpoint of philosophy, and on this occasion chose as his starting point the fact that the latest Soviet dictionary of philosophy omitted the category of "semblance," which in Lenin's explanation of the dialectical process of cognition is given great attention and which Gerry considered to be of crucial methodological importance.

The next morning we went to the Vakhtangov Theatre in the Arbat to see the first public preview of Mikhail Shatrov's *The Peace of Brest*. It had been banned in the Soviet Union since it was written in 1969. Here, for the first time since 1927, Lenin was portrayed on the stage as a human being of flesh and blood. No special lights announced his appearance. Here, also for the first time, the whole of Lenin's Central Committee were presented, likewise as human beings, and when Lenin argued, in a minority against the majority among them, he won the argument not by fiat or command, nor by superhuman intelligence, but by the democratic weapons of political argument and persuasion. We were astonished by the force and vitality of the acting—Ulyanov as Lenin, Filipenko as Bukharin, and Lanovoy as Trotsky—and by Robert Sturua's direction. There and then we decided to do everything in our power to bring the company to London.

I walked up a flight of rickety wooden steps to a tiny studio. Our guide was a dear friend, the great actor Sergei Yursky. Our host was a painter; Yursky was determined to introduce us to him and to show us some paintings that none but the artist's closest friends had seen. Pyotr Belov was a scenic designer by profession who had spent most of his working life designing sets for the Red Army Theatre. In his spare time, and only for his own pleasure, he took his easel to the woods and fields outside Moscow and painted landscapes. He must have been a very handsome young man, as I could see from an early self-portrait, and a happy young man, for the most part, who enjoyed his work and did it very well. Almost everyone you meet in the Soviet Union has lost a father, a mother, grandparents, aunts, or uncles in the wave of terror, or in the postwar purges, or in the war itself. But there are those, and Pyotr's family was one, whose lives were blessedly unscathed by the repressions. Nothing in his work until 1984 seemed to indicate the painter he has now become. But in that year he had a heart attack, and in convalescence he began to paint allegories against Stalin. In one, the familiar features of Stalin, head and shoulders, are seen peering impassively at an hourglass. Everything looks normal and composed except—look closer—these are not grains of sand but tiny human skulls. I wanted Pyotr Belov to design a production of *Orpheus Descending* by Tennessee Williams, which I was planning to do the following year, and we talked of arranging an exhibition of his work in London, but he died the following spring of a second heart attack.

We flew back to London on November 10, and Corin drove to meet us. "There are more real Trotskyists in the Soviet Union than I have met anywhere in my life," Gerry said as we landed.

CHAPTER 25

In simple arithmetic, two plus two invariably equals four. In higher mathematics it is not necessarily so. In acting, if acting is to be creative, the rules of simple arithmetic and their logical expression, the law of identity—A equals A—do not suffice, and the actor who relies upon them will be limited to producing Stanislavsky's "stencils." Stanislavsky's teachings, in this respect, may be compared to higher mathematics, in which the rules of simple arithmetic are contained, terminated, superseded, and simultaneously preserved. In political life and struggle, formal logic, a method of thinking in fixed opposites, is dangerous and even downright reactionary: "a clock without a spring," Trotsky called it. The spring is dialectics. This problem preoccupied all his attention in the last period of his life, during 1939 and 1940.

The same problem had presented itself very acutely in November 1987, the day before Gerry and I left for Moscow. Savas Michael, secretary of the Greek section and of our International Committee, telephoned London urging us to call off our visit. Gorbachev had delivered his speech in the Kremlin, commemorating the seventieth anniversary of the October Revolution, and it was reported in the press and on television that he had attacked Trotsky. "It's not safe for you to go," Savas Michael said. We were not inclined to heed his advice. It was true, Gorbachev *had* criticized Trotsky, and also Bukharin, repeating many of the old Stalinist lies about them. They constituted the form of his speech, but within it a new and powerful content was stirring. He announced that a commission had been set up, under the Politburo, to investigate the crimes of Stalin and the Stalinist Comintern. Dialectics here, therefore, was "the teaching which shows how opposites can be, and how they happen to be—how they become—identical, becoming transformed into one another." The old, historical past, sixty years of Stalinist lies and distortions, was contained within the living immediate present, as a unity of opposites. But the dominant opposite was now the new. Three months after Gorbachev's speech the first results of the commission investigating Stalin's crimes were announced. Bukharin, Rykov, Christian Rakovsky, and all the victims of the 1938 Moscow trials were rehabilitated.

Two other decisions were made at this time, February 1988, that we considered crucially important, and that determined much of my activity in the months that followed. The first was the decision to withdraw Soviet troops from Afghanistan, after a decade of occupation that had claimed hundreds of thousands of lives, including those of fifty thousand Soviet servicemen. The second was the declaration by Gorbachev recognizing the PLO as the sole legitimate leadership representing the Palestinian people, and calling on Israel to withdraw from the occupied territories, the West Bank, Gaza, and the Golan Heights, which it had annexed since the 1967 war in defiance of every resolution of the United Nations.

In March, I organized a concert at the Adelphi Theatre in aid of the Arab Women's Association. It was a great success, raising £100,000 for children and orphans in the occupied territories. Nigel Kennedy played an unaccompanied Bach partita, the most beautiful sound imaginable. Julia Migenes and Kris Kristofferson sang. My friend Katharina Wolpe, the daughter of Stefan Wolpe, whose compositions, along with all the Viennese School of Alban Berg, were banned under the Nazis, played Scriabin. And Elisabeth Welch sang "It Had to Be You."

Elisabeth is a remarkable singer and a woman for whom I have the greatest admiration. She will be found in any gathering of artists who have come together for a purpose that is good and necessary. "Oh Lord, it's you, Vanessa," she says. "What is it this time?" And before I have completed three sentences she interrupts, "Okay. Count me in." She has never refused, from the first time I asked her to sing at the Round House in a cabaret to raise funds for youth training. In 1990 she went to Leningrad to raise money for rebuilding the Russian Theatre Workers' Union, whose fine old building and Actors' Club in Gorky Street had been burned to the ground in what was suspected to be an arson attack. There I discovered the secret of Elisabeth's beauty, which is that she never goes to bed. In the white nights of Leningrad she sat up every night till four in the morning, talking and singing.

I learned a lot from the Adelphi concert. Arab and Jewish artists had gathered together with artists from Europe and America, united for one cause: the children who were the victims of the Israeli occupation. That was an achievement of great practical and political significance. For what brought them together, and singled out this cause as the common aim of their endeavors, was the intifada, the Palestinian uprising in the West Bank and Gaza, with sticks and stones confronting the enemy, a war machine armed with all the most modern sophisticated weapons.

In Ramallah and Nablus, and in every town and village of the occupied territories, committees of young men and women had sprung up, organizing the intifada with leaflets distributed to the whole population. They were the heart of the intifada, the political head of which was Khalil al-Wazir, "Abu Jihad," deputy commander of the Palestinian armed forces and second in command to Chairman Arafat.

I had known Abu Jihad and his family for eleven years. We had met in the Bekáa valley in Lebanon, in Beirut, and in Tunis. There are men, and he was one, whose every breath, thought, and action are dedicated to the liberation of the oppressed, not only their own people but the poor and oppressed of all nations. Every fighter in every national liberation struggle loved Khalil al-Wazir. He was an internationalist in every drop of his blood, and through his leadership, and Yasser Arafat's, the PLO was recognized in all continents and languages as the friend, ally, and teacher of those who were struggling for their freedom.

I gasped and cried aloud when I heard he had been assassinated. It was April 16, 1988, and I could hear the radio announcement on the landing outside my front door, where workmen were repairing the stairway. "In the early hours of the morning . . . a group of gunmen . . . at his home in Tunis . . ."

I flew immediately to Tunis to pay my respects to Um Jihad and her children. Hanan, her daughter, showed me what had happened. Her father had been shot before her eyes. The little boy, the youngest child, was asleep in his parents' bedroom when the assassins raked over his cot with submachine guns. It was forty-eight hours before he could sleep again. The assassins spoke French and Hebrew. There were sixteen of them. They shot Abu Jihad's two bodyguards and a gardener and rushed the house. Abu Jihad managed to reach his pistol to defend himself and the women and children, but the assassins got him before he could fire, and pumped scores of bullets into his body. When they left, Um Jihad and Hanan ran out onto the balcony and screamed for help. The house was in the diplomatic quarter of Tunis, and no one came. Every telephone line in the surrounding area had been cut, and Um Jihad had to walk almost a mile before she could telephone for an ambulance.

Um Jihad sent me a message to read at a memorial meeting we held at the Chelsea Town Hall on May 8. Talal al-Nasry spoke for the General Union of Iraqi Students in Britain. Another speaker was David Kitson, who had been imprisoned for almost twenty years in Pretoria as a founder-member of the African National Congress and a founder of Umkonto We Sizwe, the ANC's armed-struggle section; also Mohammed Arif, for the Afro-Asian Solidarity Committee, and Harpal Brar, for the Indian Workers' Association. Gerry spoke for the Marxist Party. He recalled the time when he had first met Abu Jihad, in the Bekáa in 1976, and a later occasion, in Beirut, when Abu Jihad had asked him to give lectures on dialectical materialism to a group of military cadres in Fateh. His voice rose in pitch and urgency as he spoke about the assassins. They escaped by sea. It must have been a major international operation, he said, involving not only the Israelis but the Americans, providing radar cover and an electronic blackout.

"Why was our brother so lightly guarded?" he asked. "Why? Two men and an old gardener." In a situation like the present, "they will always strike at the leadership."

When Gerry spoke of a revolutionary situation, he meant not only the intifada but, above all, the political revolution in the Soviet Union: "I've fought for this political revolution for fifty-two years, and now it's under way, and it interacts within the Gaza Strip and the West Bank."

The more I thought of this connection, the more I realized that the key to the whole situation, both for the Palestinian revolution and for the struggle against anti-Semitism, lay in the political revolution against Stalinism. For years I had wrestled with this problem, which in its starkest and simplest form may be expressed thus: You are against the persecution and oppression of Jews? Then you must support Israel, because Israel is the Jewish state. You are against the oppression and persecution of the Palestinian Arab people, and you condemn Israeli occupation and demand a Palestinian state? Then you must be anti-Semitic. This simple syllogism torments the consciousness of millions. It is false through and through, and every honest person knows it, if only instinctively, to be wrong. But it is one thing to know it and another thing to be able to prove, in practice, that the struggle against anti-Semitism and for the self-determination of the Palestinians form a single whole. For that, something more than honesty is needed. A thorough knowledge of history is essential, especially the history of what has happened since the October 1917 revolution, whose first decree and declaration was for the right of all oppressed nations to their self-determination.

For the next five months, from April until August 1988, I devoted almost all my time and energy to preparing an international concert and conference in Moscow opposing the Israeli occupation of the West Bank and Gaza. There were to be two organizing principles—an end to the occupation, and opposition to all forms of racism, including anti-Semitism. Why Moscow? I found myself thinking again and again about Sasha Oskaldov, whose film *The Commissar* had been banned for twenty years. But why was it banned? It told a story of the civil war, when the "White" armies of Deniken, Yudenich, Wrangel, and Kolchak terrorized the country. Everywhere these armies rampaged, they slaughtered Jewish communities in an orgy of revenge against the revolution.

Gerry's speech in tribute to Abu Jihad at our meeting, Oskaldov's film, and the anxiety we both found when we visited Moscow in May that year about the activities of the fascist organization Pamyat—these were the parts I could now reassemble in a new whole, from which came the idea for the assembly and concert in Moscow against the occupation.

≡

As I began to rehearse Tennessee Williams's *Orpheus Descending* that autumn, I read everything I could find about Sicilian immigration to the southern states of America. I listened to recordings of Kentucky coal miners and Sicilian copper miners and farmhands. I played them to the director, Peter Hall, who was astonished, as I was, by the similarity of their themes and expressions, and even of their rhythms and cadences.

In *Orpheus Descending,* Tennessee, at the height of his powers as a poet of the theatre, concentrated all his fear and hatred of oppression. The Klan that set fire to the "wop," Lady Torrance's father, was the same Klan that lynched and burned "niggers," and the same that daubed swastikas on the doors of Jews.

I spent a weekend with Franco and Carlo on the seashore outside Rome and asked Salvatore, a friend from Naples, about the songs that Tennessee mentions in his play. Salvatore had never read Tennessee Williams or seen his plays. He had never even heard of him. We were sitting in a tiny garden, surrounded by bamboo bushes and oleander. I told him the names of the songs, "Cor Ingrata," "Come le Rose," not even sure that they actually existed or had ever been sung.

"These songs are in your play?" Salvatore looked at me with sudden, keen interest.

"Yes, they are, but I don't know them, and I don't know where to find them."

"This is a very great writer indeed," Salvatore said.

"Oh yes, he is, but why do you say that?"

"Because he understands a people who have had to leave their country. They long to return. People think when they hear these songs they are just love songs. No. They are so popular because they express people's love of their land, their homes, their history, their longing and their love for what they have lost."

So there I was, on the first day of rehearsal, near the Chelsea Embankment, loaded down, as I always am at rehearsal, with as many bags as a packhorse could carry, filled with books, papers, and memorabilia, out of which I triumphantly produced the songsheets of "Cor Ingrata" and "Come le Rose." Peter was thrilled. Then I gave him a cassette of a musician playing the *marranzano*, a Sicilian instrument that you hold between your teeth and twang with your fingers. It originated in North Africa, and I know of no instrument other than the mandolin that has such a range of expression, with both male and female tonalities. Alas, the score for Peter's production was electronic, from a synthesizer. It was a powerful score, creating an atmosphere of oppression and fear that served the play well. But however remarkable a synthesizer is, it cannot in all its range of sounds reproduce the sound of the *marranzano* or the mandolin.

I worked at this problem, not finding the answer until we re-rehearsed *Orpheus* for the Broadway production the following summer. I paid a call on Hugo D'Alton, the great mandolin teacher, in his home above Kenwood on Hampstead Heath. He and his wife, Micky, understood my determination to learn the instrument, despite the terribly slow progress I made. I consider myself quite musical, and I liked to think my fingers could learn new movements, even at fifty. I had learned the cello for John Schlesinger's film *Yanks*. Many people had patted me on the back for my accomplishment, and not all their compliments were patronizing, I thought. But the mandolin tortured me and I tortured it. I became exhausted with the effort, and one night I slumped fast asleep in Hugo's sitting room and woke up next morning in his spare bedroom. But despite all, I knew that if I could play a few phrases of "Cor Ingrata," the sound of a real mandolin would bring a note of the true heartbeat of Sicily.

Lady Torrance was the most difficult part I had ever played, and I needed all Peter's help and encouragement. He is an alarming man to work with, if ever you stop to think that his calendar is filled for years ahead. Then, momentarily, your efforts and those of your company shrink before the vast space of his activity. But his commitment and his concentration are inspiring. In the second week of our pre-London tour, at Bath, I spoke to Tony on the telephone. He loved the play and had directed its first production in England at the Royal Court, with Lea Padovani, in 1959. He had not been to see me in Bath, but Tasha had, and I knew she must have given Tony a full report. He was laconic. He considered the play almost impossible, but he knew how much I wanted it to succeed, so he didn't say anything too deflating. But then he added, as an afterthought, "I hear you're not playing her Italian; you must be out of your mind."

I paused for a full minute.

"Hello. Are you there?"

"Yes," I said wearily. As a matter of fact I was croaking. My voice often gives way in the first week of performance, what with the tension and the shameful habit of smoking too many cigarettes. And I was trying to expand the range of my voice as Lady Torrance, hoping to find some new notes in my upper register.

"You must be out of your mind," he said again. He was not being helpful.

"She's an immigrant," I replied, "but she came over on the boat with her father as a child. She should speak Italian?"

"Of course," Tony persisted. "You must be out of your mind."

I really loathed this expression at third hearing. "I'll think about it," I said.

"You better had," said Tony, laughing. "Tennessee wrote the part for Anna Magnani."

"You know that?"

"Of course. He was with me all through rehearsal."

It was Saturday, the last performance in Bath. Next stop Cardiff. I rang Corin.

"Tony says Lady should be played Italian. He says Tennessee wrote the part for Anna Magnani. I don't think so, do you?"

"Of course not," Corin said. "She came over on the boat with her father as a child. Naturally she'd speak American."

"Ye-es," I said, "that's what I thought."

On the train to Cardiff I pored over the text. Why was she called "Lady" Torrance? Because "Lady" is the English translation of "Madonna." I looked hard for signposts, turns of phrase, expressions, that would prove Tony right or wrong. The train to Cardiff takes an hour and fifty minutes, but when we reached Newport, eight miles from

Cardiff, I was no nearer to finding an answer. As the train pulled into our station I realized that there was only one way to find out. If you want to learn to swim, you must get into the water.

There was an hour scheduled for rehearsal onstage before our first performance. Without telling anyone or explaining what I was doing I began to speak in an Italian accent. I noticed a few of my fellow actors registering silent looks of surprise and shock. After fifteen minutes we had to stop for a technical adjustment and Peter came up onstage.

"I think I must go on trying it this way," I explained.

"Yes, I think you must," he answered, with his sexy and engaging smile. At the end of the performance he said, "Yes, you *must*. Something is releasing in you that is Lady, that wasn't coming out before."

The company divided sharply on the question, as companies do, getting deeply involved in one another's acting problems. But I knew that the only issue now was to get my Italian accent right, using definite Sicilian expressions.

Maria St. Just, who was Tennessee's dearest woman friend and his executor, and one of the best people to turn to for advice and good, clear, detailed suggestions, was also encouraging.

"You must talk a lot of Italian, the more the better. Then people will understand completely. That's how we Russians are. We talk English, but all the time we use our Russian blessings and exclamations, and we talk to ourselves in Russian when we're alone."

For good measure she rang Franco Zeffirelli and got him to sing "Come le Rose" to me over the telephone late that night.

It had been a fearful week. One night at Bath, during the performance, I heard from a desperate Franco—my Franco—that Carlo had been in a car accident and was in the hospital. Every accident I had ever seen in Rome swam in front of my vision and I almost fainted. Tasha and Joely flew out the next morning and promised to let me know immediately if I must leave the play. Peter was wonderfully understanding; he assured me I must go and miss a performance if necessary. That evening the girls telephoned. Carlo was in hospital, badly cut, and with a possible concussion. He had been sitting in the back seat of the car and had been thrown out through the back window onto the road. I shuddered to think what impact the crash must have had to force Carlo, six feet three inches tall and weighing

175 pounds, through the rear window, and how near we were to losing him. But he was all right, the girls said, and promised me his cuts would heal, and they did. Carlo spent two years at the Centro Sperimentale in Rome studying to be a director and scriptwriter. When he, Natasha, and Joely were growing up, the fact that we had split families seemed to mean that whenever I had free time and could be with them, it coincided with the children rightfully going off to spend their holidays with their fathers in Italy and America. We dealt with this by never arguing about it but accepting it, and as a result, over the years they not only had some wonderful times with their fathers but I was also very good friends with both Tony and Franco.

≡

I first met Gennady Abramov at the Actors' Club in Gorky Street in November 1987. A young man tapped me on the shoulder as I was telephoning. "Are you Vanessa Redgrave?" He had the most beautiful eyes and looked much as I had pictured Daniel Deronda, George Eliot's hero. I asked him if there was a Jewish theatre in Moscow. There was a group, he said, but they had no theatre, and they were not rehearsing.

By May the following year they had a theatre, out in the Moscow suburbs, on Warsaw Boulevard. Gennady and his director, Alexander Levenbyk, welcomed Gerry and me and introduced us to the company. The three oldest actors in the troupe had been in Stalin's gulags, up by the White Sea Canal. Specially selected Jews, they said, were put in charge of the Jewish prisoners. "They were the worst of all." When Emanuel Nelin, the eldest of the troupe, had returned from the war, decorated for bravery, he had auditioned for the great actor and teacher Solomon Mikhoels, still wearing his army uniform and boots. Mikhoels put a phonograph record on the turntable. "Show me what emotions are aroused in you by this music." The tune was very stirring, Emanuel said, but he could think of nothing except throwing hand grenades at German tanks, so he got up and mimed that. Mikhoels accepted him. He spent two years at his school and then joined his company.

Then, in 1948, the pogroms began again. Every Jewish theatre, museum, and cultural centre was closed down. Mikhoels was assassinated in what was called, officially, a car accident. Nelin and Iosip Lefkovitch were imprisoned, along with many other Jewish artists. Svetlana Alliluyeva, Stalin's daughter, writes about this terrible period in her memoirs, *Twenty Letters to a Friend.* Thousands of Jews were arrested, tortured, and shot, charged with membership in an illegal "Zionist Center." At exactly the same time as this was happening in the Soviet Union, Communist Party newspapers abroad, on Stalin's orders, were denouncing Palestinian Arabs as "fascists" and applauding Palestinian Jews as "freedom fighters."

After 1953 Nelin and Lefkovitch were released from the gulags. But still they were not permitted to form their own theatres and companies, so they worked together privately in their homes, striving to keep alive a great tradition. Individually they worked wherever they could: in cabaret, TV, or radio. When we met in May, the actors were paid a weekly salary by the state, as variety artists. It was certainly an advance on pre-perestroika days, when they had no regular income at all, but there was still a long way to go. The company had no funds, no lights, no costumes. "We must tell Ulyanov about this," Gerry and I said. "He'll do something." Indeed, as president of the Theatre Workers' Union, he did. When we returned in November the company had self-accounting status and could keep a large percentage of their box-office income for their own purposes. They had a name, the Moscow Jewish Theatre Shalom Company, and a show, *The Train to Happiness,* by their resident writer, Arkhady Khait, based on stories by Isaac Babel, which told, in songs and sketches, the history of their people from prerevolutionary times until the present. There and then they staged a performance for us, but it was interrupted by a power cut so we came back a few days later and saw the second half. "You must come to London," we urged, "with the Vakhtanghov."

That was how the Soviet Theatre Season came about, which Vanessa Redgrave Enterprises presented at the Lyric Theatre, Hammersmith, in February 1989. Both companies were a revelation to London audiences. Robert Sturua's work had been seen in a legendary production of *Richard III* by the Rustaveli Company some years before, and all who knew something of theatre history had heard of the Vakhtanghov. But Soviet Jewish theatre? Shalom was a sensation.

≡

All through the summer of 1989 faxes and telephone calls hummed to and fro between New York and London, arguing whether or not our production of *Orpheus* should descend on Broadway. Frank Rich had reviewed the London opening in *The New York Times,* saying that I was a great actress and how shameful it was that I had not been asked to appear on Broadway because I supported the Palestine Liberation Organization. Jimmy Nederlander, the New York theatre owner, saw the review and decided he wanted me, and Peter's production, for one of his theatres. I was in hard financial difficulties and knew that the first salary that was proposed would only make my problems worse. But I wanted to go, not only because I believed in our production and passionately loved Tennessee's play, but because I thought Frank Rich was right—to be invited to play on Broadway would, in its way, strike a blow against the victimization and censorship of artists that was the great danger of the judgment in the case of the Boston Symphony Orchestra. When the Supreme Court in Washington finally refused my right to appeal, I was even more firmly of that opinion.

≡

In June, July, and August I played a three-month limited season of Martin Sherman's *A Madhouse in Goa* at the Apollo Theatre on Shaftesbury Avenue. This was composed of two plays. The first was set in Greece just before the Greek colonels' coup in 1967, and the second on the Greek island of Santorini in 1989. The connecting theme was about a young writer who evaded his responsibility to write the truth of the world of the 1960s, which would have done much to help the generation of the 1980s. Martin's brilliant quantum-energy writing seized on fundamental aspects of a whole era, which trembled and shook with questions many felt unable to answer. The writer in the play could see all too clearly but had become unable to speak or write except in dyslexic sentences that no one could understand. Robert Fox, our producer, had T-shirts made up with a picture of a white rhinoceros, one of the world's endangered species, above the title of the play.

On June 3, the Chinese Stalinist regime ordered the massacre of the young students in Tiananmen Square. I was in little doubt that they had received assurances from President Bush and his colleague ex-president Nixon that the United States would take no action against Deng's powerful and corrupt apparatus if the Chinese political revolution was crushed. I joined the candlelit protest vigil of young Chinese students outside the Chinese embassy in London. Until the end of the run of the play, the photograph of the young student facing down the tanks in Bejing hung on the wall of my dressing room.

Dr. Swee Chai Ang came one afternoon to our theatre between shows. This tiny lady of epic strength had been working in a hospital just outside the Palestinian camps of Sabra and Shatila throughout the siege of Beirut. She had witnessed the massacre of Palestinian families in those camps following the withdrawal of American troops. Dr. Swee had then been assigned by UNRWA, the United Nations Relief and Works Agency, to work in a hospital in the Gaza Strip. Here she fearlessly defended her Palestinian patients from raids by the Israeli Defense Forces. She was now in the middle of a world tour raising money for the hospital and clinics in Gaza. Having listened to her and asked many questions, our cast decided unanimously to give a midnight benefit performance of *Madhouse* for the Arab Women's Association and for Centre Point, a charity that provided overnight shelter in central London to young homeless people. Each charity received about five thousand pounds. The money the AWA received went to buy an operating table for the Gaza hospital.

The Apollo is next door to the Lyric Theatre, where Joely was starring in *Steel Magnolias*, playing Rosemary Harris's daughter, who dies of diabetes. Many evenings I would call at the stage door of the Lyric with a bunch of flowers. I saw three afternoon performances and was amazed each time by the fresh spontaneity of Joely's work, and especially touched by her gaiety and gentle gravity. In the four years since she had left the Royal Academy of Dramatic Art to play the young Jean in David Hare's film *Wetherby*, she had done a considerable amount of work in theatre, film, and television. Both she and Natasha, who had just finished *Patty Hearst*, had become, in their own individual and unique ways, steel magnolias. Unlike my generation, my daughters and their friends, both in Europe and the United

States, were seeking work under extremely harsh conditions. There were very few films in production and less and less dramatic work for television, and the subsidies of theatres in the provinces and London were being drastically cut by Mrs. Thatcher's government. I thought, and still think, that my daughters are part of a remarkable generation that can teach us a lot, and they need all the support we can give them.

It was finally agreed that I should go with *Orpheus* to New York, yet more proof, I thought, of the great political changes brought about by perestroika and the intifada. On the day the box office opened, our producer, Liz McCann, came into rehearsal and announced that there were lines all round the block. I had not changed my views, but, clearly, a lot of people were changing theirs. Almost every American I met and talked to had been profoundly impressed by Chairman Arafat's speech at Geneva the previous November, accepting the State of Israel, calling for a two-state solution, with an independent Palestinian state in the West Bank and Gaza, and rejecting terrorism in the name of the PLO. Many of the young Americans who were lining up at the Neil Simon Theatre wrote notes saying they were looking forward to the production and were glad that I was coming, and adding, "We agree with your political convictions." I had long known that many would agree with my political support for the Palestinians if they could know what I really said and did, instead of the half-truths and lies in the press. For a year I had given interviews only to newspapers and magazines whose editors and journalists had signed an agreement I had drawn up with my lawyer. The document stated that there should be no political questions or political comments, and that I had the right to see the copy or to be given a tape of a recorded interview. Some journalists and editors refused to sign this, which was fine. Others wrote articles saying that I was attacking their rights and freedom of speech, which was nonsense. They were free to write anything they wanted about me. They had the time, the money, and the space to print truth or lies about me. They were denied only the right to waste my time and misrepresent what I said to them.

That document had served its purpose well, on the whole. It provided a basis for mutual trust, and, I dare say, it protected those journalists who wanted to write something decent and objective but were told by their editors to "get" me. I deeply regret the two or three occasions I waived the agreement, accepting an oral promise from the editor that, while their house rules forbade agreeing to any preconditions, they guaranteed that the "spirit" of my document would be adhered to. Every time, I was misrepresented, and abused into the bargain.

I had somewhat dreaded going to New York. I was proud of our new company for *Orpheus Descending* and was excited and happy that the Nederlander organization had agreed to present us. I had the support and friendship of Maria St. Just and I would also have my son's company during our rehearsal period. But as I said good-bye to the girls and to Corin I felt a gut-wrenching loneliness all the same. This stopped as soon as we started technical rehearsals at the Neil Simon Theatre. The stage crew was extremely friendly and coopera- tive, although our work was complicated by a computer board that exploded every light onstage, and by the size of the theatre. Peter Hall had decided that the actors should have no microphones. He was right. Amplification divorces the actors from their voices, which emerge instead out of speakers at the side of the stage. However, to speak quiet passages in a play so that every single person in a twelve-hundred-seat theatre can hear you, even when you whisper, takes practice and a giant reserve of energy. Kevin Anderson was now playing Val, and when he gave the speech about "those little birds, they don't have no legs. They go to sleep on the wind, and their wings are so transparent you can see the sky through them," the thoughts and words had the real poetry of Tennessee's heart.

We celebrated Carlo's nineteenth birthday, and our press night, at Ted Mann's Seventh Avenue apartment. The reviews were excel- lent, and there were between twenty and thirty people outside the stage door every night wanting to talk for a moment as well as get autographs. My bodyguard, an ex-cop of Sicilian parentage, became a special friend. We never had any trouble, either in the theatre or outside; on the contrary, only friendship, welcome, and hospitality.

The political revolution in the Soviet Union was spreading throughout Eastern Europe. When Erich Honecker, the East Ger- man Stalinist leader, demanded that Soviet tanks in East Berlin be sent into the streets to save his regime, President Gorbachev refused. The mass demonstrations of the revolution mounted in Leipzig,

Dresden, and East Berlin. At midnight on November 9, the Berlin Wall, for over forty years a monument to Stalinist repression, was breached and broken. I began to work at breakneck speed for a concert called *The Wall Breaks,* which would celebrate this great event. The Nederlander organization agreed to let me take the Marquis Theatre on December 10. That gave us four weeks to pull together what would normally take five months. I telephoned Mikhail Shatrov in Moscow. Would he come and speak on behalf of the Memorial Society? The Memorial Society for the Victims of Stalin's Repressions had held its founding conference in January 1989, although it had begun to organize before then. One of its most important aims is to collect all the evidence, written and oral, concerning Stalin's victims. It has many branches in the former USSR. Gerry and I had met its leading members, including Professor Lev Ponomariev, in May the previous year. We had organized a concert in London in November 1988 that raised £5000 for them. And in spring 1989, during our last visit together to Moscow, I had been made an honorary member.

Shatrov agreed to come. Ekaterina Maximova and Vladimir Vasiliev said that they would dance. I began work with a group of students from the Circle in the Square on scenes from Vasiliev's play *Tomorrow Was War.* We assembled an extraordinary cast for the concert: Joanne Woodward, Christopher Reeve, Sigourney Weaver, the Manhattan String Quartet, Raul Julia, Harvey Fierstein, Allen Ginsberg, and Dmitri Shostakovitch, son of the composer.

Lynn agreed to come and play Masha, in a scene from *The Three Sisters,* with me as Olga, Sigourney as Irina, and Chris Reeve as Vershinin. On the night of December 10 every seat at the Marquis was sold.

CHAPTER 26

Gerry Healy died on December 14, 1989, aged seventy-six. I wrote an obituary for him, which was published in *The Guardian*. I sat on the divan in my underground dressing room at the Neil Simon Theatre trying, in a few lines, to do some justice to a unique life, a human being of exceptional courage and integrity.

In his book *The Great Game*, Leopold Trepper, the leader of the "Red Orchestra," the Soviet spy ring that operated in Nazi Germany, paid tribute to the Trotskyists as the only political group who fought Stalin and Stalinism. He explained that it was their theoretical outlook and breadth of mind that enabled them to understand and withstand the terror, the mass purges, the falsification of everything Lenin and the Bolsheviks stood for. I thought of that as I wrote about Gerry.

In the sixteen years since I had joined the Workers' Revolutionary Party, I had met many members who were exceptionally gifted and able and sincerely devoted to socialist ideals. But I also noticed how many intellectuals and academics, despite the great advantage of their education, lived a life in which their thinking became almost petrified. For want of any real effort to develop creatively, they became dominated by old dogma and quite a lot of mysticism. But Gerry never let a day go by without some serious study of philosophy, backed up by his constant interest in developments in science that could throw new light on the law-governed processes in nature and society and how they are reflected in dialectical thought. He never sought relaxation: he had no private life of the kind so often yearned for by bureaucrats and professional politicians. At the same time, I have never laughed more than I did with Gerry. The main point was that Gerry never said or did anything for personal advantage. His life was a single piece of steel, and that was why he was feared and hated by the state and by political opportunists.

We held a memorial concert for Gerry at the Adelphi Theatre in March 1990. Um Jihad, at whose husband's memorial Gerry had spoken two years before, sent a beautiful message of support and condolence. James Waddell, the miner from Kent whom I had met in prison on the Isle of Sheppey, spoke on the platform. Feisal Oweida, the PLO representative in London, was there, and Mikhail Shatrov, Robert Sturua, Mariana Belov, Alexander Levenbyk, and Galina Vollchek came from the Soviet Union. Ken Livingstone, the Labour MP for Brent East and former leader of the Greater London Council, spoke about his friendship with Gerry and the support he had given when the state moved against the GLC. And then Livingstone came to the state attacks against Gerry and the party he led.

> I haven't the slightest doubt that the upheavals which split apart the Workers' Revolutionary Party were not some accident or a clash of personalities. They were a sustained and deliberate decision by MI5 to smash that organization, because they feared it was becoming too pivotal in terms of domestic policies, linking too many international struggles with progressive elements both inside and outside the British Labour movement. Nothing that I have seen causes me to question that basic assumption, and it may very well be that one day we will see the evidence drawn out that shows the work of MI5 agents that was put into actually damaging and trying to roll back so much of what had been done.

These few words had a profound effect upon the audience. I knew that great pressure would be put on Livingstone to retract his remarks. But I also felt confident that he had an independent spirit that might well resist such pressure. He speaks with a clowning, self-deprecating irony, which is a useful weapon in debate but sometimes masks the seriousness of what he is saying. But when he spoke about MI5 it was without a hint of irony or sarcasm. It was considered and deliberate. And, above all, what he said was true.

I flew to Florida a week later to film *Orpheus Descending*. I became convinced that Tennessee had really written for the cinema. In a very large theatre his story and his words become stretched out and distorted, no matter how brilliant the production. But on camera, where you can play at the speed of light, everything falls into place. Kevin Anderson and I had worked well together in the play, but we both worked twice as well in the film. Kevin's great quality as an actor is the inner life you can see in his eyes and hear when he speaks. Miriam Margolyes played Vee Talbot, the sheriff's wife. She had played the same part in our London production at the Haymarket. But now I was very struck by her playing of the "visions," and the remarkable way she showed the mysticism and the poetry of a human being who is tormented by the cruelty of the society she lives in.

In April I returned to England, to East Grinstead in Sussex, where we had booked a hotel for a week for a symposium on the historical truth of the 1920s and 1930s in the USSR. Since November 1987 we had engaged in many discussions with Soviet historians—first with those of the Memorial Society for Victims of Stalin's Repressions, subsequently with many others. Our concern, and most especially Gerry's, was to assist the process by which the history of Stalinism could emerge and be published—not only Trotsky's role, nor only Trotsky's historical accounts and documents, but all documents, and the work of all historians and researchers, regardless of their political viewpoint. We agreed that we should found an association for the study of the origin, cause, and consequences of Stalinism, and since our first symposium had been planned to take place in 1990, we simply called it Symposium 90. *Historia magister est vitae*—History is Life's teacher. The Soviet historians agreed that the most thorough research, discussion, and education was required on this question, so that Stalinism and its terror could not reassert itself. Besides the historians, the brilliant Soviet eye surgeon Sviatoslav Fyodorov came. There was the thin, frail figure of Nadezhda Joffe, eighty years old and one of the first signatories to the platform of the left opposition in 1926. There was Ivan Vrachev and his wife, Rebecca Boguslavskaya. He had joined the Bolshevik Party when he was sixteen and at the age of twenty-four was one of the delegates from the Transcaucasus who signed the December 1922 treaty that founded the Union of Soviet Socialist Republics. There were members of the Academy of Sciences, and the young members of the Memorial Society. There was Keti Dolidzhe, the woman film director from Georgia, and the actor Sergei Yursky. There was the editor of *Znamya*, Grigory Baklanov, Otto Latsis of *Kommunist*, and Andrei Karaulov from *Ogonyok*.

In discussion at the symposium, all kinds of dogmatic views would arise and then fall apart as more objective reports overcame them. And all the way through, the ninety-two-year-old Ivan Vrachev would intervene: "No, this is what happened. I was there!"

Taken as a whole, the reports presented at the symposium, many of them based on documents never before released from state archives, provided a new understanding of the nature of the problems that faced the Soviet Union, and the forces that gave rise to the bureaucratization of the party. Some of the members of Memorial were convinced that Lenin was responsible for the crimes of Stalin, a view held by many Western historians and academics. I would say that this is the most terrible of all the historical lies perpetrated by Stalin and the bureaucracy. The Soviet historians' extremely detailed and thoughtful studies proved that this was not the case. What was most striking to me was how the symposium clarified so many of our contemporary problems. It became clear that they had their source in the 1920s and 1930s and that only an honest and scientific examination of the truth of that period could help to clarify their exact nature. At the close it was agreed by all that this work must continue, and that a further symposium be held the following year. We, for our part, decided to invite Ivan Vrachev and his wife to give a series of lectures in Athens, Greece, and London.

In the first week of May I set off to Leningrad to film a miniseries about the young Catherine the Great. Leningrad was the most beautiful city I had ever seen. I marveled at how its long classic streets, laid out by Peter the Great and all but destroyed by the Nazis, had been reconstructed, stone for stone. I read a wonderful account of this in Vladimir Pozner's autobiography, *Parting with Illusions*. No international treaty, such as had saved Rome from bombardment, protected Leningrad. The Nazis spared nothing when they invaded Russia, and the Soviets knew that all the treasures of the Winter Palace would be looted and Leningrad razed to the ground if the siege was broken. A Red Army commissar chose a woman attendant to take charge of hiding the treasures and making sketches of the Winter Palace so that it could be rebuilt. She was a small, very ordinary-looking woman who sat at a door collecting tickets, and not one of the millions of visitors before the war would have given her a second glance. But the commissar had noticed that she spoke two or three languages, and found out that she had been an aristocrat and a member of the tsar's court before the revolution. He told her to choose three assistants, and to tell no one where she was hiding the treasures. After the war Pozner asked her if she had ever been tempted—times were so hard—to take just one of the priceless treasures and smuggle it out to the international art market. After all, she alone knew where all the objects were, and no one could have found out. She said nothing but looked at Pozner with withering contempt.

At the Pribaltiskaya Hotel I found to my great delight that Franco was also playing in *Young Catherine*. I was feeling tired and constantly unwell from the attentions of a tiresome amoeba I had picked up. Foolishly, I had overlooked the advice of Leningraders not to drink tapwater. Franco always travels with an entire pharmacopoeia in his trunk, and that helped somewhat. Looking after his needs, with boxes of pasta sent out by the production office, helped to distract me from mine.

Times were hard now in Leningrad. Perestroika was entering a period of protracted crisis and struggle. Shops were becoming emptier and every necessity was in short supply. The bureaucracy was deliberately choking the supply of food and everyday supplies, conducting a war of attrition against Gorbachev and the political revolution. I was organizing a concert in the October Hall to raise funds for the Theatre Workers' Union, with a brilliant young musician called Sergei Kuryokhin, and his group, Pop Mechanica. Elisabeth Welch had come over, as had Maria Farandouri from Greece, and Patti Allinson from New York. One morning before the concert my friend

Professor Startsev from Leningrad University took them on a tour of the Winter Palace, reconstructing step by step and blow by blow the storming of the palace by Bolshevik troops at the climax of the 1917 revolution. As usual, there were hundreds of visitors and tourists in the palace that day, with their official guides, winding their way through the immense buildings. As they heard Professor Startsev, they detached themselves from their guides and soon, like the Pied Piper of Hamelin, he had gathered a huge audience, which followed him around, straining to catch his account.

From Leningrad to London, and two days later to Austin, Texas, where I arrived in June 1990 on a "starry, starry night" in the middle of a wooden town on Willie Nelson's ranch. As I walked down the street of Willie's film town I saw lights and heard the strains of music. Three of India's top musicians, the Khan family, were seated on the porch of what was to become Miss Amelia's Sad Cafe, singing a long cadenza from a thirteenth-century Indian song. I thought of some lines from *Orpheus Descending:* "Something is still wild in the country. This country used to be wild, the men and women were wild and there was a wild sort of sweetness in their hearts, for each other, but now it's sick, with neon, like most other places. . . ."

Austin and its surrounding area was reputed to be the liberal region of Texas. Oil money had endowed a university and stocked it with some priceless manuscripts. I sat in the reading room for a couple of days, studying Carson McCullers's typed manuscript of *The Ballad of the Sad Cafe,* written and sent to *Harper's Magazine* in 1940. I was struck by the number of deleted paragraphs, scored through by the editor, perhaps for length, perhaps for political reasons. The two races, black and white, were bound by poverty, trapped with debt, the divisions between them maintained by that narrow but untraversable margin on which stood the white foreman or shopkeeper, who can support his family only as long as he takes the food out of the mouth of the black migrant worker or the fourteen-year-old cotton-mill hand. That was the Sad Cafe—and that was also Miss Amelia, a woman who fought like a man, who mercilessly made those who worked for her pay their ever-increasing debt, the same woman who culled and distilled wild herbs and flowers to cure the ailments and diseases produced by hard, unceasing labor in the cotton mill. Just as a ballad will tell you only a few very simple but essential facts—for instance, "Old Meg, she was a gipsy"—so Carson McCullers draws a very simple picture of the extraordinarily strange Miss Amelia. She does not explain, and so, bearing the ballad of the title in mind, I thought I should make very simple, clear choices about how to play Miss Amelia. I discussed each choice with Simon Callow, our director. I had to make a choice about her appearance, and I am still not sure I made the right one. Carson McCullers specifically writes that Miss Amelia has dark hair, but I thought I should have as little disguise as possible in the part. Given the fact that I am blond and basically fair, with blue eyes, I decided to go for looking like a real straw-headed Southerner. I wanted to make Miss Amelia look as her father might have done when he was a young boy.

Again bearing in mind the lack of explanation in the book, I did not change my clothes as you normally would to mark the passing of time. I thought that Miss Amelia should be presented like a cartoon image, looking the same way until something very significant happens in the story. When it does, she changes out of her dungarees and wears a red dress to mark the fact that she has become a woman.

I wanted her to appear to have remained rather like a twelve- or thirteen-year-old boy emotionally. She was trained by her father to work like a boy, to take over the business and the farm, and that is how she is. But she is also a woman. She is rather shy and awkward, and her instincts tell her to hit out at people, although she holds back some of the time. Her reactions are young and immediate; her hatred and her love are absolute. She has stopped developing and reacts with a readiness to fight, like a teenager. When she is betrayed by Cousin Lymon in the fight with Marvin Macy, it is as though everything she ever cared for had died. Her life becomes tragic. And like a child without defenses or the ability to dissemble, she bawls and cries and cries for her loss when the fight ends. Like all human beings, Miss Amelia is full of contradictory tendencies. Her father has taught her to squeeze the local people for their last penny, and yet the same poverty that drives her to keep others poor also produces a fellow feeling in her for their suffering. And so she heals them with her herbs.

The Ballad of the Sad Cafe was Simon Callow's first film as director. He was wonderful with the actors and spent considerable time explaining the life and the background of each of the townsfolk. Ismail Merchant came down periodically to give him encouragement. Ismail is unusual indeed in today's world. Whatever the circumstances, and wherever the location, he will seek out and find all the most rare and gifted people and bring them together, from the girl who feeds and tends the mule to the mysterious investors and academics whom he draws into each of his fascinating projects. For instance, George Burns, who lectured in the English department at Austin University, coached me for the Southern dialect and accent of Miss Amelia. Not only that, he knew how to wiggle and flap his ears, and he made an electrical device that, placed behind Cork Hubbert's ears, produced a wiggle for the camera that convinced all spectators that Cousin Lymon could flap his ears.

Early one August morning we heard the news that Iraq had invaded Kuwait. I had been following the press reports closely and had read of the Geneva OPEC meetings, especially the joint statement by the Saudi and Iraqi oil ministers announcing that Kuwait must cut back on its massive overproduction of oil. Suddenly President Bush announced massive airlifts of U.S. troops were on their way to Saudi Arabia, and the United Nations Security Council passed a resolution demanding the withdrawal of Iraqi troops from Kuwait.

It was not until late in September that *The New York Times* published the transcript of the July 25 meeting in Baghdad between the U.S. ambassador, April Glaspie, and Saddam Hussein. According to the transcript, which was leaked to ABC-TV, April Glaspie gave Saddam the green light to take whatever action he considered necessary in an inter-Arab question and assured him that the United States would not intervene. In March 1991, Ms. Glaspie maintained before a Senate committee that the transcript did not accurately reflect her conversation with Saddam Hussein. Several committee members and most of the press were incredulous, especially since the State Department placed a thirty-year ban on her notes of the meeting.

It became clear that the American and British governments wanted war, for every peace initiative was failing. U.S. planes were in the air heading for the Saudi kingdom before the State Department had requested permission for them to land. Suddenly Saddam Hussein was the "Hitler" of the Middle East, and the governments of the United States and Britain presented themselves as the liberators of Kuwait. The United Nations was used as a cover for an all-out military attack on an Arab country and occupation of Arab lands.

I was unconditionally opposed to the Iraqi occupation of Kuwait, and also unconditionally opposed to a war against Iraq. Millions of ordinary people in the United States and Europe and in the Middle East were politically ambushed for a short but crucial period. They were denied information and the means to express their political views; the British and Americans feared that the example of the Palestinian intifada would be followed throughout the Middle East on the same scale and with the same speed as the revolution in Eastern Europe.

By November, I was in the midst of rehearsals of a new production of Chekhov's *The Three Sisters,* directed by Robert Sturua. Months earlier, Thelma Holt had suggested that I should work with Robert, who wanted to do *The Cherry Orchard.* But so did Tony Richardson. It seemed best, therefore, to consider another play. Joely was out of work at the time, and it occurred to me she would be the most exceptional Irina, youngest of the three Prozorov sisters. Later, after *The Wall Breaks,* I suggested to Lynn that she might like to play Masha and I could play Olga. Thelma, our producer, and Robert both liked the idea. The financiers were ready to put up money on the three Redgraves. As it turned out, Joely was offered a marvelous film and was released to play a role opposite Melanie Griffith. I rang up Corin's daughter, Jemma, and asked if she would agree to play Irina. Both of us knew that half the best chances an actress gets are when another actress has dropped out. Maggie Smith and I were continually picking up parts that one or the other had been offered first, and very glad I was that some of them came my way.

I was thrilled at the chance to work with Lynn and for us to have more time together. After she decided to move to the United States in the early seventies I virtually lost touch with her. Once in a while she would telephone me, and once in a while, on a very rapid visit to Los Angeles, I would visit her. Her daughter Kelly had lived with me in Chiswick for a year while she finished at the American school in London, and that had helped Lynn and me to see more of each other, because it made Lynn come to London more often.

We had only five weeks for rehearsals, although Robert usually never rehearsed for less than ten. Our preparation began as usual around the table, with our scripts in front of us. We had an exceptional cast, and we all looked at Robert with great expectations. He spoke very little at the beginning. "The play is set when it was written, in 1901, but we live, think, and act as if it were now. It would be good if we succeeded in making people in the audience think about their own lives, what they are doing with their lives; some are helping others, some are only living for themselves."

I read two sentences: "Father died exactly a year ago today—the fifth of May, your saint's day, Irina." Robert stopped me. "Olga loved her father, but she's already forgotten him, she's forgotten that day. Some people say, 'Thank goodness we forgot!' Others say, 'How terrible.' To Olga it's a terrible shock." So the reading continued, very slowly, with many stops so that we could analyze the context of the words.

When it came to the doctor's presenting the silver samovar as a gift to Irina, Robert explained that Olga was horrified. Love mustn't be connected with presents or it is debased. She is afraid that Irina will accept the present and become corrupted. There was not one line that Robert had not analyzed. All his decisions were deeply thought out, and were surprising and quite contradictory, just as in life, especially in the life Chekhov understood and wanted to write about. When we began physically to "block" the first act we stopped as often as we had during the reading. Every physical action had been prepared, and very often it was in contradiction to the inner thought of the previous moment. Again, just like life.

Some of the actors became concerned. "Supposing I don't want to do this?" one queried. "Then you would have to get another director," Robert replied, calmly and with a big smile. There were several moments when an actor protested, not used to this way of working. One of them said, "The trouble is, his ideas are so brilliant," which I found hilarious: most of the time we would all be happy to have that kind of trouble. I was trained to follow a director's concept, and I was perturbed. I could see problems if even one of the cast was unwilling to give all he had to adapt himself and his ideas to Robert's. But Robert stayed calm, concentrated, and enthusiastic, and the detail of his work demanded all the concentration we possessed. Lynn, Jemma, and I were exhausted after the day's work. We would not go out to eat. As days passed we found ourselves using the tea breaks and the lunch breaks to think about, discuss, and explore every moment of the play. Robert noticed immediately when concentration slipped, and we took in deep breaths of excitement and nerves, knowing that he would miss nothing.

The first time I saw Act II assembled and run through, which was not until the end of the third week, I was absolutely lost in the world I saw before me. Every moment and every movement was rich with life and full of changes. Not once could I anticipate what would happen or what would be said. There was none of the dread familiarity that settles so often in the theatre. I was not watching Lynn, Stuart, Phoebe, Aden, Adrian, Jemma, or Graham "being good" but was seeing real people, Chekhov's people.

After the first run-through of Acts I and II we felt quite pleased. We all looked at Robert. "Quite good, but rather bad," he said. He is the only director I have worked with who can say "bad" and you know he means it but do not feel crushed.

In the last week he asked us all to make cuts. Some of us moaned, some pretended to be cheerful, but we all came up with cuts in our lines. To my surprise it was good to make cuts so very late in rehearsal. I had a copy of the play in Russian, as did Robert and his assistant, Helen Molchanov. We had agreed, quite early on, that our translation, like other published translations, was far too wordy and, in a very English way, did not get directly to the issue, as Chekhov always does. Chekhov's sentences are short and very direct. Olga does not speak much. However, I found that the shortened version was all the sharper. I forced myself to speak faster than I could think at first. Ellen Terry's advice in her autobiography remains correct. Actors speak too slowly, and the truth of the characters in *The Three Sisters* is that they are often saying the first thing that comes into their heads, without thinking. To play this required a great deal of work and total concentration.

I made a few notes in my script of Robert's advice on the day of our press night, December 11, 1990. One note was for Lynn: "Masha is crying like an unfortunate child who has been hit." Lynn was wonderful—first, because she worked to do everything that Robert wanted, second, because she did not once attempt to portray Masha in a sympathetic light. Masha didn't care what anyone thought of her, and neither did Lynn. She didn't cry romantically or beautifully or tragically. She cried just like a small child who has been hit—wailing and shrieking, and as if her nose was running and saliva spurting and she needed a mother who would wipe her face and put her on her knee, only there was no longer such a mother.

Jemma was also remarkable, and she, too, worked to do everything Robert wanted. In all the rehearsals and in all the performances of a fourteen-week run I never heard one false note in her voice. That is the highest praise I would ever hope to receive myself.

For my own part, during our two weeks of performances at the Yvonne Arnaud Theatre in Guildford I became concerned that I was "acting." Then Joely came to the play and asked afterward, "Do you think this Olga is really a schoolteacher?" I thought this over, and made a big mistake. A few days later, Robert wrote me a letter.

> You are now playing a schoolmistress—a rather ordinary, even dull person. Whilst Olga is an unusual character—a romantic, full of illusions, who believes that good will conquer evil. She wants to bring everyone happiness and good fortune. In order to do that she is prepared to sacrifice herself. She is how you created her. Her actions are different to those of humdrum people ... what you were doing before our conversation was unusual and at the same time painfully familiar. Portraying a woman, open to the world, full of a passionate desire to help everyone, to sacrifice everything for the sake of others. I do not know what has happened, it is either the pains of creation or labour pains—but I beg you to believe me that the way you used to play Olga was a *chef d'oeuvre* ...

Well, enough said. I abandoned my gray idea of the "schoolmistress." Robert, Lynn, and Jemma were happy, and I found a new conviction in what I was doing.

Robert's last words on the press night were: "This play for a lifetime has been performed in a bad mood [I think he meant a tragic or mournful mood], which is why it has never worked. These people like life. The actors say they like life. You must fight, not just for yourselves. You are fighting for others. Maintain the main freedom you have. The heroes want to live, they deserve happiness from the smallest events. They want happiness, not to be afraid of life."

In Guildford, one of Jemma's friends overheard a married couple: "Just like life," the wife said. "I hope *not*," exclaimed her husband. One director said to me after a performance, "I hope you're very proud of this production." Another said, "Fifty percent I liked, fifty percent I hated." I took both as compliments. The drama critics were 50 percent ecstatic, and 50 percent did not like us. One critic wrote: "Thank goodness *Three Sisters* never got to Moscow." Thelma Holt put that one on a board outside the Queen's Theatre.

≡

On the morning of January 13, 1991, I flew to Barcelona and spoke at a rally of about sixty thousand people who had marched through the narrow streets of the seaport bearing banners: NO WAR! FOR PEACE! U.S. TROOPS OUT OF THE GULF! On the same day there were enormous demonstrations in London, Berlin, and the United States. In Rome about a hundred and fifty thousand people demonstrated.

I spoke at another public meeting in the evening, a memorial tribute to Gerry. That meeting was packed, with all seats taken and many people standing. The next morning I got to the airport and bought *La Vanguardia*, which carried a headline on its report of the antiwar rally: VANESSA SUPPORTS SADDAM HUSSEIN. The UN deadline for Iraq's withdrawal from Kuwait was the following day, January 15. I rang *La Vanguardia*, and then Corin, who spoke to the newspaper's political editor. He got them to agree to publish a correction by way of a letter. But *La Vanguardia*'s headline was landing on news desks around the world, and this was the way the news media treated those who were against war: "If you don't support us, you support Saddam Hussein." I was totally opposed to the war and to the destruction of Iraq and the Iraqi people. I was also opposed to the invasion of Kuwait and had called for the withdrawal of Iraqi troops. But I knew that the Kuwaiti people would not be liberated by the war. They would be in a worse situation, and when the war brought back the emir, the democratic forces in Kuwait would be prevented from achieving any of their objectives, such as the right to have political parties and contend in elections.

The saturation bombing of Iraq began. If one counted the sorties from Saudi Arabia it was simple to calculate how many civilians must be dying. Even if only one died in each raid, one hundred thousand such sorties would kill that number of civilians. The British press and television became intolerable to read, watch, and listen to. There were racist caricatures in the newspapers, and very few voices in opposition. Systematic destruction of Iraq was proceeding, and the antiwar demonstrations that still took place got no publicity at all. Seven trade unions in Britain, including the National Union of Journalists and the Fire Brigades' Union, declared themselves against the war.

A hail of bombs was drowning the land and the people of Iraq in blood. Still, efforts were being made to find a way to a cease-fire and a peaceful solution. I am sure I was far from alone in thinking, as I sat late at night watching the panels of experts enjoying their roles on the TV programs, how atrocious it is to see beings dressed like ordinary men and women, completely unconcerned about sending soldiers to die, or killing civilians. If the governments and their bloodthirsty media spokesmen had given any thought either to "our boys" or to the Arab people, there would have been no war, and a solution would have been found by the Arab people themselves.

Months after the end of the war, a Harvard study team and UNICEF reported the tragic consequences of the bombing of Iraq, and the UN sanctions—tens of thousands of children in northern, central, and southern Iraq dead from hunger and disease, babies with irreparable physical damage to their bodies and brains from prolonged malnutrition and dehydration. Also, families of British servicemen discovered how many of their sons—seventeen- and eighteen-year-olds!—were killed in "friendly fire." The UN specifies that you are a child until you are eighteen. The U.S. government prevented American airmen from attending an inquest in Britain and giving evidence so that the truth about the "friendly fire" accident could be established.

I believed that people in the United States and Europe would realize the truth about the Gulf War. The fact that so many lies are told only shows, to my mind, that the present governments are extremely frightened of their own people. As I played in *The Three Sisters* in our closing weeks and spoke Olga's lines "Our sorrows will turn into happiness for those that come after us. Peace and happiness will come to the earth. They will think kindly of us and they will thank us," I cried for and with all those who will not see happiness again: for the suffering of those who are alive, for "man's inhumanity to man." But I also see the opposite of all this cruelty and suffering—millions of human beings who do not accept that life should be like this for anyone. We want peace and only need to know the truth, and we will go on insisting on the truth so that we can ensure that all oppressed peoples have justice and a real human life. The key to this lies in our history. As long as we do not know our history we cannot solve our problems. So, you see, what Chekhov wrote in 1901 in *The Three Sisters* is very much what millions of people feel today, over ninety years later: "We must see more and know more." We must know the truth.

CHAPTER 27

The American playwright Martin Sherman, whom I had known, loved, and admired from afar since 1984, shortly after his play *Bent*, a love story between two men in Auschwitz, began appearing in almost every capital city in the world, was to become my dearest and most treasured friend. We had worked together on many occasions: at the benefit for the Arab Women's Association in November 1988, during the Soviet Theatre Season at the Lyric Theatre, and in his own play *A Madhouse in Goa* in the summer of 1989. In April 1991 we met again in Robert Fox's office and agreed that I would play Isadora Duncan in *When She Danced*, Martin's play about Isadora and the young Russian poet Sergei Essenin during their short and terrible time in Paris in 1923. The year before, Robert had invited me to come with him to a small pub-theatre in North London "to see the best play I've seen in years." It was *When She Danced*, and at the end of the play I wholeheartedly agreed with him. The performance was so extraordinary that I did not think for one second that I should play the part of Isadora. Sheila Gish and Angela Pleasance—in the role of the exiled Russian interpreter—were both totally amazing, and my only thought was that their production should be seen in the West

End. Robert's asking me to play Isadora was most unexpected and came about in an interesting way.

In the middle of February, my American agent, Sam Cohn, was invited to a meeting at the offices of the Shubert Organization in New York. The contract terms had all been agreed to for my appearance in *Lettice and Lovage,* a play by Peter Shaffer. A tour of major U.S. cities was to start in June. However, the producers told Sam that reports in the U.S. press of statements I had allegedly made at a peace rally in Barcelona on January 13, two days before the Gulf War started, and a statement I had placed as a paid advertisement in *The New York Times* on February 8, had caused them to cancel my contract.

On January 14, reading the Spanish newspapers at the Barcelona airport on my way back to London, I had found a report in *La Vanguardia* headlined VANESSA SUPPORTS SADDAM HUSSEIN. A few minutes before boarding the plane, Corin and I telephoned the editor. He published a letter from me the next day by way of correction, but the headline had already been taken up by the press around the world.

For those who would like to know what I actually said in Barcelona on January 13, and what I published in *The New York Times* in February, I include the full text of the *Times* advertisement (it cost me $23,000) in an appendix to this book. The typesetter made a significant mistake in the advertisement that I did not spot until weeks later, when I was sent a copy of the paper. The word "troops" was substituted for my word "aggression."

My statement in Barcelona before the war, and the *Times* ad published during the war, should have made it clear that I supported a peaceful and just negotiated settlement of the crisis, and that I was unconditionally opposed to the Iraqi invasion of Kuwait and war as a solution. Quoted out of context, my words "we demand the withdrawal of U.S., British, and all imperialist troops from the Gulf and we must unconditionally defend Iraq against American, British, and Israeli *aggression* [not *troops*]" could only be taken to mean that I supported the Iraqi invasion of Kuwait.

I appealed to the American Actors' Equity Association, and on March 19 their executive council met in New York, with a live link to the West Coast. They listened to Sam Cohn and me and then questioned us. The council decided that my contract had been broken for political reasons and that Equity would take my case to arbitration with the Broadway Producers' Association. Under rules established between Equity and the Producers' Association after the McCarthy period, there can be no blacklisting for political reasons. This was an important test case for a few American artists who had lost work because they opposed the Gulf War. But it had been clear for some time that whatever the outcome of the arbitration, there would be no tour for me in *Lettice and Lovage*, and that was how it happened that Robert Fox decided to produce *When She Danced* and I came to play Isadora Duncan again.

I stare at my bundle of airline tickets from this time in disbelief. I was in Zurich with *The Three Sisters* in early March. Then New York, then London in April for a concert, *Jerusalem for Reconciliation*, which I produced to benefit UNICEF's Emergency Appeal for Children in the Middle East and the Arab Women's Association. I was filming *Howards End* in the long green grass of Hertfordshire in May, and in early June was back in New York, receiving a medal from the UN Writers' Association for my work for human rights, and rehearsing for four special performances at La Mama of *Collateral Damage: Meditations on the Gulf War*, a benefit for War Resisters International directed by Leonard Shapiro. The collage of poems, plays, and sketches began with George Bartenieff wheeling an empty supermarket cart onto the stage as one of New York's homeless. He then recited "Passport," a poem by the Palestinian poet Mahmoud Darwish. I chose as my contribution six verses from Dante's *Inferno* that describe the poet's horror as he turns his eyes back to the highway which has led him into a deep valley. I carried a bundle of black cloth in my arms as I came onto the stage, and at the end of the last verse I sat down with the audience to watch four minutes of film that had not been shown on TV anywhere. A European news cameraman had filmed the road to Basra a few hours after cars and trucks jamming the highway in the rush to get out of Kuwait City had been fire-bombed by allied forces.

I then turned and laid the black bundle on the stage in front of me. While Simon Shaheen played an ancient tune on his violin, I recited the lament for Dinun, a shepherd seized from the fields and taken to the underworld. His wife sees his trousers hanging from a nail on the wall of their hut, and she cries for him, knowing that he will never come to her again. The story and the lament are contained in ancient Sumerian writings that foreshadow the biblical narrative of the Flood.

Every ticket was sold for these four performances. On the last night, I was due to drive immediately after my appearance to JFK Airport, to get the flight to London. As I waited offstage, I stood next to a young dancer who was to appear as a cheerleader in *Bomb!*, a piece written by Allen Ginsberg. "What do you think about tonight?" I said. "I thought that nobody felt the same way I did," she replied. "I feel a real catharsis." I think it was the first time I really knew what the word "catharsis" meant.

In London the next day I joined Thelma Holt and a first-class documentary-film cameraman, and we flew via Tunis to Amman. There we spent the evening in the palace being briefed by H.R.H. Crown Prince Hassan and representatives of the United Nations International Children's Emergency Fund. At dawn the royal helicopter flew us to the border, and from there we drove for eight hours, reaching Baghdad around six in the evening. For the next four days we traveled with Dr. Gianni Murzi, UNICEF director in Iraq, down to Basra, the next day on up to Samara, and then back to Baghdad, where we spent another day and night, visiting hospitals, clinics, small villages, and suburbs. UNICEF and the *UN Special Report* had warned of the devastation to children's lives and health, and I had spent some hours in New York with a member of the Harvard study team that had returned from Iraq a few weeks earlier. This was how I learned that the allied bombing had been of a surgical precision, destroying most of the main electrical grid that supplied the whole of Iraq, and thereby destroying the sanitation, water, and irrigation systems that depend upon a regular and continuous power supply. The UN sanctions in fact deprived Iraq of medical supplies, although on paper the sanctions were not supposed to include humanitarian commodities. The result was that the Harvard study team expected five hundred thousand children to die of severe malnutrition and disease by the end of 1991. Those children who could be got to hospitals or clinics could not be given any treatment beyond a saline drip. Supplies of UNICEF rehydration salts had to be mixed with safe water, which hardly existed anymore. Incubators and computers for analyzing blood could not be used. Even the UNICEF and Oxfam generators, each one of which had to be approved by the UN special council overseeing the sanctions, could not keep advanced hospital equipment functioning.

The whole world had seen close-ups of children dying from starvation and dysentery in Africa, but the suffering children of Iraq were not on the nightly news. Thelma and I saw baby after baby in torment or comatose. We spoke with their mothers and with nurses and doctors, most of whom had been trained in universities and hospitals in Britain. They found it impossible to believe that Britain and the United States could inflict such horrible misery on children. The ones that survived would be physically and mentally retarded for the rest of their lives.

Leaving our cameraman behind to spend some days up north in the Kurdish country, Thelma and I flew back to London and went straight to a television studio, where producers had agreed to show some of our film and interview us on the ten o'clock news. The next morning, Sunday, I stood with Emma Thompson on the platform at the St. Pancras main line railway terminal, ready to film one last scene of *Howards End*. Thus I fulfilled my personal and contractual agreement with Ismail Merchant that I would get back from Iraq on time. The first day of rehearsals for *When She Danced* began the next day, June 16.

A month earlier, Robert Fox, Martin Sherman, and I, accompanied by our director, Robert Alan Ackerman, had flown to Moscow as guests of the Theatre Workers' Union to meet, see, and read with as many young Russian actors as possible. We were looking for Isadora's Essenin.

May is the time when purple lilac bushes bloom along the boulevards and in the gardens and parks of Moscow and the trees in front of the public buildings and apartment blocks are in full leaf. We walked over to the Kievski station from our hotel, wandering in the sunshine through crowds of vendors selling fruit or flowers or cigarettes. Martin and I bought an ice cream from every kiosk or cart we encountered. Arm in arm we wandered into the massive old station, called the Kievski because all the trains go somewhere in the Ukraine. As we gazed at the railway carriages heading for Kharkov, Odessa, or Kiev itself, Martin talked about his grandparents. They had fled the tsar's pogroms and their shtetl, heading for Odessa and a ship bound for New York. Martin's father and uncle were still living in New York. To that very day in 1991, neither of them had ever got into a boat again, not even a rowboat in Central Park. The memories of the voyage over the Black Sea, into the Mediterranean, and then across the Atlantic were unendurable.

One night in the studio space at the top of the Mossovieta Theatre, which overlooks Mayakovsky Square, where Yevtushenko and his friends gave their first mass poetry readings in the 1960s, we watched a brilliant young actor playing Caligula in Camus's play. Oleg Menshikov was already highly respected, and Robert thought he had the physical energy and charisma of the young Gérard Philipe. Offstage he was quiet and friendly and reminded me of the famous drawing of Keats. We celebrated his agreement to play Essenin over a Chinese lunch at the Peking Hotel, and then celebrated again at dinner in the apartment of the painter Reuben Vardzigulyants and his wife, the drama critic Svetlana Donskaya. They were the parents of one of my closest friends and colleagues, Misha Donskoy.

When Svetlana was sixteen she worked day and night with the firefighters as the Nazis shelled Leningrad during the siege. You cannot meet one Soviet woman in her late sixties or early seventies who did not quite literally fight the Nazis and help to bring about the defeat of the Third Reich, which began decisively with the defeat of the Nazis in the territories of the USSR. Out of every high school class of sixteen-year-olds in 1941, only two or three survived to see April 1945. Many of those who did survive saw their remaining friends and family members returned to the gulags, or were themselves imprisoned.

I have seldom laughed so much as when in Reuben and Svetlana's company, unless it is when Robert Fox and Martin Sherman get together. That night we were all around Svetlana's supper table, so it somehow seemed inevitable that our hilarity had us rolling on the floor as our combined efforts and ingenuity failed for half an hour to release Martin from the toilet, where he had locked himself in.

Before we left Moscow, Martin talked to me about Isadora. "She was brave in her statements and in the way she lived her life; for me, she embodies the best of America and the potential America once had. Even some of her naïve aspects represent aspects of America that are fast disappearing. Her life has always moved me very, very deeply—her vision, her sense of freedom, the way she embraced life."

By the middle of July we were performing our play in Brighton, with Oleg astounding us with his Essenin, and my dear friend Frances de la Tour quite haunting as well as extremely funny as the Russian émigré interpreter Miss Belzer. On our first night we were visited by a Russian playwright who was in London as a part of Gorbachev's delegation for the G7 summit. He was enthusiastic about our play, and quite pessimistic about the situation developing in the Soviet Union. Gorbachev had made an urgent and public appeal to the G7 leaders for normal trade credits, debt relief, and development loans, but nothing concrete had been conceded. Such normal commercial interbank terms require government approval, no matter what banks or brokers might wish. China had development loans, trade credits, and a high level of Western investment, even after Tiananmen. To me it seemed obvious that Western governments supported dictatorships, where profits were high and strikes and human rights nonexistent. Is there any other possible conclusion?

On the positive side, the draft of the new union treaty for all the republics of the USSR had been agreed to and would be signed in August. This would be vital for the peoples who lived in the republics, because they would then have far greater freedom to make decisions independently of the bureaucratic apparatus that still controlled the wealth of all the republics.

On August 19, in the early hours of the morning, Oleg had a call from his family in Moscow. A state of emergency and martial law had been declared. The coup committee included Anatoly Lukhyanov, a known anti-Semite and the bitter Stalinist opponent of both Gorbachev and Yeltsin. I rang friends in Moscow. Some did not answer the telephone, some did. They did not know much beyond what was on the TV news, but they knew that the situation was very dangerous. Gorbachev, as we all heard later, was under house arrest with his family, but he held true to his principles and refused to capitulate, although he certainly knew that KGB doctors could at any time give him drugs to induce illness or death. Teachers at the Russian University of Humanities told me their students went down to the square to stop the tanks. Grandmothers with shopping bags said to them,

"Go away—leave this to us. We know how to talk to the lads." Three men were killed: Dimitri Komar, Ilya Krichevsky, and Vladimir Usov. There is no doubt that their deaths were a turning point, for the soldiers in the tanks would not accept orders to kill their own people. The actor Rupert Everett, who was in Russia making *And Quiet Flows the Don,* was standing in the crowd. He told Corin that he had been filming with one of the tank regiments the previous week. Then one day the tanks did not turn up for filming. As Rupert stood in the square with the masses who had gathered with the courageous Boris Yeltsin to defend the White House, the soldiers in one of the tanks rolling by recognized Rupert and called out, "Don't worry, Rupert. We're not going to shoot!"

Thirty days later I flew to Moscow, arriving at the stage door of the Bolshoi Theatre, when I joined Elaine Paige, Chrissie Hynde, Michael Ball, and Frances de la Tour in a memorial concert for the three young Russians killed during the coup. Elaine sang "Memory" and I read out messages of support for their families from Timothy Dalton, Mick Jagger, Cher, and many other artists. On October 6 we held the *For the Fallen Heroes* concert in London. Vladimir Usov's widow, Ludmila, and their daughter, fifteen-year-old Marina, were guests of honor, with a representative from the mayor of Moscow's office. Sixteen-year-old Thomas Carroll from the Yehudi Menuhin school played the cello, and we donated £1,000 to the Yehudi Menuhin school to help finance the tuition of a Czech student. We asked Marina if she would like to see a musical. She chose *Joseph and the Amazing Technicolor Dreamcoat.* She told us that Jason Donovan was the hero of her class at school. She and all her friends had his photo on their desks.

Though it was decisively defeated, and the Stalinist leaders were arrested, the August coup accelerated the breakup of the USSR. Leaders and middle-level bureaucrats in the republics who had supported the coup openly or equivocally hastened to declare independence, changing the names of their parties, wrapping themselves in the national flag, and securing the apparatus of political and economic control.

The banning of the Communist Party of the Soviet Union provided a protective cloak for the bureaucrats. The Stalinists are still among the first to enrich themselves at the expense of millions of ordinary people, and wherever conflicts rage between nationalities long oppressed by Stalinism, the cause is both ex-Stalinist leaders and the history of what Stalin set out to do. In 1928 Stalin acknowledged that he intended to change the USSR and its economy in a way that would make it impossible for any republic to secede. Mass deportations and forced migrations of peoples of all nationalities were organized. All this, and more, makes the tasks of the political revolution complex, producing the great hardship and tragedies we see all over the republics of the former USSR and Eastern Europe.

The speed of the coup and its defeat, the intensity of the processes and problems that were both the cause and the consequence, created an explosion of accumulated problems that brutally and tragically, like Ibsen's "ghosts," strangle and suffocate the efforts of millions to build a new life. To find a solution to these problems we have to study their history in a new way. The answers we seek cannot be found in the study of Bolshevism or Stalinism or Trotskyism, or even in the study of the USSR itself outside of the whole international context. Thus the theme of the second Symposium 90 conference, held in Athens that October, was "The USSR in the 1930s in the Context of World History."

Was Stalinism the inevitable product of Lenin's Bolshevik Party and the October Revolution, or was it, on the contrary, a betrayal of those principles, a counterrevolution, both cause and effect of the brutal and dictatorial regimes that emerged, not simultaneously, but within the same historical epoch and framework, in many different countries? This is not an academic question. No one can dispute that the October Revolution did change the world, and Stalinism has shadowed us for decades. My own view is that October 1917 was both betrayed and falsified by Stalinism. Now, more than ever before, we need serious study and research into the origins and causes of both Stalinism and fascism. The second cannot be understood without a knowledge of the first; and neither can be comprehended if studied independently of the world context in which they emerged.

≡

Events in Russia in 1991 made the story of Isadora's and Essenin's lives and struggles even more relevant to us. Isadora was only one of the international artists who recognized and rejoiced in the freedom and creativity unleashed by the October Revolution of 1917. Among the Americans who went to Russia then, for the first time, were Mary Pickford and Douglas Fairbanks, Sr., who brought back to the United States the news about the amazing Sergei Eisenstein and his films.

Both Isadora and Essenin believed that through her dance and his poems, the American people would understand the need to support the revolution and send wheat to the famine-stricken Russia of 1923, to the millions who were starving after the American, British, French, and Japanese armies had fought to defeat the first state in the world where workers and peasants had democratic power.

Martin's play takes place in 1923. At this time the German workers' revolution had been defeated by an army carrying out orders of the workers' own leaders, the Social Democrats. A rapid political degeneration and reaction was establishing bureaucratic control over the Soviet Communist Party and the soviets, taking away workers' and peasants' political power. In the United States, too, political reaction had developed. Isadora and Essenin found their art rejected and repudiated both in America and in the new USSR. Lenin was paralyzed and dying. Only Trotsky defended and encouraged the desperate Essenin; only one editor had the courage to print his poems. In Boston, Isadora and Essenin were attacked for being "Reds." In Moscow, they were attacked for being "decadent." This is the historical content of Martin's play about two great artists who find themselves bewildered and penniless in Paris.

Before each performance of *When She Danced* our company, actors and understudies, met in Oleg's dressing room. We lit a candle, turned off the lights, and sat for five minutes, concentrating our thoughts, and focusing our attention on one another. The premiere in London, at the Globe Theatre, was on August 6. I thought, at our candle call, of the letter I had received from an eighty-year-old English actor. I had written to him requesting his memories of his thoughts and concerns in 1923, and he replied: "We inherited Rupert Brooke's innocent vanity and hoped his example would be enough to teach people to be world citizens through the League of Nations. The power of competition and greed, through 'market forces' led us to war again, as it will now, sooner or later."

When Oleg heard, via his family in Moscow, of the killing of the three young men during the August coup, our candle call was full of thoughts for all our friends in Moscow.

> The gates of Heaven are narrow
> Hasten up towards them
> Two of the lads were Russian
> The third one was a Jew.

These are the first lines of a poem by a Russian woman, Alla Gelikh. She handed a copy of it to Frances de la Tour at the door of the theatre, to read at the *For the Fallen Heroes* benefit concert in October. Oleg read a poem by Osip Mandelstam, and Martin Sherman read Nekrasov's "Liberty."

As our candle flickered and steadied, and the sound of machine-gun fire from the amusement arcade behind the theatre threatened us, "This is the Terminator! I will be back!," our thoughts were full of those artists and poets who had been murdered and censored by Stalin or by the tsar, and their lives and thoughts entwined in our minds with the lives of Vladimir Usov, Dimitri Komar, and Ilya Krichevsky.

≡

Late in October, ten days after the *For the Fallen Heroes* concert, Tasha, Joely, and their half sister, Catherine, flew out to Los Angeles to be with Tony, who was seriously ill. Now the evening candle became Tony's candle. On November 12, when Princess Diana gave me the *Evening Standard* Drama Award for Actress of the Year for *When She Danced*, Martin Sherman was my escort. Only he and my dear friend Frances de la Tour knew that I was wearing the Russian skirt and smock decorated with cherry-red embroidery as a talisman for Tony, who was now in the hospital.

For two weeks Martin came home with me to my kitchen and sat and held my hand. He talked to me about AIDS, which I discovered I knew little about, in spite of having lost good friends in America. Robert Fox had joined the girls and Catherine's mother, Griselda, in Los Angeles to be with Tony. We telephoned them each night. When Magic Johnson announced he had the AIDS virus, Robert had T-shirts made up with the slogan WE LOVE MAGIC. I flew to Los

Angeles on the thirteenth, but Tony was already unconscious, and he died at one-thirty in the afternoon on November 14, 1991.

He had been planning a production of *The Cherry Orchard* for me. We were to rehearse together in January. In September, when he was casting the production in London, he had shown me the model of the set, designed by Askander Timeon: Act 1—bare branches; Act 2—white blossom; Act 3—red cherries, a festival of cherries; Act 4—the green trees that will be cut down to build an estate of villas for summer tourists. The most simple concept; the most organic to the story. I had looked at the model in Tony's hotel room. Baskets of cherries, piles of cherries on white cloths. Trees heavy with cherries, wooden poles garlanded with cherries, ropes of lights hanging from tree to tree, beneath which Lliuba Ranevskaya, her daughters and friends would dance to the music of the Jewish orchestra. Tony had lain on the bed, watching and sharing my excitement. He was ill and very tired, but his brown eyes were sparkling with the mischievous look I knew so well. "Did they use to have cherry festivals in Russia?" I had asked, already expecting his reply. He giggled with great pleasure. "I don't know, but they will in this production."

I found a painting by an elderly Russian artist at Roy Miles's gallery in London and bought it for Tony and our production. The painting now hangs in Joely and her husband's flat. A grandmother, a mother, and a little girl are gathering cherries in their baskets. It was painted in the 1930s, but there is no doubt about it—it is a small cherry festival for three generations.

Joely gave birth to a baby daughter, Daisy, just after one in the morning on Saturday, March 28, 1992. Carlo and I heard the telephone ring. We were lying on our beds with our clothes on expecting the call. "Listen to this," Joely's husband, Tim, said, and I heard the "Miaow" of the newborn. Carlo and I ran down to the street, into a taxi, and then up to the third floor of the hospital. Carlo held the baby while Joely and Tim hugged each other, laughing and crying with the triumph and relief of two warriors who had won a long and hard battle. The West Indian nurse and the midwife were full of admiration. Joely and Tim had taken natural-childbirth classes together, and she had given birth after a long labor without any drugs or medication. She said she had almost given up and asked for medication just before the end, but Tim had urged her on, shouting instructions: "Go on! Push now, push now, Joely, the baby is almost here." I remembered that the night Joely was born Tony was at my side all the way. "Go on. You look beautiful. You look like Monica Vitti."

All of us, Tasha, Joely, Catherine, Griselda, and I, have a color photograph of Tony taken by Lartigue, the French master photographer. Tony is by a tree at his home in the hills and forest outside La Garde Freinet. A great white-and-yellow wide-winged parrot is lifting off into the sky from Tony's upstretched arms.

≡

I held Jim Ivory's hand as we walked up the stairs of the Grand Palais at the Cannes Film Festival for the presentation of the prize for *Howards End,* and I thought of Tony, who gave me my first sight of Cannes, and who took me water-skiing in the bay for the first time in my life. I crashed into the water pretty quickly, and the tow rope caught my engagement ring, a star sapphire, which sank and was lost.

In his work and life Tony did battle to prevent the old from strangling the new; he gave countless young people encouragement and confidence and often their first job. I was twenty-two years old when I first worked with him in his production of *Othello* at Stratford-upon-Avon and when I saw his film of *Look Back in Anger* with Richard Burton as Jimmy Porter. Jimmy's passionate invective, his infectious jokes, his noisy, joyous, and lamenting trumpet cadenzas, made me certain that the energy and creative lust for life of the young would shatter the stifling and deadly philistinism and bureaucracy of England in the 1950s.

His work and his approach to life have always inspired me. I fell in love with his independent spirit, his eyes that searched the human beings around him, and the confidence and excitement he generated in all who worked with him. He lives in his daughters, although they must now live without him.

CHAPTER 28

About six months before Daisy was born, Joely and Tim invited me to join them at the hospital to see the first magnetic-resonance scan of the fetus in Joely's womb. The magnetic waves pulse from the tiny heart, brain, legs, and arms and are instantly translated by the computer into a black-and-white moving image. To be able to watch the baby swimming safely in the waters of the womb is a miracle, no less divine for being human. Today, as throughout our century, scientists and engineers create extraordinary technology to guide and preserve the development of the human species. Meanwhile governments pursue policies that have already led to a worldwide economic disaster, with catastrophic social and ecological consequences.

On April 6, 1992, ten days after my granddaughter was born, the Serbian regime of Slobodan Milošević launched the war to seize the territories of Bosnia-Herzegovina. That same month, Corin and I and our Marxist Party colleagues, together with the Afro-Asian Solidarity Committee, organized a public meeting in defense of Bosnian Muslims. The small Quaker Hall off Trafalgar Square was full to overflowing. Two Labour members of Parliament joined the plat-

In 1986 Timothy Dalton
and I performed together
at the Haymarket
Theatre, London, in
Antony and Cleopatra
(*above*) and *The Taming of
the Shrew* (*right*).

As Miss Jean Brodie in my dressing room, 1966 (*top left*); as an extra for Joshua Logan's *Camelot* (*top right*); Guinevere in *Camelot* (*center right*); Sylvia Pankhurst in Richard Attenborough's antiwar film *Oh What a Lovely War*, 1968 (*bottom left*); acting for Sidney Lumet again in *Murder on the Orient Express*, 1974 (*bottom center*); and (*bottom right*) Julia says goodbye in a Berlin café.

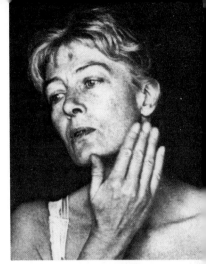

Playing for Time (*top left*); *Agatha* (*top center*); as Olive Chancellor in the Merchant-Ivory film *The Bostonians* (*top right*); Nora, the wife of Con Melody, in *A Touch of the Poet,* 1988 (*above*); Tennessee Williams's "Lady" in the Broadway production of *Orpheus Descending,* directed by Peter Hall (*center right*); and in October 1990 with crew cut again after *The Ballad of the Sad Cafe* and Lynn's scissors in *Whatever Happened to Baby Jane?*

As Mrs. Alving in *Ghosts,* with Adrian Dunbar as Oswald, in London in 1986 (*top*); with Jean-Marc Barr in *Orpheus Descending* at the Haymarket, 1988 (*left*); and as Mrs. Honey in Martin Sherman's *A Madhouse in Goa* at the Lyric, Hammersmith, 1989.

With Gerry Healy and
Selwa Abu Khadr in Kuwait,
1979 (*right*); Gerry and me
backstage at the
Sovremennik Prisoners'
March, Moscow, with
Marina Nielova and the cast
of *The Steep Route,* about
women prisoners in Stalin's
Gulag, February 1989
(*center*); and (*below*) January
1991, two days before the
end of the UN deadline and
the start of the war against
Iraq, at a public meeting for
Symposium 90 in tribute to
Gerry Healy.

Corin and me outside the courtrooms in London in 1978 during the hearings of our libel case against *The Observer* (*above*); playing Arkadina, the famous actress, with Natasha as Nina, the would-be actress, in Chekhov's *The Seagull* at the Queen's Theatre, 1985 (*right*).

Me, Joely, and Tasha,
summer 1990 (*right*); a
family snapshot of Lynn and
me (*center*); and (*below*) a
walk on Hampstead Heath
one Sunday in summer 1990
with Rachel and Carlo.

Lynn as Masha, me as Olga, and Jemma as Irina in *The Three Sisters*, directed by
Robert Sturua in 1990 at the Queen's Theatre, London.

form. Ours was the first, and remained the only, public meeting or rally organized during the war, until the UK All-Party Alliance held a rally in Trafalgar Square in February 1994. In May 1992 we assisted a determined Bosnian woman in mounting a picket line for one day outside the Foreign Office. In July we joined the picketing outside the hall in Westminster where Milošević had come to meet with Lord Carrington, who was trying to broker a peace agreement. That month, in the green parkland of Kenwood, where we gave a recital of Russian poetry, we met again our dear American friend from Actors' Equity, Stefan Fittermann. He told us that no one was organizing protest meetings in New York either. "Does no one realize that this is like 1938 in Europe? Does no one understand anything at all?" He almost cried with pain and frustration.

In Buenos Aires that August, thanks to a remarkable woman film director, Lita Stantic, I met the Madres de Plaza de Mayo. Hebe de Bonafini and her friends were as courageous as ever. Hebe had been accused by President Menem of using insulting language against him, thus breaking, he alleged, some law in the Argentine constitution. The same president had granted amnesty to the murderers of the *desaparecidos,* an entire generation of seventeen- to twenty-year-old boys and girls. The mothers, however, were still campaigning to bring the dictators and their accomplices to trial for the kidnapping, torture, and murder of their children. They also told me that the leader of the murderous junta, General Videla, could be seen jogging in the park on Sundays. The political parties and groups that had formerly marched with the mothers, and supported their cause, had fallen silent and no longer held meetings or rallies, although the mothers still received help from their international support groups. They were concerned that unless the murderers were brought to trial, the story of what had happened would not be on official records. History would be buried, their children would be forgotten, and another dictatorship could take power again in Argentina.

In late September I was in Hamburg, on a publicity tour for my German publisher. I was to visit Berlin, Munich, and Frankfurt. "Why have no East German cities been included—Dresden or Leipzig, for instance?" I asked. "No one can afford to buy books there," my publisher replied. I realized that this might well be the case, but still, in my view, I should have gone there. The Wall had now literally vanished, but it still existed in the minds of even the most progressive people.

The German Social Democrats were preparing, amid heated and anguished discussion, to agree to the Kohl government's proposal to delete Article 16 from the German constitution. Article 16 made Germany the only country in the world that defended the basic democratic rights of all persecuted peoples to seek shelter, refuge, and asylum—whether from racist persecution, political repression, or civil war. Five hundred thousand refugees from the former Yugoslavia had been given temporary asylum in Germany. The city government of Hamburg had found shelter and housing for many, but racist attacks on "foreigners" were rapidly increasing. "We won't abolish Article Sixteen," a leading Social Democrat, Herr Duve, told me. "But we will agree to change it. We've done all we can. What can I tell our own people? There are fewer and fewer jobs." He was genuinely upset and bewildered. The burning of Turkish shops and the desecration of Jewish graves and synagogues disturbed him deeply, but he could find no other answer than to close the door to refugees.

On the night of September 25, I was on a TV talk show in Hamburg. Will Quadflieg, the leading actor of Hamburg's Thalia Theatre, a genial man in his seventies, said during the discussion that as a young actor he had stood by and watched the horrors of Kristallnacht without intervening. "I won't do that this time." After the show I met Jürgen Flimm, the artistic director of the Thalia, and we discussed what artists could do to oppose the rising tide of fascism in Europe.

The next evening, as I set off for the Thalia Theatre from my hotel, my interpreter, Heidi, told me that some fascists had burned down Barrack 38, the Jewish memorial museum in the former Nazi concentration camp Sachsenhausen, just outside Berlin. As soon as I met Jürgen in the theatre, we found we had both drawn the same conclusion. The burning of Barrack 38 meant that the next attack would kill people. Every seat and every aisle was full that night, which celebrated the beginning of the Thalia's new season. Halfway through the cabaret, Jürgen told the audience that we had decided to invite artists from all over the world to join us in a conference and concert against racism at the Thalia on January 30 and 31, the sixtieth anniversary of the Nazis' taking power in Germany. Then he asked me to speak. I climbed up onstage and took the mike from him. "You probably all know that I have supported the Palestinians, and I still do. You may not know what I said when I received an Oscar for Fred Zinnemann's film *Julia*. I promised to continue the fight against anti-Semitism and fascism. I am glad I can be here with you in Hamburg on this night to fulfill that promise." I left for Berlin the next morning, agreeing with Jürgen that I would draw up a statement. The next day Jürgen received an anonymous letter from some fascist, threatening both of us.

In Berlin, on the hotel typewriter, I drafted a manifesto, which I read to guests at a reception given by my publishers in Frankfurt.

"WE WILL NEVER FORGET—WE WILL NOT LET IT HAPPEN AGAIN"

AN OPEN LETTER TO ARTISTS IN ALL COUNTRIES

Dear friends,

The burning of the Jewish Memorial Museum "Barrack 38" at Sachsenhausen on Saturday night, September 26, is not, in our view, only one more racist atrocity, following the attempted murder of Romanian gypsy and Vietnamese families in Rostock.

We are at a crossroads in our lives and in our history.

We cannot exclude that these crimes are clearly systematic, an organized and financed plan of terror—to back up and drive on politicians of all the parties which are demanding a change in the asylum rights and laws connected to article 16 in the constitution of the Federal Republic of Germany. By changing article 16, these leaders will be agreeing with the demands of terrorists.

Germany is the only country in Europe, or the world, with a constitution which defends the basic democratic rights of all persecuted peoples to seek shelter, refuge and asylum—whether from racist persecution, political repression or civil war.

If article 16 were removed from the German constitution an avalanche of fascist reaction would follow throughout Europe, and throughout the world.

We emphasize, we are at the crossroads.

October 3, the day chosen by the German government for the celebration of the re-unification of the German people in November 1989—is also the fiftieth anniversary of the first launching of the Nazi V2 rocket in 1942.

Two celebrations for the Nazi V2 were planned. The first, sponsored by the German Aerospace Industry Federation, has been cancelled after international protest.

The second, sponsored by the Society of the "Peenemünde Centre for Historical & Technical Information," has not been cancelled. The celebration has taken place at the Peenemünde Information Centre, which includes a museum.

The Nazi Peenemünde scientists built the V2s with the deaths of 20,000 slave labourers at Nordhausen. Slave labour was the basis for the Nazi concentration camps and the Final Solution. The Holocaust of 6 million Eastern European Jews, and countless other peoples of all nationalities, politics and religions, including the Moslems.

The Peenemünde Centre Museum which celebrates the Nazi V2s, and does not commemorate the torture, starvation and deaths of 20,000 slave labourers, is safe and standing.

The Jewish Memorial "Barrack 38" at Sachsenhausen was burned down: exactly two weeks after Premier Yitzhak Rabin's visit. Exactly one week before the Peenemünde Nazi V2 celebration, and the official day of celebration of the re-unification of Germany.

This is why we are all at the crossroads.

We will not stand by in protest.

We will never forget—we will not let it happen again.

1. We oppose the governments who deny entry to refugees and asylum seekers, and deport the defenceless, man, woman or child. We will not permit that our governments deny civic and social protection, as the majority of the Jews were denied entry and assistance by the USA and Britain before World War II.

2. Practical solutions for the economic questions exist. We know that, according to the UNICEF report "The State of the World's Children 1992," that as of 1990, $800 billion are being spent every year for defence, by the United States, Britain, France, the USSR and China. Three quarters of this gigantic sum is spent on the defence of Europe.

   We know therefore that the military budgets of our countries could be substantially cut, to provide the finance for new jobs, for debt cancellation, for old-age pensioners, for health, for education, training and culture for all the youth in our cities, and for all refugees.

3. We artists must say that all racist crimes must receive the maximum penalties.

4. We artists can assist our fellow citizens in organizing a twenty-four-hour civilian watch in all areas where the persecuted peoples' lives, homes, businesses, offices and sacred places are in danger.

5. We can and we must remove all the growing economic and cultural barriers that feed fascism: we will allow no more walls.

We will not allow youth to be left in ignorance, deprived not only of jobs, but also of the best we can give them of our cultural heritage: our heritage from all the peoples in the world.

We are inviting you, for these reasons, to join us in a rally and concert at the Thalia Theatre in Hamburg on January 30–31, 1993.

January 30 is the sixtieth anniversary of the coming to power of the Nazis in Germany.

This is what we mean when we say:

WE WILL NEVER FORGET—WE WILL NOT LET IT HAPPEN AGAIN.

Jürgen Flimm, Vanessa Redgrave, Will Quadflieg, Günter Grass

≡

When I finished reading, Hilde, the wife of my German publisher, came up to me and put her arms around me. She introduced me to Charlotte Dürrenmatt, the widow of Friedrich Dürrenmatt, and I told them about what I had seen on my arrival in Berlin. I had wanted to go immediately to Sachsenhausen but was told that the police had cordoned off the area. So Heidi, my interpreter, and I took a taxi to the Putlitzbrücke, where a Jewish monument had been desecrated by fascists that August. The bridge was deserted and dimly lit. When we got out of the taxi I saw the monument, two rectangular steel plinths, some eight feet high, that supported a crooked flight of steps that rose, turned, and rose again toward the sky. I bent to read the inscription at the base. Ten thousand Berlin Jews had descended the stairs from this bridge onto trains that took them to the extermination camps. There was a crack and some holes in the steel. I looked between the two plinths. A powerful bomb had shattered the inside walls of the plinths, tearing a large hole in the steel, puncturing holes through to the front. I stood up and saw that the bridge spanned at least ten railway lines, which stretched ahead far, far away. If the bomb had been successful, the plinths would have collapsed, and the stairs would have crashed onto the railway tracks. The message left by the fascists was a threat and a warning: "We will do it all over again."

≡

A few weeks later, in London, on a pale, cool, typical October day, I walked down Kensington Palace Gardens to the Russian embassy with a letter Corin and I had written to Andrei Kozyrev, minister for foreign affairs. Our letter, which was signed by several other people, including Tony Kushner, Antonia Fraser, Harold Pinter, Robert Bolt, Sarah Miles, John Hurt, and Fred Zinnemann, was published in *The Guardian* on October 13. (See Appendix 2, page 397.) We sent a copy to *Izvestia*, faxed through to Moscow, and delivered to the editor in person. The text was not published there, only our signatures, and a note that a protest letter had been received.

We were protesting restrictions imposed on Mikhail Gorbachev that forbade him to travel abroad. Corin had been following reports on Russian radio and television about the debate over whether Gorbachev should, or would, appear before a constitutional court investigating the August coup. This was not a criminal proceeding, and it was clearly illegal for Gorbachev's passport to be removed because of it. What was particularly outrageous was that the real criminal proceedings, against the leaders of the coup, had been delayed for months. "The right to travel freely inside and beyond the borders of one's country," we wrote, "was one of the greatest victories of the political revolution against Stalinism which was heralded by the authors of perestroika and glasnost. That right must now be upheld in the person of Mikhail Gorbachev."

On October 14 I received a reply from the ambassador. He had good news from Moscow. Mr. Gorbachev would be able to fly to

Germany to attend the memorial ceremony for Willy Brandt. Nothing more was heard of a travel ban, and those responsible withdrew from this line of attack. So we flew to Barcelona for our third symposium with high hearts.

In order to change the course of events at a dangerous corner, it is necessary to have paid the closest attention to developments on a daily basis. Corin's meticulous study of the BBC Monitor reports from Moscow was essential to understanding the main issue in a tangled conflict, and to unraveling the problem so that everyone could see and, if they wished, solve the problem correctly. The daily study of history reveals a thread, like Ariadne's in the Cretan labyrinth, which we can follow to go forward without losing our way.

The theme for the third Symposium 90 was "The Twentieth Century and the Right of Nations to Self-Determination." Four distinct periods had been chosen for papers and discussion: (1) World War I, the October Revolution, and the struggle for national liberation; (2) National Socialism in Germany and National Communism in the USSR, and their effect on liberation movements and national minorities; (3) World War II, the defeat of fascism, and the consequences for the oppressed nationalities in Palestine and Eastern Europe; (4) October 1917 in light of present conflicts and problems for the national question today.

I was especially impressed by the papers and presentations of the American professors, who included Dr. Ronald Suny, who holds the Alex Manoogian Chair of Armenian History at the University of Michigan. Stephen Cohen had suggested that we invite him, and he proved an extremely energetic and wise participant in all the discussions. The lively and passionate interest the Americans took in their own and everyone else's work brought out the best in everybody. They, in turn, were particularly impressed with the clear and thoughtful presentations from the Palestinian historians. Neither the American nor the Russian professors knew much of Palestinian history, and they said so. This surprised our Palestinian colleagues, but they deeply appreciated the professors' questions. Dr. Budeiri from Bir Zeit University, Dr. Sulatha Hijjawi from the General Union of Palestinian Women, and Dr. Naseer Aruri from Dartmouth, Massachusetts, gave key papers on the second, third, and fourth days. Pierre Broué made an outstanding presentation on Stalinism and anti-Semitism. Esteban Volkov, Trotsky's grandson, also gave a personal testimony, and Annette Muller presented an oral history of the mass arrest of thirteen thousand Jews by the French fascist police on July 16, 1942.

While we were all in our hotel one evening we saw a documentary film on Catalan TV that proved, with the help of papers newly studied in the KGB archives, that the GPU intelligence chief known in Spain as General Orlov had been personally responsible for the kidnapping, torture, and murder of Andres Nin, the Catalan POUM leader of the Barcelona uprising in the Spanish Civil War. This was corroboration of research I had done on the available documents on General Orlov given to a House Judiciary subcommittee in Washington in 1957. These had originally been studied in the mid-seventies, during our party's investigation into how the GPU killed Leon Trotsky. My position was that, given Orlov's role in the Spanish Civil War as a GPU butcher, which he had omitted from his testimony in the United States in the 1950s, and given that he was in charge of intelligence in connection with the international brigades that came to Barcelona, which he admitted himself to the subcommittee, the question had to be posed: Was he in fact the key controller of the network that assassinated Leon Trotsky, and was this the reason that he came to the United States in 1938?

As far as I am concerned, the question of the assassination of the only Bolshevik central committee member who steadfastly opposed Stalin and the bureaucracy that created the nightmare the world came to know as "Socialism" is similar to the issue of bringing fascists to trial for their crimes. It is not a question of revenge. Without the most thorough evaluation of events, another generation, if not the present one, will be condemned to repeat the same mistakes and undergo similar horrors.

We saw an aspect of this problem when we heard a Serbian professor at our symposium justify the policies and the war that Milošević was waging to carve a Greater Serbia out of Bosnia. This took us by surprise. The problem, however, was much larger than the opinions of one history professor. Milošević is the leader of the Socialist Party of Serbia, formerly the Communist Party of Serbia. How many socialists are there in Europe who are somehow condoning or justifying in the name of "socialism" the ethnic cleansing of Bosnia—if not in words, by their silence?

We were all alarmed at the situation of the historical archives belonging to the ministries in Moscow. For large sums of money, some person might be tempted to sell parts of the archives to those who could withhold them from historians who did not have similar funds at their disposal. Or they could be abused, as in the case of the Goebbels diaries that had been discovered in the Moscow archives. The London *Sunday Times* paid the historian David Irving to select the ones they would publish. This was particularly scandalous, since Irving claims the Holocaust never happened, and his choice of diary sections showed Goebbels as a sincere politician and family man, with no mention of his hideous activities. We resolved to do all we could to help the archivists and historians in Moscow maintain and preserve the archives in a proper fashion.

≡

It was now January 1993, and at Ismail Merchant's urgent request I agreed to fly to the Delhi Film Festival for two nights with James Wilby, who played my son in *Howards End*. Our flight was diverted to Bombay, where members of the Hindu fascist party were in the midst of a ferocious pogrom against the Muslims. James and I spent four hours obtaining a permit so we could leave the airport and get to a hotel, from which we might make a phone call to Ismail. We got into a taxi, surrounded by swirls of small children, who darted like flocks of swifts in whatever direction seemed to promise a few coins. The taxi drove quickly past the tin shanties between the airport and the coast of the Arabian Sea, where the Holiday Inn stretched its white concrete above the sands.

James and I put a call through to the only number he had that might lead us eventually to Ismail. It was the phone number of a carpenter who was constructing the set for Ismail's next film. Around two in the morning my phone rang. "Ismail! Well done! How can we get to you?" This was complicated—Delhi was five hundred miles away. However, Ismail was cheerful and reassuring, and around five that morning we were boarding a flight. Ismail met us, took us to a palatial hotel, and got us to the ten o'clock press conference. It was then I met the beautiful actress Shabana Azmi. We seized the chance to sit on the sofa in my suite for an hour. Shabana told me what was happening in India. "You must understand, these pogroms have nothing to do with religion. This is fascism. The streets of our cities are covered with graffiti: 'Muslims! There is only one place for you to go—Pakistan or Hell!' " She and a number of her young friends had been going into Muslim neighborhoods to try to protect the women and children. She told me that some of the police were siding with the fascists and were standing by as Muslim shops and homes were burned. "The problem is," she said, "that liberal and progressive people are silent and are staying at home. They could do so much to prevent what is happening." So I learned from Shabana's story that indeed it was the same problem everywhere.

After the festival's opening ceremony, Ismail took my hand and we slipped into an old car and sped off into the night. "I am going to take you someplace very special," he said. I could hardly keep my head upright on my shoulders or walk without crumpling at the knees, but I would never dream of saying no to Ismail. Some time later the car stopped, and I followed him unsteadily into the dark, passing by a multitude of little stalls and booths lit by small kerosene lamps. Figures and shadows moved slowly in and out of other shadows as we began to walk down a narrow arcade, picking our way from stone to stone across puddles of water. The air seemed damp and smelled of roses on an English night in midsummer. As we walked, the vendors and their families in the doorways and windows watched us. The distinct smell of the kerosene lamps was now entirely overcome by the scent of the garlands and baskets of blood-red roses heaped on display. Ismail bought some garlands, and now we were walking into a dark, quiet courtyard with worn paving stones, surrounded on all sides by high marble walls with shuttered windows. Before us lay a low mausoleum, the shrine of Nizamuddin Aluya, a Sufi saint who had been buried there about four hundred years earlier. We took off our shoes, and then I waited while Ismail entered the shrine.

As we walked back, Ismail began to talk. "You see, this shrine where this very good man is buried is the center of this monastery. The priests look after the shrine and they look after all these people. All the poor families are given a meal once a day; otherwise they would have nothing. This is how it was in medieval times. Visitors would come to see the saint's shrine. Priests came to look after the shrine. Then they built a monastery, and people set up their stalls if they had something the visitors would buy. Then they make their dwellings, or they sleep beneath their stalls, and soon there is a small town. This is how life still is, all over India."

Two nights later I was in the Thalia Theatre in Hamburg, watching Will Quadflieg play King Lear.

> Poor naked wretches, whereso'er you are,
> That hide the pelting of this pitiless storm,
> How shall your houseless heads and unfed sides,
> Your loop'd and window'd raggedness, defend you
> From seasons such as these? O, I have ta'en
> Too little care of this! Take physic pomp;
> Expose thyself to feel what wretches feel,
> That thou mayst shake the superflux to them,
> And show the heavens more just.

Shakespeare was writing in early seventeenth-century England. How is it possible, over four hundred years later, when science is able to accomplish so much, that people in Sarajevo and other Bosnian cities can be denied food off the relief convoys by Serbian and Croatian born-again Chetniks and Ustashi, their ranks joined every day by young fascist mercenaries from all over the world, including Britain?

As I watched the Thalia production of *Lear*, the story of the division of England into two territories, and all that followed, ending in death and war, appeared in a contemporary way, analogous to our world.

> Love cools, friendship falls off, brothers divide: in cities, mutinies;
> in countries, discord; in palaces, treason; and the bond cracked
> 'twixt son and father.

In the Thalia, we were now making final preparations for our program against racism, *We Will Never Forget—We Will Not Let It Happen Again.* The theatre directors had won the sponsorship of NDR-TV, which would televise both the conference and the con-

cert, Spiegel TV, the publishers Gruner and Jahr, and *Stern* magazine. In the rehearsal studio Jürgen rehearsed his company in the
final chorus of *Antigone*. In his office we prepared the agenda and the
running order for the concert. Every single assistant director had
been allocated a special task: transport, meeting guests at the airport,
preparing the front-of-house display of long banners bearing the
names of the German, American, Russian, French, Italian, Greek,
English, and Indian artists who had signed our manifesto. Tickets
were being sold, refugee families and schools contacted, and in the
midst of this Jürgen took the time to rehearse the popular TV actress
Marie Louise Marjan, who would read a letter written in a cellar that
winter by a child in Sarajevo.

By Saturday, the hotel was filling hour by hour. The glorious
Mercedes Sosa was there, and Roger Moore, who made an excellent
speech the next day. Bono and Edge arrived and immediately went
into a room to rehearse with the great Indian musician Shankar and
his wife, Caroline. Matti Megged, the Israeli novelist, arrived from
New York and met for the first time the daughter of his old friend
in Palestine in the 1930s, Katharina Wolpe, daughter of the composer
Stefan Wolpe, a refugee from the Anschluss and the Gestapo. She
would play the Mozart Fantasy in C minor. Annette Muller and her
husband, Daniel Bessmann, had come to speak. The next minute
there was Harvey Keitel, Kris Kristofferson, and John Trudell.

I woke about six on the morning of January 30 and found a note
with flowers from Elena Bonner. "Dear Vanessa, Happy Birthday and
best of luck in all you do." Elena gave me the Sakharov medal that
day, the greatest honor I have ever received. I will try to be worthy
of it for the rest of my days.

We assembled on the Thalia stage and listened to the testimony
of Flora Neumann, Trudi Simonsohn, and Artie Goral, three Holocaust survivors, as if our lives depended on remembering every word.
We all had simultaneous-translation headsets. We collectively
relived with the survivors those first four days when the Nazis took
power, the Nazi concentration camps, and the post-liberation
trauma. Two partisans, one French, one Greek, followed. Both had
been Communist Party members of small combat groups in the
maquis, in the hills and forests above the Côte d'Azur, and in the
parched mountains near Thebes.

There were presentations throughout the day. Elena Bonner spoke of the new fascism in Russia: the red hammer and sickle of the new Communist Party, and the black, yellow, and white of the fascist alliance, the National Salvation Front. Both parties were anti-Semitic, and both blamed Jews and dark-skinned "foreigners" from Tajikistan and Azerbaijan for crime, unemployment, and everything else. Professor Mikhail Gefter, a frail seventy-five-year-old philosopher and historian, spoke as president of the Holocaust Society of Russia. Thanks to the personal support of former president Gorbachev, they had just held their first public exhibition in Moscow. Prisoners' letters, photographs, and drawings about the Holocaust were displayed, and President Yeltsin had agreed to the official registration of the society. Only those who lived through the decades of persecution and repression of the Stalin-Khrushchev-Brezhnev period can know the significance of this official recognition. I will never forget Professor Gefter's soft voice, which grew firmer with every word.

> People's rights for life, shelter, and food are endangered. Women, children, and old people suffer most. The chaos of mass migrations is held in check by restrictions that, while unable to get to the core of the problem, promote nationalist and racist isolationism. Xenophobia is gaining strength again. To our shame, new pogroms bring back memories of the Holocaust. The hour of decision is at hand. It is high time to take steps toward establishing an informal alliance of supporters of social justice and the protection of human dignity all over the world.

We had invited Richard Reid, acting executive director for public affairs at UNICEF, to give us a report on the state of the world's children in 1993. UNICEF was founded, with the charter of the United Nations, following the defeat of fascism in 1945, to protect and defend the lives and rights of all children regardless of race, politics, or religion. We were pleased to be able to raise about a hundred thousand dollars for UNICEF's Emergency Appeal for the Children of the Former Yugoslavia. The money was urgently needed.

In the brief period of discussion toward the end of our eight-hour conference, a Muslim leader of the Sunni Mosques in the Midlands of Britain, Dr. Bustan al-Qadri, spoke. His community of fifty thousand members had voted to support our manifesto and had taken up a collection to pay for his airline ticket. Interestingly, their decision had been made at a meeting to which Corin and Rabbi Ralph Solomon had been invited. A handful of young Islamic fascists had tried to prevent the rabbi from speaking, but Dr. Qadri and his colleagues had physically protected him and insisted that he be heard. Their extremely firm and principled stand had taken the fascists totally by surprise. After talking some rubbish for three minutes, they ran out of the mosque with their tails between their legs. This happened a few days after the courageous Israeli peace campaigner Abie Nathan met President Arafat in Tunis and pushed the peace process ahead by two thousand years in a two-minute radio linkup. He passed the radio mike to the president, who then spoke directly on Israeli radio, appealing for peace talks between both peoples. This foreshadowed the historic accord between the PLO and the Israeli government, which was announced eight months later.

CHAPTER 29

R ade Serbedzija was the most popular film star and theatre actor
in Yugoslavia until the war started there. In 1978, he and a group
of directors, writers, and performers cofounded the KPGT Zagreb
Theatre Company. KPGT is an acronym formed from the first letter
of the word "theatre" in the languages of Yugoslavia. The Croatian
"K" for Kazalište, the Serbian "P" for Pozorište, the Slovenian "G"
for Gledališče, and the Macedonian "T" for "Teater." The choice of
this word and its acronym is a history in itself.

One of the KPGT brochures explains their purpose: "Yugoslavia
is a country of many nations, ethnic cultures, and distinctive languages. There is no 'melting pot' theory; on the contrary, each ethnic
group is encouraged to develop its potentials and to set up its own
cultural and educational institutions and enjoys equal political representation in the Federation. But the consequences of this system is
that culture becomes segmented, self-centered, and locked in its own
ethnic, linguistic, or regional boundaries. The KPGT wants to respect all these ethnic and cultural differences, but at the same time
to oppose the disintegrative, parochial tendencies in Yugoslav cultural and public life. The idea is to develop contacts, collaborations,

exchanges, and circulation of artistic products across the boundaries of the republics, provinces, and nations and languages. . . ."

When the war between Serbia and Croatia came, Rade continued to try to work this way. But in spite of the tens of thousands, mostly young people, who had attended and applauded the KPGT productions, xenophobia got the upper hand, intensified by the atrocities of the war. Two of Rade's last productions with the KPGT were the immensely successful *Croatian Nightingale,* about Miroslav Krlezà, and *Brecht in Exile,* about Bertolt Brecht's exile in Denmark as a refugee from the Third Reich, his discussions with Walter Benjamin, and the scenes he wrote for *Mother Courage. Brecht in Exile* was prepared in Sarajevo and performed in Belgrade in the winter of 1991. It had a great influence on the many young students opposed to Milošević's savagery.

On April 6, 1992, when Rade stepped onto the platform in front of several hundred thousand people at an antiwar rally in Sarajevo, he told the assembled press and TV crews: "Europe, are you listening? War is coming here, send some UN people at once." The crowd started to sing his famous antiwar song:

> The second call is out to go to war.
> New recruits are going off to war
> To defend our home from our home,
> To defend our people from a people that's our own,
> To defend the sea from the land
> And the land from the sea that's its own.
> But I won't. I won't, and I won't.
> Never against friends I've known.
> But I won't. I won't, and I won't.
> I can't against friends unknown.

Just as Rade was coming down from the platform to join his friends, Serbian fascist snipers starting shooting at the peace rally from the top of the Holiday Inn.

Eight days later, Rade managed to board the last bus leaving Sarajevo for Belgrade. His wife, Lenka, was about to give birth to their baby. Taxi drivers at the Belgrade bus terminal, who all knew Rade, refused to take him in their cabs. A few nights later, in the restaurant where he was celebrating the birth of his little girl, Nina, a group of young fascists pulled a gun on him and tried to shoot him. He and Lenka had never had time to set up a home in either Belgrade or Zagreb, and now he could not live in either city. There were growing numbers of fascists who condemned him as a traitor for not waving their flag.

Rade and Lenka left for Ljubljana, in Slovenia, and there, in January 1993, Rade met a friend who had escaped from Sarajevo. Together they wrote "Wake Up, World," an appeal addressed to artists and writers in Europe and the United States. They sent it to Joseph Brodsky, among others, but couldn't find me anywhere, since I had gone to Moscow. So Rade and I didn't meet until that June. He rang me backstage at the Royal Exchange Theatre in Manchester, where I was rehearsing a new Russian play directed by Braham Murray. The next day, after rehearsals, Braham and I were sitting with Rade and Lenka and their year-old Nina in the theatre bar. That was when I first read the appeal. By then Rade's friend was dead, killed by a piece of shrapnel when he returned to Sarajevo.

> Sarajevo was once a golden example of tolerance; here East mixed with West; here the deep-rooted amalgam of cultures and religions was the wellspring of exceptional creativity. Sarajevo is today no more than rubble and ruins, with 300,000 people trapped under conditions no better than a concentration camp. And an equal number have escaped with nothing but their bare lives intact. . . . Sarajevo is only the largest community that has met this fate; there are many, many more. Millions of men, women, and children who until yesterday were bakers, writers, salespeople, engineers, factory workers, builders, hairdressers, waitresses, teachers, pre-schoolers, pupils, students, mothers, fathers, beloved children, are today no more than refugees, mostly unwanted. The flames of evil burning here could easily and quickly spread to neighboring countries, to all of Europe and the world. Three years ago these horrors were not possible even in our worst nightmares. There is little left to say except "Wake up, world!"

As a result of our talk with Rade, Braham and I immediately booked our theatre for an International Artists Against Racism meeting and concert on July 18, one week after the press night for our new play, which we had commissioned from Mikhail Shatrov. The very first scene concerned a young American student preparing to leave her home in Boston to join a students' peace convoy to Sarajevo. Silent and immobile in a wheelchair, her grandmother watched her, unable to speak of the evening in 1937 when she welcomed a Jewish refugee from Poland, a young communist girl who was escaping Stalin's purges of the party and the advance of Hitler's Third Reich across Europe. I played the grandmother in flashbacks to 1937 and 1938, and her daughter in 1993, who was determined to prevent *her* own young daughter from being destroyed by politics in the new European war.

On July 18 our theatre was full. At least four hundred young Bosnian refugees had come up from London on buses organized by Corin, his wife, Kika, and our friends. Serious young faces ringed the stage, listening without one movement to the testimony given by Esther Brunstein, a survivor of the Lódź ghetto and Auschwitz. Lódź had been the second largest city in Poland in September 1939, with 750,000 inhabitants, of which a third were Jews. Esther's father, a well-known trade unionist, escaped. Her uncle, who wrote for a liberal Yiddish newspaper, was arrested and shot in prison. Her oldest brother went to the Soviet Union. Esther, a young child, was herded into the ghetto with her mother and another brother.

"Very soon starvation and disease claimed the lives of my dear ones," Esther recounted.

All my uncles, cousins, and friends were either deported or dead. Little children did not wake up in the winter because they froze to death. But I also want to point out that we did not succumb. We tried to hold on to some semblance of human dignity. We formed some groups and tried to learn. We thought the war would be over soon and we must not fall behind with our education. We learned Yiddish literature and Polish literature, and we even managed to feel sorry for characters in our books. I remember reading *Les Misérables* and feeling sorry for Jean Valjean. We said, Well, history has placed us in even worse conditions but we will hold on and we will try to survive. I want to say we did not go like sheep to the slaughter. We resisted. Picking up arms is not the only form of resistance. To live one day as a decent human being, and to care, was an act of courage and a great act of resistance. We would not let them totally demoralize us.

Then I introduced Anita Lasker, who had been a member of the women's orchestra in Auschwitz, and whom I had at last met, many years after I portrayed Fania Fenelon in *Playing for Time.* Anita rose to speak. "I was asked by Vanessa to come here today," she said, "and I am happy to do so, although I admit I would much rather be somewhere else, and wish that the reasons for holding this meeting were no longer topical because the world had learned something from the past." She continued:

As we all know, this, alas, is far from being the case. Anti-Semitism is as rampant as ever and nationalism is truly out of hand. To cap it all, we have a new concept in our vocabulary, ethnic cleansing. . . .

I do not identify with causes but with people, human beings, and the greatest miracle of all, life itself. But it is hard to believe, and no doubt very significant, that in the nearly fifty years which have elapsed since I was liberated in Belsen, this is only the second time that I have been asked to speak.

In my time I had a number of labels attached to my person. I started as an ordinary child. Then I became a "dirty Jew"; then I graduated to "undesirable" and "vermin," which simply had to be destroyed. Eventually, when I was liberated by the British army on April 15, 1945, I changed my status and became a "displaced person."

It took me nearly one year, but after endless refusals from the Home Office I was finally allowed to come to the only country where I still had some relatives left. I came to Britain with high hopes, convinced that the generation after me would be free from all prejudices, and that our suffering was an atonement for all time. Then I realized, like all other survivors of the horrors, that I was engulfed in silence. No one asked me any questions. At first I barely wanted to talk, but one can't just start talking; one has to be asked, be shown some interest. Nothing. Then I realized that there's actually a sort of taboo on the subject. It is uncomfortable to all concerned to speak of things that seem unbelievable the moment you utter them. You begin to feel like a liar yourself. So

I settled for a life in limbo, so to speak, isolated from normal people. I think it is fear rather than a lack of interest that produces this silence—fear that the questioner may not be able to handle the answers he may get, and fear that the survivor may have some sort of fit. "One mustn't stir up old wounds" and "Surely in time they'll forget." Let me tell you, we don't forget.

Anita had played the cello in the Auschwitz orchestra. We all listened to a young cellist who was a pupil of Anita's son, Rafael. She played an adagio composed by Nigel Osborne in tribute to Vedran Smailović, a Sarajevan cellist and the grandson of the great Bosnian cellist who founded the Sarajevo Symphony Orchestra. Since April 1992 Vedran had been playing in the streets and in the ruined National Library. The director of the library had himself urged Radovan Karadzić, the Bosnian Serb leader, to destroy it with all its ancient Bosnian manuscripts. The adagio was very mysterious, mournful. As the cellist plucked the strings with her thumb, it seemed to me the gesture echoed the thumb movement from right to left of Dr. Mengele, who had selected Esther's mother to be killed when they arrived in Auschwitz.

Around the cellist on the stage sat many rabbis and one of the Muslim leaders from the Birmingham Central Mosque. There was Anthony Andrews, Robbie Coltrane, and Daniel Day-Lewis. There was my son, Carlo, and by him Ted Mann, who had flown in from New York. Richard Reid then spoke for UNICEF, and for the children of the former Yugoslavia. By this time there were 526,000 refugees in Croatia, 460,000 in Serbia, 33,000 in Slovenia, and 32,000 in Macedonia. In Bosnia and Herzegovina there were 2,280,000 men, women, and children who had lost their homes. Including the refugees in Montenegro, nearly three and a half million people had lost their homes, their livelihoods, and, in practically all cases, members of their family. Figures and statistics can be hard to remember and almost impossible to comprehend. Leaning forward from the first and second tiers of seats surrounding the stage were adolescents and students who had lived this history. In Western Europe, and in what had been Yugoslavia until June 1991, there were now four and a half million refugees from this European war. In September 1938, there were already four and a half million refugees from the Third Reich, from Austria and Czechoslovakia. Then, as now, the governments of Europe and the United States closed their frontiers.

In May, the German Bundestag voted to restrict the asylum law of Article 16. Three days later, two young women and three young girls, all Turkish, were killed when their house was firebombed in Sölingen. Already deportations from Germany had started—of Roma and Sint people, of Turkish families. Already some good German pastors were again trying to hide these families from the authorities. Indeed, the greatest efforts against nationalist xenophobia had been made by Germans. Michel Friedman, deputy leader of the Jewish Council in Germany, urged us to remember the Germans who had resisted the Nazis. He himself had been one of Schindler's children. (At that very moment my daughter Natasha was in Poland, where Steven Spielberg was filming *Schindler's List*.) There was indeed a resistance to this new fascism, but no leaders or political parties who would speak or act for this resistance of ordinary people.

We listened to the ringing voice of Mr. Feingold, the best cantor in the North of England. I had asked him to sing the song of the Warsaw ghetto. I had never heard this song until I met Esther in her home. She had played me a recording of Paul Robeson singing it at a rally in London in April 1943:

> From lands so green with palms,
> To lands all white with snow,
> We shall be coming with our anguish and our woe,
> And where a spurt of our blood fell on the earth,
> There our courage and our spirit have rebirth.

In the evening we heard the wild, sweet vigor of Ani Schnarch's violin, followed by the duet for oud and violin played by Taiseer Elias and Nassim Dikwar, all three Israeli citizens. Ani played because she was a Jew, and because she was Israeli. Taiseer and Nassim played because they were Palestinians, and because they were part of a whole group of Jewish and Palestinian Israelis who were playing their music to create the conditions for peace. Those notes, first composed by Arab musicians in the fifteenth century, had inspired a later generation of Italians, like Vivaldi, to bring new rhythms and cadences into European music.

I read a manifesto written by Corin, Rade, and myself with Braham Murray. We took up again the main theme of the Thalia manifesto and we called for the siege of Sarajevo to be lifted. We warned that if Sarajevo was destroyed and ethnically divided, every city would be divided, and all hopes and rights of refugees to return to their homes would be crushed forever. We called on our fellow artists in the former Yugoslavia to contact us so that we could exchange ideas about how to oppose the warmongers' violence and ethnic divisions and make it possible for people to live without fear.

A journalist in the Slavonic section of the BBC World Service faxed our manifesto to *VREME*, a progressive daily paper in Belgrade, and via satellite to Sarajevo. We published it in *The Guardian* in London on July 28 at the cost of £5,000, and later, translated into Russian, in the Russian daily *Nezavisimiya* for £2,000. The *Asian Times* and *Caribbean Times* in the United Kingdom published it for free. Stefan Fittermann spent one of the last days of his life talking to the editor of a newspaper in St. Louis, Missouri; as a result they published the manifesto, also for free, the only U.S. paper to do so. Stefan died of AIDS on August 1, our dear friend who had worked with us since *The Wall Breaks* in December 1989. I remember by heart the last message he wrote, which Corin read out that Sunday: "We will never forget. We will not let it happen again. But it has happened again. Fifty years later, another Holocaust has happened in Europe. Wake up, world! Wake up the world!"

In spite of efforts made by Braham, myself, and Fred Zinnemann, and the representatives of Gerald Kaufman, a Labour Party leader I greatly respected for his declarations of support for land and peace for the Palestinians, we had failed to get the agreement of the government to bring two great Bosnian singers, Kemal Monteno and Davorin Popović, out of Sarajevo to perform in our concert. I had contacted the United Nations High Commission for Refugees (UNHCR) in Geneva and been put through to Wing Commander Bibby's office there; he was responsible to the UK government for the UNHCR aid airlifts into and out of Sarajevo. Wing Commander Bibby checked with the UK Ministry of Defence and then wrote me a courteous refusal, explaining that although our concert was for humanitarian purposes (we raised £5,000 for UNICEF's Emergency Appeal), the UNHCR flight guidelines were very strict, and they could not be seen to be possibly favoring any side in the conflict. We were not holding a political meeting, however. We were taking only one side that day, the side of the children of Sarajevo, the side of children from Vukovar in Croatia, the side of the refugee children in Serbia, Slovenia, and Macedonia.

Anthony Andrews, Daniel Day-Lewis, Corin, and I went in a deputation to the Foreign Office to urge the lifting of the siege. There was a precedent. In 1948, the British and U.S. air forces had flown in food, fuel, medicine, and other supplies to Berlin, defying the Soviet blockade of the city and ready to do battle if any plane was shot down. Twelve months later the siege was lifted, and no one in Berlin had starved or frozen to death or been fired upon. In the case of Sarajevo, the UN had brought in one food package per month for Sarajevans, with a special baby's kit if they had tiny children. Other agencies brought in some generators and plastic water cans, and some drugs, and there were many brave men and women who defied the gunfire and shelling to bring convoys through. The small amount of supplies that succeeded in reaching the people kept them alive. But UN soldiers were not allowed to intervene to stop the massacres they heard about and saw, or to use force to clear the roadblocks set up by the armed forces and militia groups under Radovan Karadzić. If I had been a UN soldier sent there, I would have hung my head in shame and grief, and I believe many did. It was in any case not the issue. The UN soldiers had to obey the politics of their respective governments.

William Pitt, undersecretary for the Foreign Office UN desk, received us and listened but would say only that the government did not rule out lifting the siege. This was the first deputation to the government, and there were at least twenty reporters and photographers outside to take pictures. The next day not even one newspaper carried a photograph. Neither did any newspaper or TV news desk show any interest in our *Wake Up, World* meeting in Manchester. We were the first to call for the lifting of the siege. Later, Paddy Ashdown and the *Independent* took it up in a big press campaign. This was very welcome, although they supported the division of Bosnia-Herzegovina, and this we never did.

I then went to the UNICEF-UK Committee and proposed that we artists should organize a series of concerts for the refugee children, and for UNICEF, in all the capital cities of the republics of the former Yugoslavia. We would go in the name of those who had been killed by fascism in World War II. We would seek meetings with our fellow artists in all these cities to discuss how we could work together for the children. UNICEF had been founded in December 1946 to care for the children in Europe who had been devastated by World War II. Indeed, UNICEF's first relief action went to Yugoslavia, bringing in powdered baby milk.

Harvey Keitel and Kris Kristofferson agreed to come, as did Daniel Day-Lewis. Three Russian actors and musicians agreed, and also three Greeks, and Turkey's most popular singer, Zulfu Livaneli. Katharina Wolpe, herself a refugee from the Gestapo in Slovenia in 1938, would also come, with Rade and myself making up the group. We were all ready to go, with passports, tickets, and our schedules agreed on, when the right-wing press in Croatia began to attack our visit. "This is a plot, hatched in London, to restore the former Yugoslavia." "Croatia is not racist, so why are International Artists Against Racism coming to Zagreb?" If we were going to perform in Belgrade, then we were not welcome in Zagreb. For the same reasons Rade had been attacked in Zagreb for going to Belgrade, in Belgrade for going to Zagreb and Sarajevo. Since our purpose was to help the children and UNICEF, I proposed we should cancel the concerts, and that I should go to the refugee camps and children's homes to learn more about the special UNICEF programs, and to meet with the artists, so we could prepare to give concerts with and for the children in December. Harvey said he wanted to come also.

Catherine Carnie, a beautiful young UNICEF special-events officer, traveled with me to Zagreb and to Ljubljana, and then we boarded the Hercules UNHCR airlift plane into Sarajevo. Catherine is the best traveling companion I have ever had, and we traveled many, many miles and long hours through the autumn and winter together. I have always been, and remain, immensely impressed by the people who work in UNICEF. The journeys I made through the former Yugoslavia filled me with the utmost respect for both officers and field-workers.

≡

It was a sunny day in early September, and the shelling of Sarajevo had stopped for a few days. A UNICEF car sped us through the city. We visited pediatric clinics, two hospitals, and a home for mentally disabled children, where forty-five boys remained out of the two hundred fifty children who had been there before the war, when this institution had been the finest in the whole of Yugoslavia. The kids, between five and eleven years old, had spent months on end in the cellars. Today, as there was no shelling, they played and chatted with us in the sun. None of them had seen their parents for a year and a half, since the parents lived in Belgrade, Croatia, or other parts of Bosnia and could not enter Sarajevo.

We drove to Radio Sarajevo Zid. Here we were welcomed by Haris Pasović, who had produced Susan Sontag's *Waiting for Godot* in the International Sarajevo Theatre Festival. Euripides' *Alcestis* and Sophocles' *Ajax* were the other two productions. Haris told me that Radio Zid had broadcast our *Wake Up, World* manifesto three times; it was the first news out of Europe that had given them cheer.

Vedran Smailović, the cellist, came out of a minute recording studio, and three quiet women of my own age walked into the lobby, dressed and made up as if they had just caught a bus from Central Park West and Eighty-third Street down to Fiftieth and Broadway. These were the mothers of three young musicians who were now asylum seekers in London. We watched the video film I had brought of our *Wake Up, World* meeting in Manchester. I sat next to an actor who had lost both legs in the shelling. Nermin Tulić was Muslim. His wife, a Serb, sat next to him. How would Serbian or Croatian fascists divide this couple, typical of all Bosnian families in which mixed marriages went back for generations? The Muslims of Bosnia are very much like the Jews of Esther's and Anita's generation in Poland—enlightened, secular, and cultured people, whether they went to the mosque regularly or not at all.

We drove at seventy miles an hour down Sniper's Alley, which had once resembled Riverside Drive in New York City and was now flanked by gutted high-rise apartment blocks from which Serbian fascists shot at children and women crossing the street. We came through the Old Town, slowly now, and Haris showed me the corner of the sidewalk where the young Serb Gavrilo Princip had shot

Crown Prince Ferdinand of Austria, who was visiting one of the most beautiful cities in the Austrian Empire. On that warm, sunny June day Princip believed his action was part of a liberation struggle for independence from Austro-Hungarian occupation. He did not know, or plan, that this assassination would trigger World War I.

Neither, I am sure, did Lord Owen and Cyrus Vance believe their peace plan, presented in Geneva on January 2, 1993, would intensify the conflict and all the horrors of ethnic cleansing. Yet how could a plan to divide Bosnia-Herzegovina into ten ethnic cantons with five corridors do anything but convince nationalists they must seize as much territory as possible?

Haris took us into the Jewish Center, which throughout the war provided free food and organized refugee convoys not only for the Jewish community but for all the citizens who came for help. We were welcomed into Ivan Čerešnješ's study. He spoke quietly and with some bitterness. "Help us? It's difficult to decide what 'help' is. Some food? Some medicine? Then you wash your hands? A year ago Sarajevo had six hundred thousand people. Now we are three hundred thousand. A year ago we had three hundred thousand children. Now we have only sixty thousand. Last winter we survived, we had reserves, we had some fuel, we had some trees, we had some food. Now winter is coming again, and we are without reserves. It is not satisfactory to say the city is surrounded; that that's why no one came to us for sixteen months. It is possible to come. It's a question of personal courage and personal will." He paused. "I remember another war. I remember how we waited and waited."

There was silence in the room. I looked over to Haris. I thought of the public meetings I'd spoken at in London. I remembered a dinner party after a performance of *Heartbreak House.* I thought of the zeppelin that bombed the coast of Sussex, disturbing a calm summer night in the England of 1914. I recalled Trevor Nunn, our director, saying to us, his cast and his friends, "We are all living in a fool's paradise." That was in March 1992, just before the war started. I asked myself how it happened that I didn't know how to come to Sarajevo, or who to contact. If I had not read of Susan Sontag's work in this city, I would never have known it *was* possible to get here. Ivan Čerešnješ looked at all of us in that room, at his friend Haris, at the UNICEF field-workers, at me, at Harvey.

"Sarajevo is a multicultural city. Within a few meters of one another in the center of our city we have a synagogue, a mosque, a Catholic cathedral, and an Orthodox church. We have all lived together for centuries. Sarajevo is the only European city where there never was a pogrom against the Jews. Come here. Let our people feel that somewhere outside are people who wish to help."

We drove later to the district of Dobrinya. We went through sandbags piled around the ground floor of a high-rise apartment building. The room inside was a library and cultural center. All the windows were boarded up to protect the children and the books. They had collected two thousand books for that library. The president of the Literary and Cultural Society of Dobrinya sat at the table with us, and we were offered *urmasica,* a sweet Bosnian cake. The president was one of the leading Bosnian writers, Nezhad Ibrišimović. A little girl started practicing on the upright piano while he talked to us. At the far end of the room, children were preparing a shadow play behind a sheet.

"We are part of a world war," Nezhad said. "Something new has started. Gunmen are using weapons to kill children—deliberately. Why does no one take away their weapons? They must take away their weapons."

"Tell me," said Harvey. "I'm an average American guy. I'm an actor, and I can reach a lot of people. What can we do?"

Nezhad was still and calm. The library was full of parents, children, the UNICEF workers, a camera crew. By his side was Pia Zmajevic-Hukic, a professor of fine arts. Her dark hair was brushed neatly off her face, and her hands were very still on the table. Then Nezhad spoke. "Please tell the Americans a kind of resistance is happening here, a resistance of people. Not Serbs, or Croats, or Muslims. Twenty-two languages are spoken in our city. There are no absolute categories of Serbs or Croats or Muslims; there are people, just people. We need good people. Come here to our city and be with us."

The children performed their shadow play, the story of a wise old Haj in a turban who sorted out people's problems with a great sense of humor. The little girl at the piano played a piece Mozart had written when he was her age. A small boy dressed in a dark blue jacket with yellow epaulettes knelt on the carpet and began to talk to a nine-year-old-girl, who wore a beautifully made mask of a fox with flowers and feathers between his ears.

"Tell me how I can make friends."

"Well, you know, making friends is not that simple. You can't walk into a shop and buy some friends the way you can buy apples."

When they had performed this scene, based on *The Little Prince*, we were introduced to their parents. The little boy, Mirsad, who was eight, was a poet, he told us, and he gave me a poem. I had it translated when I got back to London:

> The old mother wept
> On the banks of the Drina.
> The water was where
> Her only son now slept.
> Don't cry, old mother,
> Said the Drina.
> No one cries for Shiites,
> The river Drina said.

Would this war, where Muslims had been selected for deportation and slaughter by the Croat and Serbian ethnic-cleansers, where the army of Bosnia-Herzegovina, which did not *exist* when the war started, was denied arms by a UN embargo, where the world's politicians, electronic media, and press spoke only of Serbs, Croats (or Bosnian Serbs and Bosnian Croats), and Muslims—would these horrifying sieges and racist slaughter succeed in engendering nationalism where there had been none? Children knew their friends and parents were being slaughtered because they had Muslim names. If their city could survive, as well as the people, much would depend now on those with political power, civic responsibility, and those who worked in culture and education.

Pia Zmajevic-Hukic took my arm and we went out into the sunlight and descended into the trench that had been dug across the wide-open space between the apartment blocks. We walked along the trench to another block, also with boarded-up windows on the ground floor. We went into the fine-arts school. Women who had jobs had to leave Dobrinya on foot every day and walk to work in other parts of the city. Every time they went to work the Serbian militia aimed at them. The Academy of Arts and Sciences was on the other side of the city. So the teachers had improvised a fine-arts school for the eleven- to seventeen-year-old kids. In one room the youngest were break-dancing to a ghetto blaster's music. Eight sixteen-year-old boys and girls were drawing from a still life arrangement in the middle of the room. Their attention was totally concentrated as they bent over their easels. Around the corner a girl was singing "Feelings" in English and her friend was playing the piano for her.

At that moment I started to cry. Here were two teenagers, like those in any American high school, typical of the Sarajevo adolescents who ran at breakneck speed across the roads to avoid the snipers, crowded into cellars to dance and listen to jazz, made up their eyes, cracked jokes, read books more than ever before, and tried to get to classes whenever possible, thinking like Esther that the war would be over soon and they must keep up their education.

Pia told me firmly not to cry. "We don't cry," she said. "We just try to live."

Outside the production office of SAGA, the Bosnian filmmakers' group, Ademir Kenović interviewed Harvey for the video camera. SAGA was out filming every day, making documentary films, even feature films. Kenović's last documentary, *Sarajevo Ground Zero,* was shown on the last day of the 1993 Cannes Film Festival, at the request of two members of the jury. It had received quite a lot of publicity in France and New York, and some even in London. But the networks had refused to show it. "We've done Sarajevo." Ademir asked Harvey what he felt now that he had seen Sarajevo for himself.

"It's an outrage. Where in their wisdom, in their books, in their religious writings, in their culture, have they been given a mandate to shell a civilian population?"

"What do you think should be done?"

"Whoever seeks to destroy children should be stopped, in any way they can be stopped. Whoever it is. All children deserve a life. I came here for UNICEF. For an organization with the motto 'All children. No discrimination.' Children have no politics. They want to play. They want to *be.* You're either in the politics of helping them or you're not. Being here in Sarajevo is another reality. I met a friend here I knew in New York. He's Bosnian-Herzegovinian. It makes me realize how close this is to my reality, what could happen to my children, God forbid."

One of the UNICEF guys was listening to his radiophone. We had to get to the airfield. I didn't want to leave Sarajevo. Harvey didn't want to leave. "Someone said to an American reporter, Where are the artists? Why haven't they come here? Now I can say the same thing. Where are the artists? You should come."

Haris was organizing an international film festival for two weeks beginning October 22. He gave Harvey and me an invitation and asked us to invite other artists to come back with us to Sarajevo, with as many new films as possible. Winter would be hard, and the film festival would not only be a special event, it would ensure that good new feature films could be shown through the freezing dark months whenever there was some electric current to run the projectors. I read the invitation: "Sarajevo Film Festival, under the title *Beyond the End of the World,* is an artistic action directed against physical and mental violence. It is in continuity with all the efforts of filmmakers to build for a future free from totalitarianism."

Haris talked about the theatre productions, the plays they were planning for the winter: "I hate talking to journalists about art or culture in Sarajevo because it seems to me these words could be used to hide the reality—a genocide, a siege that is the most horrible thing that has happened in Europe since World War II. We are just doing our normal job. Doctors are doing a terrific job. The young people are defending us with arms, and we are doing theatre to defend our sanity in the city. I feel betrayed by the rest of Europe. But now I realize that the ordinary people there cannot do much, simply because fascism in Europe is prevailing again. And it's going to get worse and worse. I am an artist. I don't know what to do in life except this. Part of our job is a kind of spiritual defending.

"When you see people in Western civilization you are seeing people who suffer a lot simply because they are becoming robots, and the duty of art is to help people keep alive. In Sarajevo, people's lives are in danger from weapons, and we are trying to save their souls. I mean to improve all of our spiritual lives. I think we can do the same in any country, with the same passion."

We said good-bye to Haris. I said, "See you in October."

We drove through the checkpoints, past the graffiti on the wall: "Welcome to Sarajevo." We got our passports stamped in a shed surrounded by sandbags. "Maybe Airlines." We turned around to wave, walked across the tarmac, and climbed up inside the plane. There were ten seats, five for the crew and five for whomever— UNICEF, Médecins Sans Frontières, relief workers, and journalists. On this trip there were three Americans. The rest of the plane was empty. The Hercules lifted off the runway, and the city became small among the villages and the mountains. In thirty minutes we would land in Split. Others would climb into the seats, and two pallets of UN aid cartons would be forklifted into the belly and clipped and hausered down to the metal tracks, and the plane would take off again for Sarajevo.

≡

Six weeks later, on Friday, October 22, a small private plane touched down on the runway of Ancona's small airport, on the eastern coast of the Adriatic. It was a gray, windy morning. At the other end of the runway I could see three or four UNHCR Hercules lined up like fat-bellied pigeons. There were aid pallets in a row on the runway beside the planes. A young air force man with headphones was heading for our plane. He came up the steps into the cabin and introduced himself.

"Guten Tag! I'm from the German UNHCR air force here. We've been expecting you. As you know, the German air force was ready and agreed to fly you to Sarajevo, but we received this fax from Geneva, and now I'm afraid that we cannot fly you."

United Nations High Commission for Refugees
Airlift Operations Cell Geneva
From: Mike Allport, UK Representative
Date: 21 October, 1993
Subject: Sarajevo Film Festival

Your fax to UNHCR Ancona listing eight artists, film directors, and producers as journalists with accredited UNPROFOR press cards has been passed to the AOCG.

The group approached the UK government and were firmly

advised that they could not be carried on UK aircraft as this activity falls outside the very firm guidelines established for the UNHCR humanitarian airlift. This is in accord with other providing nations and we were also advised that very firm pressure would be applied to UNPROFOR to support the UNHCR line. We were also aware of the approach by this group through UNESCO for travel on UNHCR aircraft.

This group, however well-intentioned, is denied access to UNHCR aircraft. Furthermore, we feel that the accreditation of this group as bona fide press correspondents is an abuse of the system.

We clambered out of the cabin. Dieter, Hermann, and Martin, three of the German producers from New Constantin Films, were first, followed by the long, lanky blue jeans of Jeremy Irons, who was starring in their new film *The House of the Spirits*. Down tumbled the director Jim Sheridan, who looks like a gentle, untidy schoolboy under his flyaway gray hair, mainly because his shirt will never stay in his trousers. In his knapsack he had a first cut of *In the Name of the Father*, which he'd worked on with his screenwriter, Terry George. Another pair of long legs, belonging to Daniel Day-Lewis, emerged. I practically collapsed down the steps, since I'm too tall for most cabin doors. Last but certainly not least strode Volker Schlöndorff, who is reckoned to be Germany's top film director, along with Wim Wenders. Wim was not with us, but he'd sent a film for the festival.

We had all been accredited by film magazines in Britain and Germany to cover the festival, and our accreditation had been accepted by the UNPROFOR press-accreditation office in Zagreb. I had informed the Foreign Office in the appropriate way, and not one of the officials I had talked to had told me the UK government would prevent us from going to Sarajevo.

For twenty-four hours we all did what we could to get the decision reversed. Back in London, senior members of Parliament from all political parties spoke to the Ministry of Defence and the Foreign Office. Our friends in Sarajevo sent a fax to UNHCR in Geneva: "We, the organizers of the Sarajevo Film Festival and the Sarajevo filmmakers, express our protest and a bitter disappointment because our colleagues were not allowed to come to the festival. These artists have the right to come and show their films and to greet the Sarajevo audience, and we have the right to invite them. Culture is a part of humanitarian rights. It is an elementary need as much as food and medicine. We request that you allow our colleagues to come and, please, give them your full assistance." It was signed Haris Pasović, Dana Rotberg, Ademir Kenović, and Ismet Arnautalic.

When Esther Brunstein heard about this, she sent me a letter. She wrote that poetry, theatre, literature, and music are fundamental to survival. "Besides the genocide against a race, or religion, there is the genocide of the soul."

CHAPTER 30

EPILOGUE AND PROLOGUE

I lie down, watching my mother, Rachel, swimming in the blue water of the pool Tony built almost twenty years ago, after he and Jeanne Moreau walked through the forests of the Var region in southern France, to the deserted hamlet where, year by year, he built a home for his three daughters and their children to come to.

Rachel looks as if she were flying, gently and slowly, through the skies. "You are beautiful." Rachel doesn't believe me. I can see that from the timid way she glances around. Then she laughs softly and lifts her arms up high in a gesture that is sweet and joyous and rather sexy. I can see why Michael couldn't believe his luck when she told him they ought to get married, and why her lover adored her for over thirty years, until he died. All the same, she has never believed she has beauty, nor that she was, and still is, a very special actress.

The Var province is preparing for the fiftieth anniversary of the August 1944 landing in southern France of the Allied forces and the battle for liberation from the Nazi occupation. Over five hundred memorials commemorate the men of the Resistance units who slipped through the dense oaks and chestnut trees that cover these valleys and mountainsides, to undertake sabotage actions against the Wehrmacht battalions stationed in Toulon, Bandol, Draguignan, and the fishing port of Saint-Tropez.

Now Rachel lies on the couch by the open door. The sun has dipped below the ridge above the small farmhouse. The faraway hills have turned a misty color. They look like Hemingway's elephants; but this is the Var, not Catalonia, so the elephants are blue, not white. On Rachel's lap is her much-loved, much-read *Jane Eyre*. Her wooden cane is close to hand. A small brown photograph marks the page where she left off reading. It was taken in August 1914, the last summer before the First World War, when Rachel's mother, Beatrice, was twenty-eight. Lying across Beatrice's lap is her first son, Nicholas, who is nine weeks old. Rachel stands at her mother's side in a cotton frock, her short hair ruffled as if she has just run in from the garden. One arm is laid protectively around her mother's neck, the other stretched down to the baby, her fingers gently touching his long christening robe. She looks down at her brother with the same timid joy I saw for a second in the pool.

On the shelf above the couch Rachel is lying on now is an illustrated edition of *Beauty and the Beast*, the favorite story of her great-granddaughter, Daisy Carmen Bevan, who was here a few days ago. Daisy's name becomes her; her blue cornflower eyes follow everything, and she lies on the floor and sobs tempestuously when she is thwarted or misunderstood. Daisy watches the video of Walt Disney's *Beauty and the Beast* once a day if possible. She knows by heart the words of Belle's first song, which climaxes "There must be more than this provincial life," and when she sings she mimes every gesture Belle makes. Since Tasha's marriage to Liam Neeson a month ago, Daisy has grown two inches; since April, when she realized that the question "What's that?" brings her a wealth of information, her vocabulary has increased by about sixty words a day.

I turn the pages again and again of *I Dream of Peace*, a book of children's paintings and writings gathered by UNICEF from teachers and child specialists in counseling centers, refugee camps, schools, hospitals, and cellars in besieged enclaves in all parts of what was Yugoslavia. A fifth-grade class from a school in Zenica writes:

War is here, but we want peace. We are in a corner of the world where nobody seems to hear us. But we are not afraid and we will not give up.

Our fathers earn little, just barely enough to buy five kilos of flour a month. And we have no water, no electricity, no heat. We bear it all, but we cannot bear the hate and evil.

Our teacher told us about Anne Frank, and we have read her diary. After fifty years, history is repeating itself right here with this war, with the hate and the killing, and with having to hide to save your life.

We are only twelve years old. We can't influence politics and the war, but we want to live! And we want to stop this madness. Like Anne Frank fifty years ago, we wait for peace. She didn't live to see it. Will we?

These children living in one of the worst enclaves in Bosnia have good teachers, and they have taken strength from Anne Frank's story. Many children are younger, and many suffer trauma from horrors they cannot bring themselves to speak about. Their paintings and drawings are part and product of the essential healing process of sharing what they have witnessed, what they have lost, their nightmares. Through this process of painting and playing games and singing—making things that counselors can analyze—the children regain their powers of communication and can begin to think and hope for the future.

Physical damage is not too difficult to estimate. Thousands of children have been killed and wounded in Bosnia alone. Psychological damage has to be assessed and remedied over a long period. UNICEF estimates that about 1.5 million children have been traumatized by the war. By the spring of 1994 at least 281,000 children were living in besieged enclaves and war zones, and 620,000 children had been forced to leave their homes. Many people know that these children need food and medicine. Very few know anything about the psychosocial programs that are fundamental to the emergency aid UNICEF is coordinating.

The simple activities of singing, dancing, painting, and playing are essential to children's mental and physical development, as they are to the development of the human race and civilization. When I read the manuscript of *I Dream of Peace* and studied the paintings before I wrote a foreword to it for UNICEF, I realized that these pictures contain the key to all peace processes, and the first key to the survival of what we call civilization. We must listen to the children, to all children.

On an impulse, I take Tony's old Funk and Wagnalls dictionary (published in 1951; first edition 1910) from the bookshelf. What is "civilization"? "Condition of organization, enlightenment, and progress." *Synonym,* see "humanity." I turn the pages—"The state of being humane." I read on. "The *humane* man will not needlessly inflict pain upon the nearest thing that lives, a *merciful* man is disposed to withhold or mitigate the suffering even of the guilty. The *compassionate* man sympathizes with and desires to relieve actual suffering, while one who is *humane* would forestall and prevent the suffering which he sees to be possible." *Antonyms:* "barbarous, brutal, cruel, inhumane, merciless, pitiless, savage, selfish, unmerciful, unpitying."

What is happening to the children in all our cities? The majority have already been dispossessed of textbooks, literature, drama, dance, music, and decent sports and social facilities. Governments are cutting teachers and school funding, and spending more and more on prisons and police to punish the children they have deprived. Parents are traumatized by lack of work and the fear of not being able to pay bills, and traumatized parents make traumatized children who have no assistance or counseling elsewhere.

I read with anger and horror that a living-wage program in New York, projected for a thousand kids in the Bronx in 1992, was scaled down in 1994 to a mere twenty-five minimum-wage jobs. Meanwhile, in Brownsville, the city is spending $30 million on a youth detention center. This sort of thing is happening all over Britain as well. Earlier this year a British children's charity reported that the daily subsistence of gruel and bread, with meat three times a week, which was given to children in Victorian workhouses, would now be too expensive for the 1.5 million families who try to survive on state benefits. Chemical warfare is prohibited by the Geneva Convention, but chemicals used in food production and for preservation are poisoning our children. Health and safety legislation has been bypassed, expenditure on sanitation and safe water dropped. We in Britain have lost one of the outstanding reforms of our century, and not one leading politician has spoken out.

I read that children in the Bronx and other poor neighborhoods are being poisoned by lead-based paint. In an article in *The New York Times* a doctor is quoted: "Such exposures are linked to neurological disabilities in children, like reduced I.Q., hyperactivity, and the increased likelihood of antisocial behavior later in life." The newspaper reports the story of a woman who came to a Bronx clinic with her two-year-old son. Peeling lead-based paint in her apartment was so prevalent that she had to pick pieces out of the water in his bathtub. "He is having a lot of trouble walking," she told a reporter. "He stumbles a lot. He has a speaking problem. The doctor says it could be because of the lead." A consultant on a Housing and Urban Development committee concerned with this told the *Times,* "Money isn't the problem; political will is the problem."

UNICEF's annual report for 1992, "State of the World's Children," shows an enormous increase in child poverty in the United States and Britain in the 1980s. It is not hard to see the connection between the increase in unemployment and poverty in Europe and the United States and the desperate situation in the African countries. During the 1980s these countries were paying out to Western banks more money as interest on bank loans than all the aid they received, reaching a level of debt that in 1992 had become, in the words of the UNICEF report, "a new form of slavery." Surveys published by philanthropic trusts and nongovernmental aid agencies report that in the last decade the incomes of the wealthiest 10 percent of the population in Europe and the United States have vastly increased, while the incomes of the bottom 10 percent have drastically decreased. War on Want, a British relief agency, reported that "one in three of the world's children are hungry; one in five of the world's population is trying to survive on less than 50p a day; while 1.5 million pounds is spent *every minute of every day* to arm the world against itself."

Stories of the consequences for children of neglect of the urban environment are to be read every day in the British newspapers. Britain's newest jail, H.M. Doncaster, was built at the cost of nearly £80 million, and is run by an American company. It is already known as "Doncatraz." Privatization of the prisons brings a new and serious concern. Our elected representatives in Parliament have lost the right to obtain full information on the conditions in such institutions.

There are now more private security firms, with armed employees, in Britain than there are police. Unlike the police, who are responsible to some degree to Parliament, through the Home Secretary, these private policemen are accountable only to those who contract them. We have the potential, therefore, for a new kind of *Stürmabteilung,* private storm troopers. The new criminal-justice bill seeks to remove the right to silence. In the United States, the Constitution (we have no constitution in Britain) provides the right not to incriminate yourself. The right to silence is the only defense against the torturer. Interestingly, the chief opposition to this bill comes from some of the peers in the House of Lords, and not from the Labour Party in the House of Commons.

The historian Hippolyte Taine wrote of Napoleon's France that it became a gigantic prison. He said that you could analyze the fundamental character of a nation-state by studying its penal laws, institutions, and the condition of prisoners. I would add to this list only the study of the actual provisions for children in our countries, the chances for education and employment, and the conditions of those places where children under eighteen are incarcerated.

≡

Rachel opens her eyes. The sun has gone down, and I turn on the lamp at the table where I am writing. I ask her about her father, Grandpa Eric, who left his family behind in the First World War when he went to fight under General Allenby in Palestine. "He had an old pony," Rachel tells me, "and he used to swim in the sea with it, holding on to its mane. Father said General Allenby was mad. He told his men, 'Sweep the desert.' " Suddenly I recall Grandpa Eric cackling with laughter as he recited the verse from Lewis Carroll's *Through the Looking-Glass* about the Walrus and the Carpenter walking on the beach.

> "If seven maids with seven mops
> Swept it for half a year,

Do you suppose," the Walrus said,
"That they could get it clear?"
"I doubt it," said the Carpenter,
And shed a bitter tear.

Rachel pauses and looks at me. "Do you suppose it could happen here?" "What do you mean?" I ask. "A war?" And then we have a long talk. It will soon be the fiftieth anniversary of the defeat of fascism, and we can all see the conditions here again in Europe that brought fascist governments to power in the 1930s. However, we have some great advantages today that our fathers and mothers did not have. The first is the Israeli-PLO peace accord, the Declaration of Principles signed by President Arafat and Prime Minister Rabin on September 13, 1993, ending the historic conflict between their peoples. This conflict was deliberately created, principally by the British government in 1917, and later by Stalin and his successors, Khrushchev and Brezhnev. Now, in spite of all the problems and tragedies, Palestinians and Israelis, with Jews in all countries, will find their rightful historical destiny as allies against fascism and oppression everywhere.

In 1994 we watched millions line up at polling stations in South Africa to vote for Nelson Mandela and the African National Congress. Apartheid and white supremacy were built into the constitution of the Union of South Africa by the British government in 1910, and it was this constitution that remained fundamentally unchanged when the Republic of South Africa was formed in 1960. The Israeli-PLO peace accord and the great changes in the government of South Africa signify a quantum leap, and nothing and no one can reverse this. For these developments were not only the consequences of the conscious decisions of courageous people, they were first and foremost the outcome of historic processes and objective laws. Neither would have occurred at this time but for the political revolution that ended the Stalinist regimes in 1989. I was on my way to Sarajevo when I heard the amazing reports of the coming peace accord between Israel and the PLO, and the next day I told Haris Pasović that this was a harbinger of change and a cease-fire for Sarajevo. "How could that be?" he said. But it was. Sometimes you know something before you can explain it.

During these few days in Tony's house, I am in contact with the headquarters of UNESCO in Paris. They are arranging for me to go to Sarajevo to attend the "Baby Universe" International Theatre Festival that Haris has organized under UNESCO's auspices. The highlights of the Festival will be the opening of the Hamdija Kreševljaković library, and the premiere of a play Haris has directed based on a book by Paul Auster, *In the Country of Last Things*. In January, when the shelling was terrible and the political situation just as bad, a student gave this book to Haris. He discovered to his amazement that Paul Auster, who had written it in 1987, and had never been to Sarajevo, had described the psychological and physical conditions of life and death under the siege of the city where Haris was born.

In March, Haris and I met Paul Auster in New York, and he gave the go-ahead for a production based on his book. Then in early May we met Peter Brook and Richard Eyre at the National Theatre in London, and Peter invited Haris to bring his company to perform their plays at the Bouffe du Nord in the fall. That night Haris and I watched *The Man Who*, directed by Peter, based on the book *The Man Who Mistook His Wife for a Hat*, by the neurologist Oliver Sacks. "For Sacks, those who suffer from the hardest and most painful complaints are not diminished human beings: they are warriors struggling across inner chasms and abysses with the courage and determination of tragic heroes," Peter wrote in the program. Haris and I were enthralled by the production and by the acting—above all by the way the territories of the human mind were explored, challenging commonly held myths and prejudices. That night we ate with Oliver Sacks and one of his warriors, Richard Sorrell. But for Oliver, Richard's neurological disorder would have doomed him either to a drugged state in some hellhole of a public institution, or to jail. We four talked for a long time over a pasta meal. Then we exchanged addresses. When Richard finished putting his name in my book, he noticed that the opposite page was blank. He took back the pen, and from his quick strokes on the page a tiger appeared, looking out as if to say, "Follow me, if you can." Another quantum leap.

Rachel and I have eaten our supper at the wooden table under the cypress and the aspen tree. The earth has turned and now the moon appears over the hills. Neige, Tony's shepherd dog, appears through the shadows, hopefully sniffing for the remains of our meal. We return to the salon and sit there reading. I am wondering how Haris will make a play from Paul Auster's book, and whether I will get there to his city and see it. I pick up *In the Country of Last Things* and start to read.

"When you live in the city, you learn to take nothing for granted. Close your eyes for a moment, turn around to look at something else, and the thing that was before you is suddenly gone. Nothing lasts, you see, not even the thoughts inside you. And you musn't waste your time looking for them. Once a thing is gone, that is the end of it."

≡

Seven days later, I have flown into Sarajevo on the big white UN Ilyushin. It seems like a miracle, but it is not. The miracle worker is Maria Elena Mueller, the director of UNESCO's new office in Sarajevo. At Svrzo's house in the old quarter of the city I find Haris and his actors rehearsing. Lejla, Haris's young sister, rises to her feet and sings the opening words of *In the Country of Last Things*, to a melody I realize later is "Amazing Grace."

> These are the last things.
> One by one they disappear and never come back.
> I can tell you of the ones I have seen,
> Of the ones that are no more,
> But I doubt there will be time.

Paul Auster says his book is about the struggle to remain human in the face of dehumanizing terror and catastrophe. Haris and the actors and musicians have found the content and forms that connect the vast mental perspectives, the agony, and the delirium of Euripides' tragedies with the simple, everyday moments of the English Miracle plays. There are melodies, notes, and rhythms from many times and many countries: a cadence from Indonesia, Billie Holiday's rendition of "In My Solitude," Abraham Lincoln's campaign song, and the frightening, deep-below-earth thudding of David Byrne's "Nineveh." Anna Blume, in search of her brother in a dark, starving European city at the end of the twentieth century, writes her story, and sings, and she and her friends try to continue a human life in a place where every human action, however simple, is achieved in spite of continual violence and disintegration.

Since the company has prepared the whole text in English, and Haris is trying to read the narrative as well as direct, I offer to take the part of the Storyteller. We have six days of rehearsal before us, as well as press conferences, the opening of the library, my lecture, and the launching of Paul Auster's book, translated into Bosnian and printed here in Sarajevo. Plus we have to obtain all the documents that will permit the company to leave Sarajevo for its European tour.

By the light of the moon—the same moon that shone when Rachel and I sat together a few days earlier—we all set off on foot to return home. Haris and I walk down the hill past the great old Beg's mosque, across Princip's bridge and up the hill to Haris's house. We discuss then, as we will many times again, the extraordinary nature of this production. For Paul Auster is an American Jewish writer, and Haris's family name is a Muslim name, and Svrzo's house, where we will premiere the play, was built by a Sarajevo merchant in the Turkish style of his day. *Historia est magister vitae:* History is Life's teacher.

Near Svrzo's house is the Jewish center, the hub of the Jewish community of Sarajevo, the community whose forefathers were expelled from Spain by Ferdinand and Isabella. We go there one morning to invite Ivan Čerešnješ and Jacob Finzi to our first performance. They give me a book in which I read the story of the Moslems of Sarajevo who protected the Jews from the persecution of the Turkish governor Mehmud Ruždi in the early 1800s.

We rehearse most of the day, until the evening, when we have to stop because of the curfew. On one of our last mornings, Haris takes me to Kovači, on the outskirts of the city. The roadside is bordered by a grassy space in front of a group of small houses like those found near Heathrow Airport in London, or Newark Airport in New Jersey. About one hundred graves fill that space, covered with golden marigolds. The dates on the graves show how young the boys and girls were who have been killed by the mortars. I watch a woman walking down the road toward us. Her arms carefully and tenderly hold a little girl, whose head nestles in the comfort of her mother's shoulder. I turn to look again at the graves. One million mortar shells were fired on the city in the first year of the war, more than were fired in the whole of Yugoslavia during World War II. I look back at the mother, who is now a few feet away. I see her eyes then, black with grief. She stares ahead and passes by, putting one foot slowly in front of the other, and then the other foot in front of the first. I cannot speak to her, for at that moment I see that she is holding a doll in her arms.

On Sunday, at five in the afternoon, I take my place among the actors on the rush carpet. Before us on chairs and a wooden "divan" is our audience, those who have come to see and listen. I look at their faces: the prime minister, Dr. Haris Silajdzič; a few seats away Jacob Finzi from the Jewish Center; Nermin Tulič in his wheelchair, with his black-haired Serbian wife, who is now pregnant. There is the senior doctor from Koševo Hospital. The man in military fatigues is the Serbian general Jovan Divjak. He left the Yugoslav National Army to join the small number of men who had no weapons to defend Sarajevo, or any of their cities, in those first terrible April weeks that became summer, then winter, and then a new year, and then another. These people, and all the citizens of this city, under the same blue firmament and sun that fills the streets of Rome, Berlin, Paris, and London at this same hour, are the survivors of the second European genocide.

Faruk plays the Bach prelude on his flute, and then Lejla sings again.

> I am not sure why I am writing to you now.
> To be honest, I have barely thought of you.
> But suddenly, after all this time,
> I feel there is something to say,
> And if I don't quickly write it down,
> My head will burst.
> It doesn't matter if you read it.
> It doesn't even matter if I send it.
> Perhaps it comes down to this.
> I am writing to you because you know nothing.
> Because you are far away from me and know nothing.

The audience is silent. They could speak, for this is their story— the story of members of their families, their friends, and citizens of nearby towns that are still under siege. This is the requiem for all men, women, and children in all the cities of our civilization. Sarajevo is what Stephen Hawking calls a "baby universe."

Not far from here, one hour's flight away, is Macedonia, the land where Euripides came as an asylum-seeker, a refugee from Athens. This play, its author, its performers, and its audience are the products of agonized peoples—a civilization in agony. Our civilization. The word "agony" is derived from the Greek word for struggle. The struggle of human beings to be humane, to restore humanity to those who are in danger of being dehumanized. The struggle to forestall and prevent the further suffering they see is possible.

AGAVE: What cause have I for wretchedness?
CADMUS: Come here. First turn your eyes this way. Look at the sky.
AGAVE: I am looking. Why should you want me to look at it?

And so we spend these few hours together in Svrzo's house, thinking of the lives that are gone and the lives that are coming into being.

≡

Rachel is in the water by my side. Through the glass walls that surround the pool we can see that Sarajevo moon shining over English trees. The moon is now waning into September, and I have promised Rachel a few more days together before I fly to Canada to start work on a film. I may not see her again for four or five months. I probably won't see Haris and the actors until the spring.

"You are swimming so well," I tell Rachel. "I'm very medium," she replies. "I think if I'd learned to swim properly when I was young, like you did, I wouldn't be afraid of the water." She is afraid of the water, but she is swimming nevertheless. She is afraid when she goes onstage, but once there, she gives herself to her character. I saw her early this year, using her cane to get onto the platform for a recital. She laid the cane down, that gentle profile lifted, and the years vanished from her face and body. Fourteen-year-old Juliet stood before us.

Farewell! God knows when we shall meet again.
I have a faint cold fear thrills through my veins,

That almost freezes up the heat of life;
I'll call them back again to comfort me.
Nurse!

In the early hours of the morning Haris phones me. The company has arrived safely in Ljubljana. The wife of the president of Slovenia, Milan Kučan, has kept her warm promise and provided accommodation for them all so that they can rest and eat before they fly to Paris for their performance. Peter Brook's people have also kept their promise. Whatever hardships lie ahead of us all, however few there are who understand what must be done and do it, we are living in the time of the quantum leap. Modern physics teaches us that one discrete change alters the whole field, no matter what barriers separate the parts. "Well, Haris," I say. "We had better stop talking. Phone calls are expensive, and the dawn is on its way." "That's how you must end your book," he says. "The dawn is on its way."

APPENDIX 1:

Statement About the Gulf War, February 8, 1991

APPENDIX 2:

Letter Protesting Travel Ban on Mikhail Gorbachev, October 13, 1992

LIST OF PRINCIPAL THEATRE WORK

LIST OF FILM AND TELEVISION WORK

A P P E N D I X   1

THE NEW YORK TIMES,
FRIDAY, FEBRUARY 8, 1991
(Paid Advertisement)

I would like to clarify the misunderstanding that has arisen on account of a statement I made at a peace rally in Barcelona on Sunday, January 13th, 1991, two days before the expiration of the United Nations deadline for the withdrawal of Iraqi forces from Kuwait, and prior to commencement of the present hostilities.

In my statement that I read in Barcelona I said:

> We support those Arab leaders, including Yasser Arafat, who are seeking a peaceful solution, a guarantee of no reprisals against Iraq, agreement to withdraw Iraqi forces from Kuwait, a peace conference to discuss and resolve all the main problems of the Middle East. We demand the withdrawal of U.S., British and all imperialist troops from the Gulf and we must unconditionally defend Iraq against American, British or Israeli aggression [printed as "troops," because of a typesetting error]. We must prevent deportations and detentions of Arabs in our own countries.

In context, the statement fully supported a peaceful, negotiated settlement of the crisis; a position taken by all the American church organizations, twelve American trade unions, His Holiness Pope John Paul II, Cardinal Hume, Crown Prince Hassan of Jordan, and millions of peace-loving individuals throughout the world.

Out of context, and taken on their own, the words "we must unconditionally defend Iraq against American, British or Israeli aggression" could only be taken to mean that I supported the Iraqi invasion of Kuwait and that I opposed any action undertaken by the United Nations or its members to effect a peaceful solution to the crisis, which must include the withdrawal of the Iraqi forces from Kuwait and the restoration of the Kuwaiti people's right of self-determination. I unconditionally oppose the Iraqi invasion of Kuwait.

The sentence quoted above was intended, as the full context of my statement made clear, to affirm my *unqualified* opposition to war in the Middle East, as distinct from those whose support for the war was qualified by the demand that more time should be allowed, and further use of economic sanctions, before going to war.

My statement was made on January 13th. Since January 16th, when allied saturation bombing of Iraq commenced, thousands of Iraqi civilians are dead and injured, allied and Iraqi troops have been killed, Israeli civilians have been killed by missiles from Iraq, Palestinian families in the Israeli-occupied territories of the West Bank and Gaza Strip are being killed, wounded, imprisoned and kept under 24-hour curfew, and the entire Gulf area is a disaster from oil spills.

Arab citizens are being imprisoned and deported from Britain without charges or legal process; the Muslim and Jewish communities are under attack from fascist groups and others.

Now, therefore, new initiatives for a cease-fire and peace in the Middle East must be made. One such proposal was advanced, in their recent communiqué, by Secretary of State James Baker and Foreign Minister Alexander Bessmertnikh.

I support wholeheartedly all efforts to end this war, and to establish peace in the Middle East. The Iraqi invasion of Iran in 1980 (which I opposed), its invasion of Kuwait in 1990 (which I oppose), and *all* conflicts in the Middle East have as their source the unresolved conflict between the Arabs and the Israelis. As Sir Yehudi Menuhin wrote in the London *Independent* on Saturday, February 1st: "I am convinced that the key to the future of humanity is the reconciliation of Israeli and Palestinian, and the sharing of Jerusalem."

I hope all my fellow artists will give their best endeavors to this cause.

Vanessa Redgrave

Letter to Andrei Kozyrev, Russia's Minister for Foreign Affairs
(Published in The Guardian, *October 13, 1992)*

TRAVEL BAN ON MIKHAIL GORBACHEV

CONDEMNED AS ABUSE OF POWER

The following letter has been sent to Andrei Kozyrev, Russia's Minister for Foreign Affairs:

We protest against the restriction imposed upon former President Mikhail Gorbachev, forbidding him to travel abroad. We demand that this ban be immediately lifted and his passport returned, and the premises of the Gorbachev Foundation be restored.

We request the Constitutional Court, the Foreign Ministry and the Ministry of State Security make known by what law Mikhail Gorbachev is forbidden to leave Russia. We request that all written instructions, orders, and correspondence on this subject be published. We do not believe that the Constitutional Court has powers to compel witnesses to attend a hearing of the kind presently being conducted. It is clear that until recently the Court did not presume to exercise such powers, and that it did not consider them necessary or appropriate.

The Court's chairman, Valeriy Zorkin, said: "The Court is not engaged, as you can understand, in criminal or legal affairs (June 28, 1992)."

On July 23, the Court proposed to invite additional witnesses, including Gorbachev. A panel of 13 judges voted by a majority of one to issue such invitations. Judge Vedernikov gave the following reasons: "I should like to remind you, esteemed colleagues, that as long ago as May 26, the issue of representation according to office was examined, and we decided, I hope unanimously, that in his official capacity the General Secretary should represent his party here. However, he expressed his reluctance to do so as the case was prepared and we silently agreed with this reluctance. We did, however, declare our agreement at a sitting of the Court. Subsequent investigations, however, during the sitting of the Court have completely and unequivocally convinced me, for example, of the need for Mikhail Gorbachev to be present here since a whole series of questions, primarily that of the events of 19–21 August, have not been clarified."

Surely it would have been illegal for questions to be asked on the August Coup in the Constitutional Court, since this is the subject of criminal proceedings?

Procurator General Stepankov's argument is absolutely clear and unequivocal. The hearings in the Constitutional Court are in no way analogous to proceedings under criminal or civil law. Yet it is precisely such an analogy which is being attempted in the illegal removal of Mikhail Gorbachev's passport to travel. The law provides for such a measure only in certain very specific criminal or civil cases. If the powers of Russia's parliament, or the Ministry of Foreign Affairs, or the Ministry of State Security must be invoked to make good an absence of powers belonging to the Constitutional Court, then the government's powers are being abused in order to supplant the rule of law. It was to ensure that the rule of law should prevail in a law-governed state, that the people of Russia followed President Yeltsin's call and defeated the coup. The great victory is in danger of reversal by the delay in bringing the leaders of the coup to trial.

The right to travel freely inside and beyond the borders of one's country was one of the greatest victories of the political revolution against Stalinism which was heralded by the authors of perestroika and glasnost. That right must now be upheld in the person of Mikhail Gorbachev.

Vanessa Redgrave, Trevor Nunn, Robert Fox, John Hurt, Corin Redgrave, Tony Kushner, Mikhail Shatrov, Sarah Miles, Fred Zinnemann, Theodore Mann, Braham Murray, Robert Bolt, Miriam Karlin, Harold Pinter, Antonia Fraser, Timothy Dalton, and Buck Henry.

PRINCIPAL THEATRE WORK

1957

The Reluctant Debutante (Clarissa) Frinton Summer Theatre,
Frinton-upon-Sea. Directed by Peter Hoar.

Look Back in Anger (Helena) Frinton Summer Theatre,
Frinton-upon-Sea. Directed by Geoffrey Edwards.

Come On, Jeeves (Mrs. Spottsworth) Arts Theatre, Cambridge.
Directed by Peter Hoar.

A Touch of the Sun (Caroline Lester) Provincial tour, 1957; Saville
Theatre and Prince of Wales Theatre, London, 1958. Directed
by Frith Banbury.

1958

Major Barbara (Sarah Undershaft) Royal Court Theatre, London.
Directed by George Devine.

Mother Goose (Colin) Leatherhead Theatre, Leatherhead, Surrey.
Directed by Jordan Lawrence.

1959

Hippolytus (Artemis) Leatherhead Theatre, Leatherhead, Surrey.
Directed by Jordan Lawrence.

A Midsummer Night's Dream (Helena) Shakespeare Memorial Theatre,
Stratford-upon-Avon. Directed by Peter Hall.

Coriolanus (Valeria) Shakespeare Memorial Theatre,
Stratford-upon-Avon. Directed by Peter Hall.

1960

Look on Tempests (Rose Sinclair) Provincial tour; Comedy Theatre,
London. Directed by Lionel Harris.

The Tiger and the Horse (Stella Dean) Queen's Theatre, London.
Directed by Frith Banbury.

1961

The Lady from the Sea (Bolette) Queen's Theatre, London. Directed
by Glen Byam-Shaw.

As You Like It (Rosalind) Shakespeare Memorial Theatre,
  Stratford-upon-Avon; Aldwych Theatre, London, 1962. Directed
  by Michael Elliott.

1962

The Taming of the Shrew (Katharina) Shakespeare Memorial Theatre,
  Stratford-upon-Avon; Aldwych Theatre, London. Directed by
  John Barton.
The Hollow Crown (The Queens) Shakespeare Memorial Theatre,
  Stratford-upon-Avon; Aldwych Theatre, London. Directed by
  John Barton.
Cymbeline (Imogen) Shakespeare Memorial Theatre,
  Stratford-upon-Avon. Directed by William Gaskill.
Beatrice and Benedict (Beatrice) Royal Festival Hall, London.
  Conducted by Colin Davis.

1963

In the Interests of the State Royal Court Theatre, London. With
  George Devine, Robert Stephens, and Jack MacGowran.
  Devised and directed by Vanessa Redgrave.

1964

The Seagull (Nina) Queen's Theatre, London. Directed by Tony
  Richardson.
Saint Joan of the Stockyards (Joan) Queen's Theatre, London. Directed
  by Tony Richardson. (Vanessa Redgrave rehearsed the play, but
  left the production to have her second baby, Joely Kim; Siobhan
  McKenna took over the role.)

1966

The Prime of Miss Jean Brodie (Jean Brodie) Provincial tour;
  Wyndham's Theatre, London. Directed by Peter Wood.

1969

Daniel Deronda (Gwendolyn Harleth) University Theatre,
  Manchester. Directed by Michael Elliott.
Gandhi Centenary Concert (Producer) Royal Albert Hall, London.
Pierrot Lunaire (Narrator) Queen Elizabeth Hall, London. Conducted
  by Zubin Mehta.

1971

Beatrice and Benedict (Beatrice) Los Angeles Music Center. Conducted by Zubin Mehta.

Cato Street (Susan Thistlewood) Young Vic Theatre, London. Produced by Vanessa Redgrave, Robert Shaw, and Michael White. Directed by Peter Gill and Vanessa Redgrave.

1972

The Threepenny Opera (Polly Peachum) Prince of Wales Theatre, London. Directed by Tony Richardson.

Twelfth Night (Viola) Dolphin Theatre Company at the Shaw Theatre, London. Directed by Michael Blakewell.

1973

Antony and Cleopatra (Cleopatra) Bankside Theatre, London. Directed by Tony Richardson.

Design for Living (Gilda) Phoenix Theatre, London. Directed by Michael Blakemore.

1974

October (Performer) Alexandra Palace, London. Directed by Roger Smith, Roy Battersby, and Corin Redgrave.

1975

Macbeth (Lady Macbeth) Ahmanson Theatre, Los Angeles. Directed by Peter Wood.

1976

The Lady from the Sea (Ellida) Circle in the Square, New York. Directed by Tony Richardson.

1978

The Lady from the Sea (Ellida) Royal Exchange Theatre, Manchester; Round House, London, 1979. Directed by Michael Elliott.

1982

Two recitals of plays, songs, and poetry at the Orpheum Theatre, Boston, with Tennessee Williams and Philip Casnoff. Presented by the Arab-American Association, Washington, D.C.

Shakespeare and His Players Liverpool Playhouse, Liverpool. With Sir
Michael Redgrave, Corin Redgrave, Vanessa Redgrave, and
Rachel Kempson. Directed by Corin Redgrave.

Benefit performance for the Young Socialists Youth Training Center,
Round House, London, with Sir Michael Redgrave, Corin
Redgrave, and Vanessa Redgrave. Directed by Corin Redgrave.

1984

The Aspern Papers (Miss Tina) Yvonne Arnaud Theatre, Guildford;
Haymarket Theatre, London. Adapted by Sir Michael Redgrave
from the novel by Henry James. Directed by Frith Banbury.

1985

The Seagull (Madame Arkadina) Queen's Theatre, London. Directed
by Charles Sturridge.

1986

Antony and Cleopatra (Cleopatra) in repertory with *The Taming of the
Shrew* (Katharina) Theatr Clwyd, Mold, North Wales;
Haymarket Theatre, London. Directed by Toby Robertson and
Christopher Selbie.

Ghosts (Mrs. Alving) Young Vic Theatre, London; Wyndham's
Theatre, London; National Theatre, Oslo, Norway. Directed by
David Thacker.

1987

October 1917 (Producer) Riverside Theatre, London. Directed by Corin
Redgrave.

Tomorrow Was War (Simultaneous Translator) Mayakovsky Theatre
Company of Moscow at the International Theatre Festival,
Royal National Theatre, London. Directed by Nikolai
Goncharov.

1988

A Touch of the Poet (Nora Melody) Young Vic Theatre, London;
Theatre Royal, Brighton; Comedy Theatre, London. Directed
by David Thacker.

Orpheus Descending (Lady Torrance) Theatre Royal, Bath; New
Theatre, Cardiff; Haymarket Theatre, London; Neil Simon
Theatre, New York, 1989. Directed by Sir Peter Hall.

1989

Chekhov's Women Lyric Theatre, Hammersmith. Devised and performed by Vanessa Redgrave, Frances de la Tour, and Rachel Kempson. Directed and performed by David Hargreaves.

Soviet Theatre Season, Lyric Theatre, Hammersmith: Vakhtanghov Theatre Company, *The Peace of Brest,* directed by Robert Sturua; Moscow Jewish Theatre Shalom Company, *The Train to Happiness,* directed by Alexander Levenbyk. Produced by Vanessa Redgrave and Corin Redgrave.

A Madhouse in Goa (Heather/Mrs. Honey) Lyric Theatre, Hammersmith; Apollo Theatre, London. Directed by Robert Alan Ackerman.

The Wall Breaks: A Tribute and Requiem (Producer and Director) Marquis Theatre, New York. A benefit for the Memorial Society for Victims of Stalin's Repressions, Moscow.

1990

The Three Sisters (Olga Prozorov) Yvonne Arnaud Theatre, Guildford; Queen's Theatre, London. Directed by Robert Sturua.

Master Class Queen's Theatre, London. Vakhtanghov Theatre Company benefit in aid of the Ulyanov Fund for Nadia Samoilova. Produced by Vanessa Redgrave and Corin Redgrave. Directed by Roman Victyuk.

Perestroika (Performer) Adelphi Theatre, London. Memorial concert for Gerry Healy in benefit of Symposium 90. Directed by Corin Redgrave and Vanessa Redgrave.

1991

Collateral Damage: Meditations on the Gulf War (Performer) La Mama, New York. Benefit performances for War Resisters International. Directed by Leonard Shapiro.

When She Danced (Isadora Duncan) Theatre Royal, Brighton; Globe Theatre, London. Directed by Robert Alan Ackerman.

For the Fallen Heroes (Producer and Performer) Bolshoi Theatre, Moscow; Globe Theatre, London. Memorial concerts honoring Vladimir Usov, Ilya Krichevsky, and Dimitri Komar, killed in the August 1991 coup attempt against Mikhail Gorbachev.

1992

Heartbreak House (Hesione Hushabye) Haymarket Theatre, London.
Directed by Trevor Nunn.

Cloud in Trousers: From Pushkin to Pasternak. Circle in the Square, New
York; Adelphi University, Garden City, New York; Trinity
Church, Pittsburgh. Devised and performed by Vanessa
Redgrave, Corin Redgrave, and Kika Markham.

Attendez-Que Je Revienne (Director and Performer) Comédie
Champs-Elysées, Paris. Katharina Wolpe, piano.

1993

We Will Never Forget—We Will Not Let It Happen Again (Associate
Producer and Performer) Thalia Theatre, Hamburg. Concert of
International Artists Against Racism Benefit for UNICEF,
Emergency Appeal for Children of the Former Yugoslavia and
Somalia.

Wake Up, World: International Artists Against Racism (Producer and
Performer) Royal Exchange Theatre, Manchester. Concert
benefit for the UNICEF Emergency Appeal for Children of the
Former Yugoslavia.

Concert for UNICEF Emergency Appeal for the Former Yugoslavia
(Producer and Performer) National Theatre of Slovenia,
Ljubljana. Directed by Dušan Jovanovič.

Maybe (Pat/Lynn) Royal Exchange Theatre, Manchester. Directed by
Braham Murray.

1994

Brecht in Exile (Producer and Performer) Moving Theatre Company,
Bridge Lane Theatre, London. Directed by Lenka Udovicki.

Letter from London (Performer) Bridge Lane Theatre, London; Verbier
Festival, Switzerland. A concert with Rade Serbedzija. Directed
by Rade Serbedzija.

In the Country of Last Things (Storyteller) Sarajevo International
Festival Theatre Ensemble, Sarajevo, Bosnia. Directed by Haris
Pasović.

Vita & Virginia (Vita) Union Square Theatre, New York. Directed
by Zoe Caldwell.

FILM AND TELEVISION WORK

(the dates refer to the year the film was made)

1958

Behind the Mask, directed by Brian Desmond Hurst.

1966

Morgan!, directed by Karel Reisz (released in Great Britain as
   Morgan—A Suitable Case for Treatment).
A Man for All Seasons, directed by Fred Zinnemann.
The Sailor from Gibraltar, directed by Tony Richardson.
Blow-Up, directed by Michelangelo Antonioni.
Camelot, directed by Joshua Logan.

1967

A Quiet Place in the Country, directed by Elio Petri.
Red and Blue, directed by Tony Richardson.
The Charge of the Light Brigade, directed by Tony Richardson.
The Loves of Isadora, directed by Karel Reisz (released in Great
   Britain as *Isadora*).

1968

The Seagull, directed by Sidney Lumet.
Oh What a Lovely War, directed by Richard Attenborough.

1970

The Trojan Women, directed by Michael Cacoyannis.
The Body (Narrator), documentary directed by Roy Battersby.
Drop Out, directed by Tinto Brass.
La Vacanza, directed by Tinto Brass.

1971

The Devils, directed by Ken Russell.
Mary, Queen of Scots, directed by Charles Jarrott.

1974

Murder on the Orient Express, directed by Sidney Lumet.

1975

Out of Season, directed by Alan Bridges.
The Seven-Per-Cent Solution, directed by Herbert Ross.

1976

Julia, directed by Fred Zinnemann.

1977

The Palestinian (Interviewer and Producer), documentary directed by
  Roy Battersby.
Agatha, directed by Michael Apted.

1978

The Fifth War (Interviewer and Producer), documentary with the
  participation of the Palestinian Film Institute.
Vanessa Talks to Farouk Abdul Azziz (Interviewer and Producer),
  documentary directed by Roy Battersby.

1979

Bear Island, directed by Don Sharp.
Yanks, directed by John Schlesinger.
Playing for Time, directed for television by Daniel Mann.

1980

Occupied Palestine (Producer), documentary directed by David
  Kott.
My Body, My Child, directed for television by Marvin Chomsky.
Wagner, directed for television by Tony Palmer.

1983

The Bostonians, directed by James Ivory.
Snow White and the Seven Dwarfs, directed for television by Peter
  Medak.

1984

Peter the Great, directed for television by Marvin Chomsky.
Steaming, directed by Joseph Losey.
Three Sovereigns for Sarah, directed for television by Philip Leacock.

1985

Wetherby, directed by David Hare.

1986

Second Serve, directed for television by Anthony Page.

1987

Comrades, directed by Bill Douglas.
Prick Up Your Ears, directed by Stephen Frears.

1988

Consuming Passions, directed by Giles Foster.

1990

Orpheus Descending, a television film adapted from the stage
    production, directed by Sir Peter Hall.
Young Catherine, directed for television by Michael Anderson.
The Ballad of the Sad Cafe, directed by Simon Callow.
Diceria dell'Untore, directed by Beppe Cino.
Stalin's Funeral, directed by Yevgeny Yevtushenko.
Whatever Happened to Baby Jane?, directed for television by David
    Greene.

1991

Howards End, directed by James Ivory.
Can't They Put Human Beings First?, documentary produced and
    directed by Vanessa Redgrave.

1992

Great Moments in Aviation, directed by Beeban Kidron.
Mother's Boys, directed by Yves Simoneau.

1993

Crime and Punishment, directed by Menachem Golan.
Wake Up, World: Lift the Siege of Sarajevo (Producer), documentary
    directed by John Tolley.
They, directed by John Korty.
The Sparrow, directed by Franco Zeffirelli.

The House of the Spirits, directed by Bille August.
Little Odessa, directed by James Gray.

1994

A Month by the Lake, directed by John Irvin.
Down Came a Blackbird, directed for television by Jonathan Sanger.

INDEX

Abdul Azziz, Farouk, 250
Abramov, Gennady, 311
Abu Jaffar, 226–28
Abu Jihad, 232, 248, 304–7
Academy Awards, 155, 235–37, 349
Ackerman, Robert Alan, 337
Actor Prepares, An (Stanislavsky), 82–84
Actors' Equity, American, 241, 266, 334–35
Actors' Equity, British, 76–77, 87, 175–76, 208–10, 212–13, 239–41, 246
Actors Studio, 64–65, 67, 84
Actor's Ways and Means, An (M. Redgrave), 49, 82
Addison, Jock, 223
Aeschylus, 152
Afanasiev, Yuri, 297
African National Congress, 132, 239, 305, 386
Agate, James, 95
Agatha (film), 176, 218
Ainley, Henry, 95
Akhmadulina, Bella, 299
Albery, Donald, 149
Ali, Tariq, 161, 163
Alliluyeva, Svetlana, 312
Allison, Patti, 322–23
Allegranza, Helen, 118–19
Allende, Salvador, 184, 193
Almani, Dawood K., 238
Anderson, J. P., 92
Anderson, Kevin, 316, 320
Anderson, Lindsay, 104, 135, 141, 150
Anderson, Margaret (VR's grandmother, formerly Daisy Scudamore), 15–16, 68, 88, 92, 96, 218
Andrews, Anthony, 366, 369
Andrews, Eamonn, 212
Andrews, Harry, 164
Andrews, Julie, 164
Antonioni, Michelangelo, 149–50
Antony and Cleopatra (Shakespeare), 48, 49, 95, 176, 194, 287–88, 290
Arab Women's Association, 303–4, 314, 333, 335
Arafat, Yasser, 56, 232–33, 241, 242, 252, 281, 304, 315, 360, 386
Armstrong, Neil, 169–70
Arnautalic, Ismet, 379
Aruri, Naseer, 353

Ashcroft, Peggy, 49, 60, 62, 78–79, 134, 296
Ashdown, Paddy, 369
Ashwell, Beatrice, *see* Kempson, Beatrice Ashwell
Asner, Ed, 266–67
Aspern Papers, The, 272–73
Assad, Hafez, 222
Astor, David, 171, 245
As You Like It (Shakespeare), 101–3, 109–10, 111, 115, 147
Audin, Maurice, 166
Auster, Paul, 387–91
Aveling, Eleanor Marx, 291
Aytmatov, Chingis, 293, 295
Azmi, Shabana, 356

"Baby Universe" International Theatre Festival, 387–91
Bachardy, Don, 138
Bacon, Francis, 74
Baklanov, Grigory, 321
Baksi, Joe, 39
Ball, John, 121
Ball, Michael, 340
Ballad of the Sad Cafe, The (film), 272, 323–25
Ballad of the Sad Cafe, The (McCullers), 323–24
Ballet Rambert, 42–43
Banda, Mike, 280–81
Bandar Bin Sultan, 269
Bannen, Ian, 103, 146–47
Barker, Ronnie, 113
Barnes, Clive, 218
Bartenieff, George, 335
Barton, John, 102
Bashir, Mounir, 255
Bassiak, Serge, 150
Bates, Alan, 68
Battersby, Roy, 208, 222–24, 234
Baylis, Lilian, 5
Beaton, Cecil, 275
Beatrice and Benedict (Berlioz), 177, 178
Beaumont, Hugh, 92
Beauvoir, Simone de, 120, 121, 167
Beckett, Samuel, 69, 114
Bedford, Duke of, 119
Bedford House, 32, 38, 55, 85
Behind the Mask (film), 89–90, 141

Bell, Gertrude, 254
Belov, Pyotr, 300–301
Benedetti, Jean, 82
Bernhardt, Sarah, 68
Bevan, Daisy Carmen (VR's niece),
    344–45, 346, 381
Bevan, Tim (VR's son-in-law), 344–45, 346
Bevin, Ernest, 20
Bewell, Bill, 263–66
Bhutto, Benazir, 248
Bibby, Wing Commander, 368–69
Bikel, Theodore, 241, 242
Billington, Michael, 296
Bird Talisman, The (Wedgwood), 12
Blair, Betsy, 141, 171
Blake, William, 98–99
Blood Wedding (Lorca), 79–80
Blow-Up (film), 149–50, 152, 155
Blunt, Anthony, 25
B'nai B'rith, 265–66
Boguslavskaya, Rebecca, 321
Bolam, James, 113
Bolt, Robert, 98–100, 106, 109, 145, 213,
    352
Bonner, Elena, 358, 359
Borromeo, Friar, 172
Bosnia-Herzegovina, 346–47, 354–55, 366,
    368–69, 371–79, 388–91
Bostonians, The (film), 269, 272–73
Boston Symphony Orchestra (BSO),
    262–71, 313
Bowles, Anthony, 159
Bradley, Buddy, 59
Branagh, Kenneth, 296
Brando, Marlon, 64
Brecht, Bertolt, 67–68, 120, 135–36,
    180–81, 362
Brecht in Exile (Serbedzija), 362
Brezhnev, Leonid, 194, 386
Bridgewater, Leslie, 46
British Broadcasting Corporation (BBC),
    27–28, 68, 103, 114, 353
Brittain, Vera, 119
Bromyard, 6–9, 12, 17–19, 39
Brook, Peter, 150, 160, 387, 392
Broué, Pierre, 353–54
Brown, Harmer, 81
Browne, Maria, 40–41, 51
Brunstein, Esther, 364–67, 379
Budberg, Baroness Moura, 164
Budeiri, Dr., 353
Bull, Peter, 116
Buñuel, Luis, 172
Bunyan, John, 13
Burgess, Guy, 25
Burns, George, 325
Burnstein, Arthur, 268
Burton, Richard, 48, 78–79, 262, 345
Bush, Alan, 28

Bush, George, 225, 314, 325
Byam-Shaw, Glen, 61, 88, 98, 100
Bykov, Rolan, 297

Calley, John, 139
Callow, Simon, 324–25
Camelot (film), 153–55, 161
Cameron, James, 160–61
Campbell, Sir Jock, 133, 135
Cannes Film Festival, 150, 155, 167, 345,
    375
Carnie, Catherine, 370
Caron, Leslie, 150
Carrington, Lord, 347
Carroll, Thomas, 340
Carten, Kenneth, 82
Carter, Jimmy, 239
Casnoff, Philip, 267
Castro, Fidel, 122, 124, 184
Cato Street (Shaw), 47, 186–87
Central School of Speech and Drama,
    60–62, 66, 69–70, 73, 75–84, 112
Čerešnješ, Ivan, 372–73, 389
Chamberlain, Neville, 4, 26–27, 71
Chamoun, Camille, 221
Chamoun, Danny, 225
Charge of the Light Brigade, The (film),
    158–59, 175
Charleson, Ian, 275–76
Chekhov, Anton, 93–94, 109, 134, 283–84,
    326–29, 344
Chekhov, Michael, 61
Chernobyl, 288–89, 290
Cherry Orchard, The (Chekhov), 326, 344
Chesshyre, Robert, 246
Chichester Festival Theatre, 109, 111
Churchill, Sir Winston, 7, 20, 23–24, 27,
    28, 31
Churchill, Winston S., 194
Cilento, Diane, 63–64
Cinderella (play), 116–17
Circle in the Square, 215–19, 268, 269, 317
Clark, George, 118
Clark, John (VR's brother-in-law), 37,
    154–55, 181
Clark, Kelly (VR's niece), 326
Clurman, Harold, 63, 64
Cocteau, Jean, 263
Cohen, Stephen, 353
Cohn, Sam, 334
Collateral Damage, 335–36
Collins, Canon, 100
Collins, Jack, 212
Comacho, Ralph, 177
Commissar (film), 306–7
Committee of 100, 100, 104–10, 118–19,
    152
Connery, Sean, 209, 210
Conran, Terence, 125

Coriolanus (Shakespeare), 97, 294
Council for Civil Liberties, 28
Courtenay, Tom, 114–15
Coward, Noël, 132, 194–98
Croasdell, Gerald, 176
Croft, Stephen, 18
Cromwell, Oliver, 121
Cronin, A. J., 5
Crozier, Roger, 197
Crucible, The (Miller), 69
Cruickshank, Andrew, 100
Crutchley, Rosalie, 68
Curtain Up (Streatfield), 17
Cymbeline (Shakespeare), 116

D'Alton, Hugo, 308
D'Alton, Micky, 308
Dalton, Timothy, 176–77, 203–4, 217, 235, 287, 288, 290, 296
Daniel, Larissa, 166, 168
Daniel Deronda (Eliot), 169, 263
Dartington, 61
David Copperfield (Dickens), 41, 42
Day Is Longer than a Century, A (Aytmatov), 293, 295
Day-Lewis, Daniel, 366, 369, 370, 378
de Bonafini, Hebe, 347
de la Tour, Frances, 339, 340, 343
Del Guidice, Filippo, 49
Dench, Judi, 76, 78–79, 82
Deneuve, Catherine, 172
Denham Film Studios, 28
De Niro, Robert, 297
Design for Living (Coward), 194–98
Devils, The (film), 174–75, 218
Devine, George, 33, 37, 61, 62, 67–68, 84, 113–22, 125, 126, 134–36
Devine, Sophie, 33
Devlin, Bernadette, 181–83
Diana, Princess of Wales, 343
Dickens, Charles, 41, 42, 247
Dikwar, Nassim, 367
Disney, Walt, 44, 54, 381
Divjak, Jovan, 390
Dolidzhe, Keti, 321
Doman, Glenn, 148
Donovan, Jason, 340
Donskaya, Svetlana, 338
Donskoy, Misha, 338
Dremliouga, Vadim, 166
Drowning by Numbers (film), 150
Drumm, Maire, 244
Duke in Darkness, The (melodrama), 15
Duncan, Isadora, 168, 333, 338–39, 341–42
Dunham, Joanna, 100
Dutt, Palme, 24
Duve, Herr, 348

Ecevedo, Del, 285
Eden, Anthony, 71–73
Edwards, Geoffrey, 88
Edward II (Marlowe), 63
Eggar, Samantha, 113, 283
Eisenberg, Alan, 266
Elias, Taiseer, 367
Eliot, George, 169
Elliott, Michael, 101–3, 168, 245, 249, 263
Éluard, Paul, 133
Emin, Artashes, 294–95
Emin, Gevorg, 293–95
Enemy of the People, An (Ibsen), 290
English Stage Company, 67–69
Essenin, Sergei, 160, 333, 341–42
Evans, Dame Edith, 5, 28, 97, 101, 105, 116–17, 132, 217
Evans, James Rose, 70
Everett, Rupert, 340
Eyre, Richard, 387

Faisal, king of Iraq, 254
Farandouri, Maria, 322–23
Farron, Stoker, 9–10
Farrow, Mia, 179
Fay, Stephen, 197
Feibleman, Peter, 271
Fellini, Federico, 143
Fenelon, Fania, 251–54, 261
Finch, Peter, 134, 167
Finch, Yolande, 134
Finney, Albert, 116, 117
Finzi, Jacob, 389, 390
Fitch, Rodney, 184
Fittermann, Stefan, 347, 368
Five O'Clock Angel (St. Just), 164–65
Flimm, Jürgen, 348–49, 357, 358
Fogazzaro, Antonio, 52
Fonda, Jane, 168, 177, 178–79, 219–22, 237, 252
Fonteyn, Margot, 42, 44
Foot, Michael, 201
Force de l'âge, La (The Prime of Life) (Beauvoir), 120
Forster, E. M., 28
Fox, Angela, 171
Fox, Robert, 313, 333–35, 337, 338, 343
Fox, Robin, 151, 171
Franco, Francisco, 26, 222
Frank, Anne, 382
Freeman, John, 133
French, Liz, 277
French, Terry, 277, 278
Friedman, Michel, 367
Frinton Summer Theatre, 85–88
Furtseva, Madame, 160
Fyodorov, Sviatoslav, 320

Galitzine, Princess Xenia, 41
Gandhi, Mahatma, 120
Gardiner, Muriel, 219
Garibaldi, Giuseppe, 54, 55–56
Garnet, Henry, 205
Garrick, David, 65
Gefter, Mikhail, 359
Gemayel, Bashir, 225
Gemayel, Pierre, 222, 224–25
George, Terry, 378
Georgy Girl (film), 155
Ghosts (Ibsen), 290–92
Gielgud, John, 47, 139–40, 158, 159
Gilbert, Victor, 245–46
Gilkes, Denne, 97
Gilliatt, Penelope, 113
Ginsberg, Allen, 336
Giraudoux, Jean, 63–64
Gish, Sheila, 333
Glascot, Miss (governess), 33–35, 38
Glaspie, April, 325
Glover, Julian, 98
Godard, Jean-Luc, 167
Goldman, Milton, 268
Goncharov, Nikolai, 296
Goodwin, Clive, 67
Goral, Artie, 358
Gorbachev, Mikhail, 289–93, 302–3, 316, 322, 339, 352–53, 359
Gordon, Judith, 265
Gordon, Ruth, 5
Gormley, Joe, 197
Gorst, Irene, 246, 247
Gould, Elliott, 207
Grainger, Gawn, 87, 88
Great Game, The (Trepper), 318
Greenaway, Peter, 150
Greene, Graham, 53, 109
Greenwood, Joan, 117
Grimes, Tammy, 121
Grody, Donald, 241
Grynzspan, Hirschel, 190
Guide to Military Rights, A, 178
Guinness, Alec, 5, 43
Guinness, Matthew, 33
Guthrie, Tyrone, 97
Gwynn, Michael, 68, 93

Haddad, Sammi, 232, 239
Haigh, Kenneth, 68
Hall, Peter, 48, 101, 103, 110, 114, 307, 308, 310, 316
Hamlet (Shakespeare), 3, 88, 93, 94–95, 176, 274
"Hanging on a Tree" (Vanessa Redgrave), 133
Hanley, Michael, 282
Harding, Olive, 82
Hard Times (Dickens), 247

Harris, Julie, 64
Harris, Richard, 154
Hartley, Neil, 139
Hassan, crown prince of Jordan, 261, 336
Healy, Gerry, 185, 189, 191–93, 202–3, 204, 211, 222, 243–44, 247–51, 254, 279–83, 288, 291, 297–302, 305–7, 311–12, 317–20
Heath, Edward, 177, 183, 185, 191, 199, 201
Hegel, Georg Wilhelm Friedrich, 188, 189
Hellman, Lillian, 19, 219–20, 237, 269, 271
Hemingway, Ernest, 124
Hemmings, David, 159
Henry IV, Part I (Shakespeare), 36, 45
Henry V (Shakespeare), 45
Hepburn, Audrey, 43
Hepburn, Katharine, 173
Herbert, Jocelyn, 33, 114, 115, 119, 125
Herzen, Alexander, 55
Heston Charlton, 180, 204
High Noon (film), 220
Hijjawi, Sulatha, 353
Himmler, Heinrich, 22
Hingle, Pat, 217
Hitchcock, Alfred, 5
Hitler, Adolf, 4, 13, 26, 28–31, 71, 120, 222
Hoar, Peter, 85
Hobson, Harold, 68, 69
Hoffman, Dustin, 218
Holt, Thelma, 91, 249, 269–70, 292–93, 326, 330, 336–37
Honecker, Erich, 316
Hoover, J. Edgar, 98, 180
Hoskins, Bob, 194
House Un-American Activities Committee, 69, 220
Howard, Leslie, 28
Howard, Trevor, 159
Howards End (film), 272, 335, 337, 345
Hunter, N. C., 90–93
Hurst, Brian Desmond, 89
Hurt, John, 283, 352
Hussein, Saddam, 325, 334
Hussey, Olivia, 149
Hynde, Chrissie, 340

Ibrišinović, Nezhad, 373
Ibsen, Henrik, 100, 215–18, 245, 272, 290–92
I Dream of Peace (UNICEF), 381–83
Ilyenkov, Evald, 298–99
In My Mind's Eye (Michael Redgrave), 94, 170, 214
Inner London Education Authority (ILEA), 181, 184
International Artists Against Racism, 363–67, 370
International Marxist Group, 163
In the Country of Last Things (Auster) 387–91

"In the Interests of the State," 121–22, 126
Ireland, John, 204
Irish Republican Army (IRA), 181–83, 185–86, 190, 244
Irons, Jeremy, 378
Irving, David, 355
Isadora (film), 159–60
Isadora and Esenin (McVay), 168
Isherwood, Christopher, 136
Ivory, James (Jim), 345

Jabavu, Noni, 104
Jaber, Sheikh, 248
James, C.L.R., 183–85
James, Henry, 272–73
James I, king of England, 205
Jamil, Mohammed Shukri, 254
Jarman, Derek, 174
Jawharieh, Hani, 224
Jeffries, Lionel, 153
Jerry Williams Show, 264
Jerusalem for Reconciliation (concert), 335
Jewish Defense League, 235–36, 237, 241, 266, 268
Jhabvala, Ruth Prawer, 273
Jihad, Hanan, 305
Jihad, Um, 305, 319
Joffe, Nadezhda, 320–21
Johnson, Lyndon B., 137, 162, 164
Jones, Jack, 212
Jones, John, 282
Jones, Russell, 276
Jonson, Ben, 63
Joss, William, 192
Julia (film), 219–21, 234–36
Jumblatt, Kamal, 221, 225

Kahane, Meir, 235, 268
Kallin, Tasha, 41, 42, 50, 51
Karadzić, Radovan, 366, 369
Karpov, Vladimir, 290
Kaufman, Gerald, 368
Keaton, Robert E., 270
Keitel, Harvey, 370, 372, 373, 375–76
Kempson, Beatrice Ashwell (VR's grandmother), 4–5, 8, 9, 381
Kempson, Eric (VR's grandfather), 4–5, 9–12, 48, 385–86
Kempson, Joan (VR's aunt), 18
Kempson, Lucy Wedgwood ("Cousin Lucy"), 6, 8, 12, 69, 70, 73–74, 101
Kempson, Nicholas (VR's uncle), 8, 11
Kempson, Rachel (Lady Redgrave, VR's mother), 3–9, 15, 17, 23, 25, 27, 37, 38, 44–46, 59, 60, 68, 70, 77, 78, 82, 110–11, 113, 115, 154, 214, 248, 380–81, 385–88, 391–92
    acting career of, 4, 42, 45–46, 48–49, 92, 93, 117, 134, 218

family background of, 4–5, 10–12
pregnancies and childbirths of, 3, 13, 48–49
in Stratford, 45–46, 48
at Whitegate, 6–9
Kempson, Robin (VR's uncle), 8, 9–10, 77, 100
Kennedy, John F., 125
Kennedy, Ludovic, 162
Kennedy, Nigel, 303
Kenović, Ademir, 375, 379
Kenyatta, Jomo, 55
Khait, Arkhady, 312
Khrushchev, Nikita, 72, 73, 190, 386
King, David, 47
King, Martin Luther, Jr., 162–63, 282
King Lear (Shakespeare), 48, 95, 183, 250, 357
Kipling, Rudyard, 40–41
Kierkegaard, Sören, 152
Kitson, David, 305
Klimov, Elem, 289, 297
Knight, Esmond, 100
Koch, Howard, 236
Komar, Dimitri, 340, 343
Kozyrev, Andrei, 352
KPGT Zagreb Theatre Company, 361–62
Kramer, Stanley, 297
Krasker, Robert, 53
Krichevsky, Ilya, 340, 343
Krige, Alice, 286
Kristofferson, Kris, 303, 370
Kučan, Milan, 392
Kuryokhin, Sergei, 322
Ky, Nguyen Cao, 143

Labadi, Dr., 228–29
Labour Party, British, 12, 20, 23, 24, 27, 29, 31, 33, 38, 127, 132–33, 138–39, 143, 163, 179, 181, 197–99, 201, 212, 213–14, 247, 249, 276, 279, 346–47, 385
Lady Chatterley's Lover (Lawrence), 114
Lady Chatterley's Lover (TV film series), 114
Lady from the Sea, The (Ibsen), 100, 215–18, 245, 249
Lasker, Anita, 253, 365–66
Lassally, Walter, 115
Latsis, Otto, 321
Lavender Hill Mob, The (film), 43
Lawley, Sue, 212
Lawrence, D. H., 114
Lawrence, Gertrude, 59
Lawson, Wilfrid, 117
Laye, Evelyn, 16–17
Lean, David, 42
Le Bonnet, Monsieur (chef), 144, 145
Lefkovitch, Iosip, 312
Leicester, Margot, 290

Lenin, V. I., 24, 30, 183, 184, 188–90, 299–300, 318, 321–22, 341, 342
Lester, Richard, 153
Lettice and Lovage (Shaffer), 334, 335
Levenbyk, Alexander, 311, 319
Levi, Carlo, 52
Levin, Bernard, 111
Libin, Paul, 217, 269
Littlewood, Joan, 62, 63, 113
Litvinov, Pavel, 166, 168
Livaneli, Zulfu, 370
Livingstone, Ken, 319–20
Logan, Joshua, 153
Logue, Christopher, 106
Loneliness of the Long Distance Runner (film), 114–15
Look Back in Anger (film), 112, 114, 345
Look Back in Anger (Osborne), 68–69, 88
Loraine, Robert, 95
Lorca, Federico García, 79–80
Louis, Joe, 39
Lousada, Anthony, 33
Loved One, The (film), 136, 139–40
Loved One, The (Waugh), 136
Love's Labour's Lost (Shakespeare), 49–50
Lukhyanov, Anatoly, 339
Lumet, Gail, 154, 164
Lumet, Sidney, 154, 164, 209, 269
Luther (Osborne), 120
Lynch, Alfred, 113
Lynn, Vera, 14

Ma'arouf Saad, 221
McBean, Angus, 44
Macbeth (Shakespeare), 41, 74, 180, 204–6
McCann, Eamonn, 182
McCann, Elizabeth (Liz), 315
McCarthy, Joseph, 69, 207, 237, 265
McCarthy, Mary, 219
McCullers, Carson, 323–24
McGinnan, Jack, 122
MacGregor, Ian, 276–77
McKellen, Ian, 275
McKenna, Siobhan, 136
McMaster, Anew, 46
Macmillan, Harold, 98
McVay, Gordon, 168
Mademoiselle (film), 144
Madhouse in Goa, A (Sherman), 313–14, 333
Magnani, Anna, 309
Malle, Louis, 167
Mandela, Nelson, 132, 163, 239, 281, 386
Mandelstam, Osip, 206
Mankiewicz, Joseph, 53, 142
Mann, Daniel, 254
Mann, John, 216
Mann, Pat, 215–16
Mann, Theodore, 215–16, 217, 269, 316, 366

Man Who Mistook His Wife for a Hat, The (Sacks), 387
Margolyes, Miriam, 320
Marjan, Marie Louise, 358
Mark, Sir Robert, 245
Markham, David, 26
Markham, Kika (VR's sister-in-law), 144, 288, 364
Markov, Georgi, 289–90
Marowitz, Charles, 249
Marsh, Sandra, 218, 235–36
Martin, Henri, 166
Marx, Groucho, 207
Marx, Karl, 152, 190
Marxist Analysis of the Crisis, The, 189–90, 191
Marxist Party, 299, 346–47
Mary, Queen of Scots (film), 176, 177, 218
Mason, James, 147, 164
Maximova, Ekaterina, 317
Maxwell, James, 169
Mazzini, Giuseppe, 55
Megged, Matti, 358
Mehta, Zubin, 178
Memorial Society for the Victims of Stalin's Repressions, 317, 320, 321
Memorial Theatre, 46–50, 60, 88, 97
Memorial Theatre Company, 70, 95, 97
Menem, Carlos, 347
Menshikov, Oleg, 338, 339, 342–43
Menuhin, Yehudi, 172, 276
Mercer, David, 144
Merchant, Ismail, 269, 337, 355–57
Merchant of Venice, The (Shakespeare), 49–50, 78–79
Merman, Ethel, 54
Michael, Savas, 302–3
"Michael Redgrave at Home," 5–6
Middlesex Hospital, 13–14
Midsummer Night's Dream, A (Shakespeare), 93, 97, 112–13, 223
Migenes, Julia, 303
Mikhoels, Solomon, 311–12
Miller, Arthur, 64, 69, 84, 251, 253, 254
Milošević, Slobodan, 346–47, 354
Miss Spalding's (Queen's Gate School), 40–42, 51, 88, 93
Mitchell, Alex, 202
Mitchell, John, 180
Moiseivitch, Tanya, 46
Molchanov, Helen, 328
Monroe, Marilyn, 84, 153
Montessori, Maria, 148
Montand, Yves, 165–68
Monteno, Kemal, 368
More, Julian, 150
Moreau, Jeanne, 144, 145, 150, 380
Morgan—A Suitable Case for Treatment (film), 141–44, 150
Morley, Robert, 162, 175

Morris, John, 104
Morris, Tom, 265, 266
Moscow Arts Theatre Company, 64, 93–95
Moscow Film Festival, 249, 297
Moscow Jewish Theatre Shalom Company, 312
Mother Goose (pantomime), 95–96
Mountbatten, Louis, 172
Much Ado About Nothing (Shakespeare), 88, 93
Mueller, Maria Elena, 388
Mulberry Bush, The (Wilson), 69–70, 73
Muller, Annette, 354
Murch, Pauline, 88
Murder on the Orient Express (film), 209
Murdoch, Rupert, 257–58
Murray, Braham, 169, 363, 368
Murzi, Gianni, 336
Mussolini, Benito, 192, 222, 256
My Body, My Child (film), 257, 264
My Life (Duncan), 168

Nagy, Imre, 72, 73
Naismith, Laurence, 286
Napoleon I, emperor of France, 34–35
Nasry, Talal al-, 305
Nasser, Gamal Abdel, 71–72, 256
Nathan, Abie, 360
National Front, 202–3, 263
National Liberation Front, Vietnamese (NLF), 143, 160, 161, 163, 179–80
National Theatre, 292–96, 387
National Theatre Company, 109, 127, 132
Nederlander, James (Jimmy), 313
Neeson, Liam (VR's son-in-law), 381
Nelin, Emanuel, 311, 312
Nelson, Horatio, 34
Nelson, Mary, 44
Nero, Franco, 154–57, 169–76, 181, 218, 307, 310, 311, 322
Nesbit, E., 41
Neumann, Flora, 358
Neville, John, 100–101
Newman, Christine, 148, 153, 157, 159, 203
Newton, Robert, 42
"New World Will Be Born, A," 25, 27
Nichols, Mike, 216
Nin, Andres, 354
Nixon, Pat, 179
Nixon, Richard M., 178–80, 206, 237, 314
Norman, Jessye, 262, 264
Norman, Kirsty, 150
Nunn, Trevor, 48, 372

O'Brien, Edna, 186
O'Casey, Sean, 63
Occupied Palestine (documentary), 255, 260–62
October (play), 197–98

Oedipus Rex (Stravinsky), 262–66, 270
O'Ferrall, George More, 89
Okhudzhava, Bulat, 290
Old Vic Theatre Company, 5, 49, 61
Oliver Twist (film), 42, 49
Olivier, Laurence, 3, 5, 42, 97, 109, 127, 165, 213, 295
O'Neill, Eugene, 177
Orpheus Descending (film), 320
Orpheus Descending (Williams), 81, 216, 301, 307–10, 313, 315, 316, 323
Osborne, John, 68–69, 88, 113, 120, 146, 149, 159
Osborne, Nigel, 366
Osborne, Penelope, 149
Oskaldov, Sasha, 297, 306–7
Othello (Shakespeare), 97–98, 345
O'Toole, Sean, 183
"Our Profession in Peril," 175
Oweida, Feisal, 319
Owen, Lord, 372
Owen, Peter, 285–86
Owen, Robert, 12
Ozawa, Seiji, 262, 266

Page, Anthony, 135, 269, 285
Page, Elaine, 340
Page, Geneviève, 42
Paine, Tom, 121
Palestine Liberation Organization (PLO), 56, 190, 203, 224, 230, 235, 241–42, 244, 303–5, 313, 315, 360, 386
Palestinian, The (documentary), 222–38, 241, 248, 255
Paley, William, 252
Parents' National Education Union (PNEU), 33–34
Parsons, Betty, 129–30, 131
Parting with Illusions (Pozner), 322
Pasović, Haris, 371, 372, 376, 379, 386–89, 391, 392
Pasović, Lejla, 388, 390
Passato e Pensieri (Herzen), 55
Pasternak, Boris, 298
Pavitt, Laurie, 186
Peace of Brest, The (Shatrov), 300
Peacock, William, 47
Peck, Gregory, 297
Pellico, Silvio, 53
Pentimento (Hellman), 219
"People's Convention for a People's Government, The," 25–31, 107
Petri, Elio, 156–57
Philipe, Gérard, 338
Philosophical Notebooks (Lenin), 188–89
Piccolo mondo antico (Fogazzaro), 52–53
Pilgrim's Progress (Bunyan), 13
Pinochet, Augusto, 184, 193
Pisk, Litz, 61, 159, 285

Pitt, William, 369
Playing for Time (film), 251–54, 261
Pleasance, Angela, 333
Plouviez, Peter, 212, 246
Plummer, Christopher, 120
Polanski, Roman, 167
Pollitt, Harry, 192
Ponomariev, Lev, 317
Popović, Davorin, 368
Potter, Madeleine, 273
Pottle, Pat, 118
Powell, Enoch, 202
Pozner, Vladimir, 297, 322
Price, Dolores, 192
Prime of Miss Jean Brodie, The (play),
    148–49, 151–53
Pritt, D. N., 29
Pryce, Jonathan, 283
Pugacheva, Alla, 297

Qaddafi, Muammar, 256
Qadri, Bustan al-, 360
Quadflieg, Will, 348, 357
Quayle, Anthony, 296
Queen's Gate School (Miss Spalding's),
    40–42, 51, 88, 93
Quiet American, The (film), 53, 82, 88, 142
Quiet Place in the Country, A (film), 157–58

Rabin, Yitzhak, 386
Radd, Ronald, 164
Rambert, Madame, 42–43
Randall, George, 35
Randall, Kathleen, 12, 15, 16, 17, 21, 22,
    23, 35–39, 42, 89–90, 127, 172
Randle, Michael, 106, 118
Ransohoff, Martin, 139
Rathbone, Eleanor, 69
Read, Sir Herbert, 100
Reagan, Ronald, 177, 178
Red and Blue (film), 150–51, 152
Redgrave, Corin (VR's brother), 24–25, 63,
    108, 109, 115, 151, 170, 175, 176,
    184–85, 187–89, 191, 207, 210, 212,
    214, 243–50, 271, 272, 280, 281,
    288–89, 291, 299, 301, 309, 330,
    346–47, 352–53, 364, 368
  acting of, 17, 18, 19, 40, 112, 158
  in Bromyard, 7, 8, 17–19, 21
  childhood of, 4, 6, 7, 8, 10, 12, 13, 15,
    17–19, 21, 33–35, 38–40, 45–49
  education of, 33–35, 40, 93, 112
  in Stratford, 45–48
  VR's acting and, 87, 88
Redgrave, Deirdre (VR's sister-in-law),
    127, 210, 211, 216
Redgrave, Jemma (VR's niece), 211–12,
    216, 326–29
Redgrave, Kika, *see* Markham, Kika
Redgrave, Luke (VR's nephew), 211–12, 216

Redgrave, Lynn (VR's sister), 115, 171, 181
  acting career of, 39, 49, 93, 112–13, 117,
    127, 132, 147, 155, 317, 326–29
  childhood of, 13, 14–15, 17, 21, 37,
    38–39, 49
  marriage of, 37, 154–55
Redgrave, Margaret, *see* Anderson,
    Margaret
Redgrave, Michael (VR's father), 3–9, 16,
    24–33, 37, 40, 42–49, 51–54, 70, 77,
    95, 104–13, 115, 218, 271–76, 380
  acting career of, 3–6, 15, 27–28, 32, 33,
    38, 44–50, 57, 63–64, 82, 88–95, 98,
    101, 109, 142, 165, 235, 250
  autobiography of, *see In My Mind's Eye*
  death of, 218, 271, 275–76
  health problems of, 25, 47, 170, 235, 250,
    271, 274–75
  politics and, 24–31, 107, 214, 271
  VR's acting and, 88–89, 98
  VR's advice from, 59, 60, 62–63
  VR's correspondence with, 52, 104–11,
    152
Redgrave, Rachel Kempson, *see* Kempson,
    Rachel
Redgrave, Roy (VR's grandfather), 218
Redgrave, Vanessa:
  awards and honors of, 85, 150, 235–37,
    284, 343
  childhood of, 3–4, 6–10, 12–25, 32–44
  early acting of, 18–19, 40, 44
  education of, 19, 33–35, 40–42, 51–56,
    60–66, 69–70, 73, 75–84, 136–37, 138
  family background of, 4–5, 10–12, 16
  film test of, 89
  finances of, 85, 87, 89, 218, 222–23,
    268–69
  Italian studies of, 51–57
  marriage of, *see* Richardson, Tony
  pregnancies and childbirths of, 116,
    126–32, 135–36, 138, 140, 169–71,
    174, 175
  reading of, 7, 12, 13, 17, 41, 52, 58–59,
    69, 120–21, 188–91
  stage fright and nervousness of, 18, 81,
    82, 89, 90, 151–52, 169
  visa problems of, 180
Redman, Joyce, 117
Reed, Carol, 5
Rees, Llewellyn, 61
Reeve, Christopher, 273–74, 317
Regester, Bob, 170, 290–91
Reid, Richard, 359, 366
Reisz, Betsy, *see* Blair, Betsy
Reisz, Karel, 141–42, 143
Reluctant Debutante, The (Heatherton), 88
Resistible Rise of Arturo Ui, The (Brecht), 120
Resnais, Alain, 166
Rich, Frank, 313
Richards, Ivor, 139

Richards, Renée, 284–86
Richardson, Catherine, 343, 345
Richardson, Cecil (VR's father-in-law), 126
Richardson, Elsie (VR's mother-in-law), 126
Richardson, Griselda, 343, 345
Richardson, Joely (VR's daughter), 19–20, 144–46, 153, 157–60, 159, 160, 169–74, 180, 203–4, 210–12, 216, 223, 262, 285, 310, 311, 329, 343–46
    acting career of, 92, 114, 150, 314–15, 326
    birth of, 131, 140, 345
    education of, 173, 204, 210, 212
Richardson, Natasha (VR's daughter), 19–20, 78, 137–38, 144–46, 153, 157–60, 169–73, 203–4, 207, 210–12, 216, 223, 262, 275, 291, 309–11, 343, 345, 367
    acting career of, 274, 283–84, 314–15
    birth of, 127–32
    education of, 148, 153, 173, 204, 210, 212, 234
    marriage of, 180, 381
    naming of, 115
Richardson, Tony (VR's husband), 111–17, 119–28, 134–41, 144–48, 150–53, 157–59, 176, 204, 218, 311, 380
    birth of children and, 128, 130, 131, 132, 136, 140
    death of, 343–45
    as director, 68, 98, 112–17, 120–21, 134–36, 144–47, 150–52, 158–59, 180–81, 194, 217, 218, 309, 326, 344, 345
    VR's marriage to, 70, 111, 115
Richard II (Shakespeare), 45–47, 62–63
Richard III (Shakespeare), 48, 64–65, 312
River Runs Through It, A (film), 177
Roberts, John, 110
Robeson, Paul, 54, 69, 95, 97–98, 367
Robeson, Susan, 95
Robinson, Joe, 113
Romeo and Juliet (Shakespeare), 45–46
Roosevelt, Franklin D., 31
Rosen, Jerome, 264–65
Rosenberg, Ethel, 54
Rosenberg, Julius, 54
Ross, Annie, 180–81
Ross-Munro, Colin, 244
Rotberg, Dana, 379
Royal Air Force, British (RAF), 71, 99
Royal Court Theatre, 67–69, 84, 112–13, 121–22, 126
Royal Navy, British, 4, 8, 9–10
Russell, Bertrand, 100, 104, 107, 119
Russell, Ken, 174

Sabah al Sabah, Sheikh, 248
Sacks, Oliver, 387
Sadat, Anwar, 194
Sadoff, Fred, 65, 79
Sailor from Gibraltar, The (film), 145, 146–47
Saint, Eva Marie, 65, 66
Saint-Denis, Michel, 57, 61, 62
Saint Joan (Shaw), 44, 49, 88
Saint Joan of the Stockyards (Brecht), 135–36
St. Just, Marie, 164–65, 310, 316
St. Paul's Girls' School, 204, 210, 234
Sambalino, Dottore, 55
Sammassimo, Silvana, 203, 210, 216, 218, 223, 262
Sandrig, Caroline, 265
Sands, Bobby, 257–59
Sarajevo Film Festival, 377–79
Sartre, Jean-Paul, 120
Savan, Bruce, 269
Scarfe, Gerald, 179
Scargill, Anne, 277
Scargill, Arthur, 277–78, 279
Schlöndorff, Volker, 378
Schnarch, Ani, 367
Schoenmann, Ralph, 119
Schofield, David, 194
Screen Actors Guild, 266
Scudamore, Daisy, see Anderson, Margaret
Scudamore, Fortunatus Augustus, 16
Scudamore, Lionel, 16
Scudamore, William, 16
Seagull, The (Chekhov), 134, 135, 283–84
Seagull, The (film), 164–65
Second Serve (film), 285–86
Sellars, Peter, 265–66, 269
Semprun, Jorge, 166
Serbedzija, Lenka, 362–63
Serbedzija, Rade, 361–63, 368
Shaffer, Peter, 334
Shaheen, Simon, 335
Shakespeare, William, 36, 41, 45–50, 60, 62–65, 74, 77, 88, 94–95, 101–3, 176, 183, 204–6, 230, 294, 357
    see also specific plays
Shakespeare's People, 235
Shankar, Ravi, 172
Shankland, Dean, 276
Shapiro, Leonard, 335
Shatrov, Mikhail Filipovich, 297–98, 300, 317, 319, 364
Shave, Dulcie, 3–4, 6, 7, 12
Shaw, George Bernard, 44, 49, 69, 88
Shaw, Robert, 47, 49, 63, 186–87
Sheridan, Jim, 378
Sherman, Martin, 313–14, 333–34, 337–38, 342, 343
Shoufani, Elias, 231
Sidmouth, Lord, 186
Signoret, Simone, 164–68
Silajdzič, Haris, 390
Sillitoe, Alan, 114, 125
Simonsohn, Trudi, 358

Sisulu, Walter, 132
60 Minutes (TV show), 252
Smailović, Vedran, 366, 371
"Small" (Emin), 294
Smith, Colin, 245, 246
Smith, Liz, 235
Smith, Maggie, 132, 326
Socialist Labour League, 163, 184–85,
   187–95, 261
Solomon, Ralph, 360
Soper, Lord, 186
Sorrell, Richard, 387
Southern, Terry, 136
Spalding, Miss, 40, 41–42
Sparanero, Carlo (VR's son), 131, 171–73,
   184, 203, 204, 210, 216, 223, 262, 307,
   310–11, 316, 344, 366
Sparanero, Gabriele, 156
Sparanero, Ninetta, 156
Special Branch, British, 118, 247–48
Spock, Benjamin, 166
Spycatcher (Wright), 72, 282
Squire, Ronnie, 91–92
Squire, Ursula, 91–92
Stalin, Joseph, 24, 28–31, 71, 73, 98, 189,
   190, 206, 301, 303, 311, 312, 318,
   321, 341, 386
Stalky and Co. (Kipling), 40–41
Stander, Lionel, 120, 135
Stanislavsky, Konstantin, 64, 65, 82–84,
   89, 195, 196, 290, 302
Stansfield, Walter, 245
Stantic, Lita, 347
Stars Look Down, The (Cronin), 5
Stars Look Down, The (film), 5
Startsev, Professor, 323
Stephens, Robert, 68, 122, 126
Stephenson, William, 7
Stevens, Bob, 184
Stevens, Jann, 137–38, 159, 181, 184,
   222
Stevens, Jolie, 137, 159
Stewart, Forrest, 285
Stiebel, Victor, 82
Stirling, David, 202
Stockwood, Mervyn, 186
Strasberg, Ivan, 222, 224
Strasberg, Lee, 64–65
Strasberg, Susan, 65
Strasser, Irene, 57
Strasser, Jani, 57–58, 61, 102, 121
Stratford-upon-Avon, 45–48, 60, 88, 93,
   94–95, 97–98, 101–3
Stravinsky, Igor F., 262–66
Streatfield, Noel, 17
Sturua, Robert, 312, 319, 326–29
Suny, Ronald, 353
Sutherland, Donald, 135, 168, 179
Swee Chai Ang, 314
Symposium 90, 320–21, 341, 353–55

Tabakov, Oleg, 160
Taine, Hippolyte, 385
Tal al-Zaatar, 221–22, 225–29
Taming of the Shrew, The (Shakespeare),
   103, 115, 176–77, 287, 290
Tanqueray, Paul, 77
Tassarty, Eleanor, 50
Taste of Honey, A (film), 112–13, 114
Taylor, Elizabeth, 155
Tennant, H. M., 98
Terence, 284
Terry, Ellen, 60, 328
Terry Juveniles, 17
Thacker, David, 290
Thatcher, Margaret, 20, 249, 277, 315
Theatre Workers' Union, 322–23, 337
Theatre Workshop, 62–63
Thistlewood, Arthur, 186–87
Thistlewood, Susan, 187
Thompson, Emma, 337
Thorndike, Sybil, 49
Three Mile Island nuclear accident, 253
Threepenny Opera, The (Brecht, Weill),
   180–81, 218
Three Sisters, The (Chekhov), 93–94,
   326–32, 335
Thurburn, Gwyneth, 60, 73
Tiger and the Horse, The (Bolt), 98–100
Tiger at the Gates (Giraudoux), 63–64
Timeon, Askander, 344
Times (London), 69, 73, 160, 161, 167, 171,
   213, 247, 257
Tolstoy, Leo, 41, 115
Tom Jones (film), 115, 116–17, 121
Tomorrow Was War (Vasiliev), 295, 317
Tone, Wolfe, 121
Topolski, Felix, 23
Torrance, Sheila, 289
Touch of the Poet, A (O'Neill), 176, 177
Touch of the Sun, A (Hunter), 44, 90–93,
   102, 249
Train to Happiness, The (Khait), 312
Travolta, John, 237
Trepper, Leopold, 318
Trojan Women, The (film), 173, 174
Trotsky, Leon, 183, 190, 192, 197, 242,
   291, 298–300, 302–3, 320, 342, 354
Truffaut, François, 167
Truscott, John, 153
Tulić, Nermin, 371, 390
Turner, Hillary, 149
Tushingham, Rita, 112–13, 114
Tutu, Desmond, 135
20th Century-Fox, 235, 240
Tynan, Kenneth, 68, 69, 95, 104

Ulanova, Galina, 70
Ulyanov, Mikhail, 295, 300, 312
Uncle Vanya (Chekhov), 109
Uncle Vanya (film), 165

United Artists, 117, 121, 150
United Nations (UN), 232, 238, 239,
    244–45, 303, 325–26, 330, 331, 359,
    369
United Nations High Commission for
    Refugees (UNHCR), 368–70,
    377–78
United Nations International Children's
    Emergency Fund (UNICEF), 335,
    336–37, 350, 359, 366, 368–73,
    375–77, 381–84
Ure, Mary, 113
Usov, Vladimir, 340, 343
Usova, Ludmila, 340
Usova, Marina, 340

Vadim, Roger, 177
Vance, Cyrus, 372
Vanessa Redgrave Enterprises, 312
Vanessa Redgrave Nursery School, 184,
    218
Vanessa Talks to Farouk Abdul Aziz
    (documentary), 250
Vanguardia, 330, 334
Vardzigulyants, Reuben, 338
Vasiliev, Boris, 295, 296, 317
Vasiliev, Vladimir, 317
Vaughan Williams, Ralph, 28
Veterans (Wood), 159
View from the Bridge, A (Miller), 64, 84
Vitti, Monica, 140
Volkov, Esteban, 354
Volpone (Jonson), 63
Vrachev, Ivan, 321

Waddell, James, 278, 319
Wagner, Cosima, 262
Wagner, Richard, 262
Waiting for Godot (Beckett), 69, 114
Wake Up, World (appeal), 363, 371
Walker, Sir Walter, 201–2
Wallace, Mike, 252, 264
Wallach, Eli, 64
Wallis, Hal, 176
Walsh, Kay, 42
Walton, Emma, 164
Walton, Tony, 164
Wanamaker, Sam, 98, 194, 287
War and Peace (Tolstoy), 115
Warner, David, 113, 164
Warner Bros., 153
Warren-Greene, Chris, 252–53
War Resisters International, 335
Watkin, David, 158
Watkins, David, 275
Watson, Claude, 150
Waugh, Auberon, 104
Waugh, Evelyn, 136
Weaver, Sigourney, 317
Webb, Beatrice, 69

Wedgwood, Henry Allen, 12
Wedgwood, Josiah, 12
Welch, Elisabeth, 303–4, 322–23
Weldon, Duncan, 287
Wellington, Duke of, 34
Wenders, Wim, 378
Wesker, Arnold, 100, 106
Westmacott, Caroline, 33
Weston Biscuits, 119
"We Will Never Forget—We Will Not
    Let It Happen Again," 349–51,
    357–60
Wexler, Haskell, 136
Wexler, Marion, 136
"What Is Wrong with the English
    Theatre?" (meeting), 84
When She Danced (Sherman), 333–34, 335,
    337, 341–42, 343
Whitegate, 6–9, 12
White Meadows, 207–8, 210, 211
Whitfield, Doreen, 126–27
Wilby, James, 355
Will, Ian, 183
Williams, Jerry, 265
Williams, Richard, 159
Williams, Tennessee, 81, 124, 164–65, 216,
    267–68, 301, 307–10, 320
Williamson, Nicol, 113
Wilmers, John, 243–44, 246
Wilson, Angus, 69–70
Wilson, Harold, 139, 143, 161, 163, 201
Windsor, Barbara, 181
Wolpe, Katharina, 303, 358, 370
Wood, Charles, 159
Wood, Peter, 148, 149, 204
Woodcock, Bruce, 39
Woodfall Films, 139
Workers' Press, 197, 202, 210–11, 244
Workers' Revolutionary Party (WRP), 195,
    196, 198–204, 206–8, 210–14, 218,
    222, 234, 243–50, 257, 277–83, 299,
    318
Wrede, Caspar, 169
Wright, Peter, 72, 282
Wynyard, Diana, 93
Wyse, John, 46

Yellen, Linda, 251–52, 284, 285, 286
Yeltsin, Boris, 340, 359
Yevtushenko, Yevgeny, 160, 290
Young Catherine (miniseries), 321–22
Young Vic Theatre School, 57,
    61
Youssef, Dr., 228–29
Yursky, Sergei, 300, 321

Zeffirelli, Franco, 310
Zinnemann, Fred, 219, 220, 237, 349, 352,
    368
Zmajevic-Hukic, Pia, 373–75

PHOTOGRAPH CREDITS

SECTION I

Paul Tanqueray (p. 1, center); Hulton Picture Company (p. 2, bottom left; p. 3, top; p. 6, top; p. 7, top and bottom); Rex Features (p. 4, top and bottom; p. 5, bottom left; p. 6, bottom left and right); W. R. Ayling (p. 5, top); Camera Press (p. 5, bottom right; p. 8).

SECTION II

Hulton Picture Company (p. 12, top; p. 13, top and bottom; p. 14, top; p. 16, center and bottom); Rex Features (p. 9, top and bottom; p. 12, bottom left; p. 13, center; p. 14, bottom left; p. 15, top and center).

SECTION III

Rex Features (p. 17, top; p. 21, top right; p. 22, center); Hulton Picture Company (p. 17, bottom; p. 18, top and center; p. 19, bottom; p. 20, bottom right; p. 23, bottom left); David Hurn/Magnum (p. 18, bottom); Camera Press (p. 19, top left and right; p. 22, bottom); Mander & Mitchenson Theatre Collection (p. 20, top); Donald Cooper/Photostage (p. 21, top left); Inge Morath/Magnum (p. 21, center); Mikki Anain (p. 21, bottom); 20th Century–Fox (p. 22, top); Rex/Richard Young (p. 24, top left).

SECTION IV

Camera Press (p. 25, top; p. 30, bottom); Phil Cutts (p. 25, bottom); Rex Features (p. 26, center right and bottom center; p. 27, top center, bottom left, and center right); Eve Arnold/Magnum (p. 26, top left); Rex/Warner Pathé (p. 26, top right); Hulton Picture Company, (p. 26 bottom left; p. 30, top); Inge Morath/Magnum (p. 27, top left); Mikki Ansin (p. 27, top right); Donald Cooper/Photostage (p. 28, top and bottom right); Mander & Mitchenson/John Haynes (p. 28, bottom left; p. 32).

ABOUT THE AUTHOR

VANESSA REDGRAVE was born in London in 1937. Her first great success in a long and distinguished career as an actress was as Rosalind in *As You Like It* at Stratford-upon-Avon in 1961. Redgrave's subsequent work in the theatre has encompassed the plays of Chekhov, Ibsen, Eugene O'Neill, George Bernard Shaw, Noël Coward, and Tennessee Williams. She has appeared in over fifty films, including *Morgan!, Blow-Up, The Loves of Isadora, The Devils, Murder on the Orient Express, Julia* (for which she won an Oscar), *The Bostonians,* and *Howards End.*

The Redgrave family has a long history in the theatre. Vanessa's grandparents and great-grandparents were actor-managers, writers, and actors. Her father, the celebrated stage and film actor Sir Michael Redgrave, was the son of one of the first stars of silent feature films in Australia. Her mother is the actress Rachel Kempson. In 1961 Vanessa married the director Tony Richardson, and they had two daughters, Natasha and Joely. She and the Italian actor Franco Nero have a son, Carlo.

Vanessa has been a political activist since the early sixties, when she joined the Campaign for Nuclear Disarmament and, subsequently, Bertrand Russell's Committee of 100. She has been actively involved in supporting the rights of Palestinians, Nelson Mandela and the ANC, the Irish liberation struggle, and all other oppressed peoples. She is UNICEF's Special Representative for the Performing Arts in all the republics of what was Yugoslavia, and as such has worked with the children and the theatre artists of Sarajevo. She is a member of British and American Actors' Equity, the American Academy of Motion Picture Arts and Sciences, the Screen Actors Guild, the British Film Institute, and the Writers Guild, U.K. She is an honorary member of the Memorial Society for the Victims of Stalin's Repressions and president of Symposium 90. In 1993 Redgrave was awarded the Sakharov Medal by Elena Bonner.

ABOUT THE TYPE

The text of this book was set in Janson, a typeface designed in about 1690 by Nicholas Kis.